Merleau-Ponty and
Contemporary Philosophy

SUNY series in Contemporary Continental Philosophy

Dennis J. Schmidt, editor

Merleau-Ponty and Contemporary Philosophy

Edited by
Emmanuel Alloa, Frank Chouraqui,
and Rajiv Kaushik

Published by State University of New York Press, Albany

© 2019 State University of New York

All rights reserved

No part of this book may be used or reproduced in any manner whatsoever without written permission. No part of this book may be stored in a retrieval system or transmitted in any form or by any means including electronic, electrostatic, magnetic tape, mechanical, photocopying, recording, or otherwise without the prior permission in writing of the publisher.

For information, contact State University of New York Press, Albany, NY
www.sunypress.edu

Library of Congress Cataloging-in-Publication Data

Names: Alloa, Emmanuel, editor.
Title: Merleau-Ponty and contemporary philosophy / edited by Emmanuel Alloa, Frank Chouraqui, and Rajiv Kaushik.
Description: Albany : State University of New York, 2019. | Series: SUNY series in contemporary Continental philosophy | Includes bibliographical references and index.
Identifiers: LCCN 2018059957 | ISBN 9781438476919 (hardcover : alk. paper) | ISBN 9781438476902 (pbk. : alk. paper) | ISBN 9781438476926 (ebook)
Subjects: LCSH: Merleau-Ponty, Maurice, 1908–1961.
Classification: LCC B2430.M3764 M4675 2019 | DDC 194—dc23
LC record available at https://lccn.loc.gov/2018059957

10 9 8 7 6 5 4 3 2 1

Contents

Texts of Merleau-Ponty's, Abbreviated — ix

Merleau-Ponty and Contemporary Philosophy: An Introduction — 1
Emmanuel Alloa, Frank Chouraqui, Rajiv Kaushik

Legacies

The Three Senses of Flesh: Concerning an Impasse in Merleau-Ponty's Ontology — 17
Renaud Barbaras

Vortex of Time. Merleau-Ponty on Temporality — 35
Bernhard Waldenfels and Regula Giuliani

Undergoing an Experience: Sensing, Bodily Affordances, and the Institution of the Self — 61
Emmanuel Alloa

Between Sense and Non-Sense: Merleau-Ponty and "The Silence of the Absolute Language" — 83
Stephen Watson

Mind and Nature

The Truth of Naturalism — 111
Jocelyn Benoist

The Panpsychism Question in Merleau-Ponty's Ontology 121
  Jennifer McWeeny

Merleau-Ponty and Biosemiotics: From the Issue of Meaning in
Living Beings to a New Deal between Science and Metaphysics 145
  Annabelle Dufourcq

Politics, Power, Institution

The Institution of the Law: Merleau-Ponty and Lefort 171
  Bernard Flynn

Post-Truth Politics and the Paradox of Power 183
  Frank Chouraqui

Institutional Habits: About Bodies and Orientations that Don't Fit 197
  Sara Ahmed

Art and Creation

Art after the Sublime in Merleau-Ponty and André Breton:
Aesthetics and the Politics of *Mad Love* 221
  Galen A. Johnson

Institution and Critique of the Museum in "Indirect Language and
the Voices of Silence" 253
  Rajiv Kaushik

Deleuze's "Philosophy-Cinema": A Variation on Merleau-Ponty's
"A-Philosophy"? 269
  Mauro Carbone

Strong Beauty: In Face of Structures of Exclusion 281
  Véronique M. Fóti

Epilogue
Merleau-Ponty: An Attempt at a Response 297
  Jean-Luc Nancy

Contributors	303
Index	309

Texts of Merleau-Ponty's, Abbreviated

If not otherwise indicated, and whenever available, the numbers indicated refer to the English edition of the following texts.

AD   *Adventures of the Dialectic*, trans. Joseph Bien, Evanston: Northwestern University Press, 1973 (orig. *Les aventures de la dialectique*, Paris: Gallimard, 1955).

HT   *Humanism and Terror. An Essay on the Communist Problem*, trans. John O'Neill, Boston: Beacon Press 1969 (orig. *Humanisme et terreur*, Paris: Gallimard, 1947)

WP   *The World of Perception*, trans. Oliver Davis, London: Routledge, 2004 (orig. *Causeries*, 1948. Edited with notes by Stéphanie Ménasé. Paris: Seuil, 2002)

CPP   *Child Psychology and Pedagogy: The Sorbonne Lectures, 1949–1952*, ed. James M. Edie, Anthony J. Steinbock, and John McCumber, translated by Talia Welsh, Evanston: Northwestern University Press, 2010 (orig. *Psychologie et pédagogie de l'enfant: Cours de Sorbonne, 1949–1952*. Lagrasse: Verdier, 2001)

EM   "Eye and Mind," translated by Carleton Dallery, in *The Primacy of Perception and Other Essays on Phenomenological Psychology, the Philosophy of Art, History, and Politics*, 159–90. Evanston: Northwestern University Press, 1964 (orig. *L'oeil et l'esprit* [Paris: Gallimard, 1964])

HLP   "Husserl aux limites de la phénoménologie," ed. Franck Robert, Merleau-Ponty, in *Notes de cours sur l'Origine de la géométrie de Husserl*, ed. Renaud Barbaras, Paris: Presses universitaires de France, 1998

IP	*Institution and Passivity: Course Notes from the Collège de France (1954–1955)*, foreword by Claude Lefort, trans. Leonard Lawlor and Heath Massey, Evanston: Northwestern University Press, 2010 (orig. *L' institution-La passivité: Notes de cours au Collège de France (1954–1955)*, Paris: Éditions Belin, 2003)
IPP	*In Praise of Philosophy and Other Essays*, trans. John Wild and James Edie, Evanston: Northwestern University Press, 1988 (orig. *Éloge de la philosophie et autres essais*. Paris: Gallimard, 1953)
N	*Nature: Course Notes from the Collège de France*, ed. with notes by Dominique Séglard, trans. by Robert Vallier, Evanston: Northwestern University Press, 2003 (orig. *La nature: Notes, cours du Collège de France*. Edited with notes by Dominique Séglard. Paris: Seuil, 1995)
NC	*Notes de cours au Collège de France 1958–1959 et 1960–1961*. Edited by Stéphanie Ménasé with a preface by Claude Lefort. Paris: Gallimard, 1996
PP	*Phenomenology of Perception*, trans. Donald A. Landes, London: Routledge, 2012 (orig. *La phénoménologie de la perception*. Paris: Gallimard, 1945)
PrP	*The Primacy of Perception and Other Essays on Phenomenological Psychology, the Philosophy of Art, History, and Politics*, Evanston: Northwestern University Press, 1964
PW	*The Prose of the World*, ed. Claude Lefort, translated by John O'Neill. Evanston: Northwestern University Press, 1973 (orig. *La prose du monde*. Edited with an introduction by Claude Lefort. Paris: Gallimard, 1969)
S	*Signs*, trans. with an introduction by Richard S. McCleary. Evanston: Northwestern University Press, 1964 (orig. *Signes*. Paris: Gallimard, 1960)
SB	*The Structure of Behavior*, trans. Alden L. Fisher, foreword by John Wild, Boston: Beacon Press, 1963 (orig. *La structure du comportement*, Paris: Presses Universitaires de France, 1942)
SNS	*Sense and Non-Sense*, trans. with a preface by Hubert Dreyfus and Patricia Allen Dreyfus. Evanston: Northwestern University Press, 1964 (orig. *Sens et non-sens*. 1948. Paris: Gallimard, 1996)

TLC *Themes from the Lectures at the Collège de France, 1952–1960*, trans. John O'Neill, Evanston: Northwestern University Press, 1970 (orig. *Résumés de cours, Collège de France, 1952–1960*, Paris: Gallimard, 1968)

VI *The Visible and the Invisible, Followed by Working Notes*, ed. Claude Lefort, trans. Alphonso Lingis. Evanston: Northwestern University Press, 1968 (orig. *Le visible et l' invisible*, Paris: Gallimard, 1964)

Merleau-Ponty and Contemporary Philosophy

An Introduction

EMMANUEL ALLOA, FRANK CHOURAQUI, RAJIV KAUSHIK

Despite the premature interruption of his work, Maurice Merleau-Ponty (1908–1961) has left a lasting mark on twentieth-century thinking. Thanks to a large body of scholarship on his thought after his death, he is now part of the canon and a key figure within both phenomenology and twentieth-century philosophy more broadly. In addition, his own readings of the history of philosophy continue to attract interest and he has also become an authoritative reference in many other fields of research. This last point deserves to be stressed: at a time when philosophy is increasingly being institutionalized and reduced to its so-called core competencies, we should recall that Merleau-Ponty's place in the canon is due in large part to the breadth of his studies, including his ability to implicate philosophy in the sciences and vice versa. That he steadfastly refuses to marginalize both what is central to philosophy and other practices of knowledge betrays a point about what philosophy is and what counts as philosophy. Rather than proceeding from a systematic core which he later merely applied to other fields, Merleau-Ponty engaged in a demanding encounter between philosophy and other disciplines to such an extent that he reconceptualized some of philosophy's most central concerns. He has now become, in other words, a canonical philosopher precisely because he opposes neither the traditional principles and foundations of philosophy nor the new sciences of his time and the intellectual enigmas they generated.

That the sciences are able to reorganize philosophy implies that, to Merleau-Ponty, philosophy is not the "absolute science" to which the natural sciences would merely be relative. In fact, Merleau-Ponty seems to operate with a thoroughly contemporary notion of both philosophy and all other epistemic practices. It is this fundamental reconceptualization of philosophy, and all of the new possible lines of investigation such reconceptualization opens, which seems to us most alive today.

In light of this fundamental shift, this volume is not an overarching survey of interdisciplinary interests, but it defends a central thesis that serves as a through-line: Merleau-Ponty's work involves a certain reinvigoration of philosophy that opens toward some of the contemporary issues with which we are still to this day concerned. The explorations of the relationship between philosophy and non-philosophy, as Merleau-Ponty called what might also be termed philosophy's "outside," have been praised for their methodological topicality, for a metatheoretical reflection about the relationship between forms of knowledge. Moreover, as this volume shows, Merleau-Ponty's writings not only yield metatheoretical insights concerning methods but also remain relevant in terms of concrete ideas, for example in the many inventive conceptual attempts for moving beyond the dualism of nature and culture or reconciling objective sciences and first-person experience.

It is no doubt true that, since his voice fell silent in the last century, contemporary philosophers have been turning their attention to a set of newly formulated questions that at first glance would seem alien to Merleau-Ponty's phenomenology. Most importantly, Merleau-Ponty's early death coincided with the emergence of a new generation of thinkers that defined themselves by way of a sharp demarcation from a certain phenomenological tradition to which Merleau-Ponty belongs. Some of these demarcations have become famous and might indeed give the impression that his work is obsolete. In order to motivate the thesis of this volume, it is important for us to address directly some of the arguments put forward by those who assert that Merleau-Ponty's work is outmoded. There are three such arguments we would like to mention here, all of which have to do with a misunderstanding of phenomenology or the sense in which Merleau-Ponty is called a phenomenologist.

The first kind of criticism harks back to an argument repeatedly voiced against phenomenology's naïveté since the 1960s. Michel Foucault complained that phenomenology is incapable of addressing the materiality of discourse, and thus the formations of knowledge and power or the themes of domination and exclusion. Gilles Deleuze in turn opposed "meat," with all its crudeness, to Merleau-Ponty's notion of "flesh." "The flesh," Deleuze jokes, "is too tender." More generally, phenomenology has often been seen as incapable of thinking the material, the hardness of objects and the violence of history.

The second line of criticism sees phenomenology in an essentialist and therefore genetic manner: in this view, phenomenology is determined by its origins in Husserl's transcendental idealism. This criticism has gained traction again, especially through the argument put forward in Speculative Realism that phenomenology subordinates what things are to the way they appear to a subject. According to this line of thinking, any philosophy that starts by describing phenomena ends up being caught in the spell of idealism, and proves incapable of reaching out to reality and its concrete objects.

The third kind of criticism relies on a methodological notion of phenomenology as determined and exhausted by its emphasis on description. In this view, phenomenology is of exclusive interest to the empirically-informed strands of naturalistic philosophy, and fundamentally unable to build itself into a worldview comprehensive enough to account for phenomena beyond description, or unable to draw any generalizable accounts of the world, let alone anything like an ontology or a metaphysics. In short: phenomenology would be, at best, a preliminary level on the way to a conceptual analysis, and at worst, an antiphilosophical tendency within philosophy.

While all three criticisms are misconstructions of phenomenology as a whole, it is not the purpose of this volume to restate the aims of phenomenology as a worthwhile method. In any case, our defense of Merleau-Ponty against such critiques is far simpler: this is not the kind of phenomenologist Merleau-Ponty is or thought himself to be. Indeed, his writings deliberately set phenomenology into relief as the study of phenomena that ultimately pushes phenomenology to its own limits. Some readers even go as far as to say that he is in fact not a phenomenologist (assuming that phenomenology should be understood in the terms outlined above). Merleau-Ponty himself would rather disagree with the description of phenomenology from which he seems to be excused, but he would most certainly also like to reject any ethically, politically, or metaphysically deflationary view of reality (as goes the first criticism). He would just as well dispute that phenomenology is essentially committed to transcendental idealism, and he definitely considers ontology the natural horizon of phenomenology, not an exit from it. Let us pursue this last claim a bit farther.

When Husserl describes the move from the natural to the phenomenological sphere, he remarks that, "[b]etween consciousness and reality there yawns a veritable abyss of sense."[1] While Husserl most definitely thinks that this abyss only serves as a reason to supplant the science of reality with the science of consciousness, in a certain sense he leaves the nature of such an abyss itself uninvestigated. Whereas, for Merleau-Ponty, the proper phenomenological question would have to be: What is the sense of such an abyss? To what extent is intentionality irreducible to a naturalistic conception of the real while at the same time granting consciousness its very place *within* reality? To what extent is intentionality a feature of the sensible world itself rather than just of consciousness? In what sense is the sensible world a world of differences (allowing for things to emerge in contrast to a background) and of continuity (as the very ground that allows for things to emerge)? For Merleau-Ponty, these are questions of a relation between thought and the very world that remains independent from it. They are also not merely questions of the place of human thought in the nonhuman world but also of the *separation* between them. Indeed, what makes Merleau-Ponty's phenomenology unique is that he seems to at least want to think through this separation itself—to think from within the veritable abyss of sense that Husserl claims yawns between consciousness and reality. In other words, it seems that precisely this ambiguity of separation leads Merleau-Ponty to venture to the limits of the Husserlian phenomenology he inherited, and to inaugurate a series of new problems that have proven inspirational for contemporary thought.

The first thing that must be noted, when reappraising Merleau-Ponty's legacy for the current century, is that the situation is significantly different from the time when, in the 1960s and 1970s, his thinking was by and large either ignored or thought to be hopelessly dated. In the last two or three decades, the interest in Merleau-Ponty has been continuously growing, both within philosophical scholarship and in other fields of research. Besides, intellectual history has made significant progress, and the often-polemical rejections of Merleau-Ponty by authors such as Foucault, Deleuze, Lyotard, or Derrida are now taken with a pinch of salt, as it has now become evident how influential he has been for the subsequent generation of French thinkers. Uncontestably, the richer notion of phenomenology which Merleau-Ponty's thought points to offers potent perspectives when placed against the backdrop of the current "ontological turn" that can be witnessed in anthropology and the social sciences. But other aspects of this thinking are being reconsidered too. With the publication of many of Merleau-Ponty's lecture courses and posthumous working notes over the last few years, researchers have gained access to completely new materials that clarify the ways Merleau-Ponty breathed new life into metaphysics and ontology, even before the generation of thinkers that followed him, and the uncanny way that his thinking prefigured theirs. Just as in the 1960s readers were left with the fragmentary yet fascinating working notes from *The Visible and the Invisible* collected by Claude Lefort, today the scripts from the courses at the Collège de France as well as other archival materials or interviews released in the last decade or two have provided an ever more detailed picture of the manifold aspect of Merleau-Ponty's intellectual forays. When we scan the bounty of the current secondary literature on such posthumous materials, we are struck by the fact that it is rarely just philological or historical and that Merleau-Ponty's posthumous writing always gestures to new and different kinds of thought that may not be so explicit in his published work. Whether it be the lectures on institution and passivity, nature, the sensible world and the world of expression, or on the literary uses of language, Merleau-Ponty's lecture notes are continuously—and rightfully—being mined for new insights pertaining to everything from history, to psychoanalysis, aesthetics, and evolutionary biology.

Such historical and bibliographical facts count as an invitation to consider anew the possibility that Merleau-Ponty's work still speaks to us and that the sound of his thought still rings in our ears. Not only does the criticism that Merleau-Ponty's phenomenology is merely a naturalistic worldview seem ludicrous; the recently reappraised reflections on historical dialectics show that processes of emancipation, political organization, and revolutionary events were never out of his sight. However, although the Merleau-Ponty scholarship has recently unearthed such underexplored venues, the connections to current debates still need to be made. This is what this volume aims to do. *Merleau-Ponty and Contemporary Philosophy* cuts across the different loci of contemporary continental philosophy and provides an assessment of the innovative research of today. The purpose of this book is to show how Merleau-Ponty offers hitherto unexplored resources to address some of the pressing questions of our time and to acknowledge how some of our current concerns can find unexpected resources in his work. This book aims at clarifying some of the unfinished, loose, or simply hitherto unheard aspects of the philosopher's thought, and an exploration of their less visible relevance to contemporary philosophy.

Thus, this volume chronicles the continuities that connect our current intellectual world to Merleau-Ponty's thinking without reducing one to the other. In order to gain a better understanding of Merleau-Ponty's intellectual legacy, it is necessary to draw different perspectives on his oeuvre. The present volume gathers fifteen representative voices from continental philosophy today, some from Merleau-Ponty scholars and some from others who come to his work through their own thematic interests. The point is not to propose a unified "new Merleau-Ponty," but rather to remain sensitive both to the gaps and the crossings, to the chasms and chiasms, at work between seemingly disconnected fields. Some of the key themes with which the book is concerned, as evidenced by the table of contents, include: ontology, epistemology, anthropology, embodiment, animality, politics, language, aesthetics, and art. These are but a few areas for which Merleau-Ponty's writings have opened up new and different approaches. While our attempt cannot claim to be an exhaustive resource on the work of Merleau-Ponty, it offers a selection of some of the most creative current analyses of his thought.

The Texts

This book is organized along four main sections: "Legacies," "Mind and Nature," "Politics, Power, Institution," and "Art and Creation," each of which attempts to document Merleau-Ponty's legacy for some of our present philosophical concerns. These sections are rounded off by an epilogue by Jean-Luc Nancy ("Merleau-Ponty, an Attempt at a Response").

Legacies

What are Merleau-Ponty's legacies for contemporary thinking? The contributions contained in this section do much to support what we described above as our central thesis, namely, that Merleau-Ponty's phenomenology serves to reinvigorate a set of philosophical concerns that we continue to have. To start with, due to his incessant efforts to locate our bodily condition at the heart of any sense-experience, Merleau-Ponty has most obviously contributed to rehabilitating corporeality. The body, he asserts, is our "general medium" for having a world. The world is itself, first and foremost, what we perceive through the means of our bodily condition. Merleau-Ponty's idea of embodiment already cuts through the dualisms of mind and matter, insofar as it implies a form of oriented movement which locates the birth of intentionality on a prelinguistic, bodily level.

To Merleau-Ponty, the life of consciousness is inseparable from an embodied, situated, and desiring being. The motility of the body points toward a motor intentionality (*intentionnalité motrice*) which is the primordial way to relate to a world of objects and beings. As a result, issues of cognition can never be ultimately separated from drives and other living forces, since there is a permanent interplay between life and desire, perception and action, movement and expression, depth and meaning. While Edmund Husserl stressed the necessity for the subject to "return to the things themselves," Merleau-Ponty wanted to highlight the many situations where the subject is called upon by the things themselves. The contributions of this section focus on some central concepts contemporary philosophy inherits from Merleau-Ponty, such as that of "flesh" (*la chair*), as well as his analysis of temporality; it also indicates how new insights can be gained from Merleau-Ponty's accounts of how experiences come about, both in terms of how things come into view and how correlatively subjects come into being.

Merleau-Ponty's arguably most widely known conceptual invention is arguably "the flesh" (*la chair*), which has generated many critical discussions in contemporary philosophy. As Renaud Barbaras argues in "The Three Senses of Flesh," Merleau-Ponty's own ambiguity concerning the meaning of "flesh" has led to two opposing interpretations. The first one reads *la chair* as a faithful retranslation of the Husserlian idea of *Leib* as the experiential body, but then we find ourselves with the strange concept of a "flesh of the world": the reversible structure of embodiment (my own body is both sentient and sensed) cannot be extended to the world at large without turning the world itself into a sentient being (some aspects of this hypothesis are discussed in this volume by McWeeny). The other reading takes "flesh" to be distinct from the "personal body," and to be the name for a generalized account of the texture of the world in its sensible (yet not sentient) condition. However, Barbaras states, these two senses (the ontic one and the ontological one) can only be explained through a third, transcendental one. Flesh belongs neither to the subject nor to the world alone, it is rather a dynamic of life, which shares a same structure with the dynamic of desire. Indeed, the specificity of desire is that it only ever tends to something insofar as this thing is not yet present, to desire means to project oneself toward something that evades givenness. The very notion of the world should be thought as dynamic: beyond the flesh of the subject and the subject of the world, flesh should be thought *as* world.

Barbaras's plea for a dynamic reading of flesh generally raises the question of Merleau-Ponty's idea of temporality and of becoming. In "The Vortex of Time," Bernhard Waldenfels and Regula Giuliani ponder what Merleau-Ponty's legacy can be for a radical reconception of time. Cutting into the modern opposition between objective and subjective time, the question is how to make space for both the unity and the paradoxical character of temporal structures. Against linear accounts of time, which are to be found both in the externalist and in the psychological accounts, Waldenfels and Giuliani elicit the many resources that Merleau-Ponty offers throughout his work for an alternative picture of time. From the radical ontological meditation of the late writings one can follow the temporal thread backward, into the early works: what emerges in this comprehensive reading is the idea of time as a swirling vortex. Taking into consideration insights from psychoanalysis, structuralism, and psychopathology, they show what it might entail to proceed to a thoroughly *temporal* rethinking of embodied experience. Merleau-Ponty's critique of traditional conceptions of time remains faithful to a certain idea of phenomenology: neither object nor fact, time is neither a form nor a content of experience; from a phenomenological perspective, one must say that time is what *appears in passing*. In "Undergoing an Experience. Sensing, Bodily Affordances, and the Institution of the Self," Emmanuel Alloa aims at showing why Merleau-Ponty's critique of sensation cannot be disentangled from a radical redefinition of subjectivity. Connecting the early criticism of sense data with the later explorations around the notion of "institution," the point is to show how a self is not a mere receptacle for sensory contents but is instituted as a self through the very experiences it undergoes. Experience is not a thing we "do" or "have," but something we go through and something through which we become what we are. From a recapitulation of Merleau-Ponty's account of sense-emergence as a Gestaltist process and the analysis of the negative, diacritical structure of the experiential field, the argument moves to the mute demands of sensible environments ("affordances") and the types of embodied responsivity they call for. As Alloa argues, affective, "pathic" events that touch the subject are also what brings the subject into existence. Consequently, subjectivity appears as the field of becoming, a becoming shaped through sensible requests and instituted by means of the creative responses given to the requests put forward by other beings, things, and subjects.

Among the questions left open by Merleau-Ponty's writings is how philosophical language may adequately express the reality of experience. In his chapter "Between Sense and Non-Sense: Merleau-Ponty and 'The Silence of the Absolute Language,'" Stephen Watson takes up the claim that philosophy in fact requires an orientation not only to its language but to the fact that its language fails to express its meaning. In that case, Watson writes, a "transcendence of the sensible becomes as much lure as *caesura*." It becomes both that which language means as well as that which it cannot possibly express. But this excess does not precede language so much as it is gathered within and by language. This would be a limit or break within linguistic meaning that shows up or is produced only in language, and which thus has many points of access. If philosophy is supposed to highlight its production of its own caesura, as we learn from Watson's chapter, this entails an undermining of philosophy seen as the pursuit of some preexisting absolute.

Mind and Nature

Merleau-Ponty is often credited with having ventured into a topic that has since become ever more timely: the concept of nature. Lately, his lecture courses at the Collège de France from 1956–1960, his in-depth forays into biology and animal behavior, along with his more general interrogations on a new concept of nature, have been reappraised. These lectures have set the scene for a thorough reconsideration of what life, materiality, and consciousness mean. In this second section, three authors assess Merleau-Ponty's legacy for current debates about the naturalization of the mind, the extent to which matter itself is animated (the so-called question of "panpsychism") and, finally, the debate about animal communication.

While the phenomenological idea of intentionality has often been taken as a rebuke of the ambitions of reductionist naturalistic accounts, Jocelyn Benoist suggests that Merleau-Ponty's work may be naturalized to a certain extent. In "The Truth of Naturalism," Benoist suggests that, while it would be hard to deny some truth to the thesis of the mental—i.e., "there is some intentional region in the world"—this does not exclude the possibility that there might be some ontological truth to naturalism. One does not need to wait for the late, explicitly ontological ponderings for this: already in the early book *Structure of Behaviour*, Benoist explains, we find the idea that any embodied meaning sustains a being and is sustained by it all at once. By choosing behavior as a starting point, the cards are reshuffled between naturalism and a philosophy of consciousness: behavior is nothing but consciousness in nature, mind in the world. If intentionality is an emergent phenomenon that has its origin in nature itself, it means intentionality cannot exhaust nature. Nature should then be taken as the name for that which escapes full intentional grasp, while also being that in which any meaning is steeped.

In her contribution, "The Panpsychism Question in Merleau-Ponty's Ontology," Jennifer McWeeny explores one way of saving Merleau-Ponty's ontology from the criticisms leveled at it by Barbaras by arguing that the notion of "flesh" points toward a panpsychic conception of Being. With respect to the possibility of using his philosophy for a holistic understanding of nature, much indeed hinges on whether mindlike qualities are restricted to the human realm or whether they should be extended to matter at large. In the wake of recent philosophical trends such as new materialisms, speculative realism, feminist phenomenology, and environmentalism, McWeeny discusses the available ways to give a panpsychist reading of the notion of flesh and outlines the ontological, ethical, and political consequences of such an interpretation. Showing continuities and ruptures with authors from Descartes and Leibniz, James, Derrida, Foucault, and Deleuze, the chapter also locates the point at which an interrogation of mindlike structures must impose itself in classical and phenomenological philosophies of consciousness.

In "Merleau-Ponty and Biosemiotics. From the Issue of Meaning in Living Beings to a New Deal between Science and Metaphysics," Annabelle Dufourcq confronts Merleau-Ponty's forays into animal life with the advances in biosemiotics, opening up fruitful reconceptualizations of what signification means in the domain of life at large. In a movement that reverses the traditional tendency to refer everything back to the human, Dufourcq points out that one might just as well wish to regard the human as a sign of the natural. In so doing, her contribution echoes Benoist's plea for a renaturalized phenomenology as well as McWeeny's suggestion that panpsychism need not mean anthropomorphism. This involves taking seriously the claims made by biosemioticians such as Adolf Portmann or Jakob von Uexküll, who were able to show the extent to which animals live in a world of meaning and signs, which undercuts any mechanistic understanding of their form of life. Merleau-Ponty's claim that the world is meaning, as Dufourcq shows, can be understood reductively as a statement of defiance toward any talk of the "thing-in-itself"; but conversely it could be seen to expand the world of meaning to all existing entities, including animals, and plants too.

Politics, Power, Institution

After decades in which scholarship has by and large ignored Merleau-Ponty's explicitly political writings, we can currently witness a return to these matters. As some commentators have stressed, beyond his topical articles that dealing with the pressing matters of his time, Merleau-Ponty also devised an ambitious ontology of power, the implications of which still need to be fully unfolded. "There is no power which has an absolute basis," writes

Merleau-Ponty in his "Note on Macchiavelli."[2] This constitutes the starting point for an entire line of postfoundational thinking, of which Merleau-Ponty's disciple Claude Lefort was the first representative.

In "The Institution of the Law. Merleau-Ponty and Lefort," Bernard Flynn returns to the ominous question that has haunted the tradition for so long, namely, the relationship between nature (*physis*) and convention (*nomos*). Any law is faced with the constitutive paradox that it cannot legitimate its own inaugural institution but needs to resort to an "outside" to justify itself. If the paradigm of political theology, so minutely analyzed by Lefort, is to be rejected, then the only possible "outside" available is nature. But this would be a misunderstanding of nature, one in which nature is reduced to a self-identical, static object facing human conventions. On the contrary, and echoing a theme that runs through all the previous contributions, a conception of nature as life contains the resources for an internal form of transcendence: human laws are not added on top of nature but it is by nature that humans are political. This chiasm forces us to rethink the very notion of institution as cutting across the nature-culture divide: to live is to establish, violate, contest, and abide by laws. It is the illusion that we could find an ultimately secured ground that severs us from life itself, not the reverse.

In his contribution "Post-Truth Politics and the Paradox of Power," Frank Chouraqui wonders what kind of responses philosophy has to offer to the apparent irrationality of manmade decisions (both individual and collective). For there is a form of rationalism that is refuted by the mere existence of irrationality. One such fact is the phenomenon of post-truth, in which the presumed correspondence between credibility and support is shattered. On the contrary, such phenomena demonstrate that adhesion is not indexed on trust or belief: power is not truth-sensitive. For Chouraqui, Merleau-Ponty provides the tools to contend with such radically unsettling phenomena, for his engagement with political irrationality has led him to challenge the widely accepted view that truth-recognition precedes reality-constitution and that political adhesion follows from truth-attribution. On the contrary, Merleau-Ponty shows that recognition and constitution are equiprimordial moments unified in the most fundamental structure of being called "perceptual faith." The world as it appears to us, even as it presents recognition in contradistinction to constitution, is only derived from their originary unity. The political sphere is organized by their unity and by its interactions with the illusion of their disunity.

A central, yet still insufficiently theorized notion in Merleau-Ponty's writings is that of "institution" (*Stiftung* or *Ur-Stiftung*). Merleau-Ponty understands institution in a broad and elementary way, as both the *instituted form* and the *instituting process*. Situating herself within an ongoing current discussion about the uses of Merleau-Ponty's notion of "institution," Sara Ahmed suggests connecting it with habit and its normalizing effects. In her contribution "Institutional Habits. About Bodies and Orientations that Don't Fit," Ahmed proposes a practical phenomenology of habituation, with direct reference to diversity work. By stressing all the moments where bodies do not fit into the places intended for them, a contingent moment of the emergence and shaping of an institution becomes visible. The encounter with de-oriented, *queer* bodies not only highlights implicit normativity; it also opens up a space for reorientation, inspiring ways of critically coming up against institutions.

Art and Creation

It is frequently pointed out that Merleau-Ponty's work yields precious resources for a better understanding of the phenomenon of expression. Just when Jean-Paul Sartre proposed his essentialist account of literature, Merleau-Ponty refused Sartre's alternative between (direct) prose and (indirect) poetry, and rather sought to interrogate the genesis of meaning, returning to the creative and expressive moments beneath the surface of discourse. Expression would thus not so much amount to the transference of an internal state into an outside form (*ex-pressio*). It is, rather, an occurrence wherein something already in view but overlooked is presented as if for the first time. Such a task is of course not limited to literature: besides the close attention he pays to literary expression, painting, cinema, and the visual arts in general are incontestably among Merleau-Ponty's most privileged objects of attention. He suggests in "Eye and Mind," for example: "in *paintings* themselves we could seek a *figured philosophy*."[3] Since their publication, Merleau-Ponty's writings on visual arts have always stirred keen interest, inspiring generations of viewers and theorists. The last section of the volume presents some of the latest advances in aesthetics concerning, among other things, the status of the work of art in a museological context, Merleau-Ponty's rediscovered theory of cinema, and aesthetics as a space for dissensus.

In "Art after the Sublime in Merleau-Ponty and André Breton: Aesthetics and the Politics of *Mad Love*," Galen Johnson provides an exegesis of the critical role that surrealism plays in Merleau-Ponty's thought, and more specifically André Breton's semiautobiographical novel *Mad Love* (*L'amour fou*). As a recently published volume of interviews with Merleau-Ponty confirms,[4] surrealist aesthetics were an inspirational resource for him, both in the larger context of his project of elucidating the "prose of truth" and for the sake of his reconceptualisation of dialogic philosophy. Johnson manages to explain that, against all expectations, surrealist aesthetics, so often associated with the *écriture automatique,* does not lead to soliloquy but is conceived of as dialogic from the outset ("the forms of Surrealist language adapt themselves best to dialogue," as Breton claims in the *Surrealist Manifesto*). Along these lines, Johnson stresses how, against skepticism, authoritarianism, and moralism, the confrontation with surrealism was an important step toward Merleau-Ponty's reconception of intersubjectivity, coexistence, and the "flesh of the political."

In the chapter "Institution and Critique of the Museum in 'Indirect Language and the Voices of Silence,'" Rajiv Kaushik discusses Merleau-Ponty's critique of "the museum" as a hegemonic force. Recalling the discussion of André Malraux's project of a *Museum without Walls,* Kaushik examines Merleau-Ponty's critique of decontextualization and dehistoricization. Although this critique was formulated with respect to its time, Kaushik points out, Merleau-Ponty's arguments remain valid, and contemporary curators would do well to reckon with it. However, without having to defend some sort of historicist contextualization of artworks, the point is to stress the lateral connections between objects and experiences. For the ontology at stake in Merleau-Ponty's various treatments of art is one that is inseparable from his hermeneutics and politics, since this being is *in fact opened up by* all kinds of difference (linguistic, symbolic, ethical, political) without those differences having to conform to one another.

For Mauro Carbone, the time has come to confront one of the most celebrated theories of cinema—Gilles Deleuze's—with the lesser-known developments in Merleau-Ponty's thought on the artform. As Carbone suggests in "Deleuze's 'Philosophy-Cinema': A Variation on Merleau-Ponty's 'A-Philosophy'?" Merleau-Ponty stands as something of a "dark precursor" to Deleuze's ambitious ontology of cinema. Indeed, Merleau-Ponty's lecture delivered in 1945, alongside other text fragments, lays the ground for understanding what Merleau-Ponty calls an "implicit philosophy" at work in cinematic oeuvres. This perspective not only offers precious hints for understanding the specificity of film, it also gestures towards a more general fact: against the backdrop of his own "screen philosophy," Carbone highlights that ideas can only be experienced by encountering them in one of their sensible manifestations, on some kind of "screen" or "veil." Screens are not just hindrances, then, but conditions of possibility of thinking.

In the fourth and last chapter of this section, Veronique Fóti offers some suggestions on the connections between ethics and aesthetics. In her contribution, "Strong Beauty: In Face of Structures of Exclusion," Fóti begins with asking what we are to do with the notion of beauty today. If this notion is to mean anything, she argues, it has to be understood as a radically unanticipable, event-like experience one is seized by. Although Merleau-Ponty has not made beauty a central category of his aesthetics, the confrontative dimension associated with this definition of "strong beauty" can easily be reconnected with his analyses of Paul Cézanne, while echoing the work of Agnes Martin, Ellsworth Kelly, or Natvar Bhavsar. Such experience of strong beauty is the experience of extreme strength and fragility at once, thereby opening up a space for resilience. According to Fóti, art has an ethical dimension where it produces a consciousness for "refraction," that is, that totality is shattered, leaving us with the necessity of permanently recomposing ourselves. *Sensus* has *dissensus* as its precondition.

These four sections are finally punctuated by an epilogue by Jean-Luc Nancy titled "Merleau-Ponty: An Attempt at a Response," in which, for the first time, Nancy takes the opportunity to address an often-discussed issue: how and in what way his own thinking is related to the thought of Merleau-Ponty.

Notes

1. Edmund Husserl, *Ideas* I, trans. F. Kersten (Dordrecht/Boston: Kluwer, 1982), 93.
2. S, 212.
3. EM, 168.
4. Maurice Merleau-Ponty, *Entretiens avec Georges Charbonnnier, et autres dialogues, 1946–1959*, ed. Jérôme Mélançon (Paris: Verdier, 2016).

Legacies

The Three Senses of Flesh

Concerning an Impasse in Merleau-Ponty's Ontology

Renaud Barbaras

In French, the word *flesh*—*la chair*—invites a metaphor that, as always in such cases, one should exploit: the very possibility to invest this word into fields other than its own designated one conversely reveals a depth of meaning that must sustain our thinking. In any case, it is within the field of phenomenology, in France particularly, that this notion attained the status of a major philosophical concept. In Husserl, *Leib* refers to the living and sensible body, the body I inhabit, in contrast to the body as a fragment of matter; in short, *Leib* refers to one's own body (*le corps propre*). But even though this concept plays an important role, it only designates a specific being; its reach is merely ontic. It is with Merleau-Ponty, in particular in *The Visible and the Invisible* and texts of that same period, that the flesh—discussed without any possessive article since it is no longer the flesh of anyone—comes to occupy a central place and in fact becomes the major concept of the new ontology in the making. In the *corps propre*, Merleau-Ponty discovers a sense of being that gives us access to the very meaning of being; my flesh becomes the ontological witness of an originary dimension exceeding it and of which it is only a privileged modality. It brings forward the dimension of *the* flesh, which Merleau-Ponty sometimes refers to as the flesh of the world (*la chair du monde*). Thus, with Merleau-Ponty, one moves from an ontic concept of the flesh to an ontological one, and it is in this ontological sense that we use the word *flesh* most of the time. It is also in this way that it has been understood in subsequent phenomenological enterprises—Michel Henry's in particular—so that when in phenomenology one mentions the flesh, it is generally accepted that one means something else than the mere *corps propre,* and that the emphasis is placed on a more originary dimension, which in truth determines the latter.

The whole challenge of the notion of the flesh is understanding exactly to what dimension it refers. For, insofar as Merleau-Ponty is the thinker who attempted to make that move from ontic flesh to ontological flesh, from *corps propre* to flesh of the world, any approach to this question requires that one comes face to face again with this enigmatic flesh, which seems to be Merleau-Ponty's name for being. It is precisely because of Merleau-Ponty's work that we take for granted the need to consider the *corps propre* as an ontological witness, calling out toward a dimension that is deeper and, so to speak, foundational to it. The question is, rather, that of the *modality* of this call or of this move toward (ontological) flesh. Is the way that Merleau-Ponty passes from my flesh to the "flesh of the world" satisfactory? Indeed, might we be content with a univocal concept of flesh, one that would include as part of its ownmost modality both the appearing of beings and the subject to whom they are appearing? By immersing my flesh into a general flesh, so to speak, doesn't Merleau-Ponty remain dependent on the perspective that he intends to dismiss and isn't he displaying a certain degree of naïveté? We shall attempt to show that the overcoming of ontic flesh toward its "foundation" cannot be carried out in such a simple—and so to speak direct—manner and that, consequently, this overcoming must in fact follow two divergent yet correlative directions. This is why we will have to distinguish between *three senses* of the flesh.

As is to be expected, the starting point for the notion of flesh is paragraph 36 of *Ideen II*, which deals with the constitution of *corps propre* through touch as a "ground of localised sensations." Just like other objects appearing within the world, my body is characterized by the fact that I can at once see it and touch it, at least in part. There is however a fundamental difference between visual and tactile appearances, and it is this difference that will allow one to conclude that the *corps propre (Leib)* can only be constituted through touch. By touching my left hand, I obtain appearances of the tactile kind, which present themselves as characteristic of the thing "left hand": soft, smooth, warm, etc. But Husserl continues: "When I touch the left hand I also find in it, too, series of touch-sensations, which are *'localized'* in it, though these are not constitutive of properties (such as roughness or smoothness of the hand, of this physical thing). If I speak of the *physical* thing, 'left hand,' then I am abstracting from these sensations. . . . If I do include them, then it is not that the physical thing is now richer, but instead *it becomes Body* [*es wird Leib*], *it senses.*"¹ Therefore, saying that my right hand touches *my* left hand, that is to say, touches a fragment of my flesh, amounts to saying that it reveals a certain sensitivity in this left hand, which suddenly reveals itself as sentient: my right hand doesn't uncover any objective qualities but it arouses a sensing (*un sentir*) that embodies itself and unfolds itself on the very surface being touched. Of course, it immediately follows that my left hand, now flesh, becomes itself sensible to the right hand which was touching it and which therefore becomes demoted to the rank of a thing touched. Touch, insofar as it applies to the *corps propre*, is characterized by a fundamental *reversibility*—the touching can at any moment become a thing touched by this very body part that it was touching—and it is within this reversibility that the fundamental mode of being of flesh comes to light. One must recognize the importance of this description: what it reveals isn't some physiological singularity; it is an irreducible sense of being. Indeed, the flesh is characterized by the fact that no part of it is immune to becoming actively sensible; and neither is any active sensibility immune to transforming itself into an object of touch at the very moment it becomes localized. So the ability to feel is not superadded to any preexisting objective reality, a flesh is not superadded to a body (*Körper*)—for this superaddition would amount to appealing to some objective plane of corporeity when it is precisely this plane that is always already challenged by the experience of reversibility.

Sensibility is *constitutive* of corporeity and, as Husserl himself declares, the body as physical thing can only be attained through an act of abstraction. Such abstraction applies itself to a reality that is neither corporeal nor subjective, and this is what the very concept of flesh intends to name. If the body is sensible in its very corporeity, one must also reject the idea of a subjectivity that would be, at least in principle, independent of the body. The reversibility of touch shows on the contrary that every active touch may be localized on the surface of a body, which then delivers itself over to another touch, and that it is a feeling that is incarnate; in short, corporeity is constitutive of (sensible) subjectivity. Here, we are indeed faced with a fundamental effacement of the sensing/sensed and subject/object distinction. Since no part of my body can remain pure body (touched), and since no tactile activity can escape incarnation, one must renounce the very use of the categories of subject and object: as Merleau-Ponty writes, "The distinction between subject and object is blurred in my *corps propre*" (*S*, 167, orig. 211). The critical reach of the analysis of *chair propre* seems undeniable.

The discovery of the reversibility of touch introduces us to an original sense of being, which we have hitherto only described negatively and which is precisely the first sense of the flesh.[2] The whole challenge is for us to appropriate the singularity of this sense of being, to measure its importance without surreptitiously reintroducing any of the categories that the flesh is meant to challenge. The flesh is nothing but the locus of experience itself, since its sensibility toward itself is merely a particular mode of its sensibility to what it isn't, which one might call, provisionally, "the world." But once it is recaptured from this point of view, the reversibility of touch, which initially makes apparent the carnal mode of being, signifies that the experience of the world essentially includes a fundamental *belonging* to this world. To say that my touch is essentially incarnate amounts to recognizing that feeling can be said to be thrown or deported toward that which it feels. In other words, sensible experience, of which touch is an eminent modality, is characterized by a sort of fundamental *iteration*: sensibility allows the world to appear only because it already is on its side, so that, according to a relationship that is only apparently paradoxical, it already belongs to that which it constitutes. Sensibility, on this view, is a *zero* of the world—in the sense that the zero is both something other than a number and the very first of all numbers: the flesh is not the world and yet it already is on its side. This is to say, therefore, that it stands on both sides like a step *toward* the world which would be at the same time a step *into* the world. It is this strange iteration that *chair propre* invites us to reflect upon an iteration in which the subject (since one must admit that what appears appears *to* somebody . . .) is engaged in what it sees, exceeding itself or rather existing on the mode of its own excess and therefore ahead of itself. The meaning of being of flesh is that is of an originary *advance,* unveiling the ground that it simultaneously re-covers, showing a ground that it has already presupposed and upon which it lands. This advance is deeper than the partition of perception and objective motion since it unveils itself as it approaches and advances within this that it sheds light on. Such is the meaning of being of this ontic flesh which phenomenology has discovered and it is this that remains to be thought through.

Provided one perceives its critical import, the ontic concept of the flesh unavoidably leads into an ontological reworking. In a way, it is one of two things: either one remains within the traditional ontological framework and therefore regards reversibility as merely a psychological singularity, and insists that, although the distinction between the subject and the object is in fact blurred within the tactile experience of my own body, it remains in theory indubitable. Or, taking the reversibility of touch seriously, one can no longer be restricted to one's own body alone, and must admit that if the subject-object distinction is obsolete within my body, it must be declared obsolete beyond it as well. Within this perspective, which is Merleau-Pontian par excellence,[3] the flesh (which is at this stage still only *chair propre*) is not a singularity but an ontological witness, like a window open to the meaning of being. The ontic sense of the flesh is therefore bound to be exceeded by a more originary sense. How does this move take place? By way of an extension of the carnal mode of being on the basis of my body's belonging to the world. Indeed, as soon as the boundary between my body and the world loses any ontological meaning, to say that my body is inhabited by a feeling amounts to saying that "space itself is known through my body" (*S*, 167, orig. 211): the test of tactile reversibility is a test through which "the 'touching subject' passes over to the rank of the touched, descends into the things, such that the touch is formed in the midst of the world and as it were in the things" (VI, 134, orig. 176). Thus, it is no longer the subject—that subject tempted to place herself at the source of feeling—who has the initiative, but rather it is the world itself, since this feeling is in principle immersed within a body, which is itself immersed in the world. Thus, it is not I who feels, it is the thing that feels itself within me. In other words, the blurring of the subject and the object within the *chair propre* is attributed to the world itself in the form of an essential indistinction of being and appearing: just as every part of my flesh can always escape its corporeal silence and become sensible (in the sense of sentient), so too has being always already gone over to the side of phenomenality, and any being that silently rests within itself is meaningless. It is in this way that flesh, now taken in an ontological way, is understood as Visibility: one must define it as an intrinsic visibility that is not the correlate of any act of vision but, on the contrary, determines the possibility of such an act. Once generalized, the mode of being of the *chair propre* becomes the mutual immersion of the visible into the invisible and of the invisible into the visible, an in-difference between transcendence and phenomenality.

But, just as the transcendental perspective presented the very transcendence of the world as relying on the subject's initiative, it is on the contrary the subject itself that must result from the initiative of transcendence; that is to say, from the initiative of the ontological flesh. The transcendence of the world is not constituted within a vision that confers visibility to it; it is on the contrary visibility seen as the mode of being proper to transcendence, which constitutes vision as a modality of itself. There is, Merleau-Ponty says, "relation of the visible with itself that traverses me and constitutes me as a seer" (*VI*, 140, orig. 185). One witnesses therefore a kind of intentional *reversal*, which encapsulates Merleau-Ponty's ontological turn and of which my flesh is the fundamental operator: if it is true that the sensing is collapsed into the body and therefore always already incarnate, then its activity, which once seemed to require the position of a consciousness, turns into a fundamental passivity: the sensing (*le sentir*) discovers itself to be dependent of phenomenality, of some Sensible in itself, which is the genuine actor of appearing and of which sensing (*le sentir*) is but a mode of crystallization or a completion. One can therefore ultimately describe two opposite trajectories that really amount to one and the same: the first goes from the subject to the world via the body and the second goes from the world to the subject via the very same body. Recognizing the import of the indistinction of sensing and the sensed (*le sentir et le senti*) in my flesh amounts to understanding that the direction of the two trajectories reverses itself within my body and that the second trajectory is the truth of the first: "The thickness of the body, far from rivaling that of the world, is on the contrary the sole means I have to go unto the heart of the things, by making myself a world and by making them flesh" (*VI*, 135, orig. 178).

In spite of its appeal, this ontological extension leaves us feeling uncomfortable, as if one had just witnessed an illusionist's trick. Just as the rabbit that reappears in the hat of a spectator is not, in truth, the same rabbit that disappeared in the scarf of the illusionist, one is not certain that this reversal of the circuit of phenomenality give us a point of arrival that coincides with the point of departure. In other words, when we make the flesh, as visibility, the subject of phenomenality, do we really allow ourselves to account for the subject we had started with? By way of its own flesh, the subject is dissolved in a world that thereby becomes Visible and it is in this sense that one may speak of a flesh of the world. But is one entitled to take the same path in reverse, to account for vision on the basis of the Visible and to ascend from the flesh of the world to the flesh as *mine*? Put in Merleau-Ponty's language: How can the relationship of the visible to itself traverse me and constitute me as seer? We have moved from an ontic concept to an ontological one, but does the latter allow us to recuperate what initially gave us access to it? Can the flesh in the ontological sense account for the flesh in the ontic sense?

In order to answer these questions, one must return to Merleau-Ponty's passage from *chair propre* to the flesh of the world, in order to interrogate its legitimacy. As we saw, the fundamental operation that determines the move to ontology consists in generalizing to the level of a world what had initially been evidenced at the level of the *corps propre*: to say that touch takes place in my body, and that it is its work rather than the work of some consciousness, involves in fact declaring that the touch takes place "from the middle of the world." But such an inference is informed by a presupposition that is both massive and unquestioned, namely, that the body *is part of* the world, that it is situated within it and *continuous* with it. In short, that it is a *piece* or a fragment of the world. It is only on the basis of the thesis of this belonging and continuity that the continuity between a body and the world holds. However, the very affirmation of this continuity covers a presupposition about both the world and the body, indeed, one and the same presupposition: the world is an objective reality, extended in space; and the body is a fragment of this reality, a piece of extension, extracted from it insofar as it is entirely inherent to it. By affirming that "space itself is known through my body," Merleau-Ponty presupposes that the world is extension and that the body is a fragment of that extension. In truth, such a presupposition is indispensable, for it is only from the point of view of extension that the boundary between my body and the world is indiscernible and that what applies to one can be attributed to the other. As a fragment of matter, the body is fully immersed into the world and attributing anything to it amounts to attributing it to the world itself. However, if it is to allow for the ontological extension of the flesh, this continuity comes immediately into conflict with the outcome of the phenomenological description, and everything takes place as if Merleau-Ponty had forgotten phenomenology for a second to make its radicalization possible.

In fact, he forgets it twice. First of all, the reversibility of the sensible has revealed that the distinction between the subject and the object became blurred in my flesh and that, consequently, the flesh can in no way be conceived as an objective body. Appealing to the body's massive continuity with the world in order to transfer its sensibility to the world therefore amounts to contradicting the very lessons of reversibility: as it gives itself in the act of touch, *chair propre* has nothing in common with the objective world; it possesses no spatial continuity with it. It appears rather like a singular mode of being which stands against it and cannot be simply inscribed within it. Therefore, it is one of two things. Either my flesh is indeed an original mode of being that transcends the distinction of subject and object, but then this flesh belongs to the world and is of a mode *that is itself original* and irreducible to spatial continuity (in which case it becomes impossible to extend directly to the world that which has been discovered about my flesh), or such belonging is indeed possible, but on condition that my flesh be immediately grasped as an objective body, that is to say, at the cost of putting aside the yields of the study of touch. The conditions of belonging thus destroy its very possibility: if flesh is indeed a body, then feeling becomes external to the flesh again, just as a soul is external to a body, and touch can in no way be attributed to the world, which remains an extension without soul or flesh. The chief condition for the transfer of sense is the separation—correlative to the objectification of the body—of what was once united, to wit, the sensing and the sensed [*le sentant et le senti*], and, consequently, the disappearance of what was to be transferred in the first place. It is not a matter of concluding that *chair propre* is foreign to the world, as consciousness would be—on the contrary, we have seen that the reversibility of touch involves an essential belonging to the world—but, just as the flesh escapes the categories of subject and object, this very belonging escapes the categories under which it is usually conceived, in particular the category of spatial or material inclusion.[4] The singularity of the carnal mode of being necessarily brings with it the singularity of its belonging: its way of being in the world must reflect its mode of being as flesh, and the true question, the most difficult question perhaps, is to understand *in what sense* such a flesh, which is the indistinction of the feeling and the felt, may still be situated in the world. Ultimately, by extending to the world what applies to my flesh, Merleau-Ponty gave himself from the outset what is fundamentally in question.

It is precisely here that he forgets phenomenology a second time. Indeed, nothing justifies one to conceive the world at the outset as pure extension, lest it be the necessity to move from the body to the world. As it gives itself to *chair propre*—that is to say, to touch—the world can certainly not be folded back onto a mode of being characterized by a radical continuity with my body, that is to say, onto mere extension. On the contrary, by forcing us to think anew the meaning of belonging, the blurring of dualities operated by the notion of flesh invites us to interrogate the sense of being *to which it* belongs. In short, it invites us to interrogate this world within which the flesh is involved in order to make it appear. One might as well say that the relation of flesh to the world cannot be one of mere continuity. Neither can it be, of course, a matter of belonging in the sense of spatial inclusion—another figure of continuity. If the flesh belongs to the world, it cannot be by simply being situated in it, and the world cannot be seen as the mere ground over which one steps while crossing a distance. Ultimately, everything takes place as if Merleau-Ponty remained dependent on the objectivistic philosophy which he ceaselessly challenged. For he succeeds in conceiving of the incarnation of consciousness, against reflective philosophy, only by understanding it as some sort of immersion in an objective world, and winds up demoting transcendental philosophy only at the cost of awarding the world itself a power to feel that can no longer be attributed to the subject. Everything takes place as if the weight of dualism was such that it could only be overcome by its wholesale rejection for a simple monism in which the very boundary of flesh and world is erased.

It is true that Merleau-Ponty recognizes this difficulty and attempts to ground the inference from the flesh to the world while preserving the distance opened up by intentionality, a distance without which, in truth, the very idea of feeling would lose any sense, and so too would the idea of flesh. The purpose of the text immediately following from the fragment about space cited above is, in our view, corrective.

> If the distinction between subject and object is blurred in my body . . . it is also blurred in the thing, which is the pole of my body's operations, the terminus its exploration ends up in, and which is thus woven into the same intentional fabric as my body. When we say that the perceived thing is grasped "in person" or "in the flesh" (*leibhaft*), this is to be taken literally: the flesh of what is perceived, this compact particle which stops exploration, and this optimum which terminates it all reflect my own incarnation and are its counterpart. (*S*, 167, orig. 167)

It is now a matter of accounting for carnal extension by no longer grounding it on some objective continuity but on the continuity of the intentional fabric. Merleau-Ponty takes advantage of a lexical proximity in order to justify the extension of the mode of being of my flesh into the world (now taken as an intentional pole). To say that things are given in bodily, fleshly presence (*leibhaft*) would imply that their mode of being has something to do with the mode of being of the flesh, and consequently that the distinction of the subject and the object is blurred not only in my body but also in the thing. The appeal to flesh, under its double use, aims to restore within intentional distance itself, a kind of continuity allowing for the ontological extension of the flesh. But there is both some naïveté and a *coup de force* here. Indeed, Merleau-Ponty's way of proceeding involves remaining silent about the fact that, in the expression *leibhaft*, the flesh has a *metaphorical* signification: it refers to the most intimate, that is to say, the most proper (*le plus propre*) and this is why the word is put to use in order to express the givenness of the thing itself, as it is, and to describe its living presence. But Merleau-Ponty acts as if there was no sense of flesh but the literal sense; as if therefore, *leibhaft* referred to the mode of being of the body. In truth, if this term refers to the *corps propre*, it is only insofar as its givenness indicates an authenticity, an originarity that describes intuition in contrast to an intentional act in which the object is merely signified. But Merleau-Ponty acts as if the presence *in the flesh* implied the presence *of a flesh*. He collapses the originary character onto the flesh instead of grasping the flesh as something that signifies originarity, and it is therefore easy for him, under the cover of this lexical proximity and refusing to see any distance, to attribute to the things of the world the meaning of being of the *chair propre*. One will therefore have to examine whether the mode of givenness that signifies this presence in the flesh may be described satisfactorily by Merleau-Ponty's notion of flesh: Is what the expression *Leibhaftigkeit* designates already visible or does it, rather, remain in the background to any visibility?

We may now return to the feeling of unease mentioned above. Ultimately, it comes down to the fact that Merleau-Ponty puts forward a univocal concept of the flesh to which the very distinction between the feeling and the felt—that is to say, intentional distance—appeals. Indeed, the ontological generalization of a carnal reversibility leads unavoidably to a transformation of one of the terms. My flesh reveals an encroachment between sensing and sensed, which amounts to saying that my body is always self-present through and through. But this relation cannot be transposed wholesale to exteriority because there is no meaning in saying that the world feels itself or is present to itself, like my flesh is. The transposition therefore requires a reformulation: the flesh of the world signifies that being is always and through and through on the side of phenomenality and that any being that would be foreign to phenomenality would have no more meaning than a body that would be foreign to its own sensibility, unable to feel itself. It is therefore the subject of sensing (*le sentir*) or appearing (*l'apparaître*) that disappears as the ontological transposition is carried out. In other words, the descent of subjectivity through the body and into the world corresponds to an ascent of the world toward phenomenality, but *never toward subjectivity*. The two opposite movements do not coincide; the point of departure of the one (the subject of feeling) cannot be the point of arrival of the other, for one cannot grasp how an appearing immanent to the world can engender its own subject, or how visibility can engender vision. What definitely contradicts the hypothesis of an appearing that gives rise to its own subject is the evidence that fuels the philosophies of consciousness, evidence according to which appearing has any meaning only as appearing *to* a subject.

This is what led Merleau-Ponty to reintroduce a distinction, one of *degree* this time, at the heart of the flesh. Thus, he writes about the *corps propre* that "fundamentally it is neither thing seen only nor seer only, it is Visibility sometimes wandering and sometimes reassembled" (*VI*, 137–38, orig. 181), and it is based on the very same Visibility that he shall account for the subject of the appearing. Yet, one cannot see at all how visibility, by "reassembling" instead of "wandering" or remaining "scattered," can ever turn into vision: the subject is not a *moment* or a degree of concentration of visibility but is straightforwardly its *condition*. The appeal to a difference between a reassembled visibility and a wandering visibility indeed hides a difficulty lying behind the metaphors; it doesn't solve it however. Merleau-Ponty knew this well. He in fact stresses it in a working note: "The flesh of the world is not *self-sensing [se sentir] as* is my flesh—It is sensible and not sentient" (*VI*, 250, orig. 304). Here, one gets the impression that all that had been achieved becomes abandoned at once, for by stressing that my flesh is characterized by a feeling-oneself that does not apply to the world, Merleau-Ponty radically disputes the possibility of preserving any univocal sense of the flesh. The flesh is suddenly doubled out—there is the flesh of the world and there is sentient flesh—which amounts to recognizing that the ontological concept of flesh, as thematized by Merleau-Ponty in his last work, is an inconsistent concept.

This recognition gives rise to two remarks. First, it seems that what Merleau-Ponty wanted to evade is exactly what caught up with him, and precisely because he attempted to escape it too quickly. Indeed, he sees the concept of flesh as a way of liberating himself once and for all from any philosophy of consciousness and that is why he immediately credits the world with the reversibility he discovered in touch. But in doing so, he prevents himself from giving an account of what makes the sentient, active pole different, and ends up reaffirming the specificity of my flesh in contrast to the flesh of the world. There is here something like an attempt at naturalizing the flesh which inevitably leads to a restoration of the point of view of consciousness. Once more, Merleau-Ponty wavers between a certain form of realism and a certain form of idealism: in so doing, he doesn't overcome their opposition.

But this failure shows us a way. One would be foolish to seek an ontologization of *chair propre*, for this could only lead into some sort of confused phenomenological monism. The best way to truly overcome the philosophy of consciousness may rather be to begin by recognizing what is irreducible in it, or rather, by recognizing in what ultimate phenomenological truth it is rooted. This truth is very well summed up by Merleau-Ponty in the note we just cited: the distinction of the felt and the sentient in my flesh and in general, of the subject and the world, cannot be entirely reabsorbed lest one deliberately ignores the fact that appearing only exists as an appearing-to. It is therefore not so much a matter of overcoming the polarity of the feeling and the felt in favor of a third kind of being—of which we have seen that it only brings us back to dualism—but a matter of interrogating the *meaning of being* of the feeling and of the felt world (which my body is part of) in light of their originary interlacing, as evidenced in the experience of the *chair propre*. By way of this *chair propre*, a feeling is thrown into the world and it is now a matter of understanding the meaning of being of the world and that of the sensing (*le sentir*), so that this originary advance, this fundamental iteration we mentioned at the outset, becomes possible. Thus, the *chair propre* doesn't lead into one single concept of flesh but rather into two: ontic flesh must be referred to an ontological flesh and a transcendental flesh all at once. One must therefore attempt to outline more precisely these two new senses of the flesh by reintroducing the polarity of the phenomenological correlation where Merleau-Ponty wanted to see only one mode of being. By grasping ontological flesh in its genuine sense, cut off from its subjective side, we shall acquire the means of understanding transcendental flesh, which is truly the flesh of the transcendental.

In order to answer the question of the ontological sense of the flesh, we must return to the problem of the givenness in the flesh. As we have seen, Merleau-Ponty subjects the metaphorical sense of the flesh, in the expression *leibhaft*, to the literal sense that he applies to *chair propre* and he thereby places it in the service of his conception of ontological flesh as a "formative medium of the object and the subject" (*VI*, 147, orig. 193), as an intermediary element standing between the two. Yet, this is not the use that Husserl makes of this expression. There, givenness in the flesh qualifies the perceptual act as an originary bestowing intuition (*intuition donatrice*). Hence, the flesh has the metaphorical sense of the ownmost (*le plus propre*), the most intimate, as evidenced, for example, in the expression "flesh of my flesh": the flesh is so to speak the "heart." Wouldn't it be possible therefore to move from givenness "in the flesh" to an ontological flesh, that is to say to draw from this *Leibhaftigkeit* a new sense of the flesh? It is indeed, in a sense, what Merleau-Ponty is attempting to do, but he makes the mistake of conflating from the outset the *Leib* of *Leibhaftigkeit* with ontic flesh, as it is given in the experience of the *corps propre*. It now becomes a matter of deciding whether givenness in the flesh can be understood as an indication of an ontological sense of the flesh that owes nothing to the *corps propre*, but indeed one on which the *corps propre* is on the contrary dependent in the sense that this ontological flesh exhibits the meaning of the belonging of the *corps propre*. In Husserl, the givenness in the flesh coincides with intuition, and any originary character can only suggest an intuitive character. In this context, our question remains unanswered, for givenness in the flesh becomes necessarily conflated with the positive intuition of a positive being. In this givenness, no dimension besides that of the being (*l'étant*) is given to me, no flesh is delivered over to me: the flesh is just a mode of givenness (*Leib* refers to *Leibhaftigkeit*) and it is not something liable to be given to me. But the situation becomes transformed when one separates *originary* character from *intuitive* character. This separation is required by the discovery of the fact that any intuition supposes the giving of a frame or of a preliminary scene which cannot, itself, be the object of any intuition (lest one be forced to posit a new frame within which this intuition will take place). Indeed, if perception is indeed a sketch of givenness (*par esquisses*), it demands that the possibility of indefinitely going through its sketches be given from the start alongside the *determinability* of the object, and prior to any effective determination. Patočka, as one who has pursued this question farther than anyone, declared: "The fact that I always possess anew, wherever I am, the possibility of realising the same continuation; this is not merely anticipated, it is given in the form not of a simple intention, but as a presence *independent* from the contingent filling up or of the mere empty anticipation."[5] There is indeed a donation and therefore a proper presence of this that is not intuitively given, of what remains, in this sense, a non-presence:[6] this givenness and this originary (non-)presence are the very condition of intuitive fulfilment, the element of originarity that functions as a frame or a ground for any intuition. In short, it is not because I perceive the thing by giving myself endlessly renewed sketches of it that I know that it is here; it is not because it is intuited that it is given; it is, rather, because it gives itself over to me as *here* that I know that I can perceive it by uncovering what is merely a sketch of it, that is to say, that I can have an intuition of it. This is why intuitive givenness presupposes an even more originary givenness, one that delivers the thing over to me as here and therefore as determinable, and this is exactly what Husserl calls givenness in the flesh.

Given that this originary determinability refers to a specific dimension, givenness in the flesh may now be understood as givenness *of a* flesh—it leads into an ontological meaning of the flesh. This flesh is simply a preliminary stage in which any intuited presence takes place, a form or element of originarity inasmuch this originary character is not conflated with the intuitive character but rather commands it. This form is nothing but the *world,* conceived not as the sum of the beings but rather as the frame or originary ground within which the beings may take place in order to be intuited. It is the untotalizable totality, which contains everything that may spring up and which is therefore not distinguished from what it totalizes. It is the very scenic stage of being that, since it is not itself a being, is circumscribed by the very beings that appear on it. Therefore, if Patočka is correct to say that the world is one constitutive dimension of the appearing, that any apparition supposes the co-apparition of the world, one must therefore recognize that the intuition of any being presupposes the givenness in the flesh of the world as a frame of the intuition and as the very element of originarity. One may conclude that givenness *in* the flesh indeed supposes the givennes *of* a flesh, which is nothing but the world understood as a not-being totality (*totalité non-étante*). There is an ontological sense of the flesh, which refers to the world, and one should no longer talk of the flesh *of* the world, as Merleau-Ponty did, but rather of the flesh *as* world. Let us stress that, thus understood, the mode of being of the flesh is as different as possible from that of the *chair propre.* Recapturing the flesh on the basis of givenness in the flesh involves dramatizing the separation between the being of the *corps propre* and the being of the things at which it aims. It is this very distance that Merleau-Ponty sought to reduce.[7] There is a flesh of the things, synonymous with the world organizing them and which they crystallize in return, which is given (in the flesh) without ever being visible: this is not an originary being, but originarity as being.

This ontological flesh correlative to givenness in the flesh is indeed the originary condition for the appearing of things, but it isn't the only one. It is a flesh that one could call transcendent and which, as such, requires a *transcendental* flesh,[8] corresponding to the third sense of the flesh. This transcendental flesh is merely the truth of the very sensing (*sentir*) initially grasped within the *chair propre*: the sense of a kind of being which would be specific to sensing (*sentir*) and which is characterized by the reversibility of flesh and sensing, a sense of being specific to sensing insofar as sensing implies being steeped in something sensed (*un senti*), being steeped in a body. But its characterization is subjected to a double condition that has been established in the foregoing analyses. On the one hand, as transcendental, the flesh must enable one to account for the flesh in the second, ontological sense. In this manner, the flesh is what sets transcendence free, what bestows the carnal originary insofar as it exceeds any apparition, as withdrawing itself behind everything that presents it as its nonapparent background; in short, as what givenness can in no way intuit. On the other hand, regarded as *flesh*, that is to say, as what conforms to the features brought out by the analysis of ontic flesh, it must be characterized by a fundamental iteration, by an originary advance that unveils as it approaches, so that it unceasingly passes over to the side of this whose appearing it enables. Let us stress immediately that these two conditions are perfectly consistent with each other, and are perfectly articulated together. It is indeed obvious that any transcendental flesh would be unable to deliver the invisible background of the ontological flesh if it remained mere intuition or mere vision. Its reach would never measure up to the element of originarity—that is to say, the world. On the contrary, one can see that only a phenomenalization[9] in the form of an advance that advances over itself can attain this that withdraws itself behind all appearing being and stands as the very stage of its appearing: only the indefinite character of an advance can correspond to the forever reinitiated recoil of this open totality that we call the world.

Given this double condition, it appears that transcendental flesh must be characterized as *desire*: desire is the most originary sense of the flesh and it delivers the very mode of being of what on the ontic plan, we initially grasped as sensing (*sentir*). This brings us back to a classical conception of the flesh, one with religious connotations, as evidenced in the expression "sins of the flesh," and one that construes desire as the fundamental characteristic of the flesh. This theological-metaphysical intuition contains an authentic phenomenological discovery: only desire satisfies the conditions of the problem and, in truth, the conditions to which we have submitted the transcendental flesh are nothing if not a portrait of desire. Indeed, the specificity of desire is to deliver a presence on a mode that excludes intuition: to desire means to project oneself toward a given that evades seeing, it means aiming at that which exceeds all presentation, that toward which one can only tend. The specificity of desire is that the object of desire exacerbates desire as much as it satisfies it. Thus, the opposites of satisfaction and disappointment makes no sense from the point of view of desire. One might as well say that any being, insofar as it always disappoints the desire that aims at it, outlines as its genuine "object" a dimension of pure excess or of pure withdrawal, which transcends the very order of the object and, consequently, the order of intuition too. Since nothing fulfills it, desire is properly desire for nothing and to that extent is able to provide access to everything, to that which transcends all being, that is to say, to the nothing of being that we examined as ontological flesh taken as the very element of originarity. But on the other hand, although desire is ignorant, it should not be reduced to the mere displacement motivated by its own satisfaction: it takes place at a deeper level than the distinction of seeing and moving, and thereby it informs its possibility. Desire aims at its object and makes it appear only by projecting itself toward (*tendant vers*) it and that is why its reach exceeds the reach of intuition. But such a tendency doesn't fall back onto the mere plane of spatiality; it is as if contained within itself, enclosing an infinite reserve, and that is also why no object ever exhausts it. The most positive thing we can say about the transcendental flesh as desire—or the transcendental of the flesh—is that it grounds the fundamental iteration of *chair propre* defined as active feeling assigned to a condition of belonging. Describing the flesh as ahead of itself and therefore, so to speak, wider than itself, this means grasping it as desire. Saying that it enables appearing only by advancing toward precisely the appearing it enables amounts to affirming that it entertains relations to what it isn't and is the mode of Aspiration. If *chair propre*, in its act of phenomenalization, is Advance, Desire is its essence.

There are therefore neither one nor two senses of the flesh, but indeed three. These three senses are not situated on the same level, for, although the first leads into the other two, it becomes reabsorbed within them to the extent that they are the ones delivering its meaning. There is the flesh in the ontic sense, which is merely the *corps propre*, in which feeling and felt ceaselessly pass over into each other. But if we wish to avoid construing it as a mere psychological singularity, if we are decided to recognize the specificity of the mode of being revealed by *chair propre*, we immediately look away from the ontic field toward its condition. This condition is double: ontological and transcendental. As appearing, the flesh belongs—alongside any appearing being—to the ontological flesh, that is to say, to the originary and nonintuitive element requisite for any intuition properly construed as givenness in the flesh. This flesh is the ontological counterpart to *Leibhaftigkeit*; it is undistinguishable from the pure transcendence of the world. But, in contrast to what Merleau-Ponty believed, this condition cannot be self-sufficient: by virtue of its very meaning, transcendence appeals to a transcendental flesh, that is to say, to a life able to open up ontological flesh, a life whose reach would be as wide as that of the world itself as it exceeds all beings. We think that we have found in desire the ultimate determination for this transcendental flesh, and in this sense, desire must doubtless be regarded as the very essence of life.

Notes

1. Edmund Husserl, *Ideen zu einer reinen Phänomenologie und phänomenologischen Philosophie II. Phänomenologischen Untersuchungen zur Konstitution*, §36 (tr. *Ideas Pertaining to a Pure Phenomenology and to a Phenomenological Philosophy*, book 2: *Studies in the Phenomenology of Constitution*, trans. Richard Rojcewicz and André Schuwer [Dordrecht: Kluwer, 1989], 152).

2. Following Husserl, Merleau-Ponty defines it as a "perceiving thing," and a "subject-object" (*S*, 166, orig. 210).

3. But not exclusively. Hans Jonas later adopted the same approach in the *Phenomenon of Life* (New York: Harper and Row, 1966) although from a rather different perspective.

4. Besides, Merleau-Ponty was perfectly aware of this, as shown in this passage from the *Visible and the Invisible*: "We have to reject the age-old assumptions that put the body in the world and the seer in the body, or, conversely, the world and the body in the seer as in a box" (*VI*, 182; tr. 138). yet, instead of concluding from this that there is a necessity to interrogate the mode of belonging to the world specific to the body, Merleau-Ponty gives himself this mode of belonging, and thereby contradicts this that he has just said, by adding: "[W]here is one to set the limits of the body and of the world, given that the world is flesh?" Surprisingly, Merleau-Ponty challenges belonging not in the name of any difference between the modes of being of the *corps propre* and the world, but rather for the sake of a more radical sense of continuity.

5. Jan Patočka, *Papiers phénoménologiques*, trans. Erika Abrams (Grenoble: Millon, 1995), 178.

6. "Emptiness is in no way a kind of non-givenness; rather, it is a mode of givenness" (Patočka, *Papiers phénoménologiques*, 176).

7. In all fairness, one must add that Merleau-Ponty, in his concern for a close description of the essence of phenomenality, sometimes does thematize the flesh in terms very similar to those we are using here. Thus, in *VI*, 135, orig. 175 he writes: "The *Urpräsentierbarkeit* is the flesh," and further, *VI*, 219, orig. 27: "It is hence because of depth that the things have a flesh." But it goes without saying that this sense of the flesh, which refers to visibility as such, that is to say, to the ontological condition of any visible (a condition that could be identified with the world) forbids any integration of vision within it, as well as any return to ontic flesh.

8. Here, we encounter Michel Henry's approach. In *Incarnation* (orig. 2000; tr. *Incarnation. A Philosophy of Flesh*, trans. Karl Hefty [Chicago: Northwestern University Press, 2015]), after criticizing the exteriorization of the flesh in Merleau-Ponty, Henry too proposes a transcendental sense of the flesh. Yet, this transcendental flesh is conflated with pure auto-affection seen as a revelation of life itself. Therefore, this sense of the flesh doesn't involve any rooting or any relation to externality, so that one is left wondering what justifies the appeal to the notion of flesh at all (in fact,

it is only this reference to life [*Leben*] that earns it to be qualified as flesh). The transcendental sense of the flesh that we are developing here relies on the contrary on the recognition of its constitutive relation to externality. In this sense, we stand equally as close to Henry as to Merleau-Ponty, or rather, equally as far from them.

9. "Phenomenalization" rather than constitution. Given the situation of the problem, it goes without saying that we are dealing here with a transcendental that is in no way constitutive.

Vortex of Time

Merleau-Ponty on Temporality

BERNHARD WALDENFELS AND REGULA GIULIANI

I

There are central topics that constantly accompany Merleau-Ponty's thought and therefore have a special share in the intellectual transformations characteristic of his thought. Among them are the body, expression, space, and also time. These key ideas have become part of the basic kit of phenomenology and have this point in common: what is meant through them is not merely something that appears; rather, they are involved in the very appearing of whatever appears. Time is neither one fact among others nor one essence among others, it is neither an empirical given nor one of the transcendental conditions of experience; rather, it pervades all experiencing in which everything makes its appearance and then exits. Time appears in passing by making things appear. For Husserl, it belongs to the realm of transcendental experience in which experience becomes accessible to itself in a magnified form. From the very beginning, it generates a cluster of paradoxes inasmuch as constitutive time, like everything that constitutes itself, ultimately appears among the outcomes of its own constitution. The now of the living present certainly means more than merely a temporal datum that could be deciphered by means of temporal signs; but nonetheless, it can be dated. There is a relationship between "now" and April 1, 1998—despite all the distinctions that thrust themselves upon us. Time is duplicated or replicated in a manner similar to the body, which also has a place among the physical things that owe their appearing to it. It is one of the merits of Merleau-Ponty's thought that it endures these tensions and makes them fruitful even at points where Husserl urges that the tensions be resolved. The paradoxes that have their very specific effect in the theory of time create a counterweight to fundamentalist dispositions that insist on something primary and to totalitarian ambitions that appeal to a whole. Moreover, they prevent everyday phenomena from being degraded as vulgarized variations of a genuine experience. What happens every day can "explode" at any time and open up experiences of time that in and despite their temporality breach the framework of the temporal. The late title *The Visible and the Invisible* can also be read as "The Temporal and the Nontemporal" but in such a way that the nontemporal, like the invisible, can be identified as the "nontemporal of this world" and not transported to the shadow realm of eternal ideas. The figures and sceneries of Proust's *Recherche* recur as leitmotifs in Merleau-Ponty's works; and as in *Recherche*, lost, misjudged, despised time is regained here and now hand in hand with the fundamental events of birth, rebirth, and death, of leave-taking and return that everyone undergoes, and also hand in hand with foundational historical events that do not merely bring about new things, but also change the coordinates of the world and in the end profoundly affect even our views of time and history.

If we look at the contexts in which the problem of time is addressed, it begins in the early work *The Structure of Behavior* with the description of perceptual forms and structures of bodily behavior. These basic aspects are picked up in the *Phenomenology of Perception* and interwoven not only with the temporality of bodily experience, but intensified to a self-affect that does not merely make something or other appear, but rather the self: the various things appear to the self, and also the self itself appears to the self. Finally, in the unfinished work *The Visible and the Invisible*, there are traces of the problem of time that are new in kind: a temporal architecture in which time and space unite and time inscribes itself into space. It is obvious that Merleau-Ponty's reflections arise from a sustained conversation with Bergson, Husserl, and Heidegger. If we wanted to complement the well-known titles *Phenomenology of Internal Time Consciousness, Being and Time, Time and the Other,* and *Time and Narrative* with a corresponding title, it could be something like "Body and Time" ("Le corps et le temps") or "The Flesh of Time" ("La chair du temps"). Finally, it should be mentioned that in the course of his reflections on nature in the last years of his life, Merleau-Ponty paid renewed attention to the scientific revolutions in the interpretation of time brought about by modern physics and biology. This gave rise to a counterweight to the subjectification and internalization of time that too readily lets its objectivistic adversaries define the rules of the game. Lastly, it hardly needs to be mentioned that politics and history, literature and art had a decisive influence on Merleau-Ponty's interpretation of time. All of this merges to form an outstandingly rich temporal landscape. In the following discussion, a few paths through this landscape shall be mapped with keen regard to the specific surroundings in which the temporality of phenomena and ultimately the phenomenon of time itself emerge. Generally, this takes place indirectly, often in conjunction with the repudiation of inadequate interpretations of time.

II

In our European tradition, reflection on time begins with a resounding chord on two notes: on the one hand, cosmic time with its goal-oriented courses of movement; on the other, mental time with its focus in the experienced present. In the one case, it is the recurrent circular movement that liberates from the transience of time, in the other case it is the instancy of the moment that tears us out of temporal distraction. This polarity, which to this day is associated with the classical texts of Aristotle und Augustine,[1] breaks apart in the early modern era. There ensues an opposition between measurable, homogeneous time, which only admits of relative determinations such as earlier and later, and experienced duration, which has its center in an absolute present. The objective view of time is oriented on space inasmuch as it uses the patterns of the point in time and the timeline, whereas the subjective view of time is removed from space through its link to mind, spirit, or consciousness. The opposition of body and soul continues in Kant's antithesis between outer sense determined by space and inner sense determined by time. At the threshold of the twentieth century, the efforts by authors such as Bergson and Husserl, James and Whitehead to renew thought on time are also largely under the sway of this modern problem, even in their conceptual nomenclature. It is remarkable that Merleau-Ponty begins utterly elsewhere, specifically in a "third dimension" "on this side of the pure subject and the pure object," that is, on this side of spatialized and experienced time.[2] In this respect, his approach is similar to Heidegger's except that in his bodily orientation he draws more stimulation from scientific research and innovation and that he places more confidence in the anonymity of everyday experience.

In his work *The Structure of Behavior*, the topic of time first occurs in the context of *spatial-temporal structures and forms* found on all levels of bodily behavior, even on that of animal behavior. The difference between human being and animal is not ascribed to a supplementary logos or causality of freedom, but is, rather, derived from the manner of generation of structure and form, which is characterized both by continuity and discontinuity. Merleau-Ponty knows that he is in agreement with Gestalt theory and environmental and behavioral research in biology.[3] Jakob von Uexküll's book *Theoretical Biology*, first published in 1920, received great attention from philosophers such as Scheler and Heidegger; he writes that the "temporal form with its goal-directed duration is indeed the creative rule that governs all generation of form"[4] in opposition to Bergson's antithesis of time and duration, of intellect and intuition.[5] In his work *Der Gestaltkreis* (*The Gestalt Circle*), Viktor von Weizsäcker states: "The world and its things are not in space and time, rather space and time are in the world and on the things";[6] this proposition could have been written by Merleau-Ponty, provided that "in" and "on" are not understood realistically but in the sense of a structuration process forming the world and things. In this connection, Merleau-Ponty refers to corresponding animal experiments, to detour experiments in the goal-directed behavior of dogs, to rats' orientation in space and time labyrinths, and to the motor and instrumental behavior of chimpanzees. The decisive point is the concept of a movement that is no longer understood merely as a force-dependent change of place in space, but rather as a self-moving that goes beyond the present stimuli in the form of retroaction and anticipation and imparts a temporal sense to the differences between here and there, proximity and distance that Heidegger discusses in *Being and Time* under the aspect of spatiality of being. Moving bodily, I am at once where I just was, where I am about to be, or where I could be at some time. Movement takes place in the form of motion rhythms and motion melodies that give rise to a kind of space-time (*espace-temps*).[7] This fusion of space and time, which shall play an increasing role in his later work, must be distinguished from the subsequent spatialization of time. It is not surprising that the melody, which since Augustine has been one of the standard examples of the theory of time, is readily adduced by von Uexküll to characterize movement in order to indicate the internal conjunction of various phases of motion.[8] Merleau-Ponty does not hesitate to draw on these suggestions, paying special attention to the hearing, notation, and instrumentation of music; the motif of rhythm, which has to be interpreted in terms of time, recurs later in the theory of the senses as an intermodal form of order.⁹ Thus, behavior that has a structure and generates forms does not take place outside in an objective time or in an objective space nor inside in an intellectually controllable area; rather, it is scanned through fruitful moments of restructuring and reforming; "[E]ach moment does not occupy one and only one point of time; rather, at the decisive moment of learning, a 'now' stands out from the series of 'nows,' acquires a particular value and summarizes the groupings which have preceded it as it engages and anticipates the future of the behavior; this 'now' transforms the singular situation of the experience into a typical situation and effective reaction into an aptitude."[10] The dual pattern of the a priori form of time and the empirical contents of time and the one-sided ascription of time to the inner sense prove to be inadequate even at the biological level since forms and structures materialize without being completely absorbed in the material. The detachability of behavior from the here and now results in decisive structural differences between lower and higher, animal and human behavior; however, the detachability is only relative. Just as the structures of behavior are grounded more deeply than any consciousness of structure, so too do the temporal structures of behavior precede all time consciousness.[11]

In his Sorbonne lectures on *Child Psychology and Pedagogy*, Merleau-Ponty extensively discusses structures and conflicts of the child's consciousness.[12] Among other points, he criticizes Piaget's approach, which understands the child's rationality merely as a preliminary stage of adult reason. According to this view, the child's growth is subject to a logic of development in which the successive phases are transitional and precursor stages culminating in an adult parameter. He criticizes that they were evaluated with reference to an ultimate goal and judged according to it: premature developments were regarded as positive, delays as negative. Merleau-Ponty, by contrast, entertains the idea of a "blundering logic"[13] that no longer assesses individual stages as progress or regress relative to a developmental goal, but rather accepts that loss and dwindling of possibilities is the other side of the coin in all augmentation of possibilities: "There is nothing absolutely new; instead, there are anticipations, regressions, the permanence of archaic elements in new forms."[14]

III

In the first two parts of the *Phenomenology of Perception*, the author takes bodily existence and the person's world of perception as his immediate point of departure; in comparison with the more broadly based analyses of his first work, the focus is narrower, giving more prominence to the paradoxes and the pathologies of time. Time plays a role in the bodily oriented analyses in various ways before in the end it becomes a topic in its own right in an extensive chapter.

Let us begin with the *perceptual synthesis* as discussed in the second part. The *syn-* which establishes coherence, making of many one, of parts a whole, stands for the ordering process as such, assuming order to mean a regulated (that is, nonarbitrary) connection of one thing and another.[15] Expressed in later diction, it is a problem of meaning generation (*Sinnbildung*). Kantian transcendental philosophy presents us with the alternative of assuming that the unity of the manifold is either given or posited. It is well known that Kant opts for the second possibility because in the first case order would be merely a plaything in the hands of experience. Among the necessary conditions of experience is time as a form of intuition, constituting an order of succession and simultaneity. In his critical analysis of Kant, Husserl is intent on shifting the logos back into the "aesthetic world" of experience but still adheres to Kantian formalism, for example, when he understands temporal synthesis as a basic and universal form within which the particular operations of experience take place.[16] Merleau-Ponty goes a step farther inasmuch as he does not only subject the perceptual synthesis to formal temporal conditions, but rather understands it as temporality, as itself a form of temporal development.[17] This assumption is anything but a matter of course for it presupposes that something that is experienced does not merely occur somewhere in space and time, but in a certain way has *its* time and *its* space. If this assumption were valid without reservation, we would return to old ideas of a cosmic order within which everything ultimately already has its place and all sense is pregiven. Naturally, this is not what Merleau-Ponty had in mind. The use of the concepts form and structure already showed that Merleau-Ponty is searching for a middle path that gives neither the things nor the subject the first and last word. The meaningful unity is originally neither pregiven in the things nor posited by a subject, it emerges from a *synopsis*, not a *synthesis*.[18] In the elaboration of this idea, time plays a decisive role together with corporality.

The synthesis of the perceptual world and the simultaneous appropriation of time are explicitly attributed to the body. But if the body itself were just something found in the world like a thing, nothing would be gained. Every reflection would teach us that the body presupposes a body consciousness and that bodily rooted time presupposes a similar time consciousness; quite a number of phenomenologists of consciousness have repeatedly brought this to bear against Merleau-Ponty. The response to this objection can be manifold; a first response is provided by the temporal understanding of perception and the body. The synthetic operation of the experience of time is not limited to the fact that variety is ordered in the form of concurrent and successive, that is, that something appears as earlier, later, or synchronous; rather, it also means that the givenness itself takes place temporally. In moving into focus, the gaze performs a spectacle, initially "not a spectacle of anything," and takes on a prospective and retrospective character.[19] We say that something comes into sight. This does not mean that something is already there that is prior to bodily attention and the perceptual appearances; rather, it means that they *precede themselves*. The object of perception, which the gaze prospectively grasps as something to be seen, proves retrospectively to be something "preceding its own appearance" (*comme antérieur à son apparition*), as a stimulus to which the gaze responds, as a motive by which it is guided. The gaze does not begin in itself and with itself, and it thus does not perform an active positing (*Setzung*) and synthesizing (*Zusammensetzung*). This self-precedence, this character of being concurrently prior to and beyond itself, begins with an "original past, a past which has never been a present,"[20] and refers to a "future to which I have not access," which will never be present.[21] This subjection to birth and death, repeated in a certain way in every sensation,[22] it not a mere attribute of the body; rather, it constitutes its manner of being. For precisely this reason, Merleau-Ponty does not tire of repeating that I do not perceive, but rather that "one perceives" or that there is perceiving in me,[23] that perception refers to an anonymous *prehistory* that is not accessible to any grasp or take (*prise*), but rather is *carried on* in a retake (*reprise*).[24] According to Husserl, this synthesis has a history that is "evinced in the synthesis itself,"[25] and he sees it as engrained in the passive synthesis of the perception of things; this also applies to the body, whose acquisitions, traditions, and habitualities contain a history of their own. Merleau-Ponty repeatedly speaks of a "thickness" or "density" (*épaisseur*), for example, of a "historical density" of the perceiving person and of a "thickness conferred by the present" which the perceived thing has, thus suggesting that the gaze is caught in a spatiotemporal labyrinth of perception and perpetually escapes itself; perception is not an active operation that we could ascribe to ourselves alone because it "takes advantage of work already done."[26]

This reconception of perception on the basis of time, to which Merleau-Ponty devotes all his powers, is in the long run more fruitful than much of the vociferous criticism of a metaphysics of presence that avoids the passage through the phenomena. The reconception proves its merit in diverse problem fields, for example, in the area of *depth perception*. Spatial depth plays an important role in Merleau-Ponty up to his late work, for example, in reflection on painting; it disappears if, in the double tradition of rationalism and empiricism, it is regarded as a width seen in profile, that is, if it is subjected to a gaze from everywhere which also sees what I do not see. The pseudo-problem that we can see distant objects is resolved when with Husserl we think on the basis of a "field of presence" in which the dimension of here-there crosses the temporal dimension. I see something there in the distance similarly to how my memory finds past things in the temporal distance and not just traces that belong to the present.[27] In both cases, we have to do with a "transitional synthesis" that does not link *discrete* spatial or temporal data, but rather establishes a connection in transition.[28] The puzzles of *perception of movement* are solved in a similar way. For us as perceiving people, the bird in flight is not a moving thing that successively occupies discrete locations in space; rather, the gaze accompanies what is seen as "something in transit" (*quelque chose en transit*).[29] Finally, recourse to the temporality of perception also resolves the contradiction of the *perception of the world*; this contradiction consists in the fact that perception strives toward a completed synthesis, although this presumption remains unfulfillable because of the perspectival limitation of our experience.[30] The contradiction vanishes when we shift from the level of being to that of time and understand "time as the measure of being," so that in the strict sense nothing exists absolutely; rather, everything is "temporalized" and there is in this a surplus of existence or an "additional existence" (*surplus d'existence*).[31] "Though I am here and now, yet I am not here and now."[32] The transcendence of the distant penetrates into my present, it gives the world fissures (*fissures*) and gaps (*lacunes*) in which subjectivity can lodge.[33] Time participates in the ambiguity characteristic of the body, but the body does not occur somewhere and sometime in the world, nor does it reside everywhere and at all times, that is, outside of the world. The significance of perception thus ultimately remains "confused" or foggy (*brouillé*).[34]

IV

The worlds of perception and bodily existence do not correlate in the strict sense, since we are bodily embedded in the world and bodily involved in the generation of sense and form. Thus, as we have seen, speaking about the temporality of things always also means speaking about the temporality of the body. Nonetheless, in the first part of the *Phenomenology of Perception*, which is explicitly concerned with the body, certain features of time are more prominent. The fact that the body's own movement is inconceivable without a temporal structure, that there is a kind of motion memory that retains forgotten body positions, that every starting that initiates motion anticipates future body positions is already known from the early work. But this insight is further refined in the chapter on spatiality, and comes to a head in the assertion that as bodily beings we are not in space and time, nor do we conceive them; rather, we "belong to" space and time (*je suis à l'espace et au temps*) and we "inhabit" them in various scopes.[35] Inhabiting, which takes shape in settling in, means that we belong to space-time and at the same time react to it. According to Helmuth Plessner, not only are we our living body (*Leib*), at the same time we also have it as our physical body (*Körper*); and similarly, we are not merely situated in time, we also have time to which we treat ourselves and others, time that we need, give, or waste.

However, this distance to ourselves gives bodily existence a precarious character that is manifested in a special way in pathological dysfunctions, among them a *pathology of time*. Traces of this can be found in Merleau-Ponty in abundance; here he follows authors with a phenomenological background and authors with a psychoanalytical background such as Ludwig Binswanger, Kurt Goldstein, Eugène Minkowski, Paul Schilder, and Erwin Straus. A striking example that Merleau-Ponty uses to illustrate the ambiguity of both the living body and of time is the *phantom limb*, which since Descartes has done service as a prime example for physiological-mental explanations.[36] In contrast to traditional views, which explain the occurrence of the phantom limb in physiological terms as a real awareness of a presence or psychologically as a delusional awareness of a presence, Merleau-Ponty interprets this phenomenon as an ambivalent presence of the lost body member, that is, as an intermediate between presence and absence emerging from a dissociation of bodily and temporal existence. The medical history condenses to a pathological process that penetrates into the core of the personality. The loss of a limb, in the case of a pianist, for example, the amputation of an arm, can take on traumatic dimensions and approach the affliction brought about by the loss of a person to whom one was close. The nonacceptance of the loss can be interpreted as a kind of repression. Repression has the result that things, for example, the piano, continue to appear to be manageable, but not for the present I in the first person, but rather for an impersonal somebody or One in the third person. The habitual body prevails over the presently active body because the lost present refuses to become past and thrusts itself over every other present. Merleau-Ponty aptly calls this living in the past, this secondhand living a "scholastics" of existence.[37] The ego lives the life of a past ego. One's own life trickles away in former experiences, in memories of experiences, and ultimately condenses in a general, frozen typology. Life goes on, but all new matters of experience are channeled into old structures like new wine into old wineskins. However, Merleau-Ponty does not come to a halt with this description of the disorder; rather, he draws conclusions for all embodied existence. Pathological dissociation presupposes that with the exception of moments of intensity our bodily existence is never fully integrated. Our personal, freely chosen existence, which opens a historical world to us, remains chained to the prepersonal or impersonal, anonymous existence of the organism, which follows its own rhythms and cycles in the beating of the heart, in the pulse, in breathing in and out, and also in nutrition and reproduction, in the courses of illness, and finally in aging. Here we encounter the same phenomenon that we already faced in the anonymity of the process of perception. The sublimation of nature in culture, the merger of soul and body, the centering of existence are never completely successful. This has the consequence that presents contest each others' status and that in the temporal field conflicts are fought out that simply escape a formalized view of time. "Each present may claim to solidify our life, and indeed that is what distinguishes it as the present"; it is thus like a wound that is never completely closed.[38] Normality and pathology touch each other at this point, past things are never completely dismissed, future things are never guaranteed, so that "phantoms" come to haunt us in our dreams or in moments of shock.[39]

In the chapter on sexuality, in which Merleau-Ponty approaches Freud via Ludwig Binswanger, he addresses the case of a girl suffering from *aphonia*. This speech disorder takes on the radical form of a loss of speech.[40] The author attempts to show how the story dissolves in a "natural time," how it melts off in a series of now moments that are all the same, how it always flows back into itself—up to the moment when the spell is broken, when movement toward others, toward the future, and toward the world is restored in the same manner "as a river unfreezes."[41] The proper motion of the living body is characterized by habituation, blockades and breakthroughs. The river metaphor becomes questionable when the river is regarded as a movement in space or when everything coalesces in it, but it gains in credibility when, as Merleau-Ponty does, it is used to illustrate the proper motion of life, the motion that carries us, sweeps us away, threatens to engulf us, but also the motion that produces its own articulation in the form of "temporal waves."[42] In passages such as these it becomes clear how Merleau-Ponty draws on and revises impulses from Bergson when the clarity of time consciousness or the openness of existence drifts too far from bodily existence; something similar applies to Freud's body language and corresponding motifs from the works of Proust and Valéry.[43] Even in the final chapter of the second part when the human world is the explicit topic, nature and natural time play an important role. It appears in the heart of one's own history. A being that is given to itself through its birth as a being to be understood finds within itself the outline of a natural ego and a natural time going back to the womb. This natural weakness remains, and it has the result that "my possession of my own time is always postponed [*différée*]."[44] Time can never be regarded as mine in the full sense, just as the body is never completely my own because my consciousness is always interspersed with "absent-minded and dispersed 'consciousnesses,'" it remains anchored to the sensory fields of vision, hearing, and touch, "which are anterior, and remain alien, to my personal life."[45] The alien character of the others, which is subsequently addressed, corresponds to the foreignness of a past time and a prehistory that we can never completely appropriate.

V

After these long forays through the spatiotemporal labyrinth of bodily existence, what remains for a direct discussion of time? We can find such a discussion in the third part of the *Phenomenology of Perception*, framed by one chapter each on the cogito and on freedom. It should be clear that the bodily embedding of time does not permit the shifting of time into a mental inner world nor a replication of objective time consciousness through reflective self-consciousness. All that remains is a "phenomenology of phenomenology," which again takes the phenomenon of time itself as a phenomenon without relapsing into a dualism of inner and outer temporality.[46] The paradox of time mentioned at the beginning makes itself lastingly felt in this radicalized view.

At first sight, the cogito seems to escape the vicissitudes of time in its cogitata, in the ascent to the ideas, in thinking the thoughts of God. In contrast, Merleau-Ponty insists on a "time of ideas" that is more secret than natural time: "The existence of the idea must not be confused with the empirical existence of the means of expression, for ideas endure or fall into oblivion, and the intelligible sky subtly changes colour."[47] The timelessness or the supertemporality of what is thought proves to be what Husserl called "omnitemporality" (*Allzeitlichkeit*);[48] it refers to the temporality of thought, which is characterized by forms of acquisition, adoption, and anticipation, generating the "inner history" that according to Husserl even pervades the origin and the transmission of geometry through the generations.[49]

Just as the certainty of what is seen cannot be detached from the seeing, so too can the certainty of what is thought not be detached from the thinking. Thus, the cogito itself receives a "temporal thickness" (*épaisseur temporelle*).[50] Nietzsche's Zarathustra proclaims that "every moment craves eternity"; however, this eternity "is not another order of time, but the atmosphere of time," it is expressed as a "sublimation of the present."[51] As a reader of Freud and Proust, Merleau-Ponty will not go along with a futurist activism that degrades the present to a transitional phase.

The new that the chapter on temporality yields falls like a ripe fruit. Merleau-Ponty relies largely on Husserl's lectures on internal time consciousness, on Heidegger's *Being and Time* and on Heidegger's Kant book. But here, too, he sets his own focus. The central task of a phenomenology of time consists in grasping time in the flesh (*en personne*), in statu nascendi.[52] We fall short of this task if we hope to find a solution in the physical reality of the things, in the mental reality of states of consciousness or in a synthesizing thought. A world pregiven in reality or a world preformed as an ideal would lack every elsewhere, first time, and tomorrow so that there would only be a series of now-points, more or less a time according to Zeno. But where does the phenomenon of time manifest itself to us? The double answer that Merleau-Ponty gives to this question amounts to a temporalization that is neither founded in something nor posited by someone, thus evading the subject-object distinction.

The first answer says: Time is a transition (*passage*), a jet (*jaillissement*), a thrust (*poussée*), and at the same time a breakup (*éclatement*), a rupture (*déhiscence*), a unity that is produced in transition, that is, on the way from differentiation and disintegration. Something is inasmuch as it is not yet and is no longer.[53] In this first answer, Merleau-Ponty makes use of concepts borrowed from Husserl and Fink such as operative intentionality (*fungierende Intentionalität*), transitional synthesis, passive synthesis, adumbrations (*Abschattungen*), and horizons; furthermore, Heideggerian concepts such as ecstasy and transcendence, and the Sartrean concept of the temporal escape from being. He liberally uses metaphors derived from the aqueous element such as river, fountain, wave,[54] source, and vortex, but he does so with care. On the one hand, he emphasizes the process character, on the other hand the repetitive character of wave forms and movement rhythms, which precludes a simple fusion of the discrete temporal moments, thus avoiding Bergson's drastic opposition between time and space.[55]

But the first answer is insufficient because a mere transition would again be a something *for a someone* confronted with time. Therefore, the second answer says: *Time is someone*, in traditional terms: time has to be conceived as a subject, the subject as time. It is the same capacity that keeps temporal events together and that keeps them apart.[56] With this second answer, Merleau-Ponty again draws on Husserl, who conceives time consciousness as a manifestation of itself or self-presence, that is, as presence of the self for itself; on the other hand, he also follows Heidegger, who, based on Kant, views time as a pure self-relationship (*Selbstaffektion*) and thus as an expression of a finite selfhood.[57] Accordingly, consciousness is defined as an internal "duality" of a being that is affected by itself and is given to itself.[58] Neither am I the initiator of time nor does time impinge upon me as something that comes to me from outside; the usual distinction between activity and passivity breaks down here. Therefore, as Plato once did, Merleau-Ponty takes recourse to bastard concepts such as that of an "acquired spontaneity"—an idea that Sartre mentions only to reject it—or he calls passivity a form of *investissement*—a wording that returns later in slightly modified form in Levinas when he identifies freedom as an "investiture" by the other.[59] This makes it understandable why Merleau-Ponty, in the face of the privileged status of the future in Heidegger,[60] insists that our decisions always proceed from the present and that the present for its part is always borne by the past. This has little to do with a metaphysics of presence inasmuch as the present is itself identified as a place of dispersion, of ecstasy, and also as a place of being beside *oneself*. The self-pregivenness of birth or "generativity," to use the Husserlian term, amounts to an "inner weakness which prevents us from ever achieving the density of an absolute individual."[61] As an absolute individual, I would be an incident in space and time, even though space and time are only what they are when I am at the same time elsewhere, that is, even where I have never been, in the pre-time of my birth, and where I never shall be, at the other's time-place.[62]

The theory of freedom concluding the *Phenomenology of Perception* is also characterized by this view of time. Self-pregivenness precludes a freedom that has its beginning in itself in pure spontaneity and transcends everything else. Detachment (*dégagement*) and commitment (*engagement*) are one. "By taking up a present, I draw together and transform my past, altering its significance, freeing and detaching myself from it. But I do so only by committing myself somewhere else."[63] By being outside of myself, I am already with others; the field of time thus proves to be eo ipso a social field, and thus also a historical field. However, as the works on politics and philosophy of history show, some questions remain open, for example, the question of a dynamics of the temporal process, of its orientation, of its branching and of divergent orders of time which do not readily merge into a homogeneous historical field and a homogeneous historical drama. The two mottoes with which the author heads his chapter on time—"Le temps est le *sens* de la vie" (Time is the sense of life, Claudel) and "Der Sinn des Daseins ist die Zeitlichkeit" (The meaning of Dasein is temporality, Heidegger)—suffer from a lack of determinateness in the face of the fact that there is significance, but not the one and only significance;[64] the question of the contingent conditions of the generation of sense cannot be answered with a simple reference to time.[65]

VI

In the context of his orientation on a structural thought inspired by Saussure, Lévi-Strauss, and Lacan, which focuses more acutely on differences, deviations, incompossibilities, and caesurae, Merleau-Ponty's late work further shifts the accent of his theory of time; by contrast, his early work, though open to reason and history, had a varnished surface of Hegelianism disposed to a whole, which is now repelled. In his posthumous work *The Visible and the Invisible*, there are some working notes that in condensed form hint where his path might well have led him and where it could lead.[66]

In general, the tendency becomes apparent to liberate temporality more clearly from its fixation in a consciousness of time and act, from the link to a subjective experience of time and from the pattern of simple succession. The path from *corps propre* to *chair*, from *perception* to *vision*, from acts of experience and behavior to structures and events also shapes the reconception of time, which, however, can always draw on early and very early motifs and elicit new potential from them. A very differentiated critical consideration of Husserl and a cautious approach to Bergson and to the late Heidegger are characteristic of this reconsideration; in all cases, a simple pro and contra is avoided. Certain core problems emerge in which the classical topics of the theory of time return in modified form.

The revision begins on the elementary level of *sensation and perception* where something "appears to itself." Merleau-Ponty resists the assumption that "primal impressions" and "primal experiences" are individual presents that succeed each other in the course of time. There is not something *with which* our experiencing merges, *which* it construes as temporal or *which* it nihilates (again, the rejection of a certain Bergson, Husserl, Sartre). What is referred to in speaking of a "consciousness of . . ." consists rather in "deviation from. . . ."[67] In Gestalt theoretical terms, it is the contrast of a figure to its background, that is, a differentiation that is not preceded by anything identical, neither a visible something nor a seeing someone. It is the deviation that gives rise to a sight (*vue*). The "for itself" plays a part from the very beginning, though not as the leader, but rather in a derivative form as the "culmination of separation [*écart*] in *differentiation*—Self-presence *is* presence to a differentiated world."[68] Retention does not bring about an attenuation of the "primal experience," it squeezes itself into the present present, into this "Self-presence that is *absence from oneself,* a contact with Self *through* the divergence [*écart*] with regard to self—The figure on a ground, the simplest '*Etwas.*' "[69] The self-difference, which does not by any means annul our self-affection,[70] leads us out of the circularity of a "pre-being" or a "pre-ego" that runs after itself ceaselessly and in vain in a lived form of bad infinity. If there is a pre-, it is not one that can be built upon; rather, Gestaltung always also means "*Rückgestaltung,*" (*a reversal of the course of formation*).[71] It is a matter of course that Merleau-Ponty again anchors this deviation in corporality, in the process of lodging in space by virtue of the body schema, in the arrangement of a time in the embryology of behavior.[72] The interpretation of the body schema as a Gestalt formation that generates space and time robs the body of its centering character, a character as if everything revolves around it. Something that deviates is already beyond itself, at something other than itself.

A second problem complex concerns the temporal structure of *remembering and forgetting*. Merleau-Ponty finds that Husserl's retention is only a beginning, and that the origin of forgetting is not explained by it. And indeed, forgetting is at odds with the intentional process; what is forgotten may well have a sense, but this does not apply to forgetting as a sinking into the past. The deficient elucidation of forgetting has the consequence that from Augustine to Bergson the mind always has to act as a place of storage;

and the matter is not improved when the mental process is materialized in the form of physical traces. A further problem consists in the fact that the interpretation of retention as a gradual sinking cannot explain why precisely this is retained and not that, why it often happens that things that are long gone have precedence over what is just now past. Merleau-Ponty seeks an answer to these questions in vision itself. Beyond the aspects of object and subject, perception takes place in the things, and does so in the form of a "modulation," a "winding" (*serpentement*) as Bergson puts it.[73] It is not the case that something appears, only to vanish immediately (where?); rather, something is there by deviating from a straight line in the form of a winding line, by deviating from a level, a standard, from something normative or *Maß-Gebend* (Heidegger), and the deviant exists at first only in the deviation. What becomes visible in this way is "inscribed" in the world since it leaves its traces behind in it.[74] This corresponds to a forgetting that must not be understood negatively as a mere darkening or nihilation, nor positively as a knowledge that is hidden somewhere, but rather as a "being to . . ." that is discontinuously determined as deviation from . . . , as dedifferentiation, as deforming (*Entstaltung*), as a vanishing of the deviation and smoothing of the relief. This forgetting is the reverse of attention; as imperceptions, it belongs to perception. The idea that occurs to us and what slips our minds belong together, forgetting begins now, and it has always already begun. The structural view of the process of time has the consequence that *time and space* come together. As he was earlier, Merleau-Ponty is resistant to playing a subjective time off against an objective time and to criticizing the spatialization of time on this basis. "For in fact space does not comprise *points*, *lines* any more than time does"; Gestalt makes it understandable "that a line is a vector, that a point is a center of forces."[75] The thing as difference means that there is always something "behind," beyond, distant, in contrast to classical space as the being apart of identical things. The point is no longer simply that the proper motion of the body takes place in a spatiotemporal field; the point is, rather, an *intertwining of space and time*.[76] Spatial objects thus have their specific time, for example, the house that appears on the horizon as something past or hoped for, and on the other hand, time is inscribed into space such that "inversely my past has its space, its paths, its familiar locations [*lieux-dits*], and its monuments." Underneath the order of succession and simultaneity, a "nameless network—constellations of spatial hours, of point-events" is found.[77] These ideas, which touch Heidegger's late reflections on a topology of being, also find support in the time-space view of modern physics, which replaces the strict opposition of spatial disparity and temporal succession with the construction of spatiotemporal fields, also integrating the measuring observer into the constellation.[78]

Finally, the inscription of time into space leads to the idea of an *architectural* or *vertical* past. In picking up the indestructibility and intemporality of Freud's unconscious and picking up Proust's search for lost time, which culminates in a "temporal pyramid," Merleau-Ponty resists the interpretation of time as a series of experiences or acts of consciousness and an intentional analysis that presupposes a "place of absolute contemplation" as the place of interpretation, obliging everything that is "to *present* itself to the *consciousness* across Abschattungen [*adumbrations*]."[79] To put it briefly, the criticism is directed against a reduction of time to an internal time consciousness; in this criticism of Husserl, Merleau-Ponty appeals, among others, to Eugen Fink. The justification of this criticism of phenomenology of consciousness would have to be examined in detail; however, the more important point is the substantive aspects that Merleau-Ponty advances. With the idea of a verticality of being,[80] Merleau-Ponty addresses several points. As he attempts to show, the past cannot be arrayed in the horizons of a temporal field; rather, it mounts up like architecture from which every frontal gaze rebounds. The gaze penetrates into the distance, not into the heights and depths; the heavens under which and the earth on which we move are not partial regions of the world. They belong to the constitutive factors of a world, similar to how our erect posture determines our manner of walking so that it cannot be reduced to one direction of walking among others. In speaking of a vertical or architectural past, Merleau-Ponty makes the point that past matters cannot be reduced to a consciousness of the past nor to an originary consciousness of the present: "the 'vertical' past makes the claim that it has been perceived, but by no means does the consciousness of having perceived entail consciousness of the past."[81] The past thus goes beyond present generation of sense, and at the same time it precedes it. In a certain sense, the past is simultaneous with the present, simultaneous, however, not in the literal spatial sense that already presupposes a time, but rather in the sense of a concurrence of various times that are not kept together by a universal order of time.[82] The particular present is not merely displaced by a new present, and it is not aligned to it as a modification is to its primal mode. Here, a distinction must be made between past events that take place *in time* and foundational events with a continuing effect that *inaugurate a new time*. In allusion to Proust, Merleau-Ponty writes that "the *true* hawthorns are the hawthorns of the past,"[83] but this has nothing to do with a traditionalist preference for the past. The point is rather that foundations—like our own birth—belong to a "time before time," a time that we do not encounter in the flesh, which we rather always only find *again*. They live on in the primal memory of a "monumental life" and are to be ascribed to a mythical time.[84] Singular key events are themselves not a part of the order to which they give access; they are clear of the series of normal temporal events. They prove to be overdetermined, as are early traumatic experiences, which according to Freud are only accessible in "screen memories."[85] This makes it understandable that for Merleau-Ponty the present means more than a momentary sensation, that it provides a "symbolic matrix"[86] that gives temporal processes a configuration, a constellation, a relief. Time means more than a consciousness with its processual phenomena (*Ablaufsphänomene*); time is a vortex (*tourbillon*),[87] it is a vortex or whirl which generates time and space, persistently interrupts the normal course of things, or quietly changes the accent like those "open vortexes in the sonorous world" that merge the one with the other and make patterns emerge like the little phrase in Vinteuil's Sonata.[88]

Not only the fragmentary character of Merleau-Ponty's late work, but also his very thought should keep us from seeking an ultimate statement on his tortuous path through the labyrinth of time. However, a return to his thought will always encounter moments that could be called a *praegnans futuri*, a fecundity, for example, the processual character of time that goes beyond any subjective creatorship, thus doing justice to nature; the formative power of time that in its own rhythm is richer and more elementary than all schemata and constructions; our own involvement in time, through which proximity is transformed into distance and distance into proximity; the anonymity of a time that gives names their naming power; the chiasmatic mesh of own and other's time; the priority and anteriority of our own experience of time, which continually surprises us and issues new challenges; the deviation from the true path of standardized courses of time; the indirect character of time, which refers time in the grand sense back to the polymorphous variety of specific manners of time. Questions remain such as the question of the dynamics, the driving forces of the process of time, of ruptures in historical time that are more than just temporal waves, of calendar or narrative orders of time, of the language and symbolism of time, of the time of the sexes, of the temporal dissociation of others' demands on us; and much more. But these questions, too, have a fruitful matrix in Merleau-Ponty's phenomenology of the time of the living body.

Notes

1. It is the basis of Paul Ricoeur's three-volume work *Time and Narrative*. However, the strict opposition of the time of the world and the time of the soul fails to appreciate the cosmic background of Augustine's doctrine of the soul. Cf. on this point Kurt Flasch's interpretation of Book XI of the *Confessiones* (1993).

2. Cf. "Titres et travaux" of 1951, in Merleau-Ponty, *Parcours deux* (Paris: Verdier, 2000), 13.

3. Such authors as F. J. J. Buytendijk, W. Köhler, K. Koffka, and E. C. Tolman are mentioned in the corresponding descriptions of behavioral structures (*SB*, 113–33, tr. 103–22).

4. Jakob von Uexküll, *Theoretische Biologie* (Frankfurt/M: Suhrkamp, 1973), 89. The English translation—Jakob von Uexküll, *Theoretical Biology*, trans. D. L. MacKinnon (London: Kegan Paul, Trench, Trubner; New York: Harcourt, Brace, 1926)—is based on the first edition and does not contain this passage.

5. The reception of Bergson, above all in Germany, was far too one-sidedly limited to criticism of this dualism; it recurs in crude form in authors such as Oswald Spengler: "Space is a *conception*, but time is a word to indicate something inconceivable," he writes in *The Decline of the* West, ed. H. Werner (Oxford: Oxford University Press, 1991), 122. In France, in addition to Merleau-Ponty, other authors such as E. Minkowski, E. Levinas, J. Hyppolite, and G. Deleuze ensured that the early wave of Bergsonianism, which helped prepare the ground for French phenomenology, did not completely wane. On the Bergsonian background of Merleau-Ponty's theory of time, cf. Burkhard Liebsch, *Spuren einer anderen Natur* [*Traces of Another Nature*] (München: Fink 1992).

6. Viktor von Weizsäcker, *Der Gestaltkreis. Theorie der Einheit von Wahrnehmen und Bewegen* (Frankfurt/M: Suhrkamp, 1973), 176. V. v. Weizsäcker refers to *Being and Time* here (111, tr. 146): "Space is not in the subject, nor is the world in space. Space is rather 'in' the world." When working on his early book, Merleau-Ponty could not use *Der Gestaltkreis*, which was only published in 1940, but he does refer extensively to Weizsäcker's revision of the theory of reflexes.

7. *SB*, 122, tr. 112.

8. The "myth" of the "determination of the present by the future" that is justly attacked by critics of finalism (cf. Werner Stegmüller, *Probleme und Resultate der Wissenschaftstheorie und Analytischen Philosophie* [Berlin/Heidelberg/New York: Springer 1969], vol. I, 530) only comes to be when movement is described as a series of discrete states so that a state of affairs that does not yet exist and may never exist enters into the explanation of an existing state of affairs. A revision that avoids the alternative of mechanism and finalism has to start on the descriptive level. Cf. on this point the renewed discussion of this issue with reference to modern biology in the nature lectures of the 1950s (*TLC*, especially 117, 129–37, 171–76, tr. 84, 91–98, 124–28) and the corresponding passages in the *Nature*

course. Merleau-Ponty does not argue for a simple return to teleology, but rather for a nature as "oriented and blind productivity" (*TLC*, 117, tr. 83) with regulatory and regenerative forces in which an "excess of the potential over the actual" can be recognized (*TLC*, 171, tr. 124).

    9. *PP*, 245, 247, tr. (here and throughout the chapter, the translation used is the one by Colin Smith) 211–12, 213–14. Rhythm naturally plays an important role in the treatment of the phenomena of life. Cf. on this point Bernhard Waldenfels, *Sinnesschwellen* (1999), ch. 3.

    10. *SB*, 136, tr. 126.

    11. *SB*, 239f, tr. 222–24.

    12. *Merleau-Ponty à la Sorbonne* (1988); English: *CPP*.

    13. Ibid., 85, *CPP*, 65.

    14. Ibid., 22, *CPP*, 14. In another passage (51, tr. 37) he writes: "When we move from childhood to adulthood, it will not only be about moving from ignorance to knowledge, but after a polymorphous phase that contained all possibilities, it will be a passage to a purified, more defined language, but a much poorer one."

    15. Cf. Bernhard Waldenfels, *Ordnung im Zwielicht* (Frankfurt a.M.: Suhrkamp, 1987), 17; English: *Order in the Twilight*, trans. and intro. David J. Parent (Athens, OH: Ohio University Press, 1996), 1.

    16. Cf. for example *Husserliana*, vol. I (*Cartesian Meditations*), §§ 18, 37. Merleau-Ponty rightly calls certain texts of Husserl's especially Kantian (*PP*, 320, tr. [here and after: Colin Smith], 276). But Merleau-Ponty was just as early to take notice of the revision of the interpretation pattern in Husserl's theory of time (*PP*, 178, tr. 152).

    17. *PP*, 276–78, tr. 238–41.

    18. Cf. *PP*, 320, tr. 276. The Platonic concept of synopsis can also be found in Kant, but in his work synopsis remains bound to a synthesis (*Critique of Pure Reason*, A 97).

    19. *PP*, 276f., tr. 239f.

    20. *PP*, 280, tr. 242.

    21. *PP*, 418, tr. 364.

    22. *PP*, 250, tr. 216.

    23. *PP*, 249, tr. 215.

    24. *PP*, 277f., tr. 240.

    25. Husserl, Hua I, *Cartesian Meditations*, 112, tr. 79.

    26. *PP*, 275, tr. 238. (Translator's note: Colin Smith renders "épaisseur" variously with "density" and "thickness." "Density" seems more apt in the present context.)

    27. "Traces" are here traditionally understood as real effects, for example, as brain traces that are "stored" somewhere. It looks different when traces are conceived as a temporal and bodily process in themselves as in Levinas and Derrida. In the *Phenomenology of Perception*, we do not only find footprints (*traces de pas*)

in the sand (*PP*, 400, tr. 348), but also the "eloquent relic [*trace*] of an existence" (*PP*, 401, tr. 349) and the bodily "trace of a consciousness which evades me in its actuality" (*PP*, 404, tr. 352).

28. *PP*, 306f., tr. 265. In his lectures on *The Phenomenology of Internal Time Consciousness*, Husserl speaks of a "union of the like bound together in transition (or in coexistence)" (Hua X, 45, tr. 68), of an "absolute transition" (ibid., 81, tr. 107), and the like. This usage is prefigured in Augustine's *Confessiones*: "ut id quod expectat per id quod adtendit *transeat* in id quod meminerit": "so that what [the mind] expects *passes through* what it focuses on to what it remembers" (*XI*, 28).

29. *PP*, 318, tr. 275. Merleau-Ponty is thinking of a world that does not consist of things, but rather of "pure transitions" (*pures transitions*). This makes his interest in Whitehead's process ontology understandable; he became aware of it through Jean Wahl's early work *Vers le concret* (1932). Merleau-Ponty repeatedly refers to Whitehead's characterization of nature as a pure passage (*passage*). Cf. *TLC*, 121, 131, tr. 87, 93; *N*, 162–65, tr. 119–22. The bird example is also found in Husserl, who regards the flight of the birds "as primal givenness in the now-point, as complete givenness . . . in a continuum of the past which terminates in the now" (Hua X, 69, tr. 94).

30. The following quotations are found in the important section *PP*, 381–85, tr. 330–34.

31. Respectively *PP*, 381, tr. 330, and *PP*, 383, tr. 332.

32. *PP*, 382, tr. 331.

33. *PP*, 384, tr. 333.

34. Cf. on this point Hua III, 59, *Ideas I*, 102: "Moreover, the zone of indeterminacy is infinite. The misty horizon that can never be completely outlined remains necessarily there." Indeterminacy as a "positive phenomenon" (*PP*, 12, tr. 6) is one of the most important motifs of a phenomenology of experience; it has a spatial-temporal aspect that cannot be made unequivocal by a formal logic of time and space (cf. Stegmüller 1975, 191–95). In his lectures on nature, Merleau-Ponty shows how even modern physics undermines an unequivocal and absolute spatiotemporal individuation. Cf. Whitehead's challenge to a view of nature according to which all being is unequivocally fixed at a point in space and time in the form of a "unique emplacement" without participating in other spatiotemporal entities (*N*, 153–65, tr. 113–22), or Eddington's characterization of determinism as a "crystallization on the surface of a 'cloud'" (*TLC*, 129, tr. 91–92). The passage to be discussed below on "that inner weakness which prevents us from ever achieving the density of an absolute individual" (*PP*, 495, tr. 428) is echoed by the fact that modern physics precludes an "absolute individual" (*TLC*, 129, tr. 91).

35. *PP*, 164, tr. 140.

36. *PP*, 92–105, tr. 77–89. Cf. on the medical aspects of this topic Herbert Plügge's discussion (*Herbert Plügge, "Man and His Body," The Philosophy of the Body: Rejections of Cartesian Dualism*, ed. Stuart R. Spicker [Chicago: Quadrangle, 1970],

293–311), in which Merleau-Ponty's conception of the body is productively applied.

37. *PP*, 99, 192, tr. 83, 164. (Translator's note: "scholastique." On p. 83, Smith renders this with "abstraction," on p. 164 with "a scholastic.")

38. *PP*, 100, tr. 85.

39. The traumatic character of the experience of other persons and the resultant inaccessibility (*Nichteinholbarkeit*) of a primal past receives much greater import in Levinas, but with the attendant danger of exaggeration.

40. On the general background of the aphasia debate to which Merleau-Ponty repeatedly refers in his early works, cf. Regula Giuliani-Tagmann: *Sprache und Erfahrung in den Schriften von Maurice Merleau-Ponty* [*Language and Experience in the Works of Maurice Merleau-Ponty*] (1983).

41. *PP*, 192, tr. 164–65.

42. *PP*, 318, tr. 275, as "onde"; 381, tr. 331, as "vague."

43. The body members as *gardiens du passé*, as loyal keepers of the past (Proust: *Recherche*, I, 6; English: Marcel Proust: *Remembrance of Things Past*, trans. C. K. Scott Moncrieff, vol. 1 [New York: Random House, 1934], 5) are a recurrent motto in Merleau-Ponty's work (cf. the first occurrence *PP*, 211, tr. 181; furthermore, *VI*, 297, tr. 243). Aside from Proust, Valéry is the most important literary inspiration; this also applies to the attempt to think body and time together. (Translator's note: In the cited passage from Proust, Scott Moncrieff renders the French noun "gardiens" (guards, wardens, keepers) with the verb "preserve": "and my body . . . loyally preserving from the past an impression which my mind should never have forgotten.")

44. *PP*, 398/397, tr. 346. The pre-echo of Derrida's *différance* is lost in the translations.

45. *PP*, 399, tr. 347.

46. On the methodological idea of a "phenomenology of phenomenology" (*PP*, 77, 419, tr. 63, 365), which was initiated by Husserl and Fink, and its transformation by Merleau-Ponty, cf. Waldenfels, *Deutsch-Französische Gedankengänge*, ch. 4.

47. *PP*, 447–48, tr. 390.

48. Hua I, *Cartesian Meditations*, 155, tr. 127.

49. Cf. appendix III of the *Crisis*, which Merleau-Ponty read immediately after its publication in 1939 and later discussed in detail in a lecture in 1959–60. Cf. *TLC*, 161–68, tr. 113–23, and the notes from this lecture Renaud Barbaras published (HLP). As far as the text references in the lectures are concerned, the extensive commentary that Alexandre Métraux appended to the lectures merits mention.

50. *PP*, 456, tr. 398.

51. *PP*, 451, tr. 393–94.

52. *PP*, 475f., tr. 415–16.

53. *PP*, 479–81, tr. 419–21.

54. *onde*, 481, tr. 421.

55. Many passages sound like a critical reflection on Bergson, sometimes subliminal, sometimes explicit. Cf. for example *PP*, 319, 474f., tr. 276, 415.

56. *PP*, 482f., tr. 421–22.
57. Cf. Heidegger, *Kant und die Metaphysik*, §34.
58. *PP*, 488, tr. 426–27.
59. Cf. *PP*, 488, tr. 427 [Translator's note: *investissement* is rendered by Colin Smith as "being encompassed."]; "investissement" is the usual translation of the psychoanalytical term "Besetzung" [in psychoanalysis generally "cathexis"; occupation]; the German translation uses "Belehnung" [enfoeffment, investiture (in a feudal sense)]. On Sartre cf. *L'être et le néant* (Paris: Gallimard, 1943), 194 f.; English: *Being and Nothingness. An Essay on Phenomenological Ontology*, trans. Hazel Barnes (New York: Philosophical Library, 1956), 125; on Levinas: *Totalité et infini* (Den Haag: Nijhoff, 1961), 57; English: *Totality and Infinity. An Essay on Exteriority*, trans. Alphonso Lingis (The Hague/Boston/ London: Nijhoff and Duquesne UP, 1969), 84. [The English translation of *Totality and Infinity* uses "investiture," the French original has "investiture" and the German translation uses "Einsetzung," the usual modern term for the appointment of a person to or installation in an official position.]
60. Vgl. Heidegger, *Sein und Zeit*, 329; *Being and Time*, 378: "The primary phenomenon of primordial and authentic temporality is the future." The substantive differences resulting from Merleau-Ponty's assessment of inauthenticity and from Levinas's assessment of the possibilities of Dasein cannot be dispelled by exegetical corrections; this also applies to Alphonse de Waelhens, who in his commentary to the *Phenomenology of Perception*, which is still well worth reading, treats these passages accordingly (1968, 306–308).
61. *PP*, 489, tr. 428.
62. *PP*, 495, tr. 433.
63. *PP*, 519, tr. 455.
64. *PP*, 342, tr. 296.
65. Cf. on this point the revision of the philosophy of history in *The Adventures of the Dialectic*: "If history does not have a direction [*un sens*], like a river, but but has a meaning [*du sens*], if it teaches us not a truth, but errors to avoid . . ." (*AD*, 41, tr. 28), then a new beginning is needed.
66. On the following discussion, cf. *VI*, 244–50, 296–98, tr. 190–97, 243–44. These are working notes dating from 1959 and 1960 in which the topic of time comes into enhanced focus.
67. In French, *écart* not only means a "gap," but also an active divergence, a deviation, such as a sidestep in dancing; the same word plays an important role in Valéry's poetics.
68. *VI*, 245, tr. 191.
69. *VI*, 246, tr. 192. [Translator's note: a spurious "not" has been deleted in the quotation.]
70. The narcissism of the body or of speech as a "relation to Being through a being" (*VI*, 158, tr. 118), as a fundamental narcissism of vision (183, tr. 139) open for other Narcissus (185, tr. 141), means at the same time a presentation and

a withdrawal of *oneself*: the "self in question is by divergence [*d'écart*], is Unverborgenheit [unconcealment] of the Verborgen [concealed] as such" (*VI*, 303, tr. 249). If we go a step farther with Michel Henry, appealing to a self-affection of life, to appearance as pure self-appearance, the purity of which is clouded by "no outside [*dehors*], no deviation [*écart*], no ek-stasis" (*Phénoménologie materielle* [Paris: PUF, 1990], 7), we end up with a self without difference that in its pure presence damns itself to silence—or takes refuge in ventriloquism.

71. *VI*, 243, tr. 189.

72. Cf. *VI*, 243–46, especially 246, tr. 189–92. On the concept of time and development in embryology, see the pertinent passages in the *Nature* lectures.

73. *VI*, 247, tr. 194.

74. In this context, Merleau-Ponty refers to Charles Péguy: the philosophy of history encounters the problem of perception in the "rhythm of the event of the world" (*VI*, 249, tr. 196).

75. *VI*, 248, tr. 195.

76. *VI*, 157 tr. 117.

77. As Merleau-Ponty writes in the programmatic introduction (Préface) to *Signs* (*S*, 22, tr. 15). [Translator's note: *lieux-dits*; translation slightly modified to replace "nameplaces."]

78. Cf. *N*, 144–65, tr. 106–74, for a detailed discussion; both in Merleau-Ponty's commentary on the dispute between Bergson and Einstein (cf. also the Einstein essay in *Signs*) and in his discussion of Whitehead's view of nature, the connection of space and time as well as the plurality of times and the polymorphous character of space and time play a decisive part.

79. *VI*, 297f., tr. 243–44.

80. On the motif of verticality, which was inspired by Gaston Bachelard, cf. Bernhard Waldenfels, *Antwortregister* [*Responsive Register*], 420–25.

81. *VI*, 297, tr. 244. [Translator's note: The passage quoted has been retranslated. The French original reads: "le passé 'vertical' contient en lui-même l'exigence d'avoir été perçu, loin que la conscience d'avoir perçu porte celle du passé." The translation reads: "the 'vertical' past contains in itself the exigency to have been perceived, far from the consciousness of having perceived bearing that of the past."]

82. cf. 157, tr. 117.

83. *VI*, 296, tr. 243.

84. These reflections also have a background in the philosophy of nature when, with Whitehead, nature is called the "memory of the world" (*N*, 163, tr. 120) and the "time before time" with its peculiar "architectonic" is traced into embryology and ontogenesis (*N*, 276 f., tr. 213–14).

85. Cf. the programmatic reference to psychoanalysis: *VI*, 293f., tr. 240: "memory screens." Here we encounter a series of motifs with a temporal aspect that have already been mentioned, for example, the retrograde movement of what is true, the assumption of symbolic matrices and the "ominous" sense of overdeter-

mined phenomena, which from a great distance are reminiscent of the aporias of the Augustinian theory of time: "Quoquo modo se itaque habeat arcana praesensio futurorum, videri nisi quod est non potest" (*Conf.* XI, 18): "How can I divine what is not somehow now and which I do not expect, but which expects me?"

86. *VI*, 246, tr. 192.
87. *VI*, 298, tr. 244.
88. *VI*, 199, tr. 151. On this point, cf. Levinas's praise of Nietzsche's poetic writing that it "reversing irreversible time in vortices" (*"renversant, le temps irréversible, en tourbillon"*) (Emmanuel Levinas, *Otherwise than Being. Or Beyond Essence*, trans. Alphonso Lingis [Pittsburgh: Duquesne University Press, 1974], 8). In Merleau-Ponty the tracks go back to Hegel, as they so often do. In his essay "Vie et prise de conscience de la vie dans la philosophie hégélienne d'Iena," from which Merleau-Ponty once quoted (*SB*, 175, tr. 161–62), Jean Hyppolite speaks of a "vital vortex" (*tourbillon vital*) prior to the consciousness of life and its conceptual development. See also Hyppolite, *Etudes sur Marx et Hegel* (Paris: PUF, 1955), 22; cf. in a similar vein *SB*, 166 tr. 153. Furthermore, let me call Bergson to mind; for example in his work *L'évolution créatrice* (*Œuvres*, 1959, 732, tr. 293) he writes: "On the greater part of its surface, at different heights, the current is converted by matter into a vortex [*tourbillonnement sur place*]."

Undergoing an Experience

Sensing, Bodily Affordances, and the Institution of the Self

EMMANUEL ALLOA

How should the relationship between the self and its sensory experiences be theorized? Are sensory events contents of the mind? Or are they instead located inside the body, just as the protagonist of a Faulkner novel says that the "sum of experience" is collected inside the body and its envelope of skin?[1] In any case, these two approaches—mentalist and physicalist—both ultimately dovetail in their conception of sensations as *data*, that is, as that which is "given" to an already existing, constituted subject. In Merleau-Ponty's work, this chapter argues, the premises for a different understanding of both sensory experience and the self can be found. What is at stake is an adequate appreciation of what Merleau-Ponty calls *l'épreuve du sensible*, which shall be the phenomenological starting point of a general shift in the respective determinations of what it means to sense something and what it means to be sentient.

Epreuve and *éprouver* are words that only roughly translate into English. Generally, they are rendered as "having a sensation." But what does it mean to *have* a sensation, and who is the subject here? The very notion of "having" seems awkward: "having a sensation" or "having an experience" implies the idea of an ownership or sensory acquisition, of something already fully constituted that could be shoved into our satchel. This problem can be sidestepped by translating *éprouver* as "making an experience," thereby accounting for the fact that there is a generative process taking place. But who is the subject fashioning the experience? Experiences certainly are not of our own making; rather, they are traversals, things a self goes through. Which leads to a third and last understanding of *épreuve* that is closest to the original etymological sense. *Épreuve* is not only a form of feeling; the French word also means putting something to the test, an experiential trial of sorts. Experience would then amount to an ordeal whose facticity is not dependent on the subject's spontaneity. Wherever an experience takes place, a crossing happens, which is indicated in this English word *experience* by the proto-Indo-European root *per-* (*per* means "through," "by means of"; *dia* in Greek). Undergoing an experience is tantamount to going "through" it, which is confirmed by the etymology: undergoing links the event to an act of "submitting to, enduring," which might have two different outcomes, either that of emerging greater and stronger from it or of being ruined by it (such as in Old High German *untargān*). But in any event, it has to do with "passing through" and being altered in this very process.

By turning the *épreuve* into the starting point of his analysis of sense-events, Merleau-Ponty immediately does away with some of the cumbersome barriers that hindered traditional epistemology and also paves the way for a more realistic description of processes of individuation. This chapter focuses on what has not received sufficient attention so far, that is, the link between his reconception of sensory experience and his understanding of its correlate, the self. As a matter of fact, rather than dismissing the notion of sensation altogether, as has often been erroneously claimed, Merleau-Ponty points at a specificity of sensation which is its nonobjective, transitive nature.

This transitivity is not restricted to sensation, however, but rather points to a hallmark common to experiential processes at large. This chapter sketches a connection between Merleau-Ponty's investigations into the structure of the experiential field and his reflections in his later work on the logic of "institution" in order to highlight the ways in which selves, just like the perceptions they have, are "instituted." This chapter's argument moves from a recapitulation of Merleau-Ponty's critique of traditional accounts of sensation via his own redesigning of sense-emergence as a Gestaltist process (section 2) and the analysis of the negative, diacritical structure of the experiential field (section 3) to the demands that sensible environments yield (*affordances*) and the types of embodied responsivity that they call for (section 4). We don't perceive qualities, unities, or abstract features, but instead availabilities, dangers, and threats—rather than things that *are*, we encounter things that expect us to *do* certain things, to interact with them, respond to them or avoid them. In short, our exposure to sensible encounters forces us to give an answer we didn't even know we had: aesthesia begins as hetero-aesthesia; our initiative is already the result of a primordial responsivity (section 5). In the last section of the chapter (6), the notion of "institution" is brought into play, so as to offer a broader account for processes of creation and habituation. Affective, "pathic" events that touch the subject are also what contemporaneously brings the subject into existence, and institutes it as an inventive subject who develops specific styles of responding to inescapable demands. The notion of institution also crystallizes Merleau-Ponty's need for an ontological reframing of sensible existence: as sensible Being, Being both precedes my experience of it and only exists thanks to a retroactive process of institution or invention. As a result, subjectivity appears as the field of becoming, a becoming shaped through sensible encounters and instituted by means of the creative responses given to other beings, things, and subjects. The experiential I, as it were, proves to be the result of an acquired originarity, an "instituted," second nature of sorts.

1. What Are Sensations About?

Philosophies of sensible experience are usually confronted with one chief problem, which is the question raised by skepticism: How to make sure it is indeed a sensible world—*the* world—we refer to, and not some sort of private mental abstraction we might project onto it? The classical answer has been to suppose that there is a level that precedes that of representations and which is therefore inaccessible to error, the level of sensation: the act of perceiving should not the conceived as a representation of external objects, but instead the immediate result of sensory impressions caused by them. In such an approach, external reality is saved by paradoxically focusing only on what is immanently sensed. Phenomenology inherits this empiricist line and adopts different stances with regard to its strategy. While Husserl displays affinities with empiricism and maintains the necessity of distinguishing between sensation and perception, Merleau-Ponty is generally considered to reject the notion of "sensation" altogether as misleading. Indeed, *Phenomenology of Perception* is often referenced as setting about a thorough deconstruction of the notion of "sensation," which is supposedly made superfluous. However, as will become clear, Merleau-Ponty rather criticizes the conception of sensation as a datum. Sensation is never given, because it doesn't have the structure of an object. We never perceive sensations as such; it is, rather, through sensations that we perceive. However, imperceptibility doesn't amount to inexistence, and what there is to be understood is the transitive, generative character of sensation. This argument results from premises that have to be successively reconstructed.

Merleau-Ponty's *Phenomenology of Perception* starts off with a critical discussion of the concept of sensation. The main problem with classical approaches to perception, Merleau-Ponty states, is their prejudicial acceptance of something like the reality of sensations. In everyday language, we take it indeed for granted that there are sensations: we say that we "sense" (more colloquially, we see or hear or feel) green, noise, or cold, and we are able to inform others whether we currently have a sensation of green, noise, or cold. But do we really know what we mean by that? In fact, Merleau-Ponty asserts, sensation is "the most confused notion there is."[2] Prima facie, there seem to be plausible reasons to speak of "sensing" rather than of "perceiving." We might easily imagine cases where we sense perceptual environment as fully tinted green, because we are looking through colored lenses, or that we sense a room temperature as icy due to a feverish flu. We might be told that things around as are not actually green or chillingly cold; we might even know due to previous experiences, and yet, we can't help but sense green and cold. Thanks to its indubitable nature—its presencing effect—sensation could readily become a key argument against idealist and representationalist accounts of knowledge, according to which all we know for certain comes from within or through "innate ideas" (Descartes). For British empiricism, sensation indeed offers a secure ground we must start with, both logically—all ideas hark back to sensations—and chronologically—in experience, we start with sensations: I sense a certain sound, which I will then subsequently recognize as that of a violin. Although all of this might sound reasonable, the argument is flawed, as Merleau-Ponty explains. The colors and temperatures I sense "are not sensations, they are the sensibles, and quality is not an element of consciousness, but a property of the object."[3]

Let's return to a locus classicus: When Locke defines sensation as the most basic qualities affecting our sense, he doesn't speak of qualities in general, but gives specific examples, such as the "hardness of ice" and of the "whiteness of a lily."[4] Nonetheless, the kind of particularity Locke is aiming at, which supposedly grounds all experience as that which provides the basic "ideas," is nowhere to be found. We do not sense ice cubes and lilies in general; we never experience "hardnesses" or "whitenesses" in general, but *this* hardness and *this* whiteness. In order for the experience to be specific, it must be a sensation *of* an object, the hardness of *this* ice or the whiteness of *this* lily. While it is thus always particulars that are sensed, their qualities are not items to be found within consciousness, but *sensibles,* as Merleau-Ponty holds, and as such, they are already properties of something that exceeds consciousness. Paradoxically, the very attempt to isolate minimal units of sensation forces the empiricist to reach out beyond givenness: purportedly, the Maori language boasts three thousand color names; however, this is not because their members would have a more accurate perception, but rather because they do not identify them when they belong to structurally different objects.[5]

Now, of course, this is not to say that the properties of sensible objects have nothing to do with sensations: if we refer to certain empirical things by names such as "orange," "violet," "salmon," or "lime," it bespeaks the fact that their innermost being is indissolubly tied to their sensible chromatic feature. It makes no sense to attribute qualities to things as mere objective attributes, independent of any form of appearance. These qualities are never *in themselves,* but insofar as they *appear;* a phenomenal quality without phenomenalization would be a nonsense. Not only do we have to acknowledge that sensations are never fully self-contained but gesture beyond themselves (they are sensations *of something*), but they are also sensations that someone undergoes (they happen *to someone*). There are no abstract, detached sensations that could be contemplated from all sides—no sensation in and of itself—but rather sensations are what affects *me* in a particular way, and through them I have a certain experience of the world.

Sensations are usually held to be the testimonies of a radical and unsubstitutable first-person access to the world. While I may want to ask someone to step into the same position in order to have the same perception I have of the moon rising between two mountain peaks, there is no way I can ask someone to change places and have the same sensations of an aching tooth. For this matter, sensations have also been tied to radical *mineness.* (This common conception has implications for theories of perception too, says Merleau-Ponty: "If I consider my perceptions as simple sensations, they are private; they are mine alone.")[6] The empiricist tradition has taken this dimension of *mineness* to the most radical conclusions, considering the subject of sensations as a passive, impressible receptor. But one might take even a step farther, which is well captured by Berkeley's principle *esse est percipi*: whatever exists can be traced back to an (actual or potential) sensation. To the realist (Hylas), who surmises that the quality of "heat" must exist somewhere outside of the mind, Berkeley responds (through his alter ego Philonous) that heat is no more and no less real than the pain it becomes once it moves closer to our body.⁷ Since the point here is not that objects are actual perceptions, we can slightly rephrase the famous *esse est percipi*: sensible beings are beings that are first and foremost defined through their percept*ibility*.

2. Two Fallacies of Empiricism

However, in such a radical subjectivist account, perception and sensation tend to blend, while the point was to have the "mineness" as a marker that might distinguish between both: two individuals might see the same thing or witness the same event, they might even swap positions to compare their perceptions, but they would be hard-pressed to swap their sensations: however vividly I describe my pain, it will always and irrevocably be *my* sense of pain. This has led to the first fallacy denounced by Merleau-Ponty in his analysis of sensation, the *internalist fallacy*.

The Internalist Fallacy

In empiricist conceptions, there is widespread support for the idea that sensation is a nonconceptual, noninferential, and, most importantly, presuppositionless sensory experience generated by an external agent. While itself presuppositionless, such a sensory experience will serve as a base for founding secure knowledge: we never experience an orange tree, but only an aggregate of raw sense-data—a certain colored sensation—from which we might infer other things, such as the existence of a tree in front of us with its associated properties. While empiricism claims to reject intellectualist constructions and return to sensory experience of the world, it actually does the opposite, Merleau-Ponty claims, and sensation turns out to be itself a retrospective illusion, which "corresponds to nothing in our experience."⁸ When foundationalist accounts pretend to base knowledge about the external world, which is generally problematic, on the certainty of an immanent realm of supposedly self-evident sensations, they are not acting presuppositionless at all, but in fact presume an entity whose existence is yet to be proven. The most radical sensorialist stance turns out to be a speculative, mental construct. If experience is to be the starting point, there is hardly any such thing as a private, inner realm of sensations; sensing is already an event of opening. While it might well be that there are sensations without an identifiable object, agent, or cause—sense hallucinations are a textbook example here—this doesn't mean that the subject coincides transparently with its own sensations. To be sure, "directly observing a sensation" is tantamount to having a sensation, though the nature of such "having" needs to be clarified.

Merleau-Ponty points to the fundamental contradiction inherent to empiricist approaches: either sensations are "immediately before the mind" (but in this case, one might wonder where the difference lies between sensations and representations, and we are faced with a new dualism) or there is no difference between sensation and subjectivity at all (in that case, it would be impossible for a subject to refer to its own sensation). If to speak of "qualities" is to refer to anything at all, they mostly display some minimal difference to the being who experiences those qualities; the quality of smoothness and the awareness of smoothness couldn't possibly collapse into each other without both becoming meaningless. On the other hand, there is no private garden of consciousness furnished with items that would be freely available to the self; the fact that sensing is directed and that selves are being appeared-to doesn't turn consciousness into a receptacle for personal impressions. Things might appear a certain way to me, but this doesn't make their appearances personal or subjective in any respect. When a straight rod looks bent to me in the water, there is not much that is private about that experience. For that matter, when Cézanne says all he strives for is to "realize" sensations, he doesn't mean to paint *personal* impressions, as the Impressionist painters did, but rather these sensations that are among the things themselves. Sensations are distinct from personal feelings; they are transversal, transpersonal rhythms, which are processes rather than contents, events rather than contents, and signal, not for nothing, what the painter calls "this dawn of ourselves."[9] The "dative" aspect of sensing (the *for-me-ness* of sense-events) doesn't signal any form of proprietary "mineness," and shouldn't be mistaken for a title of ownership. As Merleau-Ponty fittingly notes: "Perception is always in the impersonal mode."[10] After having challenged the internalist fallacy in the classical accounts of perception, *The Phenomenology of Perception* addresses what can be described as the other, *atomistic* fallacy.

The Atomistic Fallacy

Next to isolating a domain of pure immediacy which would be that of interior states, the other main issue with reductivist accounts of perception is atomism. In the attempt to save experience and put it on firm footing, the strategy to trace it back to basic sensations is nonetheless fatal. To look out for a minimal grammar of perception as based in discrete, analyzable elements that serve as building blocks for complex wholes of sensible apprehension is to fall prey to an illusion of transparency, which is a far remove from actual experience. The overall picture of perception as a mosaic of sorts, set up from a myriad of pointillist impressions, is attractive in its simplicity, but is the most theoretical of all hypotheses, since the existence of an isolated quale remains to be proven, not to mention all the problems that emerge from the question of its spatial-temporal extension. Such an empiricist atomism reveals dubious metaphysical implications, which would then leave the space open for all speculations whether sense-data could be mind-independent while immaterial and the like. Merleau-Ponty thus criticizes the atomistic fallacy inherent to such accounts, among other things on the basis of its problematic conception of embodiment: "The pure *quale* would only be given to us if the world were a spectacle and one's own body a mechanism with which an impartial mind could become acquainted."[11] The project of founding the possibility of sense on an initial set of discrete minimal units must thus be given up once and for all: there are no identifiable "raw feels" lying around, perception is not based on ready-mades, it needs to be enacted.

A solution which has been offered is to say, rather than that we visually sense a red square, we visually sense "red-ly" and "square-ly," and that rather than being the object of sensation, it is the adverbial tonality of its act, which would be closer to lived experience. But here again, this *adverbial* approach is just a linguistic makeshift and, above and beyond, another problem remains, which is that reddishness and squareness are taken in an abstract, decontextualized manner. If the adverbial approach is to be elicited at all, it should be connected to subjective experience. The Scottish philosopher Thomas Reid already insisted upon this: instead of saying "I feel pain," we should say, "I am pained." But such an adverbial account has often been misinterpreted as radically limited to an internal first-person perspective, which Merleau-Ponty would contest. "Sensations, or 'sensible qualities,' are thus far from being reduced to the experience [*l'épreuve*] of a certain state or of a certain indescribable quale; they are presented with a motor physiognomy, they are enveloped by a living signification."[12] As *The Phenomenology of Perception* points out, sensations never come alone, but arrive in flocks and throngs, forming superposing and sometimes contradicting layers. Of course, empiricism doesn't deny that either, but the question is what the nature of the cross-relationships is made of. The problems of atomism are not solved by associationism, its second-order explanation, which explains—in a Humean framework, for example—how the real connections, which can never be perceived, can be nonetheless inferred. By positing something like the laws of association of these discrete sensory data, the associationist theory has to leap forward to the already identified whole it purported to explain in its genesis. The principles of selection and of ordering guiding the process of association only make sense from the vantage point of the constituted object, whereby associationism presupposes the very fact it claims to explain. In a way, associationism, such as the one advocated by Ernst Mach, clings to the illusion of perception as an already assembled puzzle which one could then decompose and recompose at will. Whereas Kant rejected empiricism for picturing a "chaos of sensations" (*Gewühl der Empfindungen*), Merleau-Ponty criticizes associationism for its implicit teleology: "We observe at once that it is impossible, as has often been said, to decompose a perception, to make it into a collection of sensations, because in it the whole is prior to the parts—and this whole is not an ideal whole."[13] The ordering principle is thus not given by an ideal telos of apprehension, but is inherent to the sensorial field itself, as Merleau-Ponty stresses, by drawing on the insights of Gestalt psychology.

"An initial perception without any background is inconceivable,"[14] but it is always already enmeshed with other perceptions in a field, which generate its inner differentiation, its effects of depth, scale, and relief. The figure-background relationship creates a whole that cannot be meaningfully decomposed into single atoms without losing perception altogether. As Max Wertheimer describes this principle of the *Gestalt*: "I stand at a window and see houses, trees, sky. Now on theoretical grounds I could try to count and say there: 'here there are . . . 327 brightnesses and hues.' Do I *have* '327'? No, I see sky, house, trees . . ."[15] The Gestaltist psychologists wholesale, from whom Merleau-Ponty takes a large portion of his arguments, from Christian von Ehrenfels all the way through Koffka, Köhler, and Wertheimer, staunchly reject any synthetic conception of the psyche, which would be the naturalized version of the transcendental subjectivity: if the psychological process consisted in assembling discrete bits and pieces and fitting them into an overall synthesis, there would be no way to explain how we can perceive certain sense-events as identical, although they are made of thoroughly different sensory stuff.

An intuitive example from Gestalt analyses is musical melody as a primal continuity from which the tones are progressively released. Just as a moving body is never in one single place, but rather passes through numerous places, a melody never rests in one state but passes *through* notes. The melodic element therefore cannot be reduced to the single tones or their succession, but is the very motion of the tones, which forms their *Gestalt*. This can be easily verified: if in a given melody a few notes are changed (such as the melody to open up to a new mode for example, moving from major to minor), there will be an altogether *different* melody. On the contrary, if *all* the notes are changed in an organized fashion (through a key shift, a chord, or an interval inversion), the melody can be said to remain identical, since it can be transposed. The same holds true of a picture: if we remove a few elements from the picture and substitute them with others, we will get a picture that shows something different; if we, however, modify the entire picture, for example, through an inversion of color values or solarization, the same picture is *transposed* into a different mode (black and white, chromatic reversal, etc.). What does this mean? In a way, transposability—i.e., movement—signals a native identity, which also amounts to saying that a melody is not defined in absolute, but rather in figural, terms; and that its identity stems from the structure of its inner relationships. Consequently, the perception of constancy is not achieved through continued identical stimulations of the same sensory receptors, but through a structure present in perception or—to be more precise—through a structure that emerges *through* perception.

In short, Merleau-Ponty criticizes such a piecemeal approach and opens up the perspective of a differential, processual method. Hence, the idea of the *transitive* character of sensation: sensation is not perceptible, but makes something perceptibly present; rather than perceiving redness, it is *through* the sensation of red that we perceive a red ball. Against this twofold fallacy—the internalist and the atomistic—Merleau-Ponty will thus stress the *field-character* of perception, which is organized according to a principle he calls *diacritical*. Harking back to the fact that Hegel aptly baptized the "negativity of experience," that is, the fact that what the object is about always already exceeds the realm of a particular, given experience, Merleau-Ponty stresses that the *experienced* individuals never coincide with the way in which they appear *in experience*.

3. The Diacritical Field of Experience

In his reading of Gestalt psychology, Merleau-Ponty already applies a kind of structuralist approach, which, rather than singling out a basic grammar of forms (and hence of meaning), studies the conditions of emergence of meaning. "What is profound in the notion of 'Gestalt' . . . is not the idea of signification but that of structure," says Merleau-Ponty, and thus, Gestalt is not so much the name for a given meaning but for a structure that allows meaning to emerge, "the contingent arrangement by which materials begin to have meaning in our presence, intelligibility in the nascent state."[16] A form never has a meaning *in and of itself*; meaning emerges laterally, through the relation of its parts. The holistic form, which cannot be decomposed into elements, has no substance but consists of relations, which are not inferred but real. (Therefore, one might surmise that Merleau-Ponty defends a *realism of relations*, which puts him in the vicinity of a thinker such as Gilbert Simondon.) Where such an approach parts with traditional philosophies of mind is where it rejects the distinction between *primary*, supposedly meaningless qualities belonging to the object, independently of any observer (extension, mass, speed . . .) and *secondary* qualities that don't exist "out there" but only inside the human mind ("qualia" such as color, taste, smell . . .), which would then supposedly delineate the realm of meaning. A sensation of red is less a private matter than it is tantamount to an inner representation; any *qualia* are already caught in a net of lateral relationships, which are relationships of meaning. "The color is yet a variant in another dimension of variation, that of its relations with the surroundings: this red is what it is only by connecting up from its place with other reds about it . . . or with other colors it dominates or that dominate it, that it attracts or that attract it, that it repels or that repel it. In short, [this red] is a certain node in the woof of the simultaneous and the successive. It is a concretion of visibility, it is not an atom."[17]

The sensory field is never homogeneous, rather, it is *punctuated*, and a color such as red constitutes its chromatic punctuation. Just as an otherwise illegible text, such as in the medieval *scriptio continua*, is made accessible through diacritical signs which are placed above, below, and between the letters, so as to space them and make them "breathe," the thickness of the experiential field requires diacritical punctuations too. We would experience nothing, there would be no experience at all, if the experiential field didn't open up into forthcoming elements and receding folds. Merleau-Ponty sees an immanent logic at work in the sensual world, and this logic commands the way in which textures, tones, levels, and intensities are distributed, how things acquire their "grain." Any perception requires a preceding differentiation. A red dress, says Merleau-Ponty, is nothing but a "punctuation in the field of red things," and it will diverge from other red things, such as a bishop's robes, a revolutionary flag, the ochre fields of Madagascar, or the garments of the gypsies on the Champs Elysées, each of them freighted with their corresponding load of semantic and affective associations.[18]

But the diacritical nature precedes the level of identifiable objects. What needs to be understood, says Merleau-Ponty, is the fact of a "relative imperception of a horizon or background which it implies but does not thematize,"[19] or, to put it differently, visibility implies a certain *non-* or *in-*visibility. As the manuscript on *Nature and the World of Silence* has it, philosophy should be sketching a "theory of perception as divergence."[20] Perception is *diacritical,* both with respect to what surrounds it and internally: on a stretch of grass, the green will not only be experienced in contrast to the surrounding environment, but also by virtue of its inner rhythmicity, such as the darker and lighter kinds of green, the light browns and pale yellow that ripple within it. Differences are differences of level or of intensities: within the field of the sensible, thanks to minimal—chromatic, acoustic, tactile, etc.—variations, the field opens up. There is an originary negativity, which has to be recaptured in sensible terms: "This separation [*écart*] which, in first approximation, forms meaning, is not a no I affect *myself* with, a lack which I constitute as a lack by the upsurge of an *end* which I give myself—it is *natural negativity.*"[21]

Sensation itself is not "disorganized chaos," but already manifests an inner ordering that orients it toward certain retranslations as this or that apprehension. Shifting to another context—that of language acquisition—allows us to gain a better understanding of this fact. Already in his early analyses, Merleau-Ponty states the following: "If language did not encounter some predisposition for the act of speech in the child who hears speaking, it would remain for him a sonorous phenomenon among others for a long time; it would have no power over the mosaic of sensations."[22] Sensible experience always gestures toward a meaning yet to come, because of the blanks within the perceptual field, but also by virtue of the subject whose response it solicits. The lacunae beckon to be filled, the dots of the ellipsis issue an invitation to be taken farther. In short: the diacritical structure is not closed onto itself, but requires an embodied, pragmatic subject to get involved, which explains why the diacritical structure is also one of *affordances*.

4. Affordances

The idea of an affordance-character of the perceptual field is, once again, anticipated by Gestalt psychology, which assumes that the perceptual field is not populated with constituted signifying units, but rather makes for a network of sensible saliences that invite the attribution—or invention—of meaning. This point was already highlighted by the Gestaltists themselves, for example, when Kurt Koffka invoked the "demand character" of sensory environments, which latched on Kurt Lewin's *Aufforderungscharakter*,[23] but was taken a step farther by Merleau-Ponty. Unlike the Gestaltists, who ultimately subordinate the affordances to the subject's interest—the postbox only "requires" us to post a *letter* when we planned to send one anyway, and loses this quality of affordance once we have done it—from a phenomenological standpoint, the solicitation precedes my intentions. Whereas for Koffka the initiative lies with the human mind ("I have a need which for the moment cannot be satisfied; then an object appears in my field which may serve to relieve that tension, and then this object becomes endowed with a demand character"),[24] for Merleau-Ponty, this results in a strange subjectivist ventriloquism whereby we only lend inanimate objects with agency for the sake of retaking what we had initially transferred unto them. Even the later perspective, that of James Gibson's ecology of perception, which decisively helped promote the concept of "affordances" and which jibes with Merleau-Ponty on a surprising number of points, still evinces a strong belief in a spontaneously acting subject when Gibson translates the affordances of the environment as options "offered" to an animal, and thus as "opportunities for action."[25] While affordances must indeed be distinguished from causes (the affordance-character is not of mechanical, causal type) they are solicitations, rather than opportunities; although they do not necessarily stir a certain action, they actively steer and invite behavior (one might think of Leibniz's principle of the *inclinat non necessitat*—while not being necessary, they orient). Objects suggest how they are to be handled: paintings require to be watched in a certain way; the terrain of a landscape invites to be crossed along certain paths, etc. Rather than a backdrop for theoretical contemplation, the sensible environment is interspersed with cues exerting practical constraints and traversed by patterns and vectors guiding agents in their behavior, if not steadfastly soliciting an agent's behavior.

Affordances thus have a double component, a *normative* and an *affective* one. Affordance would thus be the name for a kind of preconceptual normativity which might always be disrespected, but whose force is only yet confirmed through their subversion. Certain given perceptual objects channel attention accordingly, and even the most unspectacular ones—such as the basic color "blue"—will create a certain normativity: "Blue is what solicits a certain way of looking from me, it is what allows itself to be palpated by a specific movement of my gaze."[26] But affordance also names a primal affective force at the level of the things themselves. Referring to the viscous, sticky quality of honey is not only to qualify a thing in its inner properties (such as containing a certain amount of glucose), but to already bear witness to a certain quality of the reaction it stirs in us. Therefore, to give an account of the honey's viscosity is "to describe a particular relationship between us and the object or to indicate that we are moved or compelled to treat it in a certain way, or that it has a particular way of seducing, attracting or fascinating the free subject who stands before us."[27] Affordance-affection means a sort of *inverted intentionality*, rather than being directed *toward* a goal, an object, an *intentum*, it is the object that draws the perceiver's attention to it. In a yet undifferentiated field, something comes to the fore, and is lifted off from a background, and comes to touch (*ad-ficere*) an embodied subject in a particular, non-primarily cognitive way.

Insisting on the demands coming from the sensible itself tallies with an imperceptible, and yet profound shift with respect to Husserl's phenomenology. It is not as if Husserl hadn't mentioned such occurrences at all. Especially in *Ideas II*, a certain number of remarks of his seem to point in a similar direction.[28] But all things considered, Husserl's account remains that of a constituting subjectivity, which functions as the instance for sense-bestowal (*Sinngebung*). If in Merleau-Ponty's picture, too, phenomena still remain as phenomena of meaning, and whatever appears appears *as something* (i.e., a certain meaning is given to appearances), this process can no longer be traced back to a seminal "sense-bestowing" subjectivity. Rather, making sense of something is already a way of dealing with its puzzling demand. As it happens, we give sense to what appears to us "only by responding to a solicitation from the outside, following an orientation that a certain 'field' imposes on us."[29] As Merleau-Ponty remarks in the lecture courses on passivity, just as in dreams, where we react to something identified only in retrospect, in wakeful moments we also do not observe an interlocutor first before responding to her solicitation; the response is already part of an identificatory process in order to find out what the demand entailed.[30] Hence, the insistence on the fact that meaning is neither in the things nor in the spectator's mind, but is present in a latent, nascent state. Such insistence on the potential and hence implicit dimension of meaning in a Gestalt hints at the need for an enactive correlate, namely, a subject that actualizes it, but only ever belatedly.

The first instance reacting to such interpellation is the body schema, which responds to the affordances of the environment, allowing an "attunement" to given requirements of a situation: the inner ordering of the body echoes a normativity of the world, and we react unreflectively in suitable ways. "The subject of sensation is neither a thinker who notices a quality, nor an inert milieu that would be affected or modified by it; the subject of sensation is a power that is born together with a certain existential milieu or that is synchronized with it."[31] We don't perceive qualities and quantities, unities or abstract features, but availabilities, options, dangers, and threats—rather than things that *are,* we encounter things that expect us to *do* certain things, to interact with them, respond to them or avoid them. Sensible encounters force us, as Merleau-Ponty says, to invent an answer to faintly expressed, "poorly formulated questions."[32]

5. Responsivity

The sensory field is therefore much more than a shop shelf on which perception may serve itself at will, but an environment that calls out for bodily, prereflective responses. Rather than resulting from an active approximation, sensible encounters are most often something that happens to us unwittingly. As opposed to the figure of the self-contained Adam who Nicolas Malebrache positions prominently in his epistemology and whose senses are incapable of troubling him, confining themselves to averting him with respect, and keeping quiet as soon as he desires it,[33] Merleau-Ponty's account of sensibility testifies for the fundamental condition of exposure to unexpected, interlocutionary events. Sensible events are happenings that strike us, jolt us, affect us, and unhinge us.

The structure of the psychotic subject is not restricted to pathological cases, but bespeaks a condition of subjectivity at large, which is its being in the state of a permanent "gaping wound,"[34] that is, the target of afflictions that befall us. Such primary vulnerability is just the correlate of the capacity of sensing, as Merleau-Ponty points out in his later ontology: any sensible being is only *capable* of sensibility if it is in return subject to the *condition* of the sensible, that is to say, of being exposed to others. Rather than a sense faculty for which I would possess the initiative, sensibility is a force to which I belong and which grasps me as much as I seize hold of it. It thus involves the possibility of being turned inside out, and as a result, has to be taken literally as *ex-periri,* as a test of proof (*épreuve*) which consists of undergoing an exposure to the other: aesthesia begins as heteroaesthesia. However, it is in this exposure to otherness and in the creative response to it that the self first experiences itself, given that responding to the claims of the sensible already entails an inventive rearticulation. Sensing is not a merely passive registration of a state of affairs; it already entails a creative part, a problem solving as it were, which consists, first of all, in identifying what the problem is: "A sensible that is about to be sensed poses to my body a sort of confused problem. I must find the attitude that will provide it with the means to become determinate and to become blue."[35] Such a process of attunement has to find an answer that one never had before the question emerged. For sure, it is *I* who senses, but the *address* of appearances should not be confused with *authorship*: whenever I sense a sensible quality, "I only do this in response to its solicitation. My attitude is never sufficient to make me truly see blue or truly touch a hard surface."[36]

In his later ontological rephrasing, Merleau-Ponty has this formula which remarkably sums up this entire point: "Being is *what requires creation of us* for us to experience it."[37] As sensible Being, Being both precedes my experience of it and only exists thanks to the experience through which it is made sensible, which, to Merleau-Ponty, is tantamount to a retroactive process of invention. "The sensible," he explains, "gives back to me what I lent it, but this is only what I took from it in the first place."[38] Merleau-Ponty's extensive elaborations on the creativity of response bear witness to another shift he undertakes in the Husserlian framework. Demands cannot be fulfilled the way intentions are fulfilled, since demand and response are never symmetric and do not form a correlation in the way *noesis* and *noema* do. What is just a seminal intuition in Merleau-Ponty's writings—the temporal discrepancy between demand and response and the irreducible "time lag" that lies between them—has been worked out in detail by authors such as Levinas (with the notion of diachronicity) or Waldenfels (who speaks of an originary *diastasis*).

If we follow Waldenfels's proposal for a "responsive phenomenology," we have to acknowledge that there is a constitutive *belatedness* of the answer—to borrow a term from Freudian psychoanalysis—which corresponds to a non-anticipable *previousness* of the demand. Sense phenomena are sensory events, before acceding to the status of meaningful noematic correlates; before being objects that receive a sense, they are something that provokes sense without being meaningful itself. However insignificant, they might be highly forceful, insofar as they provoke events by which we are touched, affected, startled, and to some extent even violated.[39] As a result, that to which we respond is never that which stirred the response; what we *respond to* is not what we were *affected by,* since the cause of our affection will always elude our full grasp. Such difference between that "from which" we are affected and that "to which" we respond has been characterized by Waldenfels as "diastasis," which radicalizes his own previous conception of "responsive difference."[40] Moreover, the instance *to which* we respond is never present, but only comes to light *as* we speak and *as* we act. Just as we do not respond to fully constituted objects, but bring about their identity through the very way in which they are responded to, there is no fully constituted subject who waits to experience and to act autonomously, whereby the traditional primacy granted to intentionality in classical action theory is dislodged. The self is an "effect," albeit not in a causal sense—the effect itself is one of a responsive type. A self emerges wherever experiences are being rearticulated. From the accusative "to whom" of the affect, something like selfhood progressively emerges.

6. Institution of the Self

One of the productive, difficult, and to this day poorly tapped, resources of Merleau-Ponty's later thinking is the notion of "institution," which, among many things, decisively displaces existing conceptions of the self. First and foremost, the notion of institution aims at offering an alternative account of subjectivity than that of the transcendental subject, which functions as a blueprint for philosophies of consciousness. For Merleau-Ponty, as soon as one starts with consciousness, one cannot but attribute it a constitutive role. For consciousness, there can be only such objects which consciousness has itself constituted. Even if one grants that such objects are "never fully" constituted and keep some dimension of indetermination, as Husserl is inclined to concede as far as perceptible objects are concerned, still these objects are intimately connected to acts of consciousness of which they are the correlates (not by accident, Husserl's model is that of the "fulfillment" [*Erfüllung*] of intentional anticipations). Hence Merleau-Ponty's proposal to take a new start in the description of subjectivity.

"If the subject were taken not as a constituting but an instituting subject," Merleau-Ponty writes, "it might be understood that the subject does not exist instantaneously" but rather is the "field of my becoming." This field of becoming happens *through* sensations, through the encounter with other beings, things, and subjects, and correspondingly, "the instituted subject exists between others and myself, between me and myself, like a hinge, the consequence and the guarantee of our belonging to a common world."[41] Indeed, the reworking of a number of problems from the early to mid 1950s onward—history, ideality, truth, nature, life, and, first and foremost, selfhood—significantly benefits from the concept of "institution." Merleau-Ponty's later writings, and specifically the Collège de France lecture course from 1954–55 on *Institution and passivity*,[42] offer instructive descriptions of a specific process of *subjectivation* and of *objectivation*, which Merleau-Ponty, in contrast to a "constitutivist" approach, describes with the concept of "institution." Through a response to affects, subjects are instituted and bestow a specific sense in return to what happens to them: they are instituting and instituted at once, rather than constitutive.[43]

While initially "institution" is just an attempt to translating Husserl's notion of *Stiftung*, it quickly far exceeds his framework. In the same way that in his pondering on the phenomenon of language, Merleau-Ponty insists upon the double aspect of the stabilized, iterable content of speech (*parole parlée*) on the one side and the unique, unrepeatable act of speaking (*parole parlante*), with regard to the problem of institution he points to the twofold character of institution: institutions can both be seen in terms of stabilized, habituated frames of acting, thinking, and perceiving (the "instituted" side) and in terms of an inaugural establishment of a new order of things (the "instituting" side). However, if "institution is an opening *to*, it always precedes *from*,"[44] and the investigation of these groundless grounds of institution, of theses occluded precedents from which we take the baton, has to be a central topic for Merleau-Ponty.

Instead of denying that there are such things as stable units—practical, intersubjective experience proves that despite the difference in perspectives, subjects might refer to one and the same thing, whether in perception or in language—the point is, rather, to recall its forgotten conditions of appearance: invariance only ever emerges through differences and consequently, its putative origin is an uncovered check. We are not the origin of our own existence, of our own being. As he says in a working note from November 1959, "I am not even the author of that hollow that forms within me by the passage from the present to the retention, it is not I who makes myself think any more than it is I who makes my heart beat."[45] Sensing is not so much the action of a subject and not even the pure receptivity or impress-ability but rather the fact of "being open(ed)," as Henri Maldiney defined *transpassibility*.[46] Or, to use Merleau-Ponty's own description, it means being exposed-to (*être exposé à*),[47] echoing the conception of "exposed being" in Jean-Luc Nancy. In brief, feeling myself and the opening toward exteriority are but two sides of the same coin. Thomas Reid was correct when stressing that rather than saying "I feel pain," we should say "I am pained." This would force us to think about the "accusative" structure of subjectivity. Affective, "pathic" events that touch the subject are also what contemporaneously brings the subject into existence, as a responsive, inventive subject: being exposed is "what puts an activity en route, an event, the initiation of the present, which is productive after it."[48] Whereas Goethe spoke of a "posthumous productivity" of the genius, one should rather speak of a belated nascence of the self.

If the world of things is already riddled with demands and claims, if we feel "looked at" by inanimate things and feel required to act, what to say about the claims that originate from the others? Things themselves offer a resistance to our complete objectification, but the encounter with other subjects is an even more unsettling experience, which—as Merleau-Ponty points out with regard to Simone de Beauvoir's novel *She Came to Stay*— often leads to attempts "to subdue the disquieting existence of others."[49] Selfhood must be conceived as something that is permanently shaped through its interaction with others; personality is the result of transpersonality. This is an aspect where Merleau-Ponty's description draws close to George Herbert Mead's distinction between "I" and "Me" (which, interestingly, are both *responsive* conceptions of the Self.) One never starts with oneself, our own origins escape us. While the "Me" is the sum of the attitudes others project onto us, the "I" is the response of the organism to the attitudes of the others.[50] In a team, a subject will react to the demands of others, catch the ball and throw it over to the next player or do some other move, but selfhood (the "I") is already a response to the claims others make on us. In a ball game, such responses will be mostly bodily and prereflective, although a later elucidation can take place in thinking, as Merleau-Ponty stresses: "When I turn towards my perception itself and when I pass from direct perception to the thought about this perception, I re-enact it, I uncover a thought older than I am at work in my perceptual organs and of which these organs are merely the trace."[51]

When undergoing what happens to us, we turn this event to our own experience and appropriate it. In a process of retranslation, the ordeal with which we are passively faced is turned into something else. Through narratives, experiences are bound together into a history, though never such that it could be anticipated. My selfhood must be thought of as a type of acquired originarity, as a "second nature" of sorts. Through experience, a self is brought to be that will be recognizable in its responsive patterns, in its style and in the habituated modes of repetition. As Aristotle already underpins, personal abilities are the result of repeated actions and capacities, which one calls one's own, the outcome of bodily practices: "Men become builders by building and lyreplayers by playing the lyre."[52] A new "motor habit"—a newly acquired capacity, a different way of doing things, a newly mastered type of skillful coping—will impinge on a "perceptual habit," such as getting accustomed to using a cane or other prosthesis, which will modify the perceptual environment.[53] Hence, the paradox of habit: one only ever becomes experienced through experience, while at the same time every new experience also potentially heralds a disruption of sedimented habits. However skillful the training, something resists full grasp; an inappropriable reserve remains within experience, which infinitely relaunches the process. The flip side of such acquired originality is that it remains an originary acquisition: "Between my sensation and myself, there is always the thickness of an *originary acquisition* that prevents my experience from being clear for itself."[54] We will always, to a certain extent, remain opaque to ourselves and yet, in spite of all, another relationship to subjectivity is possible, if one moves to the level of preintentional reflexivity.

As Merleau-Ponty points out, "self-perception is still a perception,"[55] and it is precisely this feature of withdrawal, its nonrepresentational, negative dimension, that forces us to rethink altogether what it means to speak of "our" selves and of the experiences we make. Selves are just as transitive as experiences are. We might recall what Bergson had to say to those thinking of the present as something point-like which currently *is*, while there is nothing less present than the present: "You define the present in an arbitrary manner as *that which is,* whereas the present is simply *what becomes.*"[56] What Bergson says about the present could equally be claimed for the "I."

Notes

1. William Faulkner, *Absalom! Absalom!* (London: Vintage, 1995), 69.
2. *PP*, 3.
3. *PP*, 5.
4. John Locke, *An Essay Concerning Human Understanding*, ch. II, "Of simple ideas" (London: Penguin, 1997), 121.
5. *PP*, 319.
6. *PrP*, 17.
7. George Berkeley, *Dialogues between Hylas et Philonous, First Dialogue*, ed. Michael B. Mathias (New York and London: Routledge, 2007), 63.

8. *PP*, 3–4.
9. Michael Doran, *Conversations with Cezanne* (Berkeley: University of California Press, 2000), 114.
10. *PP*, 249.
11. *PP*, 52.
12. *PP*, 217.
13. *PrP*, 15.
14. *PP*, 294.
15. Max Wertheimer, "Untersuchungen zur Lehre von der Gestalt II," *Psychologische Forschung* 4 (1923): 301 (Tr. "Principles of Perceptual Organization," abridged translation by the author, in *Readings in Perception*, eds D. C. Beardsly and M. Wertheimer (Princeton: Van Nostrand, 1958), 115).
16. *SB*, 206–207.
17. *VI*, 132.
18. Ibid.
19. *TLC*, 4.
20. Merleau-Ponty, *La nature et le monde du silence*. Unpublished manuscript from Autumn 1957. Fonds Merleau-Ponty, BNF, vol. VI, f. 143.
21. *VI*, 216.
22. *SB*, 169.
23. Kurt Koffka, *Principles of Gestalt Psychology* (New York: Harcourt, 1935), 353*sqq*.
24. Ibid., 354.
25. James J. Gibson, *The Ecological Approach to Visual Perception* (Boston: Houghton Mifflin 1979), ch. 8, "The Theory of Affordances."
26. *PP*, 218.
27. *WP*, 62.
28. E.g., "The Object, as it were, wants to be an Object of advertence, it knocks at the door of consciousness taken in a specific sense (namely, in the sense of advertence), it attracts, and the subject is summoned until finally the Object is noticed. Or else it attracts on the practical level; it, as it were, wants to be taken up, it is an invitation to pleasure, etc." Edmund Husserl, *Ideas II*, trans. Richard Rojcewicz and André Schuwer (Dordrecht-Boston-London: Kluwer, 1989), 231.
29. *IP*, xx (as Claude Lefort describes this aptly in his preface).
30. *IP*, 147.
31. *PP*, 219.
32. *PP*, 222.
33. Nicolas Malebranche, *The Search after Truth*, ed. Thomas M. Lennon and Paul J. Olscamp (Cambridge: Cambridge University Press, 1997), 22. Merleau-Ponty alludes to this passage in his early work (See *PP*, 304). On his Malebranche reading more generally, see the lecture courses in Merleau-Ponty, *The Incarnate Subject. Malebranche, Biran, and Bergson on the Union of Body and Soul*, preface by J. Taminiaux, trans. Paul B. Milan (New York: Humanities, 2001).

34. *PP*, 358.
35. *PP*, 222.
36. Ibid.
37. *VI*, 197.
38. *VI*, 214.
39. Bernhard Waldenfels, *The Question of the Other* (Albany: State University of New York Press, 2007), 74.
40. Waldenfels, *Bruchlinien der Erfahrung. Phänomenologie-Psychoanalyse-Phänomenotechnik* (Frankfurt/M: Suhrkamp, 2002), 10 and 14*sq*. On the responsive difference, see *Antwortregister* (Frankfurt/M: Suhrkamp, 1994).
41. *TLC*, 40.
42. *IP*.
43. *IP*, 7.
44. Ibid.
45. *VI*, 221.
46. Henri Maldiney, *Penser l'homme et la folie* (Grenoble: Jérôme Millon, 2007), 263*sqq*.
47. *IP*, 6.
48. Ibid.
49. *SNS*, 29.
50. George H. Mead, *Mind, Self and Society* (Chicago: The University of Chicago Press, 1967), 175.
51. *PP*, 367.
52. Aristotle, *Nicomachean Ethics*, II 1, 1103a33–34 (trans. W. D. Ross).
53. *PP*, 153.
54. *VI*, 224.
55. *VI*, 249.
56. Henri Bergson, *Matter and Memory*, trans. N. M. Paul and W. Scott Palmer (New York: Zone Books, 1991), 149–50; trans. modified.

Between Sense and Non-Sense

Merleau-Ponty and "The Silence of the Absolute Language"

Stephen Watson

(Our) desired contact with things does not lie in the beginning of language but at the end of language's effort.

—Merleau-Ponty, *The Prose of the World*

Yes (there are) non-linguistic significations (*significations non-langagière*) but they are not accordingly *positive*.

—Merleau-Ponty, *The Visible and the Invisible*

There must remain significations (which the mind) does not spontaneously confer upon contents . . . a distant meaning and which is not yet legible (*lisible*) in them as the monogram or stamp of thetic consciousness.

—Merleau-Ponty, *Signs*

One is always struck when Merleau-Ponty speaks the language of absolutes. One might think that, especially granted the "existentialism" often enough attributed to him, Merleau-Ponty would speak rarely, if ever, of the absolute. Indeed, when he appropriated Husserl's own version of the absolute of transcendental phenomenology, he both stressed Husserl's ultimate departure from logicism and attributed what he termed 'existentialism' to the result.[1] His criticisms of empiricism and intellectualism in the *Phenomenology of Perception* led him to parse the transcendental experience of embodiment it presupposed otherwise, as the articulation of a "field" rather than a constitutive act. Following Kant's third *Critique*, he emphasized a prereflective teleology of experience whose unified experience emerged without the preimposition of a concept or a conceptual form. The result was an experience whose content, like figure and ground in *Gestalt* theory, "provides the text that our various forms of knowledge attempt to translate into precise language."[2] But his emphasis here upon *Gestalt* psychology and the embodied experience it again articulated still argued against their construal as psychologism—and thereby removed both from "a solitary, blind and mute life" inaccessible to rational explication.[3] Because of the operative (*fugierende*) intentionality at stake in our embodied being-in-the-world, "rationality is not a fortuitous accident that would bring dispersed sensations into agreement with each other."[4] Instead, we must reflect upon the unreflected, even the "experience of chaos" itself in order to "render intelligible the springing forth of reason in a world that it did not create."[5] It is this "presumption of reason as the fundamental philosophical problem," this "facticity," that eludes both the explanatory models of empiricism and the constitutive impositions of intellectualism.[6] "Contemporary philosophy takes the fact as its primary theme"; it does so, however, not by a reduction to a consciousness that would constitute the world from beyond it.[7] Instead, it articulates an order for which it could not be responsible in advance but can still be made explicit through "intentional analysis."[8] To do so it would rely upon "a creative operation that itself participates in the unreflected."[9] Rightly understood, this would be to grasp the transformation at the heart of phenomenology itself as a transcendental field, that is, as a transformation of the field of reflection itself.[10] And here he glosses specifically: "Only on this condition can philosophical knowledge become an absolute knowledge and cease to be a specialty or technique."[11] Thus, inherently subjectivity will be decentered: "The center of philosophy is no longer an autonomous transcendental subjectivity, situated everywhere and nowhere, but is rather found in the perpetual beginning of reflection at that point when an individual life begins to reflect on itself."[12]

Consistently, granting Merleau-Ponty's insistence upon reading him against the grain—by "coherent deformation," as he will later call it—the

Phenomenology credits Husserl himself with provisionally outlining this transcendental field as a *Präsenzfeld*, specifically citing his analyses of the temporal flux of inner consciousness. For Merleau-Ponty, Husserl's achievement was to have articulated the reflective act as inherently temporal, precisely as "actually inserted into that flux (*Einströmen*)."[13] As he cites Husserl: "The primary flow of inner-time consciousness necessarily thereby provides itself with a 'manifestation of itself (*Selbsterscheinung*);' it does so without needing to place behind it a second flow which is conscious of itself."[14] Because of the self-relation articulated within (retentional and protentional) intentionality, Husserl himself had explicitly declared that the hypothesis of an unconscious for the flow had thus been ruled out. Moreover, he claimed that the *Selbsterscheinung* manifested through the temporal flow resulted not simply in a dispersed epiphenomenon, but in self-coincidence, unity, and identity. Again, Merleau-Ponty glossed all this with a certain deformation; while granting to Husserl that the subject is "absolute self-presence" to itself, even in the *Phenomenology*, he was not satisfied, as was Husserl, to decree self-immanence upon it.[15] Time is an event of autoaffection and reflectivity; but it is not only a synthesis of transition (*Übergangssynthesis*) between the present and the past, but an intuition inevitably problematic, that is, one that must "open up to an Other and to emerge from itself."[16]

Almost in allusion to Cassirer's neo-Kantian account of symbolic forms, an allusion that he will further complicate, Merleau-Ponty claims that this "silent" identity becomes figured and inevitably symbolized. Granted such self-presence, he adds: "[I]t is true that the subject give itself emblems of itself in succession and in the multiplicity, and that it is nothing other than these emblems, since without them it would be like an inarticulate cry (*un cri inarticulé*)."[17] Having himself just alluded to the Kantian schema as an a priori monogram of imagination, Cassirer claimed similarly that "all linguistic determination is necessarily a fixation."[18] But, in accord with his claim to perceptual self-presence, or "existence itself" (*l'existence même*), Merleau-Ponty claimed that a primary view accompanies all expression without ever being surpassed or reduced.[19] Indeed, one might think it does so like the Kantian "I think" of classical transcendentalism: "[L]anguage clearly presupposes a consciousness of language and a silence that envelops the speaking world, a silence in which words first receive their configuration and meaning."[20] Strikingly, however, against classical and antihistoricist, transcendental arguments, the immanence presupposed here is again problematic: the Cogito is a Cogito only when it expresses itself within the "entire thickness of cultural acquisitions."[21]

The question, then, is to grasp how such an acquisition might decipher its own "self-presence," the so-called inarticulate cry its expression presupposes. His glosses are both extreme and complicating: self-presence here is "prior to every philosophy, but it only knows itself in limit situations in which it is threated (*situations limites ou il est menacé*), such as in the fear of death or in the anxiety caused by another person's gaze upon me."[22] The opposition between consciousness and language is founded in both cases *in extremis,* precisely, beyond it, where language begins and ends, poised almost surreally in what Jaspers or Bataille and Blanchot would concur are "limit situations": between life and death, the first and last breath, the first cry and the last.[23]

Merleau-Ponty would later characterize surrealism as "one of the constants our time."[24] Early on, both he and Sartre initially identified this preconstitutive experience, devoid of intentional engagement or human interaction, through the poetry of surrealism.[25] Even then, however, Merleau-Ponty had emphasized that "we should not forget the role which language plays in the constitution of the world."[26] And despite Merleau-Ponty's emphasis upon the silence of the perceived world "before any word is uttered," it would lead him in a very different direction than Sartre, concerning both the role of philosophical language and the status of the surrealist poetry that apparently belied it. Sartre remained critical of Bataille or Blanchot and the surrealists, claiming that they had been insufficiently attuned to the difference between reality and imagination and, consequently, insufficiently radical in their revolutions, confusing subjectivity and objectivity.[27]

By 1948, Merleau-Ponty perhaps already knew that the oppositions from which he and Sartre already departed would not be easily maintained. As he put it with respect to Mallarmé: "[T]o speak of the world poetically is almost to remain silent."[28] The early claim seemingly still remains proximate: such a poetry "is carried entirely by language and which refers neither directly to the world, as such, nor to prosaic truth, nor to reason."[29] Taken in isolation, claims to truth, reference, or reason might be construed as fictional or aesthetic effects. Following Blanchot, in any case, who had claimed that the novel and literature as a whole would need to be thought in this way, Merleau-Ponty once more linked their reflections to the rhythm of the temporal flux:

> A successful novel would thus consist not in a succession of ideas or theses but would have the same kind of existence as an object of the senses or a thing in motion, which must be perceived

in its temporal progression by embracing its particular rhythm and which leaves in the memory not a set of ideas but rather the emblem and the monogram of those ideas.[30]

The allusion to Kant seems again clear. The work of art, Kant claimed, generates aesthetic ideas through "an intuition (of the imagination) for which an adequate concept can never be found."[31] The determinations of sensibility remain restricted to appearance, to finite "sensoriality," to use a word of Merleau-Ponty's linked to the problems at the heart of the *Phenomenology*.[32] The reference of such determinations to a monogram, the sign of what lies beyond it, is equally indirect. Kant's first *Critique* had articulated the transcendental schematism, the "hidden art" uniting sensibility and understanding by means of such a reference: the schema is "as it were, a monogram of pure *a priori* imagination."[33] The transcendental categories of pure understanding are given determinate reference to sensibility through the a priori monogram; as a result the products of imagination finally achieve what Husserl would call strictly scientific and strict determination, linked both to sensation and to understanding.

Devoid of such a determinate reference to sensibility, reason and imagination suffer different fates in Kant's critical tribunal. Through reference to the already achieved *Bedeutung* of the sensibility achieved in the syntheses of the understanding, the products of reason can achieve determinate concepts by serving as a rule for synthesis for our actions and critical judgments—even though, strictly taken, reason's conceptual totalizations trespasses the limits of finite sensibility in rational illusion (*Schein*). But undetermined by such rules, imagination is shown the exit from the critical tribunal in the first *Critique*:

> The products of the imagination are of an entirely different nature; no one can explain or give an intelligible concept of them; each is a kind of *monogram*, a mere set of particular qualities by no assignable rule and forming rather a blurred sketch drawn from diverse representations, such as painters and physiognomists profess to carry in their heads, and which they treat as being an incommunicable shadow image (*Schattenbild*) of their creations or even of their critical judgments.[34]

Merleau-Ponty's own reference to the literary monogram, clearly devoid of determinate rule and communicable category (and fixed *Bedeutung*), seems poised for a similar exit from the critical tribunal. Still, Kant's third *Critique* itself articulates poetry in another guise, precisely as a monogram of the imagination that frees itself in such a way that it allows the mind "to use nature on behalf of and, as it were, as a schema of the supersensible."[35] Moreover, it does so favorably and with justification: if "poetry plays with illusion [*spielt mit dem Schein*], which it produces at will," it does so, unlike the conceptual ruses and subreptions of rational metaphysics, "without using illusion to deceive us."[36] The result is a monogram of the supersensible, albeit an indeterminate one, again the productive genesis of an aesthetic idea.

How precisely, then, does it achieve such a monogram? Kant's claim is that here the play of imagination articulates the play inherent to language itself. By means of the play between thought and language it links "the exhibition of the concept with a wealth of thought to which no linguistic expression is completely adequate and so poetry rises aesthetically to ideas."[37] The reference is equally "indirect," like all monograms—including those regulated and restricted by a priori rules of synthesis and subsumption. Here however, the very limitations of empirical expression become positive figures of transgression; indeed, "it expands (*erweitert*) the mind," precisely by allowing us to use nature as a figure for a positive trespass of finite appearance and the accompanying illusion in extending beyond the limitations of the sensible.[38] Strictly taken, this absolute cannot be "said" any more than it can be represented; it too remains, with respect to what Kant called the demands or "the voice" of reason, silent. And yet it is reason itself that is at stake in the extension legitimately authorized in the poetic figure.

Post-Kantian Romantic Idealists saw in this poetic intuition the enclave to the Absolute from which Kant had demurred. Accordingly, Schelling's 1801 *System of Transcendental Idealism* argued that the poetic gift is "the primordial intuition."[39] What we speak of as nature "is a poem lying pent in a mysterious and wonderful script," binding together the sensible and the intelligible, the conscious and the unconscious.[40] Here, genius realizes what eludes science as an endless task.[41] Finally, philosophy, born in poetry in the infancy of knowledge may now be expected "to flow back like so many individual streams into the universal ocean of poetry from which they took their source."[42]

If Merleau-Ponty's premises similarly privilege the work of art, they remain more restricted, granted his denial of apodicticity regarding phenomenological intuition; reflection requires a monogram to bring the "inarticulate cry" of intuition to expression. The problem was how to understand the relation between expression and intuition, between the "tacit Cogito" and its linguistic or cultural expression, the "read Cogito (*Cogito lu*)," as he puts it at one point.⁴³ But it was not clear how it could be understood, granted Merleau-Ponty's denial of Husserl's Cartesianism. Whatever else his emphasis on the body had discovered, it was hard to see how the lived Cartesian body, *le corps propre*, that is, *my own* body, could generate a language. He had tried, for example, to connect the meaning of "sleet" to motor sensations, a certain modulation of my body as a being-in-the-world, again "a silence of consciousness" embracing the world of speech in which words "first receive their configuration and meaning."⁴⁴ But it was not clear how, even connected to the potentials of perception, it could generate the "thickness" of the historical and cultural expression in all its syntactic and semantic complexity.

As he realized from the outset, language binds the constitutive act of consciousness: an event in which it "imprisons itself."⁴⁵ One or two phenomenologists, after all, could not constitute a language, could not bring experience to direct expression and constitution: they could at most "reconstitute" or "reject" it. Such reconstitution would necessarily proceed as much by coherence as expression or representation, as much by adherence to a norm as intuition.⁴⁶ Still, he insisted that language was not a prison to which we are condemned because we can creatively transform it, to use Kant's term, "extending" it beyond its empirical determination. But even "the break with the tradition" is no simple "liberation."⁴⁷ As he would later argue, constitution is always the "variation of a convention," involving the outcome of "a language of which he would not be the organizer."⁴⁸ The *Präsenzfeld* he sought would accordingly need to be more complex than the one the *Phenomenology* outlined.⁴⁹

Sartre had insisted, still closer to Husserl, that the problem of art was in the end the problem of re-presentation, to understand the sign as merely an expression of an intention before the regard of consciousness, "the silence that I am."⁵⁰ Merleau-Ponty now realized that the problem instead was to understand expression precisely as variation and invention—and this, of course, is what made the exploration of inventive expression and art central, albeit precisely by emerging within the hazards of an expressive matrix that is not simply our own. What is "hazardous [*hasardeux*]" in communication is the "price we must pay to have a conquering language which, instead of limiting itself to pronouncing what we already know, introduces us to new experience and to perspectives that can never be ours, so that in the end language destroys our prejudices."⁵¹ It is precisely in this regard that the notion of language as a symbolic matrix becomes paradigmatic and aesthetic expression a "clue," to use Husserl's terminology, for phenomenological intelligibility, heuristic and corrective for its rationality:

> What is irreplaceable in the work of art—what makes it not just a pleasant occasion but a voice of the spirit whose analogue is found in all productive philosophical or political thought—is that it contains better than ideas, *matrices of ideas*. A work of art provides us with symbols whose meaning we shall never finish developing.[52]

Again, the Kantian allusion may be evident but, for Merleau-Ponty, this involves not simply the free play or liberation of the mind, but an expression and a rationality explicitly hazardous and historical. And history, again, is not only a heuristic occasion, the occasion of a "transitional synthesis," but an opening out onto the Other, surpassing the limits and prejudices of static consciousness, and both are inherent to the symbolic matrix Merleau has in mind.

At the same time, if he had originally stressed "the role which language plays in the constitution of the world," he explicitly denied thereby the other Kantian interpretation of language, dominant at the time, that of symbolic form. The *Phenomenology* had insisted, in arguing with Cassirer, that we must acknowledge expressive experiences prior to acts of signification, expressive sense (*Ausdrucks-Sinn*) prior to significative sense (*Zeichen-Sinn*) and symbolic pregnancy of form in experiential content prior to subsumption of content under form.[53] Still, no more than this anteriority could be grasped through the parallel correlates at stake in Husserlian reflection, could it simply be dissolved or overcome by what Cassirer and the neo-Kantians called pure expression, logical or causal representation.[54] The latter, they claimed, underwrote not only Kant's first *Critique*, but also Wittgenstein's *Tractatus* with its strict opposition between the world of propositional form and the ineffability of silence that attends its lack, the unsayable: the opposition between sense and nonsense.[55]

Merleau-Ponty denied the internal *Aufhebung* by representation of anterior forms in Cassirer's account of symbolic forms. The *Phenomenology* responded to this issue, once again by echoing the teleology of consciousness already implicit in Kant's third *Critique*. Thus, he invoked a different "phenomenology of spirit," one articulated through the horizons of possible objectification within the flow (*flux*) of subjectivity.[56] This different phenomenology denied absolute resolutions of the rational history in question.

"Hegel is the museum," as he put it elsewhere, and, once again, we probably should not miss the echo of the *Schattenbild* of Kant's monogram: "He is all philosophy, if you like, but without their shadowy zone [*zone d'ombre*]."⁵⁷ Such a history replaces operative history with its immanent reflection.

As has become evident, he denied the Cartesian immanence Husserl had attributed to reflection. But, accordingly, Husserl's simple denials concerning the unconscious also became less certain. While the temporal flow did not entail the need for a parallel unconscious to unite its transitional synthesis, the transcendences, the inadequation static reflection encountered in its "opening up to an Other" could not, perhaps, strictly be separated from its own surpassing—again complicating the status of the symbolic matrix Merleau-Ponty was exploring.

Strikingly, in this regard, one of the first allusions to such a matrix can be found in the *Sorbonne Lectures* on child psychology. Here, it emerges in discussions of prematuration beyond the *Id* where this matrix is involved with the child's joyful fascination with her own specular image, resulting in the emergence of a new symbolic function, one characterized by narcissism, self-contemplation—and alienation. Strikingly, too, it is Lacan's mirror stage that is at stake and ultimately explicitly cited.

> The jubilant assumption [assumption] . . . seems to me to manifest in an exemplary situation the symbolic matrix in which the I is precipitated in a primordial form, prior to being objectified in the dialectic of identification with the other, and before language restores to it, in the universal, its function as a subject.⁵⁸

Like the symbolic matrices that Merleau-Ponty will explore, this one, too, is transitional and preobjective, problematically expressed only in relation to the universal, yet to be achieved.

First, we should note that this is not just a passing reference. *The Prose of the World* would claim that "there can be speech (and in the end personality) only for an 'I' which contains the germ of a depersonalization," noting that "[i]t is true that language is founded, Sartre says, but not on an apperception; it is founded on the phenomenon of the mirror, ego-alter ego, or of the echo, in other words, of a carnal generality."⁵⁹ Doubtless, none of the elements would disappear from his account. But all elements in the account would necessitate refinement concerning their "intertwining." And, granted the historicity internal to its emergence, in the first place the symbolic matrix in question could no longer be read as a transformation of the drives or instinctual "silence" or the abstract opposition between the particular and the universal, but instead as always already institutional. Both self-consciousness and instinct would henceforth be intertwined with the social and institutional.

The *Phenomenology* had argued against the Kantian claim regarding the imposition of form or rules upon the conditions of meaning that would make a world possible. Instead, "form is the very appearance of the world, not its condition of possibility. It is the birth of a norm, not realized according to a norm."[60] The same is true of a symbolic matrix whose advent would be historically explored. But no more than I am the author of time do such explorations account for a constitution of the norm whose very exploration it presupposes and which, like time "is constitutive of us."[61] If what is a stake is a norm and its transformation or deformation, "a norm around which every given utterance oscillates," as such it is difference, *écart* and still coherent deformation.[62] And this is just how he came to understand language: "I say that I know an idea when the power to organize discourses which make coherent sense [*sens coherent*] around it has been established in me; and this power itself does not depend upon my alleged possession and face-to-face contemplation of it, but upon my having acquired a certain style of thinking."[63] But, again, if I depend upon the norms of such coherence, I am not strictly bound by them, but again can transform them: "It is just this 'coherent deformation' (Malraux) of available signification which arranges them in a new sense and takes not only the hearers *but the speaking subject as well* through a *decisive step* [*un pas décisif*]."[64] The rational emerges precisely through the sequential transformation of such decisive steps.

Such is the inherently historical, institutional character of the rational, one that has not left the notion of *Präsenzfeld* behind but precisely articulated it as a symbolic matrix: "[The] institution in a strong sense [*au sens fort*], [is] this symbolic matrix that makes a field open up, of a future according to [certain] dimension or of an common adventure and a history of consciousness."[65] It is still the case: "Ipseity, sense, and reason can exist together through temporality without contradiction."[66] Yet consciousness as *solus ipse* involves at most something of a psychological reduction;[67] instead, consciousness itself is inherently intersubjectivity. He is quick to note, again, that such intersubjectivity is neither a disperse plurality nor a set of potentially rival negations but inherently *füreinander*.[68] Here "the intelligible nuclei of history" emerge through such symbolic matrices and "the outline of rationality which it bore."[69] Time itself is still held to be a model for such institution.[70] But it is further losing its immanence, further complicating what he originally sought as absolute self-presence in being understood as intrinsically historical, no longer linked by a kind of transcendental return to beginnings but to their internal transformation. The very idea of a pretext to which all meaning might be returned thus is precisely incoherent. Even the inventive exploration of language involves "decisive steps" beyond, "extensions" to use Kant's term, beyond representation, and beyond direct reference:

> Now if we rid our minds of the idea that our language is the translation or cipher of an original text, we shall see that the idea of a complete expression is nonsensical, and that all language is indirect or allusive—that is, if you wish, silence.[71]

Such silence had seemed the silence of a primordial view, existence itself, at the origin of the sayable. Merleau-Ponty had also theorized such silence prelinguistically, the nonlinguistic meanings that attach to the intentionality that accompanies our embodied being in the world: once again, *fugierende* or "operative" intentionality, to use Husserl's term. Against what Merleau-Ponty initially regarded as Husserl's logicism, he claimed such intentionality could not be ultimately adequated in the meanings reflectively appropriated and analyzed from it. It belied such reduction. Logicists, beginning with Wittgenstein's *Tractatus*, had claimed that such silence was beyond the world of propositional expression, or logical positivists, that such "metaphysical" silence was, strictly taken, meaningless—or, at best, the music of metaphysics, as Carnap put it. The phenomenological version of logicism, on the other hand had also decried the irrationalism of such claims: everything that can be determinately and intentionally meant can be expressed, that is, said, Husserl insisted.[72]

Merleau-Ponty objected to the tacit immanence at stake in all such accounts. He objected, on the one hand, to the intentional immanence of consciousness to its experienced contents, and to that "enclosed (Wittgenstein) (the British) in the immanence of language," on the other.[73] In either case, as he said with respect to Husserl's account of independent strictly iterative ideality, such immanence is a "myth."[74] What is lacking, once again, is the link to the flux, the temporality or depths of the productive history out of which speech emerges—not by simple links to the given but by inventive transformation of the inherited language. Such silence would thus not preexist language; it would be borne both in its midst and its potential. Beyond the conventional forms of the said it would emerge in the "decisive steps" inherent in the yet to be said, ones that depends upon the productive transformation (upon the "forgetting" of the said) within saying itself. Tradition in this sense is always already the forgetting of origins.[75] Language depends upon taking on the adventure of such expressivity, such latency, such laterality, such indirection—"as it were" upon such silence.

We should be careful. This is not to claim that Being will never be said but that the opposition between silence and the said is dialectical, productively its own self-overcoming, by means of the reduction proper to language as speech.[76] Hence, "we must perform a reduction upon language, without which it would still be hidden from our view."[77] But is it to claim that the saying of Being will never be anything other than "as it were," that is, poetic (or alternately, silence)? It is Kant who had claimed that poetry liberates the mind. But he did so only after having fixed the pure categories, the a priori monograms of imagination, strictly articulating, thereby, the bounds of sense, *Sinn* and *Bedeutung*—and thereby delineating the literal and the figurative. Again, the relation between the literal and the figurative, norm and deformation, has been phenomenologically rendered exploratory and problematic by Merleau-Ponty; the symbolic matrix has itself been rendered both historical and productive. Indeed, the very notion of the flux precludes the adequacy of reflection ("it would not pass into the *Strom* if it placed as at the source of the *Strom*").[78] But it also manifests the adumbrations of the *Einströmen* itself as a symbolic matrix, modeled, as was the concept of institution itself on time: "[T]ime (already as time of the body, taximeter time of the corporeal schema) is the model of the symbolic matrices, which are openness upon being."[79] Such an opening articulates the time of memory, the imaginary, the Cogito, and intersubjectivity.[80] Indeed, an early working note for *The Visible and the Invisible* suggests as much: "after the analyses of the psychophysical body pass to analysis of memory and of the imaginary—of temporality and *from there* to Cogito and intersubjectivity."[81] All are inherently temporal, inherently historical, and inherently figural; no more than there is a direct adequation of the flux is there a direct description of this Being upon which the symbolic matrix opens. Indeed, at one point he claims that it is "not compatible with 'phenomenology' " taken as a direct encounter with objects.[82]

The problem of the monogram that has structured transcendental philosophy perhaps inevitably returns. Merleau-Ponty has seemingly denied all the classical options; we have neither Kantian categories, nor strict Husserlian intuitions, nor Hegelian Notions (*Begriffe*). Against all these Transcendental *Ich*'s we have only our history and our time. Transcendental history is also empirical, accidental, hazardous, our time. In the end, "isn't Fichte *uberhaubt* simply Fichte," dependent upon the time, history, and language that a Fichte (or a Husserl) depends upon?[83] "The philosopher who advocates the reduction speaks for everyone but he implies an intersubjective universe and remains relative to that universe in the attitude of naïve faith."[84] Here, the story of the tacit Cogito belies itself; all locution is intrinsically allocutory, an intersubjective response or *écart*.[85] Language is our ever-present accompaniment, reflection belongs to the flux, the phenomenological reduction is a transformation of history.[86]

Hence, emerges the details of a new project: "[T]he inherence of the self in the world or the world in the self, what Husserl calls the *Ineinander*, is silently inscribed in an all embracing experience which composes these incompossibles and philosophy becomes the enterprise of describing, outside of the logic and the vocabulary at hand, the universe of these paradoxes."[87] This productive deformation undertaken by philosophy would arrive at last, of course, at the "ultimate notion" of our carnal being-in-the-world or abode as the flesh, albeit one he could still understand as a "mirror phenomenon."[88] The notion of the flesh, too, was a deformation of Husserl's account, of *Ideen* II's account of intersubjectivity as intercorporeality. Still, Husserl did not grasp the deformation, the reversibility entailed by its *Ineinander*, in which "pure ideality itself is not without flesh nor freed from horizon structures."[89] Nor, of course, did Husserl grasp the implication of its *Ineinander*, the intertwining of self and other, of sensibility and intelligibility: to wit, that reversibility is "the ultimate truth."[90] He did not see the "carnal existence of idea" and "sublimation of flesh" in which the possibilities of language are already given with the double relation of seeing and saying and the silence in their midst. Yet it was there so much implicitly that Merleau-Ponty claimed to be struck by the fact, beyond the still-neo-Kantian pretensions of constitutive consciousness, that "when Husserl touched on the *body* he no longer spoke the same language."[91] Indeed, Merleau-Ponty was convinced that even Husserl in his later works thought that "this word *Bewusstsein* could still lure more sense."[92] It was the very openness of the operative language that accompanied the conventional that made further exploration and extension of this word *consciousness* possible.[93] As he put it in November 1960:

> Silence of perception—the object made of wires of which I could say what is, nor how many side it has etc. And which nonetheless is there. . . . There is an analogous silence of language, i.e. a

language that no more involves acts of reactivated signification than does this perception—and which nonetheless functions and inventively it is it that is involved in the fabrication of a book.[94]

It is, of course, this "silence of the absolute language" that Merleau-Ponty had been seeking: inventive, the deformation of signification, articulated through the expressive potential of language itself.[95] It would require an account of the inherent expressiveness of the savage mind he had sought to reveal in "deforming" Husserl's *Ineinander*, the very reversibility of the flesh.

The position has had its detractors, including those close to Merleau-Ponty (admittedly, myself included at times). Marc Richir, always a sympathetic interpreter of Merleau-Ponty, once suggested in an interview that reversibility is only part of phenomenology but not universal.[96] There was almost something of the immanence of the Spinozist attribute to it that Merleau-Ponty continually criticized as an artifact.[97] As has become readily apparent, reversibility had its own theoretical history, an artifact of Merleau-Ponty's reading of Husserl's *Ineinander*. This *reading* was perhaps best conceived as a grand wager made, all the while contesting its immanence, in what he recognized were the hazards, perhaps even the "silence," of language. As a reading, after all, it has something of the wager (if not the deduction) of Kant's "anticipations of perception," albeit one he continuously linked to the "solicitations" of sensation.[98] At one point, as was the case with the "read Cogito," Merleau-Ponty claimed that all essences (and even all inductions) were dependent upon such a reading (*lire*).[99] Reversibility by definition is never more than a half truth: every phenomenologist is a realist and a phenomenalist at once: if every *Schein* is an *Erscheinung*, every *Erscheinung* is a *Schein*.[100] One doesn't need John Cage to tell us that silence is always noise, the diatonic already atonal, or Merleau-Ponty to tell us that the aleatory or the atonal already relies upon a past, a tradition.[101] It might be said then, and more in accord with its transcendental archive, that silence can be invoked only "as it were asymptotically."[102] But then, to use Benjamin's figure, such silence might seemingly be better construed as a kind of mourning:

> In all mourning there is a tendency to silence and this infinitely more than inability or reluctance to communicate. The mournful has the feeling that is known comprehensively by the unknowable.[103]

Merleau-Ponty did not follow Benjamin's account of such mourning here, its "unknowability," perhaps even its unhappy consciousness, all of which he explicitly denied in announcing his account of the silence of the absolute language and the savage mind.[104] But we should insist, in any case, that what holds true of "reversibility" is what holds true of all ideas. What is true of all ideas, as Merleau-Ponty knew: "Each time we want to get at it immediately, or lay hands on it, or circumscribe it, or see it unveiled, we do in fact feel that the attempt is misconceived, that it retreats in the measure that we approach it."[105] As the monogram or "emblem" of the visible and the invisible, "reversibility" in accord with its *Scheinung* then might only "seem to be transcendental"; construed, that is, as an *analagon* of objective determination or *Strenge Wissenschaft*, it seems the thetic posit of "Cyclopsean" vision or *Kosmotheros*.[106] Inevitably transcendentally illusory, its "synthesis" would be intrinsically not simply transitional but transgressive and subreptive. And, as noted above, Merleau-Ponty still uses the *Schattenbild* of analogy in thinking through the relation between the silence of perception and that of language.

Still, this was not the claim; it does not involve the skeptical imposition of a shadow that either bars—or assures—the route to truth, a notion Wittgenstein once criticized in the Fregean version of the logicist's *Sinn*.[107] For Merleau-Ponty, such shadowing or ambiguity *Vieldeutigkeit* is neither transcended nor guaranteed but ventured and explored.[108] "Such polysemy (*Vieldeutigkeit*) is not a shadow to eliminate truth light."[109] It is precisely the internal differentiation, the *Schattenbildung* of seeing or saying as (*Als*). Arguably, Wittgenstein still remains proximate in his own emphasis on aspectival differentiation (perhaps even the critique of abstract universalism in terms of family resemblance).[110] It is in this sense, Merleau-Ponty declared, that "nominalism is right: the significations are only defined separations [*écarts*]."[111] Here, the shadow, in any case, is not to be eliminated but the articulation of the very partiality of experience—again, the differentiation of and not the simple identification or *ascertainment* of perception itself. Hence, all the talk of chiasm, even as difference and absolute.

> The relation between phenomenology and absolute knowledge (metaphysics) is the relation between perception and the thing: partial perception is not simply reconciled with the thing. In order to be total, it must be partial. This is at least the case if one considers the "vertical," present world—and an "understanding which is not distinct from our being.[112]

Merleau-Ponty knew that phenomenology could succeed only by having abandoned "its ambition to *see everything*."[113] Hence, Merleau-Ponty denied the reductionism of its own version of *Sinn,* the *Noema*. Language could neither be simply overseen by a constitutive act nor expressed statically or directly as a simple assertion (*Sage*).

Even as inventive deformation, expression was always already coherence, conformity, rule, and norm: in short, a history, even in its attempt to articulate the thing itself. The "decisive step" undertaken by coherent deformation, the productive imagination at stake in phenomenology, was undertaken in an oneiric venture between sense and nonsense, between coherence and incoherence. Thus, we confront another of those paradoxes he claimed to be at work in the extensions of the final account, here its flirtation with its own internal limitation. Strictly taken, "phenomenology" was meaningless (*Sinnlos*): beyond convention, "the variation of convention," beyond *Sinn,* always the internal refiguration of a symbolic matrix and its transformation.

In this extension, however, phenomenology always depended upon the rational potential of the very inheritance of the "semantic thickness" that was not its own, the "halos of signification words owe to their history."[114] Importantly, Merleau-Ponty's characterization here is taken from his description of surrealism: again, "one of the constants of our time." But Merleau-Pony has stepped beyond his initial characterization. Surrealism, in short, was not, as Sartre and the early Merleau-Ponty had surmised, the world before its constitution; it was what disrupted the world *as* constituted, what called forth the decisive step beyond the world as initially constituted, what inevitably became subjected to transitional synthesis: the other, time, the wonder of experience itself. The phenomenological reduction did not precede language; it was born out of its midst, precisely as he cited Schelling as saying that we are "not in front of but in the middle of the absolute."[115] Like his characterization of Schelling's negative philosophy, this "dismemberment of reflection from the unknown," the reduction, after all, began with its tacit and all but unconscious origin in the prereflective.[116] It proceeded "step by step," always as a series of reductions, whose seriality, "whose incompleteness is not an obstacle to the reduction, it is the reduction itself."[117] The reduction is the "step by step" overcoming of such obstacles, resulting in a deepening and even "a mutation of concepts."[118] It is in this sense that

> [t]he thematization of language overcomes another stage of naïveté. Discloses yet a little more the horizon of *Selsbsterverstandlickeiten*—the passage from philosophy to the absolute, to

the transcendental field, to the wild and "vertical" being is *by definition* progressive, incomplete.[119]

The alleged silence of the tacit or perceptual Cogito was precisely that: the "supposed silence" of inner thought is already "buzzing with words" and the saying of the said was always already *sursignification*.[120] The reality it articulated was already a "surreality" a reality "always further on" (*toujours plus loin*)—not simply because it was simply excessive, the cry of a "limit situation" but part of a developing history, its sequence.[121] And the expression of its work, its objectivity, was always unfinished. As he had learned from scientists and poets, linguists and surrealists alike, such expression remained dependent upon a surobjectivity (*surobjectif*) that accompanied its history and "saved rationality" not by a return, making it foundational, but by dialectical extension making it emergent.[122]

Husserl's word *Fundierung* became then equally emergent, bidirectional.[123] Phenomenology, even granted its "hypothesis of nonlanguage,"[124] always involved a codetermination, a "zig zag" between language and description. Accordingly, it becomes incumbent "to disclose a non-explicated horizon, that of the language I am using to describe all of that—And which co-determines its final meaning."[125] Still, there remained "non-language significations, but they are not accordingly *positive*"—and it is philosophy that has to disclose them, that is, bring them to expression.[126] Hence, once again the adventure overcoming "the alleged silence" of psychological coincidence. "The taking possession of the world of silence, such as the description of the human body effects it, is no longer this world of silence, it is the world articulated . . . but will *not be the contrary* of language."[127]

But what is the status of the deformations at stake in this indirect language, inherently a decentering of conventional normativity, articulating a lateral evidence "between the acts"?[128] Initially articulated proximate to the indirect voices of silence at stake in the painterly and the literary, had Merleau-Ponty turned philosophy into a kind of poetry? After all, he had privileged Schelling on a number of occasions. Was the account simply then the reemergence of a "transcendental poetry," to use the terms of a Novalis or a Schlegel?[129] This seem to be part of his claim about indirect language, even his attempt to "figure" what Husserl had understood as the prelinguistic status of noetic experience.

The only role of signs is [for Husserl] to transmit a signification of which they are not a part [this is contrary to the definition of poetry] [my idea of presence or of *figured World* = there of that world only a poetic knowledge]. For Husserl, in perception, hyletic elements are not signifiers [I reverse: the very signifiers of language function as perceptual *hylé*].[130]

We can only begin to grasp the complications of its conceptual status here. Nonetheless, this much is clear. The "silence" that attaches to such "poetry" cannot be invoked to infer that the world simply transcends us, reaffirming the ineffability of the noumenal—the claim, in short, that nothing can be said.[131] This position would strangely and illicitly invert the logicism such poetics itself intended to subvert—perhaps even in the same moment that it inverts the simple distinction between the literal and the figurative, the real and the imaginary, in Kant. Even in Kant, the literal, after all, always depended upon the imagination, even as "a priori" monogram. In the end the attempt to timelessly maintain the static distinction between the literal and the figurative was itself better understood as implicitly subreptive. Moreover, arguably this subreption at stake in the static distinction continually reappears in post-Kantian thought—just as much as the flirtation with transcendental poetics, both illusion of a certain Transcendental Dialectic. In contemporary philosophy, we might find the former still at work, for example, in Badiou's attempt to reappropriate philosophy from irrationalism by "desuturing" philosophy from the age of the poets (from Hölderlin to Celan) and thus to recapture the *matheme* from the irrationality of poetry.[132] As even Quine realized, the suturing of philosophy from metaphor would never be more than historically emergent and heuristic, a focus *imaginarius*.[133]

Merleau-Ponty's own emergent account of the rational also staunchly denied classical inversions of the rational: the ineffable, the irrational, relativist. Being is said in many ways, of course. But, in concluding, we should not miss its critical connection to *Dichtung* in another sense and the link between intuition and intelligibility it portends: Husserl's *Crisis*-period writings' account of depth history as history-*Dichtung*.[134] Not surprisingly, Lefort notes that Merleau-Ponty's copy of this text's reference to such *Dichtung* is "copiously underlined."[135] We have already witnessed the change of language Merleau-Ponty glimpsed in Husserl's account of the body and intersubjectivity, as flesh, *Ineinander* and simultaneity. These were all "fragments of being," Merleau-Ponty declared, that "disconcerted his frame of reference."[136] The "carnal" history at work in Husserl's final writing equally transforms the phenomenal or historically received view to cipher the silence of its depths, the sedimentation of its meaning. It thus articulates the latency of its *Tiefendimension*, complicating static givenness and its accompanying claims concerning the oneirics of the literal or the intuitions of "pure" reason.

Husserl himself questioned whether such sedimentation, such "hidden reason," does not link up with the problem of instincts (*Instinkte*) and thus the problem of overdetermination.[137] Merleau-Ponty thought this meant that phenomenology was "converging" with Freud on the pivotal question of its own silence, its own "archaeology."[138] "Freud is sovereign in this listening to the confused noises of a life"—rational life included.[139] Doubtless this complicated the task of "self-reflection": the myth of the given had its own correlating myth attending constituting consciousness: "the philosopher's professional imposter."[140]

Famously, Lacan, from whom we witnessed the emergence of the itinerary of the symbolic matrix in Merleau-Ponty's thought, saw in his final writings a phenomenology that was "attaining a beauty that is also its limit."[141] As has become evident, however, Merleau-Ponty had abandoned the account of the limit situation in an attempt to explore the transcendence in his midst: it was "no longer a question of origins nor limits," but a phenomenology that emerged "*sur place*."[142] But, as a consequence, phenomenology now confronted a world as strange and "inhuman" as the one *The Structure of Behavior* originally understood through surrealist poetry. Perhaps this was part of the long farewell that befell the science of infinite tasks and its "ambition to see everything": always to be confronted in its place with "a distant meaning," one that "is not yet legible (*lisable*) in them as the monogram or stamp of thetic consciousness."[143] Without abandoning either experience or reason—or their *Dichtung*—phenomenology more and more would involve the task of interpretation of its own silence and the sedimentation that attended and complicated it. Here "Depth is *urstiftet*," preeminently "the dimension of the hidden" and the transcendence of the sensible becomes as much lure as "*caesura*."[144]

On the one hand, Merleau-Ponty knew very well that language could not be the contrary of this silence because it not only proceeded from, but accompanied it; there could be no more a question of its simple presentation or adequation than its representation. Like modern painting, "modern thought generally, absolutely obliges us to admit a truth which does not resemble things."[145] On the other hand, he knew that, just as much as the language of simple coincidence or representation, the language of poetic *ekstasis* was equally precluded.[146] "Philosophy," Merleau-Ponty knew, "does not sublimate itself in art," even if it sought out the silence of a savage history to attain a "deeper, prehuman domain of coexistence of things prior to knowledge."¹⁴⁷ This history always brought its silence, its transcendence, with it, and it is this that he had sought to articulate. Early on, as has been seen, Merleau-Ponty claimed that "[t]he novelist speaks to his reader—as every man does to another man—the language of the initiated, namely those who are initiated into the world, to the universe of possibilities that belong to a human body and a human life."¹⁴⁸ The resulting history of the rational as *Dichtung*, as Husserl also knew, was no novel (*Roman*.)¹⁴⁹ But as has become evident, it required the critical transformation of a depth semantics and, strictly taken, could not be statically correlated with the given nor resolved in the logical *Aufhebung* of logical completeness.

Neither an intention nor a name, neither *Sinn* nor *Bedeuntung*, neither *noesis* nor *noema* would suffice. At issue was not a return to "a golden age in which words once adhered to the objects themselves," but the articulation of a rational transition, of norm and deformation, the only incarnate history out of which the literal and the figural can be intelligibly demarcated and justified. Inevitably, like modern painting, modern thought is unfinished, partial, fragmented.¹⁵⁰ "The only justification of the absolute is the conquest of this order of the phenomena, the presentation of its coherence (*enchaînement*)."¹⁵¹ This rational *enchaînement* emerges out of (and as) the silent opening of a symbolic matrix, one that like time itself, recall, already the time of the body as corporeal schema, is the articulation of our "opening onto being." Fragmented and unfinished as it was, this opening was crucial both to his transformation of phenomenology and to the "decisive step" Merleau-Ponty outlined concerning its rationality.

Notes

1. *PP*, 543n.
2. *PP*, lxxxi–ii.
3. *PP*, 58.
4. *PP*, 61.
5. *PP*, 57.
6. *PP*, 64, 62.
7. *PP*, 63.
8. *PP*, 59.
9. *PP*, 62.
10. Ibid.
11. *PP*, 63.
12. Ibid.

13. *PP*, 450.
14. *PP*, 450; Edmund Husserl, *On the Phenomenology of Internal Time Consciousness*, trans. John Brough (Dordrecht: Kluwer, 1991), 109–10.
15. *PP*, 450.
16. *PP*, 443, 450.
17. *PP*, 450.
18. See Ernst Cassirer, *Philosophy of Symbolic Forms*, vol. 3, trans. Ralph Manheim (New Haven: Yale University Press, 1957), 164. For both Cassirer and Merleau-Ponty, both Bergson and Hegel were intermediaries in the Kantian problematic of the determination of the manifold.
19. *PP*, 426.
20. *PP*, 425.
21. *PP*, 424.
22. *PP*, 426.
23. For further discussion of this issue and Merleau-Ponty's participation in it, see my "Van Gogh and the Absence of the Work: Remnants of a Hermeneutic Itinerary," in *Van Gogh Among the Philosophers*, ed. David P. Nichols (New York: Lexington, 2018). Blanchot would continue to invoke the limit experience of such a cry at a distance from the ideology of language in his *The Infinite Conversation*, trans. Susan Hanson (Minneapolis: University of Minnesota Press, 1993), 262.
24. *S*, 234.
25. *SB*, 167n.
26. *SB*, 167.
27. See, for example, Sartre's analyses in *What is Literature?*, trans. Bernard Frechtman (Gloucester: Peter Smith, 1978).
28. *WP*, 100.
29. *WP*, 101.
30. Ibid.
31. Immanuel Kant, *Critique of Judgment*, trans. Werner S. Luhar (Indianapolis: Bobbs-Merrill, 1987), 215.
32. *PP*, 251.
33. Kant, *Critique of Pure Reason*, trans. Norman Kemp Smith (New York: MacMillan, 1973), 183 (A 142; B181).
34. Ibid., 487 (A570/B599).
35. Kant, *Critique of Judgment*, 196–97.
36. Ibid., 197.
37. Ibid., 196.
38. Ibid. For further treatment of Kant's account of such rational extension, see my "On the Right to Interpret: Beyond the Copernican Turn," in *Extensions: Essays on Interpretation, Rationality, and the Closure of Modernism* (Albany: State University of New York Press, 1992).

39. F. W. J. Schelling, *System of Transcendental Idealism*, trans. Michael Vater (Charlottesville, University of Virgian Press, 1978), 230.
40. Ibid., 232.
41. Ibid., 227–28.
42. Ibid., 232.
43. *WP*, 423.
44. *WP*, 425.
45. *SB*, 176.
46. *WP*, 61.
47. *WP*, 98.
48. *VI*, 125.
49. *VI*, 173.
50. Jean-Paul Sartre, "Departure and Return," in *Literary and Philosophical Essays*, trans. Annettte Michaelson (New York: Collier Books, 1955), 172. In this 1944 essay Sartre also analyzes the meaning of the word *sleet* (against Brice Parain) by founding it in the silence of consciousness; Merleau-Ponty would stress the silence of its bodily experience. For further discussion of this issue see my "Pretexts: Language, Perception, and the Cogito," *In the Shadow of Phenomenology: Writings after Merleau-Ponty* I (London: Continuum, 2009), 28ff.
51. *PW*, 90.
52. Ibid.
53. *PP*, 304.
54. See Cassirer, *Philosophy of Symbolic Forms*, Vol. 3, 68–69.
55. Here I allude to the famous analyses of the sayable and the said at stake in *Tractatus* 7.0, "Where one cannot speak, thereof one must remain silent." See Ludwig Wittgenstein, *Tractatus Logico-Philosophicus* (London: Routlege and Kegan Paul, 1922), 189.
56. *PP*, 306.
57. *PW*, 108.
58. *CPP*, 254.
59. *PW*, 19–20.
60. *VI*, 61–62.
61. *VI*, 451.
62. HLP, 22; cf. *IP*, 41.
63. *S*, 91.
64. Ibid.
65. *IP*, 45.
66. *PP*, 450.
67. *IP*, 102n.
68. *IP*, 103.
69. *AD*, 17.

70. *IP*, 36.
71. *S*, 43.
72. See Edmund Husserl, *Logical Investigations*, trans. J. N. Findlay (London: Routledge and Kegan Paul, 1976), 321–32. Already in the *Investigations* the principle functions as a regulative one: "We are infinitely removed from this ideal," 322.
73. HLP, 43.
74. HLP, 45.
75. *PW*, 68.
76. HLP, 44.
77. *PW*, 46.
78. *VI*, 173.
79. Ibid.
80. *NC*, 83.
81. *VI*, 173.
82. *VI*, 244.
83. 107.
84. *TLC*, 106.
85. *VI*, 154.
86. *VI*, 173.
87. *TLC*, 108.
88. *VI*, 255.
89. *VI*, 153.
90. *VI*, 155.
91. Maurice Merleau-Ponty, *Parcours 1935–1951* (Lagrasse: Verdier, 1997), 303.
92. HLP, 53.
93. HLP, 29.
94. *VI*, 268.
95. *VI*, 176.
96. Florian Forestier, "Entretien avec Marc Richir," *Actu Philosophia* 21 (2012).
97. *S*, 180.
98. See Kant, *Critique of Pure Reason*, 201f (A166f; B207f).
99. *PP*, 110, 71f.
100. *VI*, 41.
101. *PP*, 196.
102. Kant, *Critique of Pure Reason*, 545 (A663; B 691).
103. Walter Benjamin, *The Origin of German Tragic Drama*, trans. John Osborne (New York: Verso, 1985), 224.
104. *VI*, 176.
105. *VI*, 150.
106. A 665; B 693; cf. *VI*, 113.

107. See G. E. Moore, "Wittgenstein's Lectures in 1930–33," *Mind* 63, no. 249 (1954): 13ff. Wittgenstein himself attributes the position to Henry Johnston.

108. Arguably the account here, in Kant's language, more clearly mirrors the analogies of experience than an anticipation of perception. Such an analogy involves connections concerning time sequencing (and remains reflective, in accord with the account of judgment he had connected to Husserl's intentionality). Hence, reversibility would be neither an axiom nor an anticipation of experience, which has the former's constitutive force. See Kant, *Critique of Pure Reason*, 211 (A180; B222). In fact, Merleau-Ponty links it explicitly to "Kant's real opposition" and in denying both origin and limit, its account of synthesis *indefinitum*. VI, 264–65.

109. *PNP*, 70.

110. See Ludwig Witttgenstein, *Philosophical Investigations*, trans. G. E. M. Anscombe (New York: Macmillan, 1953), 193ff. The difference between the accounts at this point concerns Merleau-Ponty's understanding of the symbolic matrix as historical and productive.

111. *VI*, 238.

112. *PNP*, 51–52. This reference derives from his late lectures on Hegel. The point was also made in relation to what he called the Bergsonian "reduction" and the "strange absolute knowledge" borne by duration: "In any case, when the self is at issue the contact is absolute *because* it is partial. . . . Absolute knowledge is not detachment; it is inherence" (*S*, 184).

113. Maurice Merleau-Ponty, "Preface," to *Hesnard's L'Oeuvre de Freud* in *Merleau-Ponty and Psychology*, trans. Alden L. Fisher (Atlantic Highlands: Humanities Press, 1993), 84.

114. *S*, 234. A word, too is a "field," as Wittgenstein knew. See *Philosophical Investigations*, 219.

115. *N*, 47.

116. Ibid.

117. *VI*, 178.

118. HLP, 53. See my "On the Metamorphoses of Transcendental Reduction: Merleau-Ponty and 'The Adventure of Constitutive Analysis,'" in *Phenomenology and the Primacy of the Political: Essays in Honor of Jacques Taminiaux*, ed. V. Fóti and P. Kontos (Dordrecht: Springer 2017), 107–23.

119. *VI*, 178.

120. *PP*, 189; *PW*, 144.

121. *VI*, 41.

122. *PW*, 24, 148.

123. HLP, 54.

124. HLP, 39.

125. *VI*, 178.

126. *VI*, 171.

127. *VI*, 178–79.
128. HLP, 22, 26.
129. Again, see the analysis of Walter Benjamin, "The Concept of Criticism," in *Selected Writings* Vol. I, ed. Marcus Bullock and Michael W Jennings (Cambridge: Harvard University Press 1996), 172ff.
130. Merleau-Ponty, "Reading Notes and Comments on Aron Gurwitsch's *The Field of Consciousness*, ed. Stéphanie Ménasé, trans. Elizabeth Lacey and Ted Toadvine, *Husserl Studies* 17 (2001): 182.
131. The alternate claim that all poetry is about nothingness (Heidegger, Sartre) is obviously also not far off.
132. See Alain Badiou, *Manifesto for Philosophy*, trans. Norman Madarasz (Albany: State University of New York Press, 1999). Benjamin had argued against the antinomy of poetry and reflection from the beginning: transcendental poetry in Novalis and Schlegel combined a reflexive account of life and expression. See Walter Benjamin, "The Concept of Criticism," 169. Following Benjamin, thinkers such as Lacoue-Labarthe attempted to save poetry by desuturing it from myth, *Die Sage*, by acknowledging still its vocation as *dictacmen*, acknowledging again that life itself is poetic, a synthetic unity of life and intellect—once again a transcendental schema. See Philippe Lacoue-Labarthe, *Heidegger and the Politics of Poetry*, trans. Jeff Fort (Urbana: University of Illinois Press, 2007), 72ff. Here, citing Benjamin's account of its relation with reflection, the poetic "leads not to myth but rather—in the greatest creations—only to mythic connections, which in the work of art are shaped into unique, unmythological, and unmythic forms that cannot be better understood by us" (79).
133. Cf. W. V. O. Quine, "Postscript on Metaphor," *Critical Inquiry* 5 (1978): 162: "It is a mistake to think of linguistic usage as literalistic in its main body and metaphorical in its trimming. Metaphor, or something like it, governs both the growth of language our acquisition of it. What comes after as a subsequent refinement is rather cognitive discourse itself at it most dryly literal."
134. *VI*, 176; HLP, 15. See also Edmund Husserl, *Die Krisis Der Europäischen Wissenschaften und die Transzententale Phänomenologie: Ergänzungsband Texte aus dem Nachlass 1934–7*, ed. Reinhold N. Smid, Husserliana XXIX (Dordrecht: Kluwer, 1993), 394.
135. *VI*, 177n.
136. Merleau-Ponty, Preface to Hesnard's *L'oeuvre de Freud*, 84.
137. Husserl, *Krisis*, 52.
138. Preface to Hesnard's *L'oeuvre de Freud*, 85–86.
139. Ibid., 82.
140. *S*, 180.
141. See Jacques Lacan, *The Four Fundamental Concepts of Psychoanalysis*, trans. Alan Sheridan (New York: Norton, 1981), 71.

142. *VI*, 177, 265.
143. *S*, 165.
144. *VI*, 219; *PP*, 166.
145. *PW*, 66.
146. *N*, 46.
147. Ibid.; cf. *SB*, 167.
148. *PW*, 89.
149. Husserl, *Krisis*, 47.
150. *WP*, 105.
151. *PNP*, 63.

Mind and Nature

The Truth of Naturalism

Jocelyn Benoist

A central issue in the contemporary philosophical debate is *naturalism*. The achievements of modern natural science have resulted in an "image of the man in the world," in Wilfrid Sellars's words, according to which man itself is just a part of nature, understood as a realm of mere physical laws.

"By nature we understand a multiplicity of events external to each other and bound together by relations of causality."[1]

Against such a view, the most part—not all—of good contemporary philosophers, fighting under the banner of antireductionism, strive to make some room for *another truth*. The question is then of the limits of naturalism—classically rephrased as the one of the possibility of intentionality in a nonintentional world.

Now, let us take the problem the other way around, and let us suppose the rights of intentionality are established—that there is something like an *intentional region* in the world. Does not it seem that the opposite issue might arise then: *Shouldn't we acknowledge, even in that region, some truth of naturalism?*

That is the bold question that the young Merleau-Ponty asks in the final section of his early book *The Structure of Behavior*. Such a question sounds incredibly topical in the context of the present discussion about a possible overcoming of naturalism. The answer the French philosopher suggests is also extremely original, and, considering it now, it seems to us that it might renew the very terms of the problem. The question obviously makes sense only from an intentionalist point of view—that is to say, a point of view according to which intentionality is held to be an *irreducible fact*.

Now, such is definitely Merleau-Ponty's view. Some confusion in the recent discussions in philosophy of mind about that point calls here for clarification. As people, quite commonly, rest on a very limitative concept of intentionality, understood either by the Fregean standard of judging, or in the best case of "Husserlian,"[2] conscious and lucid *representative* orientation toward an object, they might have trouble recognizing the intentionalist flavor of Merleau-Ponty's whole analysis of the mind. Some people might even believe that the insistence on immediacy that is basic in the *Phenomenology of Perception* directly conflicts with the very idea of intentionality. To emphasize the role of the silent coping of our body with its surroundings in opening a world, isn't it to get rid of some myth of intentionality?

To that point, the answer is definitely: yes. It is perfectly true that, once he has gotten more acquainted with Husserl's thought, at the stage of *Phenomenology of Perception*, one of Merleau-Ponty's main targets is a certain *myth of intentionality*—an intentionality represented as detached from the world—and some *absolute* principle. However, to get rid of the myth of intentionality is not to get rid of intentionality. On the contrary, it is to disclose what intentionality really is, *intentionality in its reality*. Now such disclosure, in the first place, entails a necessary diversification of the concept of intentionality. In his main work, Merleau-Ponty consequently reveals *different levels* of intentionality, going so far as to unearth a primordial level that pertains to our mere immediate bodily involvement with the world, which he calls "intentional arc." This process, as the rich metaphor of the "electric arc" suggests, has, properly speaking, neither subject nor object. Nevertheless, as some constitutive form of orientation link between a body and that which it is unavoidable to describe as *its* world (although it is at the level of anonymity, at which ownership does not really make sense), it is a primitive form of intentionality—we might risk the hypothesis: *the* kernel of intentionality. Thus, Merleau-Ponty's purpose is not so much to overcome intentionality as to take it down the ladder, disclosing it even where the traditional intentionalist perspective cannot see any sign of it, which, of course, supposes a sea change in the concept of intentionality, but, anyway, in return for that change, it is still about intentionality.

An objection is very likely to arise in the mainstream of the scholarship that tends (excessively, in my view) to focus on Merleau-Ponty's later ontological investigations. Once the French philosopher jettisoned the "phenomenological" perspective of the *Phenomenology of Perception* and no longer adopted the point of view of "consciousness," it might seem logical that intentionality should not be that central in his approach any more.

However, without opening that debate, which raises the difficult issue of the interpretation of Merleau-Ponty's later position, we might say that such inference might seem obvious only to people endorsing a too narrow concept of intentionality—as if the fate of intentionality were really bound up with that of consciousness, as some nonontological (but supposed to be merely "epistemic," gained in the abstraction of "knowledge") principle. On the other hand, it seems also that another reading of later Merleau-Ponty's properly ontological investigations is possible. We might put it this way: it would consist in seeing in them the quest for an *intentional ontology*. What should being be in order that there might be that basic phenomenon that inhabits it: intentionality? How can intentionality be a property of being itself—what kind of constraint does such a claim put on the concept of being and on the nature of "ontological" investigation? In that sense, it is clear that the kind of ontology that is sketched in *The Visible and the Invisible* is not some brand of ontology like others—in the traditional, nonintentional sense of the term—but does entail a strong dimension of critical reflection on "ontology" itself.

Such reflection leads to some metaphysics that one might certainly have trouble buying. However, what we just need to stress here is how much it is imbued with intentionality, far from disposing of it. How can it make sense to talk of *the world's flesh* (*la chair du monde*) unless by ascribing to the world exactly the kind of primordial, bodily intentionality that the *Phenomenology of Perception* had disclosed as the basis of our relation to the world—a basis in which the world is participating as much as we are—and our body reveals itself as a piece of the world as much as the world appears as an extension of our body, in a way that qualifies both as being commonly "flesh"?[3] What is striking, then, is the anthropomorphic accent of Merleau-Ponty's later ontology. Of course, such anthropomorphism rests on a nonclassical, decentered conception of human being—the human being is, first, what it is below the level at which it might be called a human being, that is, as "flesh." However, it does not diminish, for all that, the fact that it is an anthropomorphism. It is as if the quest for an ontology that can accommodate intentionality should result in some kind of suffused intentionalization of ontology, as if intentionality should finally become the intentionality *of the being itself* (subjective genitive).

Anyway, the gist of all that is that the way Merleau-Ponty undoubtedly distances himself (more and more) from an *orthodox* intentionalist conception never amounts to a mere relapse into a nonintentionalist, *orthodox* "naturalist" position. To adopt the terms of the later "ontological" period, it is clear that from a naturalistic (in the traditional sense of the term) point of view, the world has no "flesh," and that it just makes no sense to talk like that. It would be really difficult to describe the later Merleau-Ponty (obviously more difficult than the early or even the author of *Phenomenology of Perception*) as a "naturalist" in the sense that that term has taken on now—and had already taken on at his time, as it is possible to see it as early as in *The Structure of Behavior*. However far he drifted away from the point of view of "philosophy of consciousness," Merleau-Ponty never became a "naturalist," properly speaking.

It is even more striking to read him writing of "a truth of naturalism" at the end of his early work, in a way that is not unconnected to the evolution we have just described. What kind of truth can such a philosopher of intentionality (let us say of *generalized* intentionality)[4] yield to "naturalism"?

In such a claim one might certainly hear a concern that was to be the wellspring of his subsequent evolution as well, that is to say, the refusal to leave intentionality, as it were, floating in the air and the desire to find a more earthly place for it. In other words, that claim leads to the idea, central to his mature perspective, of an *embodied intentionality*.

The explicit project of the earlier book, as Merleau-Ponty set it out in the very first pages, was exactly to overcome the dualism between the philosophy of consciousness (or "critical philosophy," as Merleau-Ponty named it in reference to French idealism of that time),[5] and "naturalism." That means that the "philosophy of consciousness" cannot remain untouched by the inquiry into the notion of *behavior*, which cannot be explained merely in terms of naturalism, or of "philosophy of consciousness," either. Merleau-Ponty's main task appears then not so much as a plea for the standpoint of consciousness[6] as a *correction to the philosophy of consciousness*: "Once the criticism of realistic analysis and causal thinking has been made, is there nothing justified in the naturalism of science—nothing which, 'understood' and transposed, ought to find a place in a transcendental philosophy?"[7]

However, prima facie, the book, in the diversity of fields explored, seems to orchestrate a triumph for the philosophy of consciousness far beyond its usual field. The main part of the book is dedicated to the disclosure of "forms" of different levels: physical, biological, and psychological. Now, a "form" always entails some kind of unity that is not to be found in mere exteriority. Thus, "forms" as such cannot belong to "nature" as previously defined—the nature of "naturalism." They always seem to depend on some *meaning*. So, "We have been moved from the idea of a nature as *omnitudo realitatis* to the idea of objects which could not be conceived in-themselves, *partes extra partes,* and which are defined only by an idea in which they participate, by a signification which is realized in them."[8] Now, as far as signification is involved, it is about consciousness: "The human order of consciousness does not appear as a third order superimposed on the two others, but as their condition of possibility and their foundation."

There is no meaning but for a consciousness. So, the disclosure of "forms" (units of meaning) in nature reveals the latter finally as *nature for a consciousness*—or let us say, nature that takes on its proper signification only for a consciousness, as (1) it cannot have any signification by itself, although, however (2), it is essential to it to have one—otherwise it could not sport those "forms."

Should it mean that all that has been said so far about the existence of "structures" in nature makes sense only as *a spectacle for an ideal spectator*—the so-called consciousness? That would amount to a mere relapse in transcendental idealism.

It is not the case, because "forms" are not mere "objects" for a consciousness, but *forms of being,* in which consciousness itself is involved and independently of which the latter could not be. Consciousness is not only a gaze; it is a concrete viewpoint in the world that participates in the being of the so-called "forms."

Thus, the highlight of the book's finale is the idea of a meaning that should be constitutively bound up with existence, that participates in the being that it makes possible to be the being it is. That theme, freely adapted from Hegelian dialectics, as Merleau-Ponty had just heard of it from Kojève's teaching at the *Ecole pratique des hautes études,* leads to a complete reassessment of the relation between consciousness and nature.

If nature should be reenchanted, and populated by something that seems to make sense only in relation to a consciousness, that is to say, meaning, then, conversely, meaning should be "realized" (*se réaliser*), in Merleau-Ponty's words, and consciousness would thus find its place in nature itself.

"The alleged conditions of existence are indiscernible in the whole with which they collaborate": the "existence" in which we are interested now, is no longer "mere existence" by itself, but existence in a *whole* that endows it with meaning, and there is no whole but from the point of view of a consciousness, or at least of something like a consciousness (no "whole" in mere nature).[9] However, on the other hand, "reciprocally, the essence of the whole cannot be concretely conceptualized without [those "conditions of existence"], and without its constitutive history."[10] That entails that meaning is not detached from that facticity to which it gives a form: it is meaning exactly *in* that facticity. Meaning is inseparable from the arrangement of the given itself.

Thus, the book ends up with the picture of *a mind that "comes into the world."*[1] Nature acquires some interiority in what the mind makes of it, by "transferring the body outside of physical space," but that does not amount to any mere "spiritualization" of the body, which would become the mere "idea" of the body and wind up lacking any spatiality. That means much more the *becoming meaningful of physical space,* and, thus, as much the externalization of the mind as the internalization of the body. Having reached the end of the analysis, *the mind is outside*. This is the paradoxical "truth of behaviourism" that Merleau-Ponty already emphasized at the very beginning of the book, in terms that could not yet be understood then: "By going through behaviourism, one gains at least in being able to introduce consciousness, not as psychological reality or as cause, but as structure."[12]

At that early stage of the analysis, that hint was really misleading, as the concept of "behavior" put forward by "behaviorism" is exactly the opposite of the one that Merleau-Ponty borrowed from interwar German-speaking biology and psychology, imbued with phenomenology. The whole demonstration given by *The Structure of Behavior*, against behaviorism, tends to establish that there is no "behavior," properly speaking, independent of any meaning. So, behavior, one more time, cannot be that mere exteriority that "behaviorism" usually takes it to be. *There is, however, a truth of behaviorism*: that is to say that the mind, understood as the source of meaning, should be looked for outside. The mind is what it is where it alone structures an existence, thus, "in behaviour."[13] Conversely, it would not make any sense to construe any behavior in terms of mindlessness, as "naturalism" usually does.

So the title of the book might be explained. "Behavior" means, precisely, *mind in the world*. Which supposes (1) that the world is such as has mindedness in it, (2) that mind is such as is in the world. The world is, as it were, imbued by the presence of the mind in it; but all that is possible only as far as the mind has a body, or, more exactly, *is* an embodied mind. That reconciliation of nature with mind put forward seventy years ago, with its neo-Hegelian flavor (already) characteristic of that time, might certainly be compared with the way out of the debate about naturalism and anti-naturalism recently attempted by John McDowell. On either side, we find the common rejection of some "orthodox" naturalism: the naturalism of mere, naked exteriority and meaninglessness. However, on the other hand, in both cases, too, we find some vindication of naturalism, at the cost of its reinterpretation. Both philosophers intend to bridge the alleged gulf between mind and nature and to recognize mind *in* nature itself, which requires a new concept of nature, which John McDowell would call a "second nature," of which it is as important that it is *second* as that it remain *nature*, properly speaking. At that level—the level of meaningful behavior, or, maybe better (that qualification is, of course, no detail at all), in McDowell's words, *action*—there remains no genuine gap between mind and nature, and the dualism linked up with the modern philosophy of consciousness as a philosophy of the spectator has at last been overcome.

As similar as both approaches may look (and *are*, definitely, in a lot of details), there remains, however, a huge difference, which incidentally surfaced in a recent debate between John McDowell and Hubert Dreyfus[14]—the latter sticking up for a Merleau-Pontian position, or at least *believing* to do so. As blurred and misleading as the terms of that exchange might have been, I think it indirectly revealed something of the peculiarity of Merleau-Ponty's view, a peculiarity that might be of great help in putting a real end eventually to the never-ending contemporary discussion of naturalism, its nature, and its limits. So, I am going to say something about that in conclusion.

It might turn out to be a strange vindication of naturalism if, in order to survive, it should just renounce its core: the very idea of a nature as *that which has no meaning*.

In some sense, it is clear, from that point of view, that in Merleau-Ponty's later thinking, which characterizes nature as "that which has a meaning, but without that meaning having been posited by thought,"[15] he turns his back on naturalism (and probably, symmetrically, on John McDowell's position as well). One more time, Merleau-Ponty's later thought, maybe even more where it overcomes it (that is to say: makes it a *metaphysics*), is deeply imbued by intentionalism.

However, at the early stage of *The Structure of Behavior*, the final appraisal of "the truth of naturalism" might be more ambiguous than that. It might not come down to the mere hijacking of the "nature" of naturalism made hostage to meaning, but entail some more substantial acknowledgment of the irreducibility of that sense of "nature" that is to be heard in "naturalism." What is basic, then, is the fact that there is something below meaning, something that is not yet meaning. And that is even more impressive inasmuch as a full capacity to imbue nature has been granted to meaning.

In that sense, there is something in the final interpretation given of "the truth of naturalism" in *The Structure of Behavior* that does not fit in with the description we have made of a mere reconciliation, and, at last, identification of nature and meaning. The fact that a nature can be meaningful does not diminish the fact that, in the very notion of "nature" there remains a residue that resists that becoming meaningful, something that should be interpreted in other terms than meaning—otherwise, it would not make any sense to call it "nature."

Now, Merleau-Ponty explicitly says: "What is profound in the notion of 'Gestalt' . . . is not the idea of signification but that of structure."[16] The philosophy of *The Structure of Behavior*, as far as there is one in that tentative work, is a philosophy of structure, not a philosophy of meaning. Merleau-Ponty makes the difference explicitly, and that difference might be good to retain. Organization, in its facticity, is not immediately transparent to meaning—it has some kind of first "neutral" value below the level of meaning.

Merleau-Ponty's point is highly critical in view of the contemporary debate. According to him, you cannot have your cake and eat it too, by endorsing the externalization of the mind and, at the same time, maintaining a Cartesian conception of its self-transparency (something it might be possible to suspect John McDowell of). If the mind is really external, it should, in some sense, be *external to itself*. That's Merleau-Ponty's point. Thus, the least interesting aspect of Merleau-Ponty's final plea for embodied meaning in *The Structure of Behavior* is not his paradoxical vindication of "dualism" at some level.

Completely in line with the neo-Hegelian conception of a "concrete," "effective" mindedness, Merleau-Ponty insists that the traditional metaphor comparing the relation between mind and body with the one existing between a concept and a word that is supposed to "express" it, might prove really misleading, insofar as it might suggest some kind of "external" relation between mindedness and embodiment. Now, as the meaning is constitutively *the meaning of a word* (the word not being a word independently of its meaning, and the meaning not being the meaning it is but as the meaning of that word), the mind is constitutively *the mind of a body*. There are, in that picture, not two realities externally connected, but just one: the one of *the embodied mind*.

However, he says, that metaphor has *more than one flaw*. One is the kind of separation it presupposes by treating the familiarity of the mind and the body as a *relation*. Another is that, relying on that idea of a relation, it tends to treat it as excessively uniform, missing the diversity of the concrete ways in which *the body might appear as minded or not*. From that point of view, in good phenomenology a lot of distinctions are to be made and there is, in some sense, completely disconnected from the traditional metaphysical basis of "dualism," some "truth of dualism."

Particularly striking is, thus, the description Merleau-Ponty makes of the variable modalities of embodiment. Sometimes, the body is exactly the bearer of an intention, so much that it might be said itself to intend, being nothing external to that intention; Merleau-Ponty will definitely talk, in *Phenomenology of Perception*, of a "bodily intentionality." However, "*Our body does not always have meaning.*"[17] There are "cases of disintegration."

Those cases of disintegration should not be interpreted as the mere separation of two things—body and soul—of which each might be by itself. It is much more some kind of *regression from one level of structure to another*, some kind of loss of integration. The possibility of such loss is essential to our body as the one that can be minded and usually *is*.

Now, it would be mistaken to believe that what becomes apparent in those situations should necessarily be some kind of "alienated" reality. That would be the case if we should be confronted then with our body as someone else's body, or more exactly no one's body—in other words, a body belonging to mere nature, in the sense posited by naturalism.[18]

It is not the case: that nature that constitutes the silent background of the mind, and which might surface in the blanks of the latter, it is not that nature that is supposed to be mere and absolute exteriority, but the presubjective nature of a living and perceiving body. From that point of view, we might oppose a symmetrical criticism to McDowell's debunking of a myth. McDowell suspects that Merleau-Ponty falls prey to "the myth of disembodied intellect," which allegedly allows the French philosopher to maintain an exteriority of the body in relation to the mind. However, all that matters then is the meaning of that "exteriority." The trouble with McDowell's position might, conversely, be that, in his view, what is not endowed with intellect can only be a mere "physical" phenomenon, what we might call *the myth of the physical*, which we can balance with the so-called myth of the mental.

In Merleau-Ponty's view, there is that strong point that nature should unavoidably be first nature as well, and first in the sense of something that should always remain in some sense resistant to full-blooded mindedness, something that should belong to the prehistory (and not only the history) of the mind, which is a point he really shares with naturalism. Now the problem is: What do we put in that *primary* sense of nature? Is it that *mere* exteriority in which there is no subject—not even either that *"anonymous"* subject[19] *of perception* that the French philosopher will call "the body" in his masterwork? Should we really exclude perception from first nature? But, if perception is not natural *in the first place*, what is?

Notes

1. *SB*, 3.
2. We shall not here enter into the question whether that picture of Husserl is fair or not.
3. One origin at least of the theme of the "flesh" is to be found in that weird passage in *Phenomenology of Perception* in which Merleau-Ponty describes perception as a kind of "coition" (!) of our body with the world: see *Phenomenology of Perception*, trans. Colin Smith (London: Routledge, 1958), 373.
4. As far as a generalization never goes without alteration.
5. A reference that still remains central, as a foil, in the *Phenomenology of Perception*.
6. In that early work, which is still written more in the language of French "critical" philosophy than in the one of phenomenology, the concept of consciousness is more central than the one of intentionality in order to characterize the mind, although the concept of intentionality already comes up as well: the book even starts with it, emphasizing how the naturalist perspective deactivates it and debunks it as an illusion. See the example of perceptual tracking, basic for the whole book. *SB*, 7.
7. *SB*, 4.
8. *SB*, 202.
9. As far as there are no *internal relations* in such nature.
10. *SB*, 208.
11. *SB*, 209.
12. *SB*, 5.
13. "The mental is reducible to the structure of behaviour." *SB*, 221.
14. See the texts collected in the special issue of *Inquiry*, vol. 50 (2007).
15. *N*, orig. 20.
16. *SB*, 206.
17. *SB*, 209.
18. As McDowell finds convenient to believe in the use he makes of a quotation from *Phenomenology of Perception* (238) in his paper "What Myth?" *Inquiry* 50 (2007): 350.
19. An anonymous subject—or anonymous level of the subject—is that of which McDowell cannot make sense in Merleau-Ponty's perspective.

The Panpsychism Question in Merleau-Ponty's Ontology

JENNIFER MCWEENY

Does Merleau-Ponty's notion of flesh entail panpsychism? Does an ontology of flesh, properly understood, imply that mind is present in all that exists? How one answers this question is of course dependent on how one conceives of the term *mind* in the context of Merleau-Ponty's philosophy, which distances the concept from its standard philosophical and scientific heritages. For the purposes of this initial consideration, we might say that Merleau-Ponty's ontology would entail panpsychism if it required that any one "mindlike quality" were ubiquitous or intrinsic to existence. Such qualities include Merleau-Ponty's notions of sentience, experience, perspective, consciousness, self-consciousness, perception, affection, feeling, thought, dimensionality, expression, subjectivity, interiority, and intentionality. Views such as pansensism (everything senses) and panpexperientialism (everything experiences) are thus specific versions of panpsychism according to this scheme. Panpsychism is not, however, synonymous with animism (everything has spirit), hylozoism (everything has life), or pantheism (everything has God). Whether a panpsychist ontology is also a hylozoist or animist one, for instance, is a further question whose answer will depend on the specific kind of panpsychism at issue as well as the compatibilities and incompatibilities of the conceptions of spirit, life, and mind that it implicates.

David Abram is perhaps the first to have offered an affirmative answer to the panpsychism question in regard to Merleau-Ponty's philosophy. In *The Spell of the Sensuous: Perception and Language in a More-Than-Human*

World, he describes prereflective perception as coincident with a kind of animism that is also a panexperientialism or pansubjectivity (everything is an experiencing subject):

> Merleau-Ponty writes of the perceived things as entities, of sensible qualities as powers, and of the sensible itself as a field of animate presences, in order to underscore their active, dynamic contribution to perceptual experience. . . . To the sensing body, *no* thing presents itself as utterly passive or inert. . . . Prior to all our verbal reflections, at the level of our spontaneous, sensorial engagement with the world around us, we are *all* animists.[1]

In the wake of Abram's remark, and in the current of philosophical trends such as new materialisms, speculative realisms, environmentalism, and the resurgence of panpsychism as a viable position in analytic philosophy of mind, other scholars have made similar gestures toward a panpsychist reading of flesh. Consider the following statements from David Morris and Michel Bitbol, respectively:

> But what if mind is in all things that it knows, if it is not local to the body? This is what Merleau-Ponty's expressive body would lead us toward: if the body is ever to have a schema or develop habits (and if we are to make sense of this within Merleau-Ponty's expressive framework), then the world must already amount to a mindful body outside our own that solicits such habits in us, and in large part this is because the world is a cultural-historical one that already speaks to our bodies, via the bodies of others. This, more or less, is implied in Merleau-Ponty's later concept of "flesh," and by his earlier thought that the philosophy of mind is an insoluble problem if it is not also a philosophy of intercorporeity.[2]

> We can see at this point some similarities [. . .] between panpsychism and Merleau-Ponty's boundless phenomenology of the world-flesh. In both cases, any difference in nature between mental and mindless, sentient and inert beings is denied. In both cases, experience suffuses what there is. This point of convergence is so deep and so striking that one is surprised to find a recent historian of panpsychism declaring that there is no equivalent of a panpsychist tendency to be seen anywhere in phenomenology.[3]

Whereas Abram emphasizes that perceived things participate actively in our perceptions and that we therefore experience these things as subjects, Morris focuses on Merleau-Ponty's notion of the expressive body. If consciousness is understood as the expression of a style of being that both institutes and annexes other styles through its worldly relationships, then the world's capacity to hold these styles as so many cultural deposits of other expressions constitutes a kind of mindfulness. In addition, although Bitbol rejects a panpsychist reading of flesh in the end, he nonetheless acknowledges that the ontological continuity between perceiver and perceived that flesh establishes implies that experience is everywhere.

At the same time that suggestions of a panpsychist reading of flesh have grown more numerous in the scholarly literature, so have refutations of this approach. Three main points have been raised against such an interpretation. First, Dan Zahavi rejects a premise that he believes is necessary to a panpsychist interpretation, namely, the admission that Merleau-Ponty's conception of the anonymous subject of experience allows for an undifferentiated (and therefore not necessarily first-personal) prereflective consciousness.[4] Second, a host of Merleau-Ponty scholars, including M. C. Dillon, Françoise Dastur, Melissa Clarke, Bryan Bannon, and Evan Thompson emphasize the difference between the flesh of the (human) body and the flesh of the world: while the former is both sentient and sensible and therefore "self-sensing," the latter is *merely sensible*.[5] Third, Bitbol and Ted Toadvine each argue that because Merleau-Ponty's phenomenological method begins in the researcher's first-personal experience and the "self-sensitivity" that is found there, it cannot be extrapolated to all existents that would purportedly exist outside of this experience.[6] Construed as fundamentally anthropomorphic, phenomenology could never let us draw the conclusion required by panpsychism.

Although the work of these and other scholars has served to raise the panpsychism question, no thinker to date has developed the problem or a response in detail, a situation likely related to the fact that Merleau-Ponty's thinking offers ample evidence for and against a panpsychist reading, most especially within the pages of his last and uncompleted work, *The Visible and the Invisible*. This chapter seeks to redress this gap by revealing and navigating this fecund and beckoning tension in Merleau-Ponty's ontology, ultimately concluding that, when Merleau-Ponty's thinking is considered holistically, there is more evidence for a panpsychist conception of flesh than not. After first motivating the question by pointing to a number of passages across Merleau-Ponty's oeuvre relevant to the discussion, the present reading attends to the ways that Merleau-Ponty's final work appropriates and modifies panpsychist elements from the respective metaphysics of Gottfried Wilhelm Leibniz and Max Scheler to account for a "universal" or "reciprocal" expression within flesh, where each body expresses every other body and the world as a whole. It is then suggested that insofar as reciprocal expression is a necessary element of Merleau-Ponty's ontology, that body and world must each possess capacities for *both* sentience and sensibility and that therefore panpsychism (specifically, pansensism) would obtain.

The Panpsychism Question

The panpsychism question is already posed with the first line of *The Structure of Behavior*: "Our goal is to understand the relations of consciousness and nature: organic, psychological or even social."[7] Rather than presume that consciousness is separate from nature as both empiricism and intellectualism imply, Merleau-Ponty follows phenomenology in reconceiving consciousness as fundamentally integrated with the world. He asserts, for example, that consciousness is "presupposed everywhere as the place of ideas and everywhere interconnected as the integration of existence."[8] He also refers to consciousness as "milieu of the universe" and "universal milieu," that which is present in each order of existence from the physical to the vital to the human.[9]

We might expect that this universal milieu to which Merleau-Ponty refers is a sum of individual consciousnesses from the different orders, and that human consciousness is an especially developed form of consciousness. But Merleau-Ponty addresses their relation inversely: human consciousness breathes its own consciousness into the other orders. He takes care to note that his view is not a return to vitalism or animism, and he emphasizes this point by referring to a passage from Hegel: "[The mind of nature] is only mind for the mind which knows it."[10] Evoking a theme that will become central in his later works, he maintains that we grasp the universal way that "consciousness lives in things" when we recognize that perspective is constitutive of perceived objects.[11] An object is perceived insofar as it invites a particular perspective from the perceiver; it establishes itself as transcendent by exceeding the present perspective. The perceiver's consciousness both brings perceived objects into a determinate existence and endows them with a mirroring perspectival gaze that looks back at what looks at them. Merleau-Ponty thus explains, "[T]he human order of consciousness does not appear as a third order superimposed on the two others, but as their condition of possibility and their foundation."[12] A distinctively *human* consciousness lives in things, individuating bodies and making consciousness and sense ubiquitous in nature inasmuch as a human is looking at it. The universal milieu that looks at first like panpsychism in *The Structure of Behavior* turns out to be a qualified transcendental idealism that would not go so far as to recognize that things have a consciousness that was not constituted by the perceiver's (human) consciousness, even if this mode of constitution is inchoate, "not yet a Kantian object."[13]

Merleau-Ponty develops the idea of consciousness as universal milieu from *The Structure of Behavior* through his notion of an impersonal or "anonymous" subject of experience in the *Phenomenology of Perception*. As a subject that "has already sided with the world,"[14] the anonymous body appears to live meanings that it did not generate itself: "I am capable (through connaturality) of finding a sense in certain aspects of being, without myself having given them this sense through a constituting operation."[15] Commentators disagree as to whether Merleau-Ponty's conception of the anonymous subject, which many consider to be crucial to the subsequent development of his ontology of flesh, would require us to admit the possibility of a collective or general consciousness and consequently of shared experiences.[16] How this disagreement is resolved comes to bear on the plausibility of a panpsychist reading of flesh.

Merleau-Ponty explicitly acknowledges the link between affirming the possibility of shared experience and panpsychism in his first Sorbonne Lecture, "Consciousness and Language Acquisition," which, as far as this author is aware, is the only place in Merleau-Ponty's writings where he uses the word *pan-psychisme*.[17] Here he charts a phenomenological account of the relation between self and other that bridges Husserl's belief in the distinctiveness and privacy of self-consciousness with the contrary view, espoused by Scheler, that in certain types of experiences, namely, emotional or affective ones, a person can access the consciousness of another. Because Husserl begins with the *cogito* and the isolation of consciousnesses, he has difficulty explaining intersubjectivity without compromising the formal structure of his starting place. Inversely, Scheler strays from the phenomenon by "level[ing] down self-consciousness and consciousness to a neutral psychic level that ends up being neither one."[18] It is at this point in his criticism of Scheler's view that Merleau-Ponty invokes the term in question: "Scheler's conception rubs elbows with a kind of panpsychism; at the heart of his conception there is not individuation of consciousnesses."[19]

In his resolution of the contrary impasses generated by Husserl's and Scheler's respective accounts, Merleau-Ponty does not choose one account at the expense of the other, nor does he embrace a third alternative; he instead combines the two by allowing for a continuous reversion between individuation and integration. On the one hand, he recognizes an experiential or epistemological difference between self and other *in most contexts*. On the other, he allows for the possibility that the self can intermittently "rejoin" the other at certain times.[20] This solution leads to the radical conclusion that although the privacy, integrity, and sidedness of self-consciousness is very frequently assured, it is not necessarily so: "We must render the self as interdependent in certain *situations*. We must tie even the notion of ipseity to that of situations."[21] Merleau-Ponty arrives at this solution by suspending the temporal-causal question of origin—of whether individuation or integration comes first in the development of consciousness. In light of this subtle and unusual juxtaposition of Husserl's and Scheler's views, Merleau-Ponty's criticism of Scheler's panpsychist tendencies in this instance should not be read as a criticism of *all* varieties of panpsychism; it only excludes those types that would not allow for the individuation of consciousnesses, that hold that existence is *only* undifferentiated consciousness. Zahavi, for example, therefore misinterprets the remark as a blanket refutation of the idea of shared experience and thus as an affirmation of Husserl's position.[22]

Scheler's suggestion that consciousnesses are not always private and impermeable presses the question of whether Merleau-Ponty's ontology would allow for aspects of my experience that do not originate with my constituting acts, of whether the anonymous subject is an occluded part of my own consciousness or something that did not begin with me. If certain aspects of my experience are not entirely mine, then we are led to wonder both whose experiences they are and what kind of ontology could adequately account for this paradox of accessible alterity. With an eye to such questions, Merleau-Ponty begins to revise his notion of phenomenological constitution in "The Philosopher and His Shadow," a lecture that Renaud Barbaras aptly labels "a sort of rehearsal of 'The Intertwining—The Chiasm.' "[23]

Of Husserlian phenomenology Merleau-Ponty writes, "Originally a project to gain intellectual possession of the world, constitution becomes increasingly, as Husserl's thought matures, the means of unveiling a back side of things that we have not constituted."[24] With this methodological shift, phenomenology becomes ontology; I find the world most deeply in experience, not only because my experience is already in the world and synchronized with it, but more important, because experience is never entirely mine. We thus begin to look for being not from the outside, but from within being itself; we begin to look for what we ourselves have not constituted, for "what resists phenomenology within us—natural being, the "barabarous' source Schelling spoke of."[25]

The consequences of this approach are born out in "Eye and Mind" in Merleau-Ponty's descriptions of an active consciousness that lives in seemingly inanimate things and is not reducible to that of the perceiver. Merleau-Ponty tells us that "it is the mountain itself which from out there makes itself seen by the painter,"[26] and he remarks of the painted wall at Lascaux that "it is more accurate to say that I see according to it, or with it, than that I *see* it."[27] The stroke of the painter's brush is directed by the mountain's self-disclosure, by the voices of the forest. The animals painted on the cave wall swim and run through the consciousness of the perceiver, leading her gaze. At this point in Merleau-Ponty's thinking, the consciousness-object distinction has been cracked, leaked, compromised in a new way; it is no longer only my consciousness that lives in things following the view of *The Structure of Behavior*—the thing's consciousness also lives in me. The panpsychism question is a question about the ontological implications of this claim.

Several scholars deny that Merleau-Ponty's proclamations of trees and mountains seeing amounts to an attribution of a kind of sentience to these things; there is instead a fundamental asymmetry between the perceiver and perceived in this regard. Dillon's analysis is paradigmatic here: "Trees and mountains do not see; they are blind witnesses to my own visibility."[28] The asymmetrical interpretation of the self-world perceptual relationship takes much of its force from a working note of May 1960, where Merleau-Ponty stresses that the notion of "the flesh of the world" is incompatible with hylozoism, the view that all matter is alive:

> The flesh of the world is not self-sensing (*se sentir*) as is my flesh— —It is sensible and not sentient— —I call it flesh, nonetheless [. . .] in order to say that it is a *pregnancy* of possibles, *Weltmöglichkeit* (the possible worlds variants of this world, the world beneath the singular and the plural) that it is therefore absolutely not ob-ject, that the *blosse Sache* mode of being is but a partial and second expression of it. This is not hylozoism: inversely, hylozoism is a conceptualization— —a false thematization, in the order of explicative-Entity, of our experience of carnal presence.[29]

Elsewhere in *The Visible and the Invisible*, Merleau-Ponty emphasizes the difference between the flesh of my body and the flesh of things by referring to the former as "dimensional of itself," which suggests an inherent capacity for reflecting the world, rather than contingently or relationally dimensional, and by stressing that, unlike the flesh of my body, the flesh of things is given as "mute."[30]

The assertion that there are multiple *kinds* of flesh—one flesh that is self-sensing, intrinsically dimensional, and expressive, and another that is merely sensible, contingently dimensional, and mute—is readily undermined by others of Merleau-Ponty's statements that proclaim a deeper ontological continuity between self and world, perceiver and perceived, sensing and sensed.[31] For example, Merleau-Ponty states that "my body is made of the same flesh as the world"[32] and that man "is made of [the] flesh [of things]."[33] He also implies that the flesh of the world is capable of a kind of self-sensing when he writes, "the flesh of the world (the 'quale') is indivision of this sensible Being that I am and all the rest which feels itself (*se sent*) in me, pleasure-reality indivision—."[34] Self-sensing thus construed is a relational process that demands symmetrical reversibility: the thing needs me in order to feel itself just as I need the thing to feel myself, the thing's sensibility calls forth my sentience and my body's sensibility solicits the sentience and sensitivity of the thing. These ascriptions of ontological continuity between the flesh of my body and the flesh of the world culminate in a crucial passage at the heart of the chapter, "The Intertwining—The Chiasm":

> When we speak of the flesh of the visible, we do not mean to do anthropology, to describe a world covered over with all our own projections, leaving aside what it can be under the human mask. Rather, we mean that carnal being, as a being of depths, of several leaves or several faces, a being in latency, and a presentation of a certain absence, *is a prototype of Being,* of which our body, the sensible sentient, is a very remarkable variant, *but whose constitutive paradox already lies in every visible.*[35]

This passage suggests that the "fundamental fission between the sentient and the sensible" runs through all beings whatsoever.[36] In other words, the sensible-sentient difference is relative to perspective—the same thing could appear sensible from one view and sentient from another—it is not an absolute distinction that designates ontological *kinds* of beings. Merleau-Ponty reminds us, "it is indeed a paradox of Being, not a paradox of man, that we are dealing with here."³⁷ Such passages indicate, contrary to the May 1960 working note, that the flesh of the world is not constitutively different from my flesh; the two possess the same "inner framework," are cut of the same cloth.³⁸

The text's indecision about the ontological capacities of the "flesh of the world" and about whether or not to think the relationship between body and world symmetrically is precisely what renders the panpsychism question a *question* in its dynamic, vital sense. Such hermeneutical complexity warns against pointing to one or two passages as a means of settling things. It is not enough to show *that* Merleau-Ponty made claims compatible with one view or the other; we must instead explain *how* each claim functions within his ontology as a whole to see whether the contradictions should be retained or abandoned, whether the thinking is complete in itself or tragically cut short, frozen in process, calling out for more. The following section pursues this systemic approach and suggests that there is good reason to read Merleau-Ponty's last thought as a panpsychist ontology.

Toward a Panpsychist Reading of Flesh

Merleau-Ponty sees Leibniz's monadology as a suitable model for his own ontological project because it describes a system that seeks to retain rather than resolve the existential ambiguities of unity and diversity, finitude and infinity, and openness and privacy.³⁹ In a well-known working note of December 1959, he remarks:

> [C]ertain Leibnizian descriptions—that each of the views of the world is a world apart, that nonetheless "what is particular to one would be public to all," that the monads would be in a relation of expression between themselves and with the world, that they differ from one another and from it as perspectives—are to be maintained entirely, to be taken up again in Brute being, to be separated from the substantialist and ontotheological elaboration Leibniz imposes on them—⁴⁰

At the same time that each monad is complete and unique in itself—is its own substance—each monad expresses all the others and the universe as a whole. In this respect, Leibniz's summary of of his own system could just as well describe Merleau-Ponty's: "I have said nothing that does not follow from my doctrine that every body expresses all other things, that every soul expresses its own body, and that through its body each soul also expresses all other things."[41] However, because Merleau-Ponty considers flesh to be "an ultimate notion," thinkable in itself, he cannot explain reciprocal expression between perspectives in the same way that Leibniz does by invoking a "pre-established harmony" that is divinely given.[42] He must conceive reciprocal expression as a function of flesh rather than God.

In order to account for a reciprocal expression that is carnal and intrinsic to the structure of flesh, Merleau-Ponty appeals to what he describes as a "co-perception" or "*Einfühlung*" (commonly translated as "empathy," "sympathy," "intropathy," or "feeling-in") between the perceiver and perceived.[43] Merleau-Ponty's notion closely parallels Scheler's concept of *fellow-feeling* (*Mitgefühl*) as he articulates it in *The Nature of Sympathy*.[44] Earlier, in "Consciousness and Language Acquisition," Merleau-Ponty praises Scheler for the way that his theory of expression challenges the privacy of perspective and links interiority with exteriority: "Scheler's essential contribution is the notion of expression; there is no consciousness *behind* manifestations; they are inherent to consciousness; they *are* consciousness."[45] Scheler relies on this notion of expression to affirm the possibility of a particular type of "fellow-feeling," which he describes as the participation in another's experience or "the case of feeling the other's feeling."[46] He explains that once bodies are considered to be "a field of expression for their experiences" it becomes difficult to differentiate one's own experiences from those of others.[47] As Scheler describes, "What we perceive are *integral wholes,* whose intuitive content is not immediately resolved in terms of external or internal perception."[48]

The concept of fellow-feeling is misinterpreted insofar as it is taken to imply the existence of an undifferentiated consciousness that blends one experiential perspective with another. For Scheler, fellow-feeling only entails an *epistemic* confusion about which experience goes with which perspective that follows from the openness and accessibility of affective consciousness. It does not indicate a *metaphysical* confusion that would allow for two particularities to combine ontologically to produce a new being, "some huge animal" whose organs consist of the former, individuated bodies.[49] Scheler emphasizes, with language that is premonitory of Merleau-Ponty's notion of *écart*, that "fellow-feeling does not proclaim the essential identity of persons, as Schopenhauer and von Hartmann allege, but actually presupposes a pure essential difference between them (this being also the ultimate basis of their difference in actual fact)."[50] If there were an identity between the two perspectives, then the one could not affect the other, invade the other, *feel with* the other. Thus construed, we find in fellow-feeling a carnal mechanism of reciprocal expression that preserves the general parameters of Leibniz's monadology: each perspective is ontologically different from every other perspective ("a world apart"), and yet necessarily gathers other perspectives within it and gives itself to other perspectives in virtue of the expressive nature of carnality ("what is particular to each is public to all").

Merleau-Ponty does not adopt Scheler's concept without modification, however, for Scheler limits the domain of fellow-feeling in two ways that would compromise its ability to ground a carnal theory of reciprocal expression. First, Scheler maintains that the experiential accessibility that occurs in fellow-feeling only applies to a small portion of the other's experience. Although fellow-feeling gives the meaning of another's pain, the other's bodily sensations constitute "a sphere of absolute personal privacy, which can never be given to us."[51] Second, Scheler believes that fellow-feeling is an intersubjective phenomenon that can only occur between two expressive beings, that is, between a human and another being that she grasps immediately as expressive, as possessing sentience and subjectivity. Insofar as Merleau-Ponty retains these original stipulations, the flow and scope of reciprocal expression throughout existence would be curtailed, since each condition demarcates a permanent realm of inaccessibility—parts of existence that could never be expressed and that therefore could never be public to all.

To avoid these consequences, Merleau-Ponty reconceives the traditional phenomenological concept *Einfühlung* to serve as the mechanism of reciprocal expression within flesh. This new notion possesses all the benefits of fellow-feeling without falling prey to its limitations.[52] In the same way that Leibniz's concept of reciprocal expression refers to a *universal* sympathy, no part of existence is excluded from *Einfühlung* on Merleau-Ponty's account; "There is an *Einfühlung* and a lateral relation with the things no less than with the other."[53]

Let us first examine the character of *Einfühlung* in the self-other relation before going on to consider how Merleau-Ponty also applies *Einfühlung* to the the self-thing relation. Merleau-Ponty writes,

> It is said that the colors, the tactile reliefs given to the other are for me an absolute mystery, forever inaccessible. This is not completely true; for me to have not an idea, an image, nor a representation, but as it were the imminent experience of them, it suffices that I look at a landscape, that I speak of it with someone. Then, through the concordant operation of his body and

my own, what I see passes into him, this individual green of the meadow under my eyes invades his vision without quitting my own, I recognize in my green his green, as the customs officer recognizes suddenly in a traveler the man whose description he had been given.[54]

Through my perception of the other's gestures and expressions, I participate in his sentience and feel his perspective and activity within my own in virtue of our difference and distance from one another. This difference is not a matter of the impermeability and fixity of preestablished perspectival boundaries as it is in Leibniz's monadology and Scheler's ontology. For Merleau-Ponty, reciprocal expression between self and other is possible "as soon as we no longer make belongingness to one same consciousness the primordial definition of sensing [*le sentir*], and as soon as we rather understand it as the return of the visible upon itself, a carnal adherence of the sentient to the sensed and of the sensed to the sentient."[55] By freeing sentience from the formal boundaries of a private consciousness, Merleau-Ponty preserves the universality of fluidity between interiority and exteriority that is required by reciprocal expression and makes perspectival difference a consequence of the paradox of Being rather than a divine distribution. Spheres of perspectival privacy—which of the other's expressions are present to me and which are distant, obscure—are *relative* to each relating perspective at a point in time, not formally given and absolute.[56] And yet, the expression of the entire world lies within each individual perspective, since the relational character of carnality not only gives the perceived expression at hand, but also the nested expression of every other perspective that is within that expression and so on *ad infinitum*.

Curiously, Merleau-Ponty's references to *Einfühlung* in *The Visible and the Invisible* are almost always about the relations between self and thing (also indicated by "perceiver and perceived"), rather than the intersubjective relationship between self and other, as might be expected from the term's legacy in the phenomenological tradition. Indeed, it seems that Merleau-Ponty bases the intersubjective relation on the sympathetic relation between self and thing and not the other way around.[57] Like the invasion of the other's perspective into my own, the perceiver-perceived *Einfühlung* is an identity-in-difference relation: the thing is in me without being the same as me, and I am in the thing while also being at a distance from it. As Merleau-Ponty explains,

> [T]he vision [the seer] exercises, he also undergoes from the things, such that, as many painters have said, I feel myself looked at by the things, my activity is equally passivity . . . not to see in the outside, as the others see it, the contour of a body one inhabits, but especially to be seen by the outside, to exist within it, to emigrate into it, to be seduced, captivated, alienated, by the phantom, the seer and the visible reciprocate one another and we no longer know which sees and which is seen.[58]

The reciprocity between the seer and the thing involves the seer's ability to emigrate into the thing and to exist within it without coinciding with it and vice versa, as my green invades the other's green without leaving my perspective. When my hand curves around the handle of the hammer and lifts to strike, the hammer's shape and mode of interacting comes into my own. When the painter looks at the forest, the trees direct his gaze with their perspectives. Merleau-Ponty reiterates: "We are already in the being thus described [the flesh of the world], [. . .] [W]e are of it, [. . .] between it and us there is *Einfühlung*."[59] Merleau-Ponty's conception of *Einfühlung* puts the three "spheres of knowledge" or epistemic accessibility—that between self and self, self and other, and self and thing—on the same level, and, in so doing, enables reciprocal expression throughout all that exists.[60]

If *Einfühlung* obtains universally among particulars within flesh, then even purportedly inanimate things would have an interiority, an expressivity, a sentience, that can invade my perspective and that my perspective can invade in turn, that can render my activity a passivity, and my passivity an activity. In the same way that a body schema is a system of equivalents that establishes a perspectival unity with an inside and an outside, a shell or a pebble gathers itself as a thing because it is "a node of properties such that each is given if one is."[61] My activity is equally a passivity in the *Einfühlung* of self and thing because things express a unity as I do, they offer "a resistance which is precisely their openness."[62] The unity of the thing that resists my gaze while also receiving it is a perspective; it constitutes a point of view that is an interiority but is not private, that invites me in and repels me at the same time. In the carnal monadology that is flesh, every being, whether human, vegetable, or mineral, is a perspective and every perspective is a being. The one is as dynamic as the other.

In reconciling and amending Leibniz's and Scheler's views in these ways, Merleau-Ponty removes any basis for marking an absolute distinction between the flesh of my body and the flesh of the world. Put simply, Merleau-Ponty's conception of reciprocal expression seems to be incompatible with the recognition of two different kinds of flesh because an asymmetry of this sort implicates the existence of formally bounded inexpressive domains, a feature that would be in tension with the dynamic, relational character of carnality. If there were at least two different kinds of flesh, then there would need to be at least two different kinds of *Einfühlung*: one that occurs between like fleshes and one that occurs between unlike fleshes. Moreover, it is not clear that there could be *Einfühlung* as Merleau-Ponty describes it with any flesh that is not self-sensing. Not only this; Merleau-Ponty's ontology would also need to explain the interaction between these separate systems of *Einfühlung* that would result in each particular, whether human or thing, being an expression of every other particular. In addition, conceiving of this distinction absolutely seems to involve thinking of flesh as distinct from being, as that which covers and lines being, folds and coils around it in such a way as to generate sentience or self-sensing on some surfaces, that is, in some beings, and not on others. But this image begs questions rather than answers them, since it leads us to wonder why flesh would fold around some beings in a way that manifests sentience and sensibility and others in a way that renders them merely sensible. We would have to introduce a further element into Merleau-Ponty's ontology to explain why sensibility is reversible with sentience in some cases (as in human flesh), but not in others (the flesh of the world). In short, a two-flesh structure would warrant a number of second-order explanations that leave Merleau-Ponty's ontology in the same place where it started: the need to explain reciprocal expression, identity-in-difference, without recourse to substantialist and ontotheological elaborations external to the structure of being. In order to sustain the radical innovations of Merleau-Ponty's ontology and its capacity to move beyond the consciousness-object and interior-exterior distinctions, we should admit that all that exists is flesh and that *all* flesh is self-sensing, that is, sentient-sensible in nature.

The Elusive Basis of the Sentient-Insentient Distinction

Further indication of the favorability of a panpsychist reading of flesh comes to light when we consider whether there are any positive reasons for upholding an absolute distinction between the flesh of my body and the flesh of the world that are convincing enough to outweigh the concerns about the mechanisms of reciprocal expression. There are two main approaches in the scholarly literature that defend the place of the sentient-insentient distinction within Merleau-Ponty's ontology: those that emphasize structural reasons and those that appeal to experiential or phenomenological reasons.

Structural criticisms of a panpsychist reading of flesh generally proceed by deriving the absolute asymmetry of self-sensing and merely sensible flesh from another feature of Merleau-Ponty's ontology, such as the noncoincidence of the perceiver and perceived. Bannon expresses this line of thinking most clearly, although versions of it are also present in Clarke's, Dillon's, and Toadvine's discussions:

> [Clarke] calls our attention to the fact that the reflexive relationship to which Abram appeals [self and world] is not *wholly* reversible; there remains an intrinsic asymmetry or imminence within the reversibility Merleau-Ponty describes. I would add that since this asymmetry is extremely important to Merleau-Ponty's philosophy—without it the resistance and alterity of the world and others is in principle surmountable in a totalizing knowledge—abandoning it is not an option without further consequences.[63]

There is, however, an unwarranted conflation at play in this logic: *noncoincidence is not the same as a difference in kind.* In the case of a person's left hand touching her right hand, the noncoincidence of the two hands does not imply that the left hand is sentient-sensible whereas the right hand is merely sensible. The hands express a reversibility in the sense that whenever one hand is touching, the other hand is being touched, *and vice versa.* Both the noncoincidence and the reversibility of the two hands are premised on their having *symmetrical* rather than asymmetrical capacities: at the very moment when my right hand is about to be fully touched, it begins to touch the left hand. In the same way, at the very moment when the perceiver is about to grasp the entirety of the perceived, the perceived offers resistance, shows that it could be perceived from another perspective, guides our vision in a different direction. Perceiver and perceived are different from one another—they are not the same being, they do not coincide numerically—but this difference does not entail that one is self-sensing and the other is merely sensible.

Another way of grounding the sentient-insentient distinction within Merleau-Ponty's ontology is to reveal its phenomenological basis, to trace the distinction to the fact that we do experience some bodies as insentient, inexpressive, and "mute." For example, Dillon and Clarke respectively assert that the sentient-insentient distinction must be given at the level of wild being in order to have an experience of insentience at the reflective level.[64] Dillon first reasons that there must be a distinction between self and other at the level of wild being because it is only in wanting to see ourselves from a different perspective that we develop reflective awareness. According to Dillon, this self-other distinction is given as an epistemic inaccessibility to the other that ensures that experience always comes with a sense of mineness or bodily sidedness, even at the anonymous or prereflective level of experience.[65] Dillon then references the specialization of human anatomy to explain why the trees do not actually look back at the perceiver but another person, whose perspective is also inaccessible, does: because trees do not have eyes, because rocks are not sensitive to light—in short, because their bodies are different *in kind* from my body—they cannot be grasped as capable of seeing.[66] The self-other distinction thus maps on to the sentient-insentient distinction whenever a body is sufficiently different from my body that I cannot recognize its expressive capacities.

Dillon's anatomical explanation of the sentient-insentient distinction seems to conflate epistemic inaccessibility with ontological asymmetry. He may be correct that trees and mountains are incapable of sight, that the flesh of the world "does not see,"[67] but this does not entail that they are not capable of any kind of sentience, that the flesh of the world could not be self-sensing or expressive in any way at all.[68] An appeal to different anatomical structures can never ground ascriptions of insentience absolutely; it can only suggest that an alternative kind of sentience is operative.[69] Abram extends this idea by pointing out that if we were really to ascribe sentience on the basis of analogy with our own bodies, then we should conclude, not that other bodies are insentient, but that they are also self-sensing, that they possess the dual relation of sentience and sensibility as I do: "Once I acknowledge that my own sentience, or subjectivity, does not preclude my visible, tactile, objective existence for others, I find myself forced to acknowledge that *any* visible, tangible form that meets my gaze may also be an experiencing subject, sensitive and responsive to the beings around it, and to me."[70] In short, the experience of anatomical, bodily, behavioral, or affective differences from oneself, or of a limit to one's own perspective, is not necessarily the same as an experience of insentience.

Scheler also approaches the problem of accounting for the sentient-insentient distinction phenomenologically, but does so from the opposite direction as Dillon. Whereas Dillon suggests that bodies that are sufficiently different in anatomical kind cannot be given as expressive to human perception, Scheler claims that insofar as a body is not given as expressive, it must be different in ontological kind.[71] At the same time, however, Scheler's refusal to base the sentient-insentient distinction on bodily or anatomical analogy complicates this claim. For example, Scheler insists that "the relationships between expression and experience have a *fundamental* basis of connection, which is independent of our specifically human gestures of expression."[72] We grasp immediately that the dog is happy when he wags his tail, the bird is joyous when she chirps a song, and the worm is in pain when it writhes after its body is severed, even if we cannot grasp the precise content of these experiences—what it is to wag a tail, chirp through a beak, feel through a pliable, limbless body.[73] Why then, on Scheler's account, would this allowance for anatomical difference apply to humans and animals, but not rocks and trees?[74] Simply because we do not try to talk to them, we do not recognize them as expressing anything, as being sentient; in Merleau-Ponty's terms, "The things are not interlocutors, the *Einfühlung* that gives them gives them as mute."[75]

However, the contextual nature of such experiences complicate Scheler's account. While it is true that some bodies are given as expressive and others are given as mute in experience, these designations are not always associated with the same bodies in all times and contexts. Recall that, contrary to our present-day views about nonhuman animals, Descartes did not believe that animals had minds, nor did he believe that they were capable of self-motion. In addition, a number of indigenous cultures readily experience life and agency in different features of the landscape, including rocks, trees, mountains, and sky.[76] We should also note that the mental capacities of many groups of humans such as people of color, the colonized, Jews, the proletariat, women, and the disabled have been denied by others at various points throughout history. Grasping the expressivity of another body is not, after all, a matter of perceiving the fixed properties of a thing-in-itself; it is a relational process by which we come to differentiate our own style of being from that of another by looking at the same landscape, spending time together, putting our bodies into contact with each other, engaging the *Einfühlung* between us. This is just as true for purportedly inanimate bodies as it is for animate ones. In the same manner that subjects in Werner Wolff's study could match persons with their handwriting in virtue of their expressive style,[77] we can find a divot on a hillside and, if we approach it wildly without preconception or assumption, sense whether it was made by a rock or a tree, whether rustling leaves are spoken by the oak or the willow, whether the cliff that I touch in the dark is granite or limestone. This capacity to devote attention and proximity to things enables the Zen gardener to grasp the unique expressivity of each rock he tends while a Western tourist sees only inanimate, merely sensible objects, and allows Mont Sainte-Victoire to speak to Cézanne but appear mute and lifeless to a preoccupied passerby.[78]

The thinness that is revealed when these arguments are scrutinized is likely a result of the taken-for-granted character of the sentient-insentient distinction, the fact that it is so entrenched in our natural attitude that its rhetorical power would render panpsychism counterintuitive even in the context of a radical ontological vision whose explicit aim is to break with the tradition's most sacred assumptions. That the sentient-insentient distinction is assumed from the outset renders less noticeable and less questionable the too-hasty equations of insentience with noncoincidence, epistemic inaccessibility, anatomical or behavioral difference, and a failure to perceive expressivity that found pretensions of ontological asymmetry.

Panpsychism and Audacity

More discussion is needed to generate a fully fledged panpsychist reading of flesh. Bannon's contention that a thing can display interiority and dimensionality without possessing sentience will need to be addressed in more detail,[79] as will the question of to what extent the viewpoint of a phenomenology of (human) perception has been retained or abandoned in the development of Merleau-Ponty's late ontology. However, seeds have been planted for a panpsychist reading in the suggestion that in order to truly move beyond the consciousness-object distinction Merleau-Ponty's ontology would need to be more panpsychist than those of Leibniz and Scheler, not less.

The panpsychism question is a question that pulls back the curtain on Merleau-Ponty's ontology since it calls us to notice the tensions and inconsistencies at play in *The Visible and the Invisible*, and to consider which should be left alone and which demand further thinking. If a panpsychist reading of flesh shows so much promise in its capacities to let go of our Cartesian inheritances, and if we can find only a thin basis in Merleau-Ponty's ontology for recognizing an absolute distinction between two kinds of flesh, then it seems that pronouncements of this division in the working notes could be a residue of the very phenomenology of the subject that his final work was intended to overcome, a monkey-wrenching stowaway that has concealed himself so well in the development of a new, radical ontology that he is sometimes mistaken for a deserving passenger, even by Merleau-Ponty himself.

This wayward presence is revealed, however, if we follow four key developments in Merleau-Ponty's thinking toward the ontology that he intimates in his last work: the notion of an impersonal or anonymous subject of experience; the refusal to choose between the privacy and openness of experience when accounting for intersubjectivity; the turn away from thinking of constitution as epistemic possession; and the reworking of *Einfühlung* as a universal and egalitarian feature of Being that can in principle open each perspective to every other. Those who maintain that experience is inescapably first-personal, necessarily given with a sense of mineness, and that therefore the other's experience is forever inaccessible to me in part or in whole, tend to resist a panpsychist reading of flesh. Alternatively, those who display less reverence at the limits of phenomenology, who would allow for a person to sometimes have experiences that she did not constitute and that are not her own, will be inclined to see panpsychism as inherent to this notion. Affirming an ontological asymmetry between the flesh of my body and the flesh of the world therefore amounts to a kind of alignment with a more traditional phenomenology. The tensions in *The Visible and the Invisible*—Merleau-Ponty's anxieties at the precipice between institution and creativity, tradition and originality, consolation and audacity—are also our own.

The first and most egregious ontological assumption in the phenomenological tradition is likely Descartes's slip from certainty in the experience of thinking to a certainty of the I in "I think." There is an assumed mechanism of individuation embedded in that substitution and, unless it is brought to light, we will never be able to move beyond a consciousness-object ontology or account for the fundamental integration of self and world, mind and body. We should instead say with Merleau-Ponty: "Our first truth—which prejudges nothing and cannot be contested—will be that there is presence, that 'something' is there, and that 'someone' is there."[80] Only in the sympathetic and antipathetic movements of flesh will it emerge whether that someone is me, or another, or something in-between, whether its limits are eternal or ephemeral, impermeable or promiscuous. It is here, in this dynamism, this inevitable reversibility, this release of the substantialist and ontotheological impositions of modernity, this transfiguration of phenomenology, that we find the realization one of Merleau-Ponty's very last intentions: "Philosophy can no longer think according to this cleavage: God, Man, creatures."[81]

Possibly the most important contribution that a panpsychist reading of flesh can make is that it moves Merleau-Ponty's thinking forward and backward past the boundaries of his death. We can read *The Visible and the Invisible* as complete in itself, as a portent that we should not go farther lest we risk distorting the ingenuity of his ideas, dishonoring his memory by filling in gaps with our anachronistic interests and selfish desires. But if there is anything that Merleau-Ponty's oeuvre should teach us, it is that *thought moves*, most especially when one is trying to fix it, to pin it down. As Merleau-Ponty reminds us, "To think is not to possess the objects of thought; it is to use them to mark out a realm to think about which we therefore are not yet thinking about."[82] The panpsychism question brings us to this as yet unthought of terrain whose trails lead horizontally and down, out of modernity and humanism, out of epistemology and classical phenomenology, toward wild-flowering meadows of sentient-sensible beings.[83]

Notes

1. David Abram, *The Spell of the Sensuous: Perception and Language in a More-Than-Human World* (New York: Vintage Books, 1996), 56–57. The panpsychism suggestion is already present in his earlier essay, "Merleau-Ponty and the Voice of the Earth," *Environmental Ethics* 10, no. 2 (1988): 101–20.

2. David Morris, "The Logic of the Body in Bergson's Motor Schemes and Merleau-Ponty's Body Schema," *Philosophy Today* 44, supplement (2000): S60–S69.

3. Michel Bitbol, "Panpsychism in the First Person," in *Analytic and Continental Philosophy: Proceedings of the 37th International Wittgenstein Symposium*, ed. Sonja Rinofner-Kreidl and Harald A. Wiltsche (Berlin: Walter de Gruyter, 2016), 243.

4. Dan Zahavi, *Self and Other: Exploring Subjectivity, Empathy, and Shame* (Oxford: Oxford University Press, 2015), 87.

5. M. C. Dillon, *Merleau-Ponty's Ontology*, 2nd ed. (Evanston: Northwestern University Press, 1998); Françoise Dastur, "World, Flesh, Vision," in *Chiasms: Merleau-Ponty's Notion of Flesh*, ed. Fred Evans and Leonard Lawlor (Albany: State University of New York Press, 2000), 23–49; Melissa Clarke, "Ontology, Ethics, and 'Sentir': Properly Situating Merleau-Ponty," *Environmental Values* 11, no. 2 (2002): 211–25; Bryan Bannon, "Flesh and Nature: Understanding Merleau-Ponty's Relational Ontology," *Research in Phenomenology* 41 (2011): 327–57; Evan Thompson, "Living Ways of Sense Making," *Philosophy Today* 55, supplement (2011): S114–S123.

6. Bitbol, "Panpsychism in the First Person," 242; Ted Toadvine, "Strange Kinship: Merleau-Ponty on the Human-Animal Relation," in *Analecta Husserliana*, vol. 93, ed. Anna-Teresa Tymieniecka (Utrecht: Springer, 2007), 17–32, and "Limits of the Flesh: The Role of Reflection in David Abram's Eco-Phenomenology," *Environmental Ethics* 27, no. 2 (2005): 155–70.

7. *SB*, 3.

8. *SB*, 184.

9. *SB*, 184, 200.
10. *SB*, 161. See also *PP*, 303.
11. *SB*, 187–88.
12. *SB*, 202. See also 223.
13. *SB*, 224.
14. *PP*, 224. See also 86, 223.
15. *PP*, 225; translation modified. See also 162, 167, 247–48, 363–64, 369–70, 372, 468, 474, 477.
16. Compare, for example, Dan Zahavi, "Anonymity and First-Personal Givenness: An Attempt at Reconciliation," in *Subjectivität—Verantwortung—Wahrheit*, ed. David Carr and Christian Lotz (Frankfurt am Main: Peter Lang, 2002), and Kym Maclaren, "Embodied Perceptions of Others as a Condition of Selfhood? Empirical and Phenomenological Considerations," *Journal of Consciousness Studies* 15, no. 8 (2008): 63–93.
17. Maurice Merleau-Ponty, "Consciousness and Language Acquisition," in *CPP*, 32, 3–67, orig. 44.
18. Ibid.
19. Ibid.
20. Ibid.
21. Ibid.
22. Zahavi, *Self and Other*, 86–87; "Anonymity and First-Personal Givenness," 87n28. See also Dillon, *Merleau-Ponty's Ontology*, 167.
23. Renaud Barbaras, *The Being of the Phenomenon*, trans. Leonard Lawlor and Ted Toadvine (Evanston: Northwestern University Press, 2003), 148.
24. Maurice Merleau-Ponty, "The Philosopher and His Shadow," in *Signs*, trans. Richard C. McCleary (Evanston: Northwestern University Press, 1964), 159–181.
25. Ibid., 178.
26. Merleau-Ponty, "Eye and Mind," in *PrP*, 166.
27. Ibid., 164.
28. Dillon, *Merleau-Ponty's Ontology*, 169.
29. *VI*, 250. See also 261.
30. *VI*, 260, 180. See also 182, 248.
31. Renaud Barbaras elaborates a version of this tension in "The Ambiguity of the Flesh," *Chiasmi International* 4 (2002): 19–26.
32. *VI*, 248.
33. *VI*, 220.
34. *VI*, 255. See also 208 and "Eye and Mind," 163.
35. *VI*, 136; emphasis added.
36. *VI*, 143.
37. *VI*, 136.
38. *VI*, 261.
39. On the place of Leibniz in Merleau-Ponty's ontology see Barbaras, *The Being of the Phenomenon*, 229–34; Véronique M. Fóti, *Tracing Expression in Merleau-Ponty:*

Aesthetics, Philosophy of Biology, and Ontology (Evanston: Northwestern University Press), 2013, 104, 107.

40. *VI*, 223.

41. Gottfried Wilhelm Leibniz, *Leibniz: Philosophical Papers and Letters*, ed. L. E. Loemker Dordrecht: D. Reidel, 2nd ed., 1970, 531.

42. *VI*, 140.

43. Merleau-Ponty uses the term *co-perception* in "The Philosopher and His Shadow," 170.

44. Max Scheler, *The Nature of Sympathy*, trans. Peter Heath (New Brunswick, NJ: Transaction Publishers, 2012). Though Scheler is only mentioned by name in two of the working notes in *The Visible and the Invisible* and, unlike Leibniz, is rarely recognized as an influence on Merleau-Ponty's ontology, I believe that his views (and especially those expressed in chapter 4, "Metaphysical Theories," from *The Nature of Sympathy*) lurk within and shape Merleau-Ponty's thinking like the memory of a first love, drawing a circle between Merleau-Ponty's first publication and his final work.

45. Merleau-Ponty, "Consciousness and Language Acquisition," 31.

46. Scheler, *The Nature of Sympathy*, 9.

47. Ibid., 10.

48. Ibid., 261. See also 246.

49. *VI*, 142.

50. Scheler, *The Nature of Sympathy*, 65. See also 246, 250.

51. Ibid., 67. See also 255. Scheler also believes that the spiritual personality is absolutely private. For him, it is only at the vital level, between the privacies of bodily consciousness and spiritual personality, where fellow-feeling can take place (ibid., 33, 75).

52. For a discussion of the history and evolving meaning of *Einfühlung* in the phenomenological tradition see Dermot Moran, "The Problem of Empathy: Lipps, Scheler, Husserl, and Stein," in *Amor Amicitiae: On the Love that is Friendship: Essays in Medieval Thought and Beyond in Honor of the Rev. Professor James McEvoy*, ed. Thomas A. Kelly and Phillip W. Rosemann (Dudley, MA: Peeters, 2004), 269–312.

53. *VI*, 180. See also 182, 215.

54. *VI*, 142.

55. *VI*, translation modified. The English translation of "*le sentir*" as "sensibility" softens the radical import of this crucial passage by obscuring the active, experiencing aspect of *le sentir*.

56. For more on this point, especially in relation to Merleau-Ponty's concept of the body schema, see Jennifer McWeeny, "Flesh Possessed: On the Promiscuity of Subjectivity in Merleau-Ponty's Ontology," *Chiasmi International* 18 (2017): 235–49.

57. *VI*, 178. See also Barbaras, *The Being of the Phenomenon*, 234.

58. *VI*, 139.
59. *VI*, 248.
60. *VI*, 245. Cf. Moran's discussion of Lipps's account of these spheres ("The Problem of Empathy," 280).
61. *VI*, 161.
62. *VI*, 219.
63. Bannon, "Flesh and Nature," 332. See also Dillon, *Merleau-Ponty's Ontology*, 167; Clarke, "Ontology, Ethics, and *Sentir*," 215; and Toadvine, "Limits of the Flesh," 170.
64. Dillon, *Merleau-Ponty's Ontology*, 167; Clarke, "Ontology, Ethics, and *Sentir*," 217.
65. Dillon, *Merleau-Ponty's Ontology*, 168.
66. Ibid., 162.
67. Ibid., 169.
68. Bannon's twist on Dillon's suggestion, namely, that each particular consists in a different set of flesh relations and that this difference is only possible if insentient behaviors are possible, falls prey to the same criticism ("Flesh and Nature," 350).
69. See William James, *A Pluralistic Universe* (Lincoln: University of Nebraska Press, 1996), 167.
70. Abram, *The Spell of the Sensuous*, 67. Barbaras makes a similar suggestion in "The Ambiguity of the Flesh," 22.
71. In his Passivity Lectures, Merleau-Ponty rejects Raymond Ruyer's conclusion that to be an organism is to be a subjectivity by appealing to the different ways organisms are "evidenced" in perception. But I believe that the ontological focus of *The Visible and the Invisible*, which requires "rejecting entirely the idea of the In Itself" (*VI*, 223), precludes him from retaining this view. For references to Ruyer, see *IP*, 125–27; *VI*, 194, 270.
72. Scheler, *The Nature of Sympathy*, 11.
73. Ibid., 11, 262n.
74. Ibid., 11, 14. Scheler claims that one cannot be cruel to plants and trees because cruelty involves the capacity to feel the pain and suffering of the other. This implies that trees possess life but not expressivity or sentience, although Scheler also has a tendency to equate life with expressivity. For his view on the expressivity of inanimate matter, see 73n.
75. *VI*, 180.
76. See, for example, Vine Deloria, Jr., "American Indian Metaphysics," in *Power and Place: Indian Education in America*, ed. Vine Deloria, Jr. and Daniel R. Wildcat (Golden, CO: Fulcrum Resources, 2001), 1–7.
77. Merleau-Ponty, "Consciousness and Language Acquisition," 34.
78. On the expressivity of rocks in the Zen garden, see Graham Parkes, "The Awareness of Rock: East-Asian Understandings and Implications," in *Mind*

that Abides: Panpsychism for the New Millenium, ed. David Skrbina (Amsterdam, PA: John Benjamins, 2009), 325–40.

79. Bannon, "Flesh and Nature," 347.
80. *VI*, 160.
81. *VI*, 274.
82. Merleau-Ponty, "The Philosopher and His Shadow," in *S*, 160.
83. This last line carries a reference to Merleau-Ponty's characterization of Husserl's audacity in ibid., 181.

Merleau-Ponty and Biosemiotics

From the Issue of Meaning in Living Beings to a New Deal between Science and Metaphysics

ANNABELLE DUFOURCQ

In this article I will investigate the relations between biosemiotics and Merleau-Ponty's philosophy. I will focus especially on one of the most challenging issues addressed by contemporary biology: what is the nature of meaning in living beings? Does it imply a dimension of ambiguity, subjectivity, and creative interpretation? Is the best explanatory model for meaning in life a computer program or artistic imagination? I will examine how Merleau-Ponty engaged these questions, especially in the *Nature* lectures. This study will involve the analysis of the specific method that best enables a rigorous and fruitful cooperation between life sciences and a philosophical and, more specifically, ontological approach.

Jesper Hoffmeyer defines biosemiotics as "an interdisciplinary scientific project that is based on the recognition that life is fundamentally grounded in semiotic processes."[1] The term emerged in the 1970s, and the discipline cannot be regarded as unified yet. On the one hand, Thomas Sebeok and Thure von Uexküll, two major founders of biosemiotics as a full-fledged discipline, in line with Charles Sanders Peirce and Jakob von Uexküll, emphasized that, through semiosis, a new nonpositivistic paradigm would be set up in the life sciences and would be able to study living beings as subjects,[2] the world as a world *for* living beings, and meaning as requiring interpretation. On the other hand, a parallel trend seeks to understand meaning in life through the model of calculus and code.[3] Biosemiotics is, as a result, a hotbed for new researches and vehement debates about two correlated questions: (1) Should and can life sciences study the dimension of subjectivity and agency in living beings? Is it possible to study scientifically the idea that an animal, for instance, has a relationship with a world that makes sense *for* it and that is defined only through a certain—specific or even individual—production of meaning? (2) What is exactly the nature of meaning in the realm of life? Does it consist in a rigid digital code determining life and its forms through a strictly one-way process of information transfer (from DNA to RNA, further to proteins, and eventually to the morphology and behavioral patterns of living beings)?[4] Or does the meaning emerge and evolve beyond the strict limits of a genome?

If the dimension of meaning in a living being includes communication processes between individuals and species, as well as a subjective perspective, in other words, the way a living being "relates" to a part of its environment *as* food, *as* prey, *as* a threat, etc. does not meaning in life include an essential part of ambiguity and is it not intrinsically liable to interpretation? These two problems are of course closely connected: an ambiguous meaning in DNA cannot ground the understanding of life as the unfolding of a predetermined program. Moreover, if the behavior of living beings takes a form that invites different interpretations, and is indeed interpreted in different ways by different individuals, then it becomes necessary to acknowledge the presence of a certain agency and individuality in living beings. Furthermore, as a consequence, the role played by natural selection will not account for the fact that a living being is not only more or less adapted to its environment, but also possesses the *ability* to modify—again in a non-predetermined way—its environment.

Let me give a quick example borrowed from Hoffmeyer: "When a bird lures a predator away from the nest by pretending it has a broken wing, and then flies away as soon as the predator has been misled a sufficiently long way," it "takes advantage of . . . the relation between a sign and its interpretant. By pretending to have a broken wing, the bird can count on . . . the predator to misjudge the situation."[5] In other words, the bird separates the appearance from the serious attitude, through referring—somehow, but the "how" here is a secondary question—to the probability that a predator will misjudge the situation. This is indeed a matter of probability, as highlighted by Hoffmeyer, since what is at work here is the formation of habits, and the predator (or some predators), may very well, and will very likely, develop the habit of distrusting the broken-wing behavior, exactly in the same way as predators actually learn to unmask mimetic animals. Moreover, the predator is thus confronted with ambiguous behaviors, possibly serious, possibly fake. Adjustments to each situation, through the contingent interpretation performed by individuals, are made necessary by this ambiguity. Neither the DNA "program" nor natural selection can solve the problem: a "good" response cannot be preprogrammed, and, as put forward in the developmental system theory,[6] the norm of the best adaptation to the environment cannot be a strictly one-way process since the environment constantly evolves through the semiotic interaction between different animals and plants. Furthermore, this interaction can become more and more profound, precisely since each stratagem can be thwarted, even through a new stratagem, and signs can change meaning (the bird *as* wounded, *as* an easy prey versus the bird *as* a pretender).

Unsurprisingly, Merleau-Ponty is mentioned, although sporadically, in the framework of the subject/interpretation trend of biosemiotics, for instance, in Hoffmeyer's work. Indeed, a fundamental convergence exists between Merleau-Ponty's work and the major principles of this biosemiotic current.[7] Of course, biosemioticians can acknowledge, like Hoffmeyer, that an Uexküllian and—later—a biosemiotic approach are phenomenological in the sense that it studies the world such as it appears *to* the animal, the world *for* the animal or more broadly for the living beings. Furthermore, Merleau-Ponty, more than other phenomenologists, can be invoked by biosemioticians so as to defuse an intellectualist objection. One will find it absurd to consider animals as subjects and as able to "regard" x *as* a prey, *as* food, *as* a tool, *as* a lure, etc. only if thought and subjectivity are defined as essentially re-presentational, conscious, and predicative. Yet, the idea of the subjectivity of living beings becomes less absurd and, at least, worth examining, if thought and subjectivity prove to be inseparable from the matter and the behavior of our living body. Nevertheless, we have here quite a broad picture of Merleau-Ponty's philosophy and I would like to examine more closely in this article the relationship between biosemiotics and Merleau-Ponty's work—in both directions, namely, by reading Merleau-Ponty through biosemiotics and vice versa.

To that purpose, I will focus more specifically on the concept of symbolism of indivision defined by Merleau-Ponty in the *Nature* lectures. My contention is that Merleau-Ponty thematizes and conceptualizes the idea of life—animal life mainly, but this approach may be extended to plants—not only as subjectivity or embodied subjectivity, but also, more radically, as a form of creative imagination engaged in an endless dialogue with our imagination. Merleau-Ponty's reflections in this matter draw heavily on the works of two of the founding fathers of biosemiotics: Uexküll and Portmann. I would like to show how exactly Merleau-Ponty backs up his theory with empirical scientific research, but also how he proposes a radical interpretation of the results of the latter on the basis of his ontological approach. In *Biosemiotics. An Examination into the Signs of Life and the Life of Signs*, Hoffmeyer certainly refers to Merleau-Ponty's concept of a subjectivity that is essentially corporeal and, as a consequence, open to others, but he also immediately adds that he doesn't want to dwell too much on Merleau-Ponty, because "we cannot let our curiosity be paralyzed by the conception of phenomenology as transcendental and as in any way eliminative of scientific knowledge."[8] It is actually unfair to move on so hastily on the basis of such an argument: Merleau-Ponty's phenomenology is in no way defined as eliminative of scientific knowledge and it is precisely the exact nature of the relationship between Merleau-Ponty's ontological reflection and scientific knowledge that I wish to study in this paper. Moreover, biosemioticians, at least in the Copenhagen-Tartu school (Claus Emmeche, Jesper Hoffmeyer, and Kalevi Kull) and (in a hermeneutic version) by the Prague school,[9] consistently emphasize the idea that the project of biosemiotics is essentially connected with a change of paradigm[10] and a new ontology;[11] as a result, this aspect of Merleau-Ponty's approach can be regarded as fully relevant also in the framework of a scientific discipline that has been compelled by its object to combine empirical research and a methodological and ontological metadiscourse. While biosemiotics mainly relies on Peirce's ontology[12] for obvious reasons, and while many connections can indeed be found between Peirce's and Merleau-Ponty's theories of meaning and nature,[13] I think Merleau-Ponty's ontological approach, starting from a phenomenological reflection about the correlation between my subjectivity and the world, can give access to an original dimension: Merleau-Ponty's analyses provide us with tools to understand and define the analogical relationship and the dialectical kinship between, on the one hand, our subjectivity and thought and, on the other hand, intentionality and meaning in the unconscious and anonymous form that they take in nature. Merleau-Ponty's ontology of a ubiquitous being (beyond the categories of monad, dyad, or triad) and his concept of institution allow us to define more precisely such a relation. Thus, it becomes possible to legitimate the assumption of the existence of subjectivity, agency, and even imagination in life and, more than that, to understand life as imagination.

Biosemiotics and the Issue of Ambiguous Meaning

Oneiric Meaning?

Biosemiotics studies meaning in life processes and in living beings. This immediately leads to the question of the exact nature—and possible forms—of meaning in this context. The ontological question here implied is whether this is genuinely *meaning*, in other words: are the concept of "meaning" in living beings and the concept of "meaning" such as human beings experience it univocal, equivocal, or analogical concepts? The issue is particularly thorny because biosemioticians—and before them ethologists, zoologists, but also geneticists—must deal with phenomena that may imply a dimension of expression, communication, and understanding, but for which the model of symbolic signs is not adequate.

In "Are Ecological Codes Archetypal Structures?" Timo Maran presents and investigates a hypothesis that has also been put forward by Bateson and Portmann: living beings think and speak, but in the same way as humans dream.[14] According to this idea, there is a deep kinship between this form of human thinking called imagination and living beings' specific relationship with meaning. Consider: "It is plausible to assume that codes on the ecological level are not strict regulations, but rather ambiguous and fuzzy linkages based on analogies and correspondences."[15] "Ecological codes do not resemble human linguistic codes or algorithms, but are rather like archetypal imagery or patterns."[16] "Ecological code . . . can be defined as the sets of (sign) relations (regular irreducible correpondences) characteristic to an entire ecosystem, including the interspecific relations in particular."[17] It is precisely because they are interspecific that these sign systems involve all sorts of perspectives, *Umwelten*, interactions, and, in their wake, adjustments through interaction and interpretation This is exactly the conclusion reached by Portmann on the basis of his work on the expressivity at work in animal morphology. Portmann's observations provide us with perfect examples of what Maran's surprising theory aims at.[18]

Portmann's Conceptualization of the Appearance of Animals

Portmann's work is a key reference both for Merleau-Ponty and for several biosemioticians.[19] I also want to emphasize in this article that within Portmann's approach biosemiotics and the phenomenology of the imaginary can meet.

Portmann's key stance has been to define the perceptive appearance of animals as a full-fledged object of scientific study. The strength of Portmann's theory resides in his concepts of "authentic phenomena" and "organs to be seen": by following objective criteria, it is possible to define a global consistent and sophisticated "strategy" of appearing at work in the animal realm, beyond limited, though already problematic for objective sciences, phenomena of camouflage and mimicry. Portman thus delineates, in animals' appearance, manifestations that cannot be only in the eye of human observers, but must be recognized as part of the very being of animals and whose source must be situated in the animals' organization.

How can we detect, according to Portmann, the presence of such "authentic appearances [*eigentliche Erscheinung*]"?[20] The first criterion is that one and the same form constitutes a consistent appearing whole, while being the result of a cooperation between diverse chemical processes, organic processes, and, possibly, behaviors. Portmann gives the example of the famous Oudemans' principle. At the natural resting position, many butterflies' hindwings are almost entirely concealed by the forewings, only the tip is still visible. Hindwings are covered with vividly colored patterns, while forewings display a cryptic pattern. But the little tip of the hindwings that is still visible at the resting position also displays the same cryptic pattern that can be seen on the forewings and in such a way that it exactly complements the pattern appearing on the forewings and composes with it a seamless pattern. These parts make a whole and, Portmann insists, this is all the more surprising that forewings and hindwings stem from two separated ontogenetic processes.[21] Diverse vital operations here contribute to one and the same oriented process giving birth to a visible whole.

The second essential characteristic of the *eigentliche Erscheinungen*, according to Portmann, is that they are always situated on the outer surface of living bodies; they cannot be found on nonvisible parts of the body, for instance, on the reverse side of feathers. Moreover, this appearance displays clearly structured, eye-catching, patterns: contour effects, strong contrasts, nonnatural colors (yellow, red), or, at the other extreme, incredibly mimetic/cryptic patterns. Portmann points out that, in animals whose external membrane is opaque, there is a striking contrast between the chaotic appearance of the hidden organs and, on the other hand, the much more "readable" visible appearance. Even an expert will have difficulty recognizing the species of an animal when contemplating its entrails, whereas a child easily recognizes a giraffe or a lion on the basis of its outer appearance.[22] Portmann also highlights that, in transparent animals, organs are always arranged in a symmetrical and clearly structured way.[23] Thus, Portmann states that, in living beings, morphogenesis also involves a consistent orientation toward the formation of structures that can be easily spotted, delineated, and recognized and that can spark off strong affects; in other words, structures for the eye, *as if* destined for a perceptual system.

Among an immense number of appearances made possible by the physicochemical processes in living beings, only a few specific forms are stubbornly reproduced by each organism. Portmann thus contends that these phenomena cannot be adequately studied through an analytical, Galilean science whose vocation is to break up the visible appearance as a whole into physicochemical invisible causal chains.[24] For such an analytical approach the appearance does not possess any meaning in itself; it is only the secondary product and, at the most, possibly, the indication of underlying physicochemical and metabolic processes.[25] Acknowledging authentic appearances as such entails the definition of a certain autonomous oriented activity; moreover, these appearances insofar as they are destined to be perceived only fulfill their function through their reception by a perceiving subject. They do not possess an immediate mechanical efficiency; they have to be apprehended. Thus, the fake eyes displayed on the wings of butterflies may certainly possess an immediate frightening power, but they can also be foiled by a predator and lose their effect. As a consequence, taking into account the organizing activity at work in living beings necessarily involves an investigation about the addressee(s), the meaning(s), the apprehension and comprehension of such appearances. Portmann has indeed engaged such issues and he was forced to acknowledge how deeply problematic and mysterious this new field of meaning is.

Fantasy in Animal Appearance. Facts and Speculations in Portmann's Work

According to Portmann, any functional study of animal appearances shall fall short. The first argument in support for this claim is that in many cases it is impossible to univocally ascribe any obvious utility to the appearance. To be sure, one can ascribe a protective or warning function to the appearance of certain animals or plants. For instance, a species can "proclaim" itself as dangerous or mimic the appearance of a dangerous species. However, such general functions can in no way account for the exuberance of colors and forms among living beings.[26] A warning or protective function would be much more efficiently achieved if all the dangerous species were signaled by white polka dots on a red background, for example. Moreover, the appearance often possesses a mixed usefulness;[27] thus, bulky adornments (the peacock's tail, the deer's antlers) may be useful in order to be chosen at the end of a courtship dance, but they are considerable handicaps in daily survival.[28] As clearly explained by K. Kleisner,[29] it is important to distinguish function and meaning, not only because it is arbitrary, and—as noted by Portmann—also ideological, to presuppose that the appearance is destined for one predetermined rigid function, but also because one cannot take into account the dimension of apprehension that is involved by appearances without considering how it is received, understood, and possibly interpreted by other animals. Again, to be sure, it makes sense to define a univocal relationship between certain signs and certain very specific addressees. And, indeed, Portmann actually studies animal appearances in the framework of the Uexküllian functional circle [*Funktionskreis*]:[30] the appearance is designed *for* the eye of *this* animal (or species), be it a predator, a prey, or a mate. The meaning of such an appearance can then be connected to a determinate apprehension. Eyes and owl faces drawn on the wings of butterflies, for instance, when displayed suddenly, very efficiently set off a momentary state of stupor in possible predators.[31]

Nonetheless, there are motives to question the model of the functional circle. To start with, processes of learning and disillusionment have been observed. The stomachs of predators are full of mimetic animals.[32] As a result, even for a given perceiving subject these phenomena cannot be reduced to one clear-cut meaning; perception must deal with fake *more or less* misleading appearances, as well as with the contrast between the form of a butterfly and eyes coming out of the blue or monstrous and chimeric faces.[33] What is more, Portmann puts forward another aspect of animal appearance that especially challenges the model of the functional circle: authentic phenomena can be found also in lower forms of animal life, in animals that do not possess eyes, or who live in the dark and cannot be seen by any mate or prey or predator.[34] Portmann propounds the claims that such appearances are "unaddressed phenomena [*unadressierte Erscheinungen*]," "sent 'into the blue' ['*ins Blaue' gesendet*]": possible receivers are innumerable and the meaning of the "signal" becomes virtually multiple.[35]

On the basis of such phenomena, Portmann puts forward several speculative hypotheses regarding the role and the meaning of animal appearance. His reflections are extremely daring, while remaining within the framework of a scientific approach: the role of science, Portmann emphasizes, is to prevent a specific hypothesis or a particular metaphysical position from limiting access to the richness of phenomena.[36] Portmann thus maintains uncertainty but leaves the field of scientific investigation open, providing room for a possible future discovery of specific addressees or determined functions of the animal *Selbstdarstellung*. Portmann's hypotheses are as follows (we will see that Merleau-Ponty has turned a few of them into key theses of his ontology).

According to the most daring hypothesis, the organism appears for the sake of appearing. Appearing is "a basic property of life [*eine basale Lebenseigenschaft*]."[37] Portmann considers reversing the classical claim: self-presentation does not serve vital functions; rather, vital functions provide the basis upon which self-presentation can occur.[38]

Portmann ventures another hypothesis, or maybe a more specific version of the first assumption: through *Selbstdarstellung* the species would present itself in the same way as a human clan identifies itself with a blazon.[39] It may also manifest, Portmann adds, the mood, the emotions, and the idiosyncrasy of a singular animal within species where individuation is further advanced.[40]

Moreover, as shown by the phenomena of mimicry, animals can "play" with other animals' appearance. Kleisner and Markos have described similar phenomena and proposed to understand them through the concept of *seme*: the *seme* is a unit of imitation; it can be a morphology, more generally a certain form, "color patterns, but also odors and kinds of behavior"[41] first developed by one species or group of organisms and "consequently extended to the other often unrelated groups that were able to receive (or imitate) and built it up on their bodies or environment."[42] This theory helps us understand the link drawn by Maran between ecocodes and archetypes; some signs are developed and taken up by all sorts of different species, they evolve through such resumptions, through the different *Umwelten*, through the various interests and behaviors brought on by each species and, possibly, each individual. An indexical sign becomes, for instance, a lure, a part of a courtship dance, or a part of a game. Moreover, human beings also take up such *semes* in art, heraldry, symbols, and myths. We actually inherit such signs through an immemorial imagery; their meaning is deeply sedimented and is fundamentally understood and understandable in the same way as we *somehow* "understand"—at the archetypal level of meaning[43]—the meaning of the face of a lion, or of the face of an owl. Likewise, on the basis of this renewed concept of understanding, it can be argued that the butterfly or the insect that displays a monstrous gaping jaw or wide open yellow eyes on its wings *understands* these *semes* fundamentally by performing a new version of them.

Portmann thus considers the hypothesis that appearing might be autotelic and self-satisfactory, like play, which can be actually experienced in everyday human existence through narcissism, fashion, heraldic practices, art, etc. Precisely because he has emphasized the apparently gratuitous abundance of fanciful forms of colors in living beings, Portmann thus ventures the idea that, beyond the possible intention of heralding the species or expressing the individual's interiority, authentic appearances may also intend to arouse in every possible observer the pleasure and the joy of contemplation that it actually often provokes, at least in human observers, and that Portmann also wants to take into account and to consider as an integral part of these phenomena.[44] Correlatively, on several occasions Portmann draws connections between the meaning of animal appearing and human fantasy: "At times, the sight of these organic forms makes us feel as if we are faced with the uncanny materialization of our dream life, the products of our fantasy."[45] Moreover, Portmann highlights that human symbolism abundantly resorts to figures and forms borrowed from animal appearances.[46]

However, the question remains open for the reader of Portmann's work whether what is at stake with *Selbstdarstellung* is an autotelic process, the pleasure of appearing, the proclaiming to the world of one's proper value, the expression of an artistic creativity, or a free fantasy? Or everything all at once? In fact Portmann also points out that the idea of an intrinsic connection between animal appearance and human imagination is a sheer inkling [*Ahnung*] that deserves attention but "cannot be more firmly founded for the moment."[47] Furthermore, another aspect of Portmann's theories hinders the defense of the claim that the production of appearances in animals follows the same motivations as human art or human fantasy: in his anthropological texts Portmann maintains a clear distinction between humans and animals. When biology moves from animals to humans, Portmann notices in "Um eine Basale Anthropologie," it must be struck by the openness of the structures of existence and the "freedom"[48] to endlessly invent new forms of existence. In animal life "on the contrary," even for more highly developed species, behaviors as well as appearances are hereditarily determined.[49] How could we not become suspicious again, then, of the legitimacy of considering our daydreams, our playful interpretations, and fantasies as an integral part of the meaning of animals' appearances?

By contrast, in the *Nature* lectures, Merleau-Ponty puts forward in a very assertive way the claim that living beings, especially through their appearance, are essentially opened to creativity, fantasy, and ambiguous meaning. Thus, an idea that was present in Portmann's work at the edge of a scientific approach, under the form of a "sheer inkling," constitutes the starting point of Merleau-Ponty's reflections and is taken up in a way that has nothing to do with idle speculation. How did Merleau-Ponty manage to build solid concepts and arguments starting from one of Portmann's most daring and conjectural intuitions?

Merleau-Ponty's Ontological Approach to Biology: The Lateral Relationship between Meaning for Us and Meaning in Other Living Beings

Merleau-Ponty's method in the *Nature* lectures is complex: what is at stake is to found a new ontology, but the latter can only be defined indirectly, through a work on beings. Hence, the study of nature and life sciences as well as the detailed review of contemporary theories and experiments must play a crucial role in the elaboration of Merleau-Ponty's ontology.[50] Merleau-Ponty does not approach the sciences on the basis of a ready-made, a priori established ontology; he unfolds the inseparable anthropological and ontological implications of scientific theories that, on the one hand, are already in themselves classical categories and paradigms, and, on the other hand, only include open, hesitant, and multiple metaphysical interpretations sketched by the researchers themselves.

I would like to schematically distinguish two steps in Merleau-Ponty's reading of Portmann's theory: (1) a preliminary descriptive stage in which Merleau-Ponty shows that several contemporary scientific works compel us to acknowledge the existence of a dimension of subjectivity and indeterminacy in the realm of life; (2) Merleau-Ponty's demonstration—via the concept of institution—that only an ontology of the continuity between humans—other animals—and nature ("ontology" as a consequence rather than "anthropology") can explain the phenomena brought to light by scientific research in biology, ethology, and zoology. These reflections shed new light on Portmann's analyses: a radical ontological foundation is provided to support an idea that was put forward by Portmann as a bold hypothesis: the idea of a multivocal and fanciful *Selbstdarstellung* that is essentially inherent to every form of life.

Life, as an Object of Study, Has Decentered our Concepts and Paradigms

Merleau-Ponty is especially interested in operative concepts that emerged in the framework of twentieth-century life sciences and which can be integrated neither into a mechanistic or vitalistic metaphysical interpretation, nor into a realist or mentalist theory.[51] To be sure, science can claim that it does not essentially have to address metaphysical questions; nonetheless, it can discover concepts that indirectly call for a reversal of the classical positivist ontology.

It is a fact that living beings themselves and their peculiar nature *forced* a traditionally objectifying and analytical science to take into account subjectivity, global *Gestalten,* and "fuzzy" open meanings. Three researchers here play a key role in Merleau-Ponty's reflections: Uexküll, Portmann, and Lorenz. An objectivist approach would certainly be clearer and more effective, but, as consistently emphasized by Uexküll or Portmann, it would leave out crucial aspects of life and many actual phenomena, so much so that life science would have to give up taking fully into account the richness of its object. It is important to emphasize that the concepts of an animal's subjectivity (Uexküll) or interiority (Portmann) are first and foremost operative rather than gratuitously speculative. By defining the animal as a subject,[52] Uexküll does not presuppose the presence of consciousness in animals for example. He simply notices, following a Kantian inspiration, that autonomous oriented processes in living beings cannot be properly described by only referring to the passivity of inert matter. "Subjectivity" here denotes such active processes instituting consistent norms of existence, specific interests, the apprehension of certain things *as* prey, shelter, territory, etc., instead of being simply determined by their environment.

It is not only the concept of subjectivity that must be integrated into the life sciences; after all it is possible, as Heidegger did, to define a subjectivity that does not ek-sist (i.e., that is locked up in predictable patterns of behaviors) on the basis of Uexküll's work. But precisely Merleau-Ponty emphasizes that contemporary research in life sciences also demonstrates the opening of living beings to possibilities and the virtual.

While Uexküll claimed that animals are somehow locked up in their *Umwelt* and only "perceive" the aspects of their environment that correspond to a precisely determined action to be achieved (for lower animals at least, as Merleau-Ponty glosses Uexküll's view, "the *Umwelt* was a closure that separated the animal from most exterior stimuli"),[53] Portmann takes a significant step farther, as pointed out by Merleau-Ponty: animals do not simply project the meaningful layout of meaning that defines their *Umwelt,* they also prove to produce a form visible by others, a form to be seen. Their body, even in its very morphology, offers itself to the gaze of other subjects. "Animals (Portmann): the body as organ of the for-other."[54]

This opening of the *Umwelt* to perception by others essentially goes together with the possibility of manifold meanings: *for* the prey, *for* the predators, *for* mates, *for* the mimic(s), *for* the predator(s) of the mimic(s), etc.

The decentering involved by the phenomena described by Portmann also takes another form highlighted by Merleau-Ponty in a way that clearly foreshadows the biosemiotic approach: these biological observations force us to look for a deepened and renewed conception of meaning. Merleau-Ponty puts forward the concept of "symbolism of indivision"[55] to describe the specificity of expression and communication in living beings. He defines such a symbolism of indivision as a symbolism "without a preliminary *Auffassung* of the signifier and the signified supposed as separated," "the body passes in the world and the world in the body."[56] In general, indeed, the *Umwelt* is correlative of the body of the living being and of the latter's behaviors. It is thus engraved, negatively [*en creux*] in them: the eyes refer to colors, the spider web indicates the fly, the claws indicate the graspable, pinchable, and scratchable. This symbolism of indivision can also be found in the phenomena described by Portmann: the image of the environment is drawn on the surface of mimetic animals, or the image of their interiority—which also includes their world, the world for them—looms in their appearance. A genuine decentering occurs here because (1) these phenomena involve symbolism and cannot be described properly when reduced to mechanical processes, and (2) this symbolism takes a form that must surprise us and contrast with our experience of symbolism. As Portmann showed, authentic phenomena are designed to be seen. Mimetic costumes are realities of the third degree following Plato's nomenclature: they are quasi-beings; their efficiency is not simply mechanical but based on apprehension, possibly mistake, and illusion. The resemblance is always partial and the deceit is also limited. Moreover, because the mimetic animal *is* an image, and since it is not a characteristic that is simply relative to a human interpretation, the mimetic animal must be in itself ubiquitous. In short it intrinsically *consists in* the reference to what this "fake" eye or fake animal would be if it were real (for instance, a dangerous predator) and also in the reference to the possibility for a perceiving subject to trust the appearance and be mistaken. The challenge here lies in the fact that such a twofold intentionality and this double reference do not take the form that they have in the realm of human fantasy, or at least in the most common and obvious manifestation of human fantasy, namely, the conscious re-presentation of an original. But this is precisely the reason why symbolism of indivision is a deeply decentering concept: the symbol can be engraved in the very morphology of the living body and may function without the support and the articulating process of an exact symbolism, which is, by contrast, always present in human existence, at least in the background. With the concept of "exact symbolism," Merleau-Ponty refers to this form of human language in which the meaning of every term is conventionally well circumscribed and fixed. Such a symbolism essentially accompanies consciousness and is a dimension of human thought that we cannot radically eliminate: human beings happen to be immersed from infancy in the realm of conventional language and their thought develops in close relation to these conventional structures. Nevertheless, the symbolism of indivision is not completely foreign to us. Indeed, Merleau-Ponty has demonstrated in *The Phenomenology of Perception* that a conventional articulated language can emerge and develop only against the background of natural symbolism (the distinction between nature and culture being thus a caricature): a part of such a natural symbolism (resemblance, affective contagion, contagion based on the morphology of words or sounds, etc.) always subsists in everyday language.[57] Nonetheless, the idea of symbols engraved in the very morphology of a body, for instance, is challenging for us and obliges us to overcome our fundamentally logocentric mode of thought. The very limits of our existence and possibilities are displaced by the scientific work on life.

However, can it not be argued that any talk of subjectivity, fantasy, symbolism, art, or dreams about such phenomena is the result of some illegitimate anthropomorphic projection? It is precisely because the study of animals has genuinely decentered us that, according to Merleau-Ponty, animals are correlatively decentered (cannot be regarded as coinciding with their own Umwelt)[58] and must be viewed as grafted upon an intersubjective analogical system of meaning and transposition.

Meaning in Life: Merleau-Ponty's Ontological Approach

The key in Merleau-Ponty's reasoning lies in the concept of institution and is based on the idea, which is central in Merleau-Ponty's ontology, that the condition of possibility of the decentering which we have just described cannot be ascribed only to human capacities, for otherwise it would be an arbitrary projection and we would not genuinely discover and quasi-experience new dimensions of existence. The first basis of Merleau-Ponty's argumentation is thus to take seriously the phenomenon of a disturbing relationship between us and other animals. Skeptics may argue that other animals remain foreign to us, or that we only discover perspectives, perceptions, concepts, and feelings that are projected onto animals but are, strictly speaking, relevant only in a human perspective. First, the anthropomorphism objection begs the question; there is no reason to simply presuppose that applying human concepts (subjectivity, cognition, feelings, ethics, etc.) to animal perspective should be in principle inadequate. Furthermore, it is important to acknowledge, in a phenomenological descriptive approach, the existence of *unheimlich* relationships with animals, namely, encounters, but certainly not encounters of the same and the familiar; rather, disturbing and baffling encounters. Heidegger claimed that the transposition into (other) animals fails, but he also asserts that we experience it as possible but not actually achieved; this is in fact a good illustration of the *unheimlichkeit* that we have just mentioned: "[T]he dog feeds [*frißt*] with us . . . no we do not feed. It eats [*ißt*] with us . . . no it does not eat. And yet, with us. A going along with . . . a transposedness, and yet not [*nein, er ißt nicht. Und doch mit uns! Ein Mitgehen, eine Versetztheit—und doch nicht*]."[59] This is a typical analogical pattern: a certain link looms, is imminent, but it is not fully achieved, not fully real. Dogs and humans do not eat exactly in the same sense of the verb *to eat*, and the German uses two different verbs, though close to each other: *fressen/essen*. However, this difference is not radical enough to fully put a stop to the use of the concept of "*mitgehen.*" Eating in these two cases cannot mean *entirely different things*. But the difference is still important enough to make impossible a full-fledged use of this concept: "*ein Mitgehen und doch nicht.*" The relations described by Merleau-Ponty between the symbolism of indivision and exact symbolism manifest the same *Unheimlichkeit*: the idea that a rich and creative meaning can be expressed through the morphology on living bodies contrasts with our "central" concept and experience of expression. The recurring themes in myths, art, and popular imagery of, on the one hand, veritable friendship and cooperation between humans and other animals and, on the other hand, animals as the source of the most ferocious threat and aggressions, also express the same obsessive uncanny motif: that of animals as our most radical *alter ego*. It is in a similar perspective that Merleau-Ponty, as I showed in the previous section of this article, uses references to Uexküll, Portmann, and Lorenz to demonstrate that we can truly unfold new worlds and new forms of meaning through the study of living beings and that humans have even been forced to modify or at least repeatedly question a stubborn objectivist scientific method by this strange *object* of study.

If the decentering actually happens, if I actually "am"[60] at the same time here in my human self and there in this animal's world, or if I "am" actually somewhere in between, then the animal that welcomes me must in its turn be decentered. It has indeed prepared, made possible, and nourished this original unexpected rediscovery of the possibilities of existence. This animal has also pursued its existence in this variation of life that is humanity.[61] It is precisely in this sense that Merleau-Ponty defines a relationship of institution between living beings and human animals. "No pure exteriority of biological space, no pure succession/sequence of biological time. There is going to be Being of ubiquity and Being of anticipation."[62]

As indicated by Merleau-Ponty in the 1953–54 lectures devoted to this concept (see *IP*), institution can never be reduced to a founding act. It is not a one-time event; institution is transtemporal. The law, for instance, is an institution inasmuch as the spirit of the law lives on through the adjustments of jurisprudence, including the questionable decisions and the transgressions of the letter of the law in the name of its spirit. Hesitations, mistakes, misunderstandings that constitute the history of a law are also part of the law itself, since it is its ambiguity that made such metamorphoses possible. And if there have been metamorphoses inspired by the law, this demonstrates that the law in itself was ambiguous.

Merleau-Ponty, like Portmann, emphasizes that mimicry and more generally animal appearances have consistently inspired human art and myths.[63] Moreover, humans keep returning to animality in order to question it about their own origins and their own nature. Acknowledging that these questions exist, keep haunting us, and remain open actually leads Merleau-Ponty to deduce that animals are first and foremost a source of questions, speculation, and a rich imagery, namely, that they cannot be reduced to a closed set of molecules, organs, and functions. The indefinite open quest downstream must correspond, upstream, to an institution, namely, to an open question. This variation of life that I am certainly does not germinate in other animals in the sense that it would find in earlier forms of life the sufficient causes of its emergence and development. Neither is it the entelechy of such earlier forms of life. Rather, it must be already present in them under the form of the questions and the desire that it still is: "It is not a positive being but an interrogative being which defines life"[64]; "Human desire emerges from animal desire."[65]

Portmann already contended that what he called the "interiority" of animals never coincides with this or that organ or group of organs.[66] Likewise, Uexküll, as mentioned by Merleau-Ponty, defined such an interiority as *unanschaulich*[67] and compared it with "a melody that sings itself."[68] In other words, it is a theme that appears indirectly, as a watermark, dynamically through an indefinite series of variations. The nature of a living being cannot be fully circumscribed; it unfolds and evolves through morphogenesis, metamorphoses, behaviors, appearances, and interactions with others as well as with its environment. A theme always calls for new variations precisely because it is never fully achieved in any particular avatar. A theme, ontologically speaking, is not a full-fledged being; it is a phantom, an open reverie. As such, living beings are institutions and are grafted upon an intersubjective field, including the field of human transpositions. Moreover, the concept of institution allows us to think both continuity and difference between human animals and other living beings; each *Nachstiftung* (reinstitution) is original and unique.[69] Rather than a pure monism, Merleau-Ponty defines a multipolar structure, in which each pole (individuals and species, for instance) is ubiquitous, decentered by the others, and never coincides with itself or with any other.

Merleau-Ponty thus defines an ontological structure that fleshes out and legitimates Portmann's idea of the manifold meaning of an appearing for X, as well as Maran's claim that biosemiotics has to study an oneiric form of meaning. Portmann's statement that animal appearances may be "sent 'into the blue' [*"ins Blaue" gesendet*]" makes more sense in the light of Merleau-Ponty's analysis: being sent into the blue is the very essence of institution and fundamentally defines meaning in general. Meaning only exists as a question posed to others. There is in animals an "outbreak of symbolism (*poussée de symbolisme*)"[70] that does not *possess* a meaning (whose meaning is not perfectly defined in advance) but whose meaning, an open theme, will be more and more richly defined through the resumptions that individuals and species will perform of it.

This ontology also strikingly enters into resonance with Hoffmeyer's theory of emergence; it is indeed a key thesis in Hoffmeyer's conception of biosemiotics that dynamic networks of correlative signs and interpretants—rather than a univocal genome, or a unique telos, or the center of the nervous system as a leading interpreter—constitute the basis of every living process, already at the level of genes, cells, and membranes, so that it is impossible to deduce which proteins will be synthesized by simply considering the genome. The way the genome is expressed cannot be described as the mechanical completion of a determining program. It also depends on the relation with the actual environment—whose nature can also be modified by the behaviors of the living being itself—and on the interaction and the communication between different cells, between each cell and its surroundings through its communicative surfaces. Agency is involved at every level, of course to variable extents, as well as what Hoffmeyer daringly calls "freedom of interpretation." Such analyses certainly "augment the insights of Merleau-Ponty"[71] and "continue Merleau-Ponty's unfinished project of redefining nature."[72] They show that it is possible to unfold Merleau-Ponty's ontological claims through a meticulous scientific investigation of life phenomena, so much so that it will be less and less permitted to regard the idea of a multipolar imagining flesh of the world as a wooly poetic phrase. But it is important as well to emphasize, as Louise Westling also does, that, in the *Nature* lectures, Merleau-Ponty already set up an original and rigorous framework for the cooperation between scientific research and ontological reflections and moreover provided the ontological detailed argumentation demonstrating that meaning must be oneiric, that anthropomorphism is not to be feared, and that human animals and other living beings are grafted onto the same multivocal field of meaning.

Notes

This article was written as part of the grant-funded project GACR "Life and Environment. Phenomenological Relations between Subjectivity and Natural World," Czech Science Foundation (GAP15-10832S). I want to thank Louise Westling, who is professor emerita of English and environmental studies at the University of Oregon, for her great help in correcting my English as well as for her encouragements and illuminating comments. I am fully responsible for all the mistakes that remain in the text.

   1. Jesper Hoffmeyer, *Biosemiotics. An Examination into the Signs of Life and the Life of Signs* (Chicago: University of Scranton Press, 2008), 3.
   2. Thure von Uexküll, "The Relationship between Semiotics and Mechanical Models of Explanation in the Life Sciences," *Semiotica* 127 (1999): 647–55; Thomas Sebeok, "Biosemiotics: Its Roots, Proliferation, and Prospects," *Semiotica* 134 (2001): 61–78.
   3. Marcello Barbieri, ed., *Introduction to Biosemiotics. The New Biological Synthesis* (Dordrecht: Springer, 2007), ix–x; also, in the same volume, Stefan Artmann, "Computing Codes versus Interpreting Life. Two Alternative Ways of Synthesizing Biological Knowledge through Semiotics," 209–33.
   4. Hoffmeyer, *Biosemiotics*, 57–68 and 71–80.
   5. Ibid., 189.
   6. See for instance Suzanne Oyama et al., eds., *Cycles of Contingency. Developmental Systems and Evolution* (Cambridge: MIT Press, 2001).

7. Maurita J. Harney, in "Peirce and Phenomenological Naturalism: A Semiotic Contribution to Merleau-Ponty's Ontology of Nature," extended version of a paper presented to "Reconceiving Naturalism" conference at Swinburne University of Technology in April 2014, lists three major points of connection: the insufficiency of a dyadic ontology; meaning is generated from biological processes rather than a product of the human mind; ecological relations are communicative relations of reciprocity. One might add: intersubjectivity and the intertwinement between the self and the world (see Hoffmeyer, *Biosemiotics*, 35; and Louise Westling, *"Merleau-Ponty and the Eco-literary Imaginary,"* in *Handbook of Ecocriticism and Cultural Ecology*, ed. Hubert *Zapf* (Berlin: Walter de Gruyter, 2016), 65–83.

8. Hoffmeyer, *Biosemiotics*, 26.

9. Barbieri thus characterizes the trend in biosemiotics that connects essentially meaning and interpretation. "Editorial. The Challenge of Biosemiotics," in *Introduction*, x.

10. Cf. Hoffmeyer, *Biosemiotics*, 4, note; Myrdene Anderson et al., "A Semiotic Perspective on the Sciences: Steps toward a New Paradigm," *Semiotica* 52 (1984): 7–47; Jesper Hoffmeyer and Claus Emmeche, "From Language to Nature—The Semiotic Metaphor in Biology," *Semiotica* 84 (1991): 1–42; Jörg Eder and Heinz Rembold, "Biosemiotics—A Paradigm of Biology: Biological Signaling on the Verge of Deterministic Chaos," *Naturwissenschaften* 79, no. 2 (1992): 60–67; Kalevi Kull, "Ecosystems are Made of Semiotic Bonds: Consortia, Umwelten, Biophony, and Ecological Codes," *Biosemiotics* 3, no. 3 (2010): 347–57; Wendy Wheeler, *The Whole Creature: Complexity, Biosemiotics, and the Evolution of Culture* (London: Lawrence and Wishart, 2006).

11. Hoffmeyer, *Biosemiotics*, 24, 46; Jesper Hoffmeyer, "Semiosis and Biohistory: A Reply," *Semiotica* 120 (1998): 471: "At least in my ontology there is no such thing as pure semiosis."

13. See, for instance, Claus Emmeche, "The Biosemiotics of Emergent Properties in a Pluralist Ontology," in *Semiosis. Evolution. Energy: Towards a Reconceptualization of the Sign*, ed. Edwina Taborsky (Aachen: Shaker Verlag, 1999), 89–108.

13. See Maurita J. Harney, "Merleau-Ponty, Ecology, and Biosemiotics," in *Merleau-Ponty and Environmental Philosophy, Dwelling on the Landscapes of Thought*, ed. Suzanne L. Cataldi and William S. Hamrick (Albany: State University of New York Press, 2007), 133–46; and Sandra Rosenthal and Patrick Bourgeois, "Peirce, Merleau-Ponty, and Perceptual Experience: A Kantian Heritage," *International Studies in Philosophy* 19, no. 3 (1987): 33–42.

14. Indeed, in our dreams, fluctuating and indecisive themes (stubborn questions, desires, existential structures, memories, characters that transform into one another through a common imago, etc.) can be found that take the form of changing appearances while, in the state of wakefulness, and in connection with the natural and realist attitude that goes with it, such themes usually crystallize into well-defined—or much-better-defined—words, objects, and concepts.

15. Timo Maran, "Are Ecological Codes Archetypal Structures?" in *Semiotics in the Wild: Essays in Honour of Kalevi Kull on the Occasion of his 60th Birthday*, ed. Timo Maran, Kati Lindström, Riin Magnus, and Morten Tønnessen (Tartu: University of Tartu Press, 2012), 149.

16. Ibid., 151.

17. Kalevi Kull, quoted in ibid., 148.

18. Hoffmeyer's analysis of the dimension of ambiguity in junk DNA, or in "semethic" interactions, can also flesh out Maran's hypothesis. See Hoffmeyer, *Biosemiotics*, 188–97; see also Hoffmeyer's articles "The Swarming Body" and "The Global Semiosphere," in *Semiotics Around the World: Synthesis in Diversity, Proceedings of the Fifth Congress of the International Association in Semiotic Studies* (Berkeley/Berlin: Mouton/de Gruyter, 1994).

19. See for instance Karel Kleisner, "The Semantic Morphology of Adolf Portmann: A Starting Point for the Biosemiotics of Organic Form?" *Biosemiotics* 1, no. 2 (2008): 207–19; and Anton Markoš, Filip Grygar, Karel Kleisner, and Zdeněk Neubar, "Towards a Darwinian Biosemiotics. Life as Mutual Understanding," in Barbieri, *Introduction*, 235–55.

20. Adolf Portmann, "Selbstdarstellung als Motiv der lebendigen Formbildung," in *Geist und Werk. Aus der Werkstatt unserer Autoren. Zum 75. Geburtstag von Dr. Daniel Brody* (Zurich: Rhein Verlag, 1958); French translation by Jacques Dewitte, "L'autoprésentation, motif de l'élaboration des formes vivantes," in *Etudes Phénoménologiques*, 23–24 (1996): 131–64 (hereafter Portmann, "Autorepresentation").

21. Ibid.

22. Adolf Portmann, *Die Tiergestalt: Studien über die Bedeutung der tierischen Erscheinung* [1948] (Freiburg/Basel/Wien: Herder, 1965); English translation by Hella Czech, *Animal Forms and Patterns* (New York: Schocken Books, 1967), 32.

23. Ibid., 56.

24. Ibid., 17–18, 137–38.

25. The cock's comb is thus understood as the "manometer in the machinery of hormones." Portmann, *Tiergestalt*, 138, Eng. tr. 127; Merleau-Ponty, *N*, 188, orig. 245.

26. Portmann, *Tiergestalt*, 220.

27. As Marjorie Grene, in "Beyond Darwinism: Portmann's Thought," *Commentary* XL (1965): 31–37, explains, "usefulness" is obviously relative and cannot constitute a rigorous concept.

28. Portmann, *Tiergestalt*, 180, see also Portmann's remarks about the formation of external gonads in mammals, in *Tiergestalt*, 188–92.

29. Kleisner, "Semantic Morphology," 212.

30. Portmann, *Tiergestalt*, 122.

31. John Langerholc, "Facial Mimicry in the Animal Kingdom," *Bolletino di zoologia* 58, no. 3 (1991): 189.

32. Roger Caillois, *Le mythe et l'homme*. Paris: Gallimard, 1938, 105; Langerholc, "Facial Mimicry," 190 and 199.

33. Langerholc, "Facial mimicry," 192.
34. Portmann, *Tiergestalt*, ch. 1 and 2.
35. Ibid., 234.
36. Ibid., 65.
37. Ibid., 233.
38. Portmann, "Autorepresentation," 160.
39. Ibid., 150: "der Organismus [hat] auch zu erscheinen, er [soll] sich in seiner Art darstellen." See also Portmann, *Tiergestalt*, 225.
40. Portmann, *Tiergestalt*, 207–208; Adolf Portmann, *Biologie und Geist* (Frankfurt am Main: Suhrkamp, 1973), 282. For instance, the color of the skin, the smells, the pupil shrinking can manifest emotions or a certain mood (287–90).
41. Karel Kleisner and Markoš Anton, "Semetic Rings: Towards the New Concept of Mimetic Resemblances," *Theory in Biosciences* 123 (2005): 218.
42. Ibid.
43. The concept of archetype, which Maran explicitly borrows from Jung, suggests that what is at stake is not only imagination as a subjective creative mental faculty, but also sedimented or even immemorial symbols, images, schemas that haunt our imaginary, recur in myths and dreams, for instance, and shape our representation of the world as well as our relationships with others. Following Maran's idea, but also Kleisner's and Markoš's theory of *semes*, and Portmann's reflections on the way our imagery has inherited signs forged ages ago through animal evolution (such as squinting, looking down as a sign of submission, begging for food, etc.), we can venture the idea of an immemorial life imaginary beyond the narrow human realm. It is indeed extremely striking to observe how biosemiotic researches also include a cooperation with ecocriticism, namely, the study of literature and the environment from an interdisciplinary point of view. In this regard Louise Westling's work on the connection between Merleau-Ponty's philosophy and biosemiotics, in relation with the *sedimentation* of meaning through living beings and human works of art, is especially inspiring. See for instance, Louise Westling, *The Logos of the Living World: Merleau-Ponty, Animals, and Language* (New York: Fordham University Press, 2014).
44. See Portmann, *Tiergestalt*, 239–40. Portmann also considers the idea that such a *Selbstdarstellung* might be an archaic form of reflection, a sort of communication to oneself, similar to the one that we can experience when increased heart rate, sensation of smothering, warmth in our face inform us about our emotional state (Portmann, "Um Eine Basale Anthropologie," in *Biologie und Geist*, 286).
45. "Zuweilen ist uns im Anblick dieser Gestalten zumute, als begegneten wir den Ausgeburten unseres träumenden Lebens, den Erzeugnissen unserer Phantasie" (Portmann, *Tiergestalt*, 240).
46. Ibid., Zum Abschluß.
47. Ibid., 240.
48. Portmann, *Biologie und Geist*, 121, 279.
49. Ibid., 279.
50. *N*, orig. 371 (not in trans.).

51. *N*, 140.

52. Jakob von Uexküll, *Streifzüge durch die Umwelten von Tieren und Menschen* [1934] (Hamburg: Rowohlt 1956), 21.

53. *N*, 170, orig. 224.

54. *N*, 218, orig. 281.

55. *N*, 212, 219, 226, orig. 274, 282, 289, and 381. Merleau-Ponty also called it "natural symbolism" (*N*, 166, 219, 226 and 219, 282, 289.) or λόγος ἐνδιάθετος (*N*, 212, orig. 274). See also, "l'animalité est le *Logos* du monde sensible" (*N*, 166, orig. 219). "Dans la physiologie la plus simple, nous retrouverons des comportements très semblables aux comportements dits supérieurs. Réciproquement, il va falloir concevoir les phénomènes supérieurs selon le mode d'existence des comportements inférieurs." ("In the simplest physiology, we will find behaviors very similar to the so-called higher behaviors. Reciprocally, we will have to conceive higher phenomena according to the mode of the existence of lower behaviors.") *N*, 178, orig. 234.

56. *N*, 211, orig. 273.

57. See *PP*, 179–205, orig. 203–32.

58. The concept of *Umwelt* essentially emphasizes the idea that a living being is the pivotal meaning-giving activity through which and *around* which a specific world emerges and is organized.

59. Martin Heidegger, *Die Grundbegriffe der Metaphysik. Welt—Endlichkeit—Einsamkeit*, in *Gesamtausgabe*, Band 29/30 (Frankfurt am Main: Klostermann, 1983), §50, 308.

60. Ubiquity deeply modifies the meaning of the verb *to be*.

61. "Décrire l'animation du corps humain, non comme descente en lui d'une conscience ou d'une réflexion pures, mais comme métamorphose de la vie" ("the object of the last part of the course was to describe the animation of the human body not in terms of the descent onto it of pure consciousness or reflection, but as a metamorphosis of life") (*N*, 380; *IPP*, 196). See also *N*, 220, orig. 282: "Le langage comme reprise de ce *logos* du monde sensible dans une architectonique autre" ("Language as the resumption of a logos of the sensible world in an other architectonic").

62. *N*, 240, orig. 305. "Pas d'extériorité pure de l'espace biologique, pas de série pure du temps biologique. Il va y avoir de l'Etre d'ubiquité et de l'Etre d'anticipation" ("No pure exteriority of biological space, no pure series of biological time. There is going to be ubiquitous Being and anticipational Being").

63. *N*, 185, orig. 242. "La question du mimétisme n'est pas encore réglée, dans la mesure où il y a une bonne part de légende dans les faits rapportés. Mais que de telles légendes aient pu être créées et aient la vie longue, c'est justement ce qui rend ces faits intéressants" ("The question of mimicry is not yet regulated, to the extent that there is a good part of myth in the reported facts. But that such

myths could have been created and have a long life is precisely what makes the fact interesting").

64. *N*, 156, orig. 207.

65. *N*, orig. 288. The revolutionary nature of such an assertion must be emphasized. Desire is classically distinguished from need and regarded as specifically human ("Man refuses to give free rein to the satisfaction of his animal needs, needs that animal will satisfy without reservations," Georges Bataille, *Death and Sensuality: A Study of Eroticism and the Taboo* [New York: Walker, 1962], 214). In line with Plato's *Symposium*, desire is regarded by Western philosophical tradition as the sign of the relationship between human beings and the infinite. Desire is essentially beyond itself, it is defined by its indetermination and its contingency. Claiming that animals desire amounts to asserting that they consist in the institution of an indefinite quest, which opens them to the consideration of *all* that is beyond them. In connection with animal desire, see also the daring reflections developed by Florence Burgat in *Liberté et inquiétude de la vie animale* (Paris: Kimé, 2006), esp. 191–93.

66. Adolf Portmann and Richard Carter, *Essays in Philosophical Zoology by Adolf Portmann. The Living Form and the Seeing Eye* (Lewiston: The Edwin Mellen Press, 1990), 25.

67. *N*, 176, orig. 231. See also: "Ce déploiement de l'animal, c'est comme un pur sillage qui n'est rapporté à aucun bateau" ("The unfurling of the animal is like a pure wake that is related to no boat") (*N*, 176, orig. 231).

68. *N*, 173, orig 228. Merleau-Ponty quotes Buytendijk, who quoted Uexküll without giving specific references. Cf. Frederik J. J. Buytendijk, "Les différences essentielles des fonctions psychiques chez l'homme et les animaux," *Cahiers de philosophie de N* IV (1930), 131. The comparison between animals and chimes composed of living bells can be found in Jakob von Uexküll, *Bedeutunglehre* (Leipzig: Verlag J. A. Barth, 1940).

69. Every *Nachstiftung* is creative (see for instance *PW*, 68, orig. 95–96).

70. *N*, 198, orig. 258.

71. Harney, "Merleau-Ponty."

72. Westling, *Logos*, 143.

Politics, Power, Institution

The Institution of the Law

Merleau-Ponty and Lefort

BERNARD FLYNN

[It is] not that political man is still animal, but that the animal is already political.

—Jacques Derrida, *The Beast and the Sovereign, Volume 1*

Animals haunt us.

—Merleau-Ponty, *Institution and Passivity: Course Notes from the Collège de France (1954–1955)*

At issue is the transcendence of the law. Once we have rejected the idea of a supersensible foundation, how is it possible to think of the law as other than an empirical instance of the operations of power? In this paper, we'll attend to the idea of the transcendence of the law, by utilizing the philosophical resources of the thoughts of Merleau-Ponty and Lefort. We wish to show that modernity, the death of god, the "disappearance of the markers of certainty"[1] do not necessarily deliver us to a nihilistic relativism. We pursue the thesis that a phenomenological genealogy of the law does not erode the form of normativity; rather, it reveals it as constitutive of life.

By the rule of law we mean the belief that there are laws that the ruler, as well as the ruled, must obey. In premodernity, the law that transcends the will of the ruler is believed to reside in another place, a transcendence, as Lefort puts it, "a massively affirmed invisible,"[2] or, in a teleological Nature conceived of as created by God.

In premodernity the default mode of rule is theocracy, defined as a mode of articulation of political power, who rules and who obeys, as having been established by the gods. Theocracy offers a solution to an enigma that was well posed by Hobbes. Due to the fact of human equality, there is no reason why anyone should rule over anyone else; and yet organized hierarchies are ubiquitous and adaptive in an evolutionary sense. Such societies, to use the expression of Castoriadis, believe themselves to be heteronomously instituted.[3] However, with the advent of modernity, the disenchantment of the world, the rise of science, and especially philosophy, the narrative of heteronomous institution becomes progressively less tenable.

The response of the major trends of political philosophy was: if the political is not heteronomously instituted, then it must have been autonomously instituted. This is found, again in Castoriadis, but not only in him, rather in all the strains of social contract theory, most eloquently that of Hobbes. The *Leviathan* is written to undermine the theological foundations of the political, and to contend that the political is a purely human invention, a product of the Contract. Hobbes's half-hearted attempt to remain within a natural law tradition was not persuasive because his nonteleological conception of Nature could not support it.

So, it seems, one should choose between heteronomous and autonomous institution. Lefort did not take up either side of this disjunctive opposition. For him, the political is neither autonomously nor heteronomously instituted. This middle way relies on the philosophical resources of Merleau-Ponty's conception of Institution as elaborated in his College de France lectures of 1955 entitled *Institution and Passivity*. Merleau-Ponty's conception of Institution was meant to replace the notion of Constitution, and thus to complete Merleau-Ponty's exit from the dimension of transcendental idealism—sometimes latent, sometimes explicit—in Husserl's phenomenology.

In *Requiem for a Nun*, William Faulkner's character Stevens declares: "The past is never dead, it is not even past."[4] Merleau-Ponty's conception of institution might be thought of as a prolonged reflection on this thought. In the lectures he writes: "Institution (means) establishment in an experience (or a constructed apparatus) of dimensions (in the general, Cartesian sense: systems of references) in relation to which a whole series of other experiences will make sense and will make a *sequel*, a history."[5] Institution leaves a trace, which engenders other experiences. It produces what Merleau-Ponty, quoting Goethe, calls "posthumous productivity." It is this productive trace that ensures that the past is never fully past. At the end of his *Humanism and Terror,* Merleau-Ponty entertains the idea that if one rejected Marxism as not one philosophy of history but *the* philosophy of history, then one would have buried reason in history. One would be left with a crude empiricist conception of history as "one damned thing after the other."

Through his critique of Marxism in *The Adventures of the Dialectic,* and also his inspired reinterpretation of Max Weber's concept of elective affinities, in the preface to *Signs,* Merleau-Ponty arrived at the notion of Historical Institution, which he called Advent as distinct from Event.[6] The institution, or advent, he declares, presides over a certain time and space, and there is no idea without a geography.[7] The Advent, therefore, is neither a timeless essence nor the unfolding of a teleology immanent in history. Rather, it is a finite center of meaning. "Signification in tufts," to use a phrase from *The Visible and the Invisible.*[8] Lefort captures well Merleau-Ponty's meaning when he writes in his introduction to the *Institution and Passivity* lectures, "We donate sense to what appears only by responding to a solicitation from the outside, following an orientation that a certain 'field' imposes on us. A field involving levels and dimensions, that open other horizons,"[9] and he goes on to show that an institution is not a residue of a past subjective experience, as one might be misled into thinking by the usage of the term *institution.*

In the second part of the lecture course on *Institution and Passivity,* Merleau-Ponty discusses at length the passivity of our activity, the body of our mind. He invites us to render problematic our most guarded prejudices, our "unmastered" Cartesianism, namely, the assumption that our thought is spontaneous. Merleau-Ponty writes, "It is not I who makes myself think any more than it is I who makes my heart beat."[10] He evokes Lucien Febvre's book *The Problem of Unbelief in the 16th Century: The Religion of Rabelais,* to show that atheism was not in "the mental toolbox" of the sixteenth century.[11] He concludes this not by trying to penetrate Rabelais's subjectivity but by examining the field in which his thought was situated, a field that did not forbid, but rather did not enable atheism. Lefort rechristens this idea *travail,* in his monumental study of Machiavelli, *Le Travail de l'oeuvre de Machiavel.* Primarily it is a reflection on the "posthumous productivity" of his text.[12] Merleau-Ponty's and Lefort's phenomenological efforts to overcome the alternative of activity and passivity enables them to pursue their political project of overcoming the alternative of autonomous and heteronomous institution.

Now let us return to our subject, the law. In an article that effects both an appropriation and a critique of the political philosophy of Leo Strauss,

Lefort writes, "Certainly the law announces itself, but in announcing itself it simultaneously effects its own retreat." And, further, he writes, "If I say I have a right" it is because I am situated in the movement of "a first law which *escapes* me."[13] The law, lawfulness, is never present as such. Lefort contends that there is both an experience of the law and an experience of its effacement. The law is not given "in flesh and blood"; rather, it is experienced as a trace, a trace perhaps of a past that has never been present, at least for us humans.

He is not alone in claiming that the experience of the law is nonpresence. Freud, in *Totem and Taboo*, tells us of a father of a primal horde who monopolizes the women, driving the sons into exile. The sons both hate the father and identify with him. They bond together and kill him and then eat him, thus incorporating their identification. Each desires to take the place of the father, thus engendering fratricidal strife. Out of guilt and a desire to exit this state of nature, they replace the father with a totem animal, and ultimately, with God. Quoting Freud, "Totemic religion arose from the filial sense of guilt, in an attempt to allay that feeling, and to appease the father by deferred obedience to him."[14] Generally, guilt is consequent on the transgression of the law, but in this instance the institution of the law comes to exist subsequent to its transgression. It comes to exist by deferred action, by *Nachträglichkeit*. The law cannot be said to be instituted by men, nor is it imposed on them from elsewhere; it is neither inside nor outside. We might therefore say that Freud, like Lefort, regards the law as a trace.

In his article "Before the Law," Jacques Derrida comments on Kafka's story of the same title, "Before the Law." Like Lefort and Freud, Derrida sees in Kafka's story both the givenness and the effacement of the law. The countryman in Kafka's story says that the law should be accessible at all times, and to everyone. Derrida notes that the door leading to the law is open; but as we know, the peasant will never gain access to the law. Access to the law is blocked by a series of guards, each more frightful than the last. It appears not only that the law is nonpresent but that, in principle, it should not be present. For if it were "present in person" we would be able to trace its genealogy. This genealogy would undermine the normative character of the law. According to Derrida, it seems that the law, as such, should never give rise to any story. "To be invested with its categorical authority, the law must be without history, genesis or any possible derivation . . . [A] narrative account of the law would try to approach the law and make it present."[15] Derrida contends that to be bound by the law (to be bound to "you must" or "you must not"), it is necessary to at least act as if the law had no history.

What a thorough reading of Merleau-Ponty's concept of institution and Lefort's use of it shows is that this is not necessarily the case. On the contrary, we wish to show that a historical phenomenology of the law does not entail the destruction of its normative character. The question of the law is posed in an exemplary fashion in another piece by Kafka, a parable entitled "The Problem of Our Laws." The parable begins, "Our laws are not regularly known: they are kept secret by the small group of nobles who rule us."[16] This situation gives rise to three schools of thought. There is a group that believes that the laws are of divine origin and are rightly administered by the nobles. Another group argues that, for now, the laws are unknown, and we need the nobles to interpret and enforce them; however, a time will come when everything will become clear. The law itself will belong to the people, and the nobles will vanish. And, lastly, there are those who believe that the laws simply do not exist: "The Law is whatever the nobles do." They see only the arbitrary action of the nobles. We might characterize these groups as conservative, millenarist, and politically nihilistic. In the second, we can recognize the Marxist idea of a society become transparent to itself. And in the last, we recognize the position of Michel Foucault, for whom the law is only a mask of power.

Lefort, like Hannah Arendt, recognizes that the first, Marxist, claim to have rendered the law *present in the real* is one of the characteristics of totalitarian thought. Thus, naturally, he rejects it, while avoiding all the possibilities adumbrated in Kafka's parables. For Lefort the *regime* is a product of a historical institution; and, as we have seen above, every institution supposes a prior institution. For Lefort, unlike Castoriadis and with Merleau-Ponty, one must appeal to Husserl's notion of horizon. He rejects the notion of creation ex nihilo. Every institution is motivated by a prior institution, albeit lacunary.

If every institution supposes a prior institution, whence comes novelty? After the showing of a film on the work of the South African artist William Kentridge, and during a discussion of his work at BAM, someone asked him to discuss his creativity. He replied by saying that one day he told his three-year-old daughter a story: The mean dog was chasing the kitty, who was very frightened and who ran and ran until she passed through the cat flap and then she was safe. Later in the day he overheard the little girl retelling the story to her mother: The bad dog was chasing the kitty who was very frightened and ran and ran until she flapped her wings and flew away and was safe. *Voilà!* Creativity. Not ex nihilo, but through a gap, a lacuna in what was given. The cultural object, like "the sensible world is full of gaps, ellipses, allusions."[17]

Now, from Kentridge's little girl to Thomas Hobbes, with a brief visit to Martin Luther. Luther was appalled not only by the abuse of power of the Roman Church, the absurd selling of indulgences, but by the fact that it exercised any temporal power at all. It was Luther's project to deinstitutionalize Christianity, by transforming it from a hierarchically structured institution to a community of believers each in direct relationship with God, without the mediation of the Church. It is almost impossible to discover what Hobbes really believed concerning religion. Whether he was the Anglican he said he was, or a deist or an atheist, he was certainly not a Lutheran. Nevertheless, he transformed the Lutheran notion of the community, and reversed its role by way of the compact from the destruction of an institution to the creation of a highly centralized one, the *Leviathan*. The fact that most of us would not be pleased to live under the regime of the mortal god should not blind us to the fact that Hobbes is a central figure in the genesis of the concept of popular sovereignty; if, indeed, not an unambiguous one. Again, novelty is not a product of creation ex nihilo but a transformation of the given.

According to Lefort, our political modernity is born of the determinate negation of the Christian monarchy that preceded it. He employs Kantorowicz's conception of the king's two bodies: through the sacrament of coronation, the grace of God doubles the body of the king: the body of nature and the body of grace. "The king is dead, long live the king." The king's exercise of authority is legitimate through his body of grace. This is to say, his relationship to the supersensible world, God.

In the very beginning of *Discipline and Punish*, Foucault misreads Kantorowicz in a very significant way. He says that the king's power effects the doubling of his body.[18] However, for Kantorowicz it is the contrary. It is the doubling of the body of the king that confers legitimacy on his power. The revolutions of modernity, French and American, mark for Lefort the threshold of our political modernity. The revolution kills the king, both body of nature and body of grace. For Lefort, there is both discontinuity and continuity between political premodernity and modernity, because the figure of the other, the king's body of grace, is effaced, while the dimension of the other is retained as an empty place. This idea is elaborated in detail in the article entitled "The Permanence of the Theological Political?" No society is coincident with itself, is integral. Lefort rejects every form of communitarianism. In premodernity it is through the body of the king that the society is incarnated, but in such a manner as to retain a relationship to the Other. The legitimacy of the king's power lies in his relationship to the

Other. In modernity the figure is effaced, no one in the future can legitimately claim to incarnate the society. However, there again, the relation to the other is retained, but the place of the other remains as an empty place. In premodernity the legitimacy of the laws, that they are not just "what the nobles do," is founded on the king's relationship to God. Whereas the source of legitimacy in modern democracies is the people, but the people must remain indefinite, it can be given no figuration.

Lefort distinguishes between the political and politics. The political refers to the nature of the regime: the putting into form, the *mise-en-forme*, and the putting into scene, the *mise-en-scène*, in which the conflicts of society can be acted out. In a detail that we cannot rehearse here, Lefort interprets modern democracy in terms of the *empty place* left by the effacement of the figure, but not the dimension of the other. The fact that democracy emerges from the historically specific Christian monarchy does not mean that it retains a belief in the Christian dogmas, for example, the mystical body of Christ, the theology on which the doubling of the king's body is based. Nor that it is only a mutation of a Christian institution. Once instituted, democracy has its own autonomy. As Weber saw, the effective affinity of Protestantism and a market economy does not imply that contemporary capitalists spend a lot of time wondering if they're predetermined to Hell.

One of the recurrent themes in *The Visible and the Invisible*, from the chapter on perceptual faith onward, is an argument against one of the contentions of skepticism, namely, that the fact that our perceptions are our own is an indication that they cannot give us access to truth, to being, that the thickness of our body precludes our access to being, that our body functions as a screen that blocks our access to being. Against this, Merleau-Ponty argues that, on the contrary, it is not in spite of the density of our body, but because of it, that we can participate in the being of the sensible. We employ the density, the thickness of our body, to participate in the being of the sensible. The sensible is open to us because we are flesh of its flesh. In *The Visible and the Invisible*, he writes, the visible can fill me and occupy me only because I who see it do not see it from the depth of nothingness, but from the midst of itself. I, the seer, am also visible. "It is the body, and it alone, because it is a two-dimensional being, that can bring us to the things themselves, which are themselves not flat beings but beings in depth." We experience a coiling up, a redoubling, fundamentally homogenous with them. The seer feels that it is the sensible coming to itself, and that, in return, the sensible is, in his eyes, as it were, his double, and the extension of his own flesh.[19]

Analogously, because we are, ourselves, the products of historical institutions, we do not view history from nowhere, in a *pensée du survol*, but from the midst of our own history. An anthropologist can map the kinship relations of a group he is studying without feeling obligated by them. Nevertheless, he is unlikely to marry his own sister. We might study the history of the interdiction against human sacrifice, and nonetheless, this interdiction is experienced as binding on ourselves. The fact that we are aware that our politics and morality are the product of a historical institution does not sever our relationship to them, positing them as objects held at the terminus of our gaze. As Merleau-Ponty wrote, Being is not in front of us but around us. Our historical institution is not in front of us, but around us. It is not the context that dissolves the normative character of the law; on the contrary, it is what sustains it.

I will turn briefly to a work of Frank Chouraqui, entitled *Ambiguity and the Absolute: Nietzsche and Merleau-Ponty and the Question of Truth*. However, I will only deal with the section on Merleau-Ponty. If I understand correctly, the general project of Chouraqui's work is to show that while profoundly problematizing traditional conceptions of truth as a stable acquisition, nonetheless both thinkers retain a conception of truth. Chouraqui insists that, for Merleau-Ponty, there is an experience of truth in perceptual faith. Our inscription into the "there is," the *il y a,* is such that any sophisticated reflection on truth must be able to incorporate this experience.

This is not at all to cede to naïveté or realism, because if perception is our opening to truth, it is, at the same time, an opening to illusion. Perception is finalized toward a fully determined object, which is impossible and if realized would be the death of perception. In the language of Merleau-Ponty in *Phenomenology of Perception*, it would transform the world into a universe. The former (world) structured in terms of a system of motivations, the latter (universe) a matrix of causality. Thus, Chouraqui writes that Being presents itself as self-falsification. Every perception presents itself as being enveloped by the possibility of its own replacement, falsification, but by another perception, truth. He notes that Merleau-Ponty carries this out only on a theoretical level.[20]

I would like to transform this idea on to an ethical and political level. This enterprise entails the rejection of the search for what Habermas, among others, calls "context-independent criteria of judgment."[21] Which is to say, criteria that are pure and unmixed with the facticity of history and institution. Since the notion of truth as self-falsification involves the rejection of any conception of a final truth, the concept of truth and political judgment is deeply fallibilistic. Nietzsche tells us that even if we wished to return to a Christian worldview, a monkey would block our return. Perhaps in our reflection on the institution of the law the monkey will extend his paw (hand). In his monumental work, *History of the Political Order*, Francis Fukuyama writes, "The primates from which the human species evolved practiced an attenuated form of politics."[22] Naturally, I can only gloss the literature of the proto-political practices of our animal ancestors. To begin with, he notes that evolutionary biology and primate studies do not support theories of the social contract, all of which suppose a presocial individual who enters into society for reasons of self-interest. He writes, "It is more plausible to assume that human beings never existed as isolated individuals, and that the social bonding into kinship-based groups was a part of their behavior from before the time when modern humans existed."[23]

The mechanism of group formation is to facilitate the survival not of the individual but of the species. Thus, there is a preference for those who will pass on one's genes. Reciprocal altruism is one of the mechanisms of the formation of group stability.

In a group of chimpanzees there is an alpha male who is "chosen" not on the basis of his physical strength but on his ability to benefit the group as a whole. This alpha male executes "what can only be described as authority—the ability to settle conflicts and to set rules based on his status within the hierarchy. Chimps recognize authority through submissive greetings, deep bows, the kissing of the feet."[24] Fukuyama traces this proto-politics from the animal kingdom (interesting phrase) to early forms of primitive human organization, and, finally, to the state. Although I am not terribly familiar with the literature that he draws on, I do not doubt that much of it can be quite reductionistic, a route that I do not wish to follow. Merleau-Ponty, in *The Structure of Behavior*, teaches us to view the relationship of humans and nonhumans in a nonreductive manner. With the evolution of language, a symbolic order is instituted, which is not reducible to the real. My point is to argue that the experience of the nonpresence of the law and its normative character, testified to by Freud, Kafka, and Lefort, among others, is a consequence of the fact that the institution of the law is prior to the existence of human beings. It exists in a past that was never present. This is not to say that the institution of the political and of the law subsumes the ancient law of kinship and blood without remainder, as Sophocles reminds us in *Antigone*.

Re-evoking Lefort's distinction between the level of the political and the level of politics, let us ask: Where does this distinction leave us on both of these levels? The discussion of the political concerns the question of the nature of the regimes. Lefort writes, "The frontiers of political philosophy are not themselves political,"[25] which is to say, political philosophy opens onto the general questions of philosophy. This brings us into the vicinity of Aristotle, who taught us that things come into being either by nature (*physis*) or by convention (*nomos*). The laws and the constitution of the city come into being by convention. However, it is by nature that we are political. Naturally, Aristotle does not take an evolutionary position, since he sees the universe as fixed essences and man is by nature a political animal. It is my contention that a naturalistic evolutionary explanation of political authority, in terms of natural selection, can stand in for Aristotle's notion of human nature as naturally political.

In a discussion of language, Merleau-Ponty says we are like glass and crystal, sonorous beings, we make noise. Analogously, given our evolution we are political beings. We seek no transcendent grounding of the law in order to ensure its normative character, since its normative character is a dimension of its institution. We ourselves, as political beings, are a product of the same institutions. Just as Merleau-Ponty argued that the thickness of our bodies does not block our access to the sensible, the fact that our laws are the product of historical institutions, and exist within contexts, does not annul their normative character. We ourselves are the product of history and exist within contexts. A content-independent position would appear only to a being without context—God or an angel, but not us. This position would purify the law of all historical traces. The relationship to the law must be always already there, or it could never be established. A human being that was not itself sensible, visible as well as seeing, could have no access to the sensible.

Although it was not universally accepted in Ancient Greece either, the notion of man as naturally political is resolutely effaced by Christianity. The attitude of Christianity toward politics is one of indifference or hostility, which is consequent on the belief in the imminent Second Coming of Jesus, which would establish a theocracy. Although this is indeed debatable, I think that without the conversion of the Emperor Constantine, Christianity would have disappeared as another Middle Eastern doomsday cult. It is thanks to Constantine's reconciliation of Christianity with the exercise of coercive power that Christianity maintained itself. When Christianity became the state religion of the Roman Empire, it became incumbent upon it to redefine its relation to the political.

Enter Augustine. For Augustine, politics is not a dimension of human flourishing. It is a consequence of Original Sin. Without the unfortunate business with the apple way back when, there would be no need of politics. But given the transformation of human nature visited upon us by original sin, Augustine reconciled Christianity with the exercise of coercive power, up to and including forced conversion to Christianity. One might view Aristotle and Augustine as two poles between which Western political thought moves. But only if we add that Augustine's notion of the contingent character of the existence of the political opens the space of a utopianism, a world without politics. Without coercive power, Kafka's second possibility, exacerbating the antinomianism of Paul in his polemic against Jewish law that becomes a polemic against law itself, Christianity contains within itself the seeds of a form of anarchism.

If, in conclusion, we turn to politics, it seems that we are led to a republicanism from Greece and Ancient Rome, through Machiavelli, to the strands in Marxist thought other than its revolutionary messianic and antipolitical dimension. A strand that morphs into the tradition of social democracy, a position recently given eloquent expression in Wendy Brown's book *Undoing the Demos*. She rightly sees neoliberalism as a right-wing attack on the political. Her counterpose is, although she does not use the expression, an Aristotelianism of the Left. It should be our project to elaborate a politics that is finalized toward human flourishing, and at the same time is mindful of the evils that humans are capable of, and is thus able to exercise coercive power.

In the intersection of Rue de Rennes and Boulevard Saint Germain in Paris, there is a wonderful piece of Public Art. The sidewalk opens up and a fountain of cool water gushes forth. It incarnates the Rousseauian slogan of May '68, *Sous les pavés, la plage* (underneath the paving stones, the beach). Had I my druthers, for the sake of balance, I would place another piece on the other side of the street, in front of the Eglise Saint-Germain. The sidewalk would open, but instead of a fountain of water, flames would emerge and give off a slight smell of brimstone. Perhaps *Sous les pavés, l'enfer* (underneath the paving stones, Hell).

Notes

1. Claude Lefort "The Permanence of the Theologico-Political?" in *Political Theologies: Public Religions in a Post-Secular World*, ed. Hent De Vries and Lawrence E. Sullivan (New York: Fordham University Press, 2006), 148–87.

2. This is an expression Lefort used in private conversation. For the same idea formulated in different terms, see Claude Lefort: *Les formes de l'histoire: essais d'anthropologie politique* (Paris: Gallimard, 1978), 236.

3. Cornelius Castoriadis, *World in Fragments, Writings on Politics, Society, Psychoanalysis, and the Imagination*, trans. and ed. D. A Curtis (Stanford: Stanford University Press, 1997).

4. William Faulkner, *Requiem for a Nun* (London: Chatto, 1919), 86.

5. *IP*, 8 ff.

6. *S*, 68.

7. *VI*, 259; see also *PP*, 131, orig. 163.

8. *VI*, 130.

9. *VI*, xx.

10. *VI*, 221.

11. *IP*, 78.

12. *IP*, 6, 9, orig. 35, 38.

13. Claude Lefort, "La Dissolution des repères et l'enjeu démocratique," in *le Temps Present* (Paris: Belin, 2007), 540.

14. Sigmund Freud, *Totem and Taboo*, trans. J. Strachey (New York: W. W. Norton, 1950), 145.

15. Jacques Derrida, *Acts of Literature*, ed. Derek Attridge (New York: Routledge, 1992), 191.

16. Franz Kafka, *The Basic Kafka*, trans. Michael Paisley (New York, Simon and Schuster, 1991).

17. *IP*, xxi.

18. Michel Foucault, *Discipline and Punish: The Birth of the Prison*, trans. Alan Sheridan (New York: Vintage, 1995), 25 ff.

19. *VI*, 136.

20. Frank Chouraqui, *Ambiguity and the Absolute; Nietzsche and Merleau-Ponty on the Question of Truth* (New York: Fordham University Press, 2014), 2 ff.

21. Jürgen Habermas, *The Theory of Communicative Action, Volume I*, trans. Thomas McCarthy (Boston: Beacon Press, 1984), 55 ff.

22. Francis Fukuyama, *The Origins of the Political Order* (New York: Farrar, Straus, and Giroux, 2011), 25.

23. Ibid., 34.

24. Ibid., 32.

25. Claude Lefort, *Le travail de L'oeuvre Machiavel* (Paris: Gallimard, 1972), 444.

Post-Truth Politics and the Paradox of Power

FRANK CHOURAQUI

So Harold put a frightening dragon under the tree to guard the apples
It was a terribly frightening dragon
It even frightened Harold, he backed away.

—Crockett Johnson, *Harold and the Purple Crayon*

One of the reasons for our dejection before the global wave of populism comes from the discrepancy between the noncredibility of certain political narratives and their political impact. The impact of some political discourses seems to be independent from their perceived or claimed truth-value. Journalists call this "post-truth" politics, creative politicians appeal to "alternative facts." Philosophers may decide that such phenomena fit the established categories, by reducing post-truth to lying or "bullshit,"[1] or they might decide to do justice to the intuition that something "different," something "new" is being displayed, and that post-truth politics is an opportunity to reexamine our basic political categories, in particular, the common cognitivist view that sees political support as dependent on truth-belief. This assumption has been central to Western political thinking. Taking post-truth seriously involves questioning it, and in turn, this involves rethinking politics wholesale. This is because cognitivism is not only the paradigm for political science, it has been the paradigm for "normal" political behavior too. Taking seriously the political success of post-truth politics involves finding a third concept between or outside the twin concepts of might (based on reality) and assent (aimed at truth). Just like in the case of assent, post-truth discourses do not constrain. Just like in the case of might, they are indifferent to truth or justification, and unaccountable to any epistemic criterion.

In this context, Merleau-Ponty can help. His entire political thought is aimed at critiquing and replacing cognitivism by overcoming the alternative of might and assent. Between these two poles, Merleau-Ponty proposes a middle term which he calls "power." In this model, truth-attribution, which Merleau-Ponty calls "recognition," and engagement, which he calls "institution," both precede and follow each other in such a circular way that political subjects' ability to engage with a discourse independently of their truth-attribution becomes understandable, indeed, it becomes one of the most fundamental mechanisms of politics. The mutual reliance and mutual rejection of institution and recognition opens up the possibility to understand how obedience or adhesion can be produced by discourses that have no claim to truth. To speak like Merleau-Ponty: they appeal to perceptual faith.

Although there is much to bet that the contribution that Merleau-Ponty's thought can make to the analysis of this current phenomenon was motivated by a similar phenomenon in his time, namely, the sort of post-truth enthusiasm that affected some communist thinkers in the fifties, I will, rather, trace the emergence of the new account of power developed by Merleau-Ponty from the perspective of his meta-ontological concern. I argue that Merleau-Ponty's quest for an ontology that can account for its own presence in the world it describes leads him to an account of being as power. I begin by examining how the project of overcoming the "*pensée de survol*" led Merleau-Ponty to establish perceptual faith as the primary and unitary ground for ontology. I note that perceptual faith can only fulfill this function if it is recognized as a formulation of the unity of recognition and institution. I then examine how this definition of perceptual faith also applies to Merleau-Ponty's concept of power in a number of texts, including his "Note on Machiavelli" (1949), *Adventures of the Dialectic* (1954), and the Preface to *Signs* (1961). I argue that in the context of Merleau-Ponty's metaphilosophy, this structure of the identity of recognition and institution involves that being and power be identified with each other. This shall allow us to find a systematic perspective from the point of view of which the entire oeuvre of Merleau-Ponty can be read as a full-fledged political theory, and it will also allow us to understand more deeply the phenomenology of post-truth politics, by rejecting the cognitivist assumption according to which recognition is not prior to assent (even in normal cases of adhesion).

My argument is in four steps:

- First, I argue that Merleau-Ponty conceives of perceptual faith as exhibiting the coincidence of recognition and institution.

- Second, I argue that the concept of power combines a reference to factuality and to legitimacy without subjecting one to the other. Early on, Merleau-Ponty declared: "Fact is never an excuse. It is your assent that makes it irrevocable."[2] This is what I call the paradox of power: the subject of power institutes the power it subjects itself to.

- Third, I suggest that power thus understood possesses the structure of the identity of recognition and institution, and therefore that both perceptual faith and power have the same structure.

- Fourth, I argue that at the ontological level appropriate for this account of both power and perceptual faith, structure and being are one and the same.

I conclude that Merleau-Ponty defines being as power. This also suggests that power is caught up in Merleau-Ponty's phenomenological-hermeneutic ontology, in other words, that power is caught up in meaning, presentation, and representation.

Introduction: Merleau-Ponty on the Outside

In a well-known article entitled "Merleau-Ponty and Thinking from Within," Françoise Dastur established the relevance to phenomenology of Foucault's critique of "thinking from within" (although Foucault himself doesn't mention phenomenology in his article). According to Dastur, Foucault's (implicit) critique expresses the worry that in phenomenology, the subjective pole of the intentional relation acts as a black hole swallowing the world, the others, praxis, and power.[3] Foucault, I think, is correct when he assumes that "thinking from within" threatens praxis. He may also be correct in accusing phenomenology of running this danger. As Dastur points out, one would be mistaken however, to apply this critique to the case of Merleau-Ponty. Perhaps this saves phenomenology from the criticism by showing that at least one phenomenologist escaped the predicament, or perhaps it makes Merleau-Ponty himself fall outside of phenomenology. This becomes a semantic problem.

A deeper insight that Dastur's reading attributes to Foucault is, I think, more promising: it contrasts thinking from within with Foucault's own thinking. Such a way of posing the problem relies on an interesting assumption, namely, that the contrast between Foucault's own thought and transcendental phenomenology is the same as the contrast between introspection and the rejection of any crude inside-outside duality. Dastur seems to maintain that Foucault is still committed to this duality, and therefore that he places himself outside, and I am skeptical of this part of her reading. What remains however, is the implication that what makes Foucault Foucault is the obverse of what makes transcendental phenomenology what it is. In short: moving away from transcendental phenomenology would lead one into Foucaldian territory. Merleau-Ponty is famous for making that move away from the early Husserl; does this make him a precursor of Foucault?

A plausible view of what is most Foucaldian about Foucault is the thesis of the autonomy of power, namely, that power *precedes* any subject or object of power. Foucault refuses to make this into an ontological thesis (for example, that power is an ontological principle), but it is hard to argue that this thesis is not somehow contained in his philosophy. If all of this is correct, we might formulate the hypothesis that Merleau-Ponty's negotiation of the relations between philosophy and its outside leads to an ontology of power. This is the thesis I shall defend here.

Philosophy and Non-Philosophy

Merleau-Ponty asks about the relations of philosophy and non-philosophy. But we would be mistaken to think of such relations as bilateral. Indeed, Merleau-Ponty's examination of this problematic leads him to recognize three, not two, regions of being. The first is non-philosophy, that is, the world that philosophy is *about*. The second is philosophy itself, which, as "*philosophie de survol*" is this that is *about* the world. It counts as a region of being insofar as it takes place in the world and has causal influence on it. The third region, however, Merleau-Ponty calls "intra-ontology," and sometimes even "metaphysics,"[4] and it is aimed at providing an account of the interactions between the other two and of the inherence of "*philosophie de survol*" in non-philosophy.

But this tripartite structure makes things very complex: if the world were truly the object of philosophy, there would be, by definition, nothing left besides the world for philosophy to investigate, and therefore there would be no need for intra-ontology. Except that *"philosophie de survol"* cannot account for its own place in the world. Therefore, it fails in accounting for the *whole of* world. It is the job of intra-ontology to finish this account. By the same token, however, intra-ontology becomes unable to account for itself, and so on ad infinitum. This forces two conclusions: first, the job of intra-ontology cannot be determined in terms of its *content*: its contents are infinite in principle, for they are transformed by being observed, and they are always one step ahead of the theory that accounts for them, be it only because theory changes the world as it describes it. Secondly and consequently, any stable intra-ontological account will be *formal*. In other words, intra-ontology can only provide any final account if such an account is structural:[5] its theme is the structure of infinite regress itself, the structure that it motivates and takes part in. As such, intra-ontology no longer fails itself, for its transformative influences only confirm the structure it describes.[6]

But this leads to a new problem: we know that the contents of the world are affected by philosophical and intra-ontological accounts ad infinitum. We know that philosophy, precisely because it is part of the world, and insofar as it has an obverse that is not transparent to itself, is a thing in the world. This means that intra-ontology must have a *second* theme: not only infinite regress but the way that this infinite regress allows it to overcome the opposition of theory and world, knowledge and action, it must ask about *praxis*.

Once this question is asked, the constraints have already been set, in drastic terms: any philosophy that believes itself to be removed from the world will be deemed *"philosophie de survol,"* and any philosophy that thinks of itself as united with its object will be unable to account for the dynamic influence of philosophy, which structures the infinite regress. In short, we must establish a ground for *both* the *continuity* of theory and reality *and* their *distinction*.

Perceptual Faith

This ground, I argue, is what Merleau-Ponty calls "perceptual faith." In perceptual faith, as we shall see, immediate experience spontaneously acquires a pretheoretical status, involving that experience never remains identical with itself, but also that theory always arises from experience itself. Perceptual faith is the name of this mixture of continuity and distinction. In the preface to *Signs*, written in the exact same weeks that Merleau-Ponty was writing his ontological account of perceptual faith in *The Visible and the Invisible*, faith is presented as the object of a "profession of faith." Merleau-Ponty writes:

> One day, one declares oneself a Christian, a Communist. What does anyone mean by that exactly? One is not entirely changed in one instant, simply, in *recognizing* an external cause to one's destiny, man receives permission, and even mission, to live within the faith of one's natural life.[7]

A profession of faith makes one into a Christian, and yet, it is uttered in the declarative mode normally used for the recognition of a *fact*: "I am a Christian." The distinct character of the initial conversion is evidenced by the fact that all subsequent utterances of the same declaration will only take place under a regime of truth: it will be informative. The first statement however, *enacts* what it declares. In it, the *recognition* of what is and its *institution* are undistinguishable. The saying and the doing are one. (Note that this doesn't make profession of faiths thus understood or, further, perceptual faith itself into any kind of speech act, as what distinguishes it is that its illocutionary force is aimed at the institution of *itself* as its own truth maker, it doesn't enact any fact in the world.)

In the opening chapter of *The Visible and the Invisible*, Merleau-Ponty presents perceptual faith, this time from the ontological perspective. Perceptual faith is characterized by a fundamental ambiguity: one is never certain as to whether it defines perception or truth. The very first sentence of *The Visible and the Invisible* establishes this ambivalence: "[W]e see the things themselves, the world is this that we see."[8] We believe what we see; is this a definition of what we believe, namely, that what we believe is defined as what we perceive? Or of the world of perception, namely, that it is defined as what we believe in? In the first case, perceptual faith is a formula of recognition; in the latter, it is the formula of institution. As one might expect, this is not a vicious ambiguity, but rather this ambiguity is the object that Merleau-Ponty is seeking as the fundamental ground of his intra-ontology. Perceptual faith, as a result, denotes *the unity of institution and recognition*. It is perceptual faith that institutes reality, and it is perceptual faith that recognizes it: "Being is *what requires creation of us* for us to experience it."[9]

This is not a statement of *"idealisme de survol,"* for if we create being, it is only under the impulse of being itself, which requires it. In any case, once it is created, we experience it, and it gains its independence. This makes perceptual faith the primary and unitary ground of ontology. More importantly, it is the primary and unitary ground of intra-ontology too. This is because the only mode of existence of perceptual faith is activity; it is, after all, recognition, institution, or both, all of which are acts. But what do recognition and/or institution *do* first of all? They recognize/institute the *difference* between institution and recognition. Their first act is to ground *"la philosophie de survol."* Examining how it does this—how the unity of recognition and institution can support the illusion of their divorce—becomes the central, unifying theme of intra-ontology.

Intra-ontology is therefore occupied with the fact that perceptual faith is always already projected toward what it emphatically is not: the distinction between institution and recognition. In this sense, we can return to Merleau-Ponty's famously defiant statement that he is "for metaphysics,"[10] that is to say, he believes that ontology will always fail if it fails to be *about objects* (and in the Heideggerean context alluded to in this text, the science of objects is called metaphysics). Intra-ontology as metaphysics is and must be about how the nonobjective, undifferentiated ground of perceptual faith always *institutes* a world of objects to be *recognized*, and does so merely by *recognizing* them. In short, the object of intra-ontology is a chimera, which is nonobjective at the back and objective at the front, it is, Merleau-Ponty writes, a "half-thing."

So, perceptual faith tells us that recognition grounds institution and institution grounds recognition. What it tells us too is that neither of them grounds *itself*. The problem of legitimacy in philosophy, that is to say, in Merleau-Ponty's terms, the problem of truth, comes to the surface here: the instituted and the recognized both legitimize themselves with reference to each other; it is because the real is recognized as such that it is the arbiter of truth, and it is because meaning is instituted that the real can be recognized as the arbiter of truth. In so doing, both the instituted (meaning) and the recognized (reality) subject themselves to the demand for legitimacy, look for this legitimacy in each other, and therefore fail to achieve any legitimacy. Recognition is legitimate with reference to reality, but of course, reality is legitimate only with reference to instituted meaning. Any ontology (or intra-ontology) that begins with the primary and unitary phenomenon of perceptual faith will have to deal with the paradoxical groundlessness and mutual grounding of institution and recognition.

Power and Perceptual Faith

I hope that this suffices to give an idea of the necessary movement from a critical project of taking the relationships of philosophy with its outside to the question of the mutual grounding of institution and recognition. Let me now move to explore the relations between this notion of perceptual faith and the question of power. Let's begin by drawing out some analogies between the way Merleau-Ponty treats perceptual faith and the way he treats the concept of power. He locates the very same ambiguous relationship to groundlessness, and the very same mutual grounding between the instituted and the recognized at the heart of what he calls "*le problème du pouvoir.*"[11] The problem of power, in his view, lies in the fact that authority *requires* obedience, and that therefore authority is never fully grounded, since obedience is a kind of belief, and since belief is a kind of obedience. I shall obey the authorities if I believe that they have a right to my obedience, but they have a right to my obedience only if I believe they do. In other words, I, as a subject of the authority, must deceive myself into thinking that the authority of the authorities is given and independent from me, and all of this disappears if I become aware of the fact that the authoirties are only authorities if I say so. As the replay of the Hobbesian theme of the *Leviathan* in *Harold and the Purple Crayon* shows it, it looks as if fictional appearings are sufficient to make one forget that the authority that keeps them in awe is of their own making. This is why Merleau-Ponty declares that "power belongs to the order of the tacit";[12] it falls apart once it is made explicit. Of course, this reference to the "tacit" is language he usually reserves to his discussions of prereflective being and perceptual faith in *The Visible and the Invisible.*[13]

In his "Note on Machiavelli" of 1949, but published in 1960's *Signs*, Merleau-Ponty proposes a phenomenological sketch of the subject's relation to authority: How does it feel to obey, to be faced with and entangled in power? There already, he declared, "There is no power that is absolutely grounded. All there is is a crystallisation of opinion. Opinion tolerates power and takes it for granted. The problem is to avoid for this agreement to fall apart."[14] That no power is absolutely grounded amounts to saying that no power is fully given, and therefore that legitimacy can never be based on recognition alone. On the contrary, legitimacy is given by the subjects of power themselves; they institute it, but they only do so as long as they remain under the illusion that the legitimacy that they *institute* is in fact the legitimacy that they *recognize*. "Tolerance" for power is proportional to the "taking for granted" of that power. That is why Machiavelli and Merleau-Ponty contend that in politics appearance is crucial ("it is therefore a fundamental condition for politics that it must take place within appearance").[15] Recognition and institution ground each other and demand grounds *of* each other.[16] Further, Merleau-Ponty adds the third determination of perceptual faith to his account of power: it is precognitive: "The relations between subject and power, just like those of the self and the other, are untied at a level deeper than judgment."[17]

Indeed, such thinking is not confined to the texts from the '40s. It is found repeatedly in the preface to *Signs*, which concludes a discussion of the unity of recognition and institution[18] with an appeal to "*virtù*," in Italian[19] and in the *Adventures of the Dialectic*, which Merleau-Ponty himself describes as "an exploration on the impossible unity of the real and power, which insists on their circularity and connivance and on the impossibility of their encounter."[20] It is there that Merleau-Ponty regards political philosophy as unable to "break the circle of knowledge and reality, but is rather a meditation about this circle."[21]

This might be enough to show that Merleau-Ponty seems to provide a treatment of perceptual faith as the ontological ground, which is exactly parallel to his treatment of power as political ground. However, this connection should not be regarded as a simple analogy where the same words would be able to describe two different realities.

First of all, one should note that the analogy in question is an analogy between two *structures*. The weakness of arguments by analogy is that they ignore differences in contents in favor of structural parallels. At this level however, at the level of the ground, the form *is* the content, or, to speak like Merleau-Ponty, the ground is structure only. This is something I take to be accepted when it comes to perceptual faith; as I have argued above, it is the fundamental (unitary and primary) ground of intra-ontology, in any case, it is not defined by any content.

Power as Ontological Principle

Let me make some steps toward showing how this is the case for power also: namely, that power, as the unity of institution and recognition, is indeed the fundamental concept of politics, and therefore is a structure (indifferent to content).

First of all, we must understand the relations between power and force, on the one hand, and between power and morality, on the other. As both force and morals are the traditional candidates for an essential (i.e., nonstructural) ground for politics, such a move is necessary if we are to establish that power is indeed the fundamental concept of politics (and therefore a structure).

As regards the relationships of force and power, Merleau-Ponty argues in several places that they are distinct, and that force is less fundamental than power. He makes this case for example in the Machiavelli text or in the preface of *Humanism and Terror*, but most importantly, it follows from his polemic with Sartre. That is to say, it requires a discussion of Sartre's views on freedom. Although he rejects Sartre's strong thesis whereby freedom is pure, Merleau-Ponty does endorse Sartre's weak thesis, whereby one is always free to an extent. Rousseau himself accepted the weak thesis: "The stronger is never strong enough to always be the stronger unless he change might into right and obedience into duty."[22] What threatens the supremacy of the stronger is the irreducibility of the freedom of its subjects. Rousseau's account should count as phenomenological; the weakness of the politics of force is that in force, recognition is grounding recognition: "Obey the powers that be. If this means yield to force, it is a good precept, but superfluous: I can answer for its never being violated."[23] *Ad absurdum*, Rousseau emphasizes that *things* cannot legitimize themselves, that we experience dissatisfaction before such kinds of grounding, that it is always the *other* that grounds. In this case, the "other" is freedom: freedom grounds power; even more, freedom strengthens force by transforming it into power, and politics should always keep freedom within its field. This is what makes politics the field of power, and not of force, since power distinguishes itself from force insofar as it is a management of freedom. Merleau-Ponty declares: "Power is not without an appeal to freedom."[24]

In short, a thorough understanding of power reveals that power is both *instituted* by freedom and *recognized* by the understanding. However, insofar as it is instituted by being "taken for granted," "tacit," and "before judgment," it is also *instituting* and insofar as it must recuperate the freedom in its subjects, it is *recognizing*. For Merleau-Ponty, this irreducibility of freedom formulated by Sartre, should lead us into an opposite direction to that which Sartre himself followed. This is because Sartre was not content with the weak thesis, and contended that freedom was not only irreducible but also pure. Sartre, Merleau-Ponty complains, is committed to "a world of men and things"[25] where the two stand face to face without mediation (in particular, without the kind of mediations proposed by Marx). This makes the political field impossible to account for, except as an extension of morals or as an extension of science. Injustice makes men into things, justice makes things into men, or at least, it spiritualizes things by subjecting them to human purposes. Sartre's response to injustice, Merleau-Ponty claims, is "[p]ure action . . . which, like it, reaches its aim from a distance. We are in the magical or moral universe."[26] Strangely, Merleau-Ponty continues, Sartre's hyper-moralization of politics leads to an hyper-mechanization of political praxis, for it transfers the categorical imperative into the duty to the Party; it requires absolute loyalty, and therefore a total relinquishing of one's freedom. The all-or-nothing alternative of justice and injustice, of men and things, leads to an all-or-nothing view of political commitment, one that ignores circumstance and consequences. As a result, Sartre's hyper-bolshevism "gives up all points of reference and sinks into the revolution as into a delirium."[27] This is what Merleau-Ponty calls Sartre's paradoxical "pragmatism in politics" (where pragmatism is meant in the etymological sense: a politics of things).[28]

Sartre presents us with the strange alternative, without mediation, between morals and *realpolitik*. With Rousseau, however, we learned *contra* Sartre that one must reject such "pragmatism": things are grounded in non-things. With Machiavelli, we learn that we must reject a "magical" politics of morals. In the Machiavelli text, Merleau-Ponty complains about the idea that humanism should necessarily imply "a philosophy of the inner man . . . which replaces political culture with moral exhortation."[29] In short, neither the objective pole of things and force nor the subjective pole of persons and morals can ground the political. They are not foreign to its grounding, however, and the tradition was right to make them the two main candidates. Simply, they are but *signs* of the deeper structure from which they both derive. That deeper structure is the circularity of institution on the side of morals and recognition on the side of force. Finally, Merleau-Ponty's reappropriation of Machiavelli and Rousseau suggests that the proper field of politics is the field of the circular grounding relation between things and meanings, between necessity and freedom, between recognition and institution.

Conclusion

The parallel between perceptual faith and power is now, I hope, clearer and stronger; the ground of intra-ontology—perceptual faith—and the ground of politics—power—are fundamental in the sense of structural. They are also contemporaneous, and they share the same structure: the identity of recognition and institution, which recognizes and institutes their opposition and crystallization. Perceptual faith and power become two expressions of the same thing, and we now find, I think, a proper grounding for the unity of philosophy and its outside, a true ground that escapes the theory/praxis opposition. Politics and ontology both serve the purpose of hinting at their common origin, which is the unified structure that determines their subsequent distinction.

Does this mean that Merleau-Ponty is committed to an ontology of power or to a politics of being? The question loses its meaning. Indeed, Merleau-Ponty himself declares that this divorce of philosophy from politics is induced by the *pensée de survol*. The preface to *Signs* is exactly structured around an understanding of the ways that moving from *pensée de survol* to intra-ontology affects the relations of thought and praxis: it grounds it. The question therefore loses its meaning, but it does some work: the work, I think, of teaching us to rethink our political concepts in an ontological light and our ontological concepts in a political one. Returning to Hegel, whom Merleau-Ponty regarded as the founder of the problematic of non-philosophy, we might note how this intra-ontological grounding, when seen as power, becomes the hermeneutic means for understanding the relations of authority and being: the fact that we experience the real as authority and authority as the real (a fact that Merleau-Ponty has traced in both Hegel and Freud—but this would take another paper) attains the status of a fundamental principle in Merleau-Ponty's hyper-philosophy.

Returning to the question of post-truth politics, we can now see how Merleau-Ponty's ontology of power allows him to refute the cognitivist assumption. We also remember that it is that cognitivist assumption, whereby support is always dependent on (perceived) truth, that made post-truth phenomena incomprehensible. We can now see not only that support, like any other kind of engagement, is not dependent on any perceived truth, but, rather, that it precedes and informs such perceived truth. This is because, as Merleau-Ponty insists throughout his career, experience precedes and institutes truth, and not the reverse.

Notes

1. Harry G. Frankfurt, *On Bullshit* (Princeton: Princeton University Press, 2005).

2. *HT*, 36, orig. 66.

3. Françoise Dastur, "Merleau-Ponty and Thinking from Within," in *Merleau-Ponty in Contemporary Perspective*, ed. Peter Burke and Jan van der Veken (Dordrecht: Springer, 1993), 25–35.

4. *VI*, 250, orig. 290.

5. *VI*, 238.

6. *VI*, 250.

7. *S*, 28, orig. 50; my emphasis.

8. *VI*, 17.

9. *VI*, 197.

10. *VI*, 250.

11. *S*, 221, orig. 359.

12. Ibid.

13. e.g., *VI*, 41.

14. *S*, 212, orig. 345.

15. *S*, 216, orig. 352.

16. See *S*, orig. 348.

17. *S*, 213, orig. 346, see also *AD*, 10, 37, 46.

18. *S*, 28, orig. 50.

19. *S*, 35, orig. 61.

20. *AD*, 8, orig. 15.

21. *AD*, 29, orig. 46–47; see also orig. 63.

22. Jean-Jacques Rousseau, *Du Contrat Social*, ed. Bruno Bernardi (Paris: Gallimard, 2001), 49.

23. Ibid.

24. *S*, 215, orig. 350.

25. *AD*, 184 ff., orig. 269 ff.

26. *AD*, 154, orig. 225.

27. *AD*, orig. 224. This is an idea almost directly taken from Hegel who opposes Kant in just the way Merleau-Ponty opposes Sartre, when he declares in the preface of the *Philosophy of Right*, that "[t]hose who regard thinking as a particular and distinct *faculty* divorced from the will as an equally distinct *faculty*, and who in addition even consider that thinking is prejudicial to the will—especially the good will—show from the very outset that they are totally ignorant of the nature of the will (a remark which we shall often have occasion to make on this same subject).—Only *one aspect* of the will is defined here—namely this *absolute possibility* of *abstracting* from every determination in which one finds oneself, the flight from every content as a limitation. If the will determines itself in this way, or if representational thought considers this aspect in itself as freedom and holds fast to it, this is *negative* freedom, or the freedom of the understanding—this is the freedom of the void, which is raised to the satus of an actual shape and passion. . . . [B]ut

if it turns to actuality, it becomes in the realm of both politics and religion, the fanaticism of destruction, demolishing the whole social order, eliminating all the individuals regarded as suspect by a given order, and annihilating any organization which attempts to rise up anew" (G. W. F. Hegel, *Elements of the Philosophy of Right*, ed. Allen Wood, trans. H. B. Nisbet [Cambridge: Cambridge University Press, 1991]). We are also reminded how Merleau-Ponty claims to cite Hegel when he declares that "the Terror is Kant put into practice" (*HT*, 119, orig. 261). There is, to my knowledge, no such claim in Hegel, but it is easy to reconstruct this view from the preface of the *Philosophy of Right*, and the section of the *Phenomenology of Spirit* entitled "Die absolute Freiheit und der Schrecken" ("Absolute Freedom and the Terror"), in paragraphs 582–95.

28. See *S*, 55, orig. 31; see also *S*, 215, orig. 350, *AD*, 95 ff., orig. 143 ff.

29. *S*, 223, orig. 363.

Institutional Habits

About Bodies and Orientations that Don't Fit

SARA AHMED

In this chapter, I explore Merleau-Ponty's model of the habitual body as a way to understand how institutions are brought into existence over time. Merleau-Ponty suggests in his lectures on the theme that time is "the very model of institution."[1] Here, he is speaking about institution in a very broad sense that includes themes such as the institution of a feeling, of a new type of knowledge, of animal morphological forms, of the coming of age in puberty, of the creation of an artwork, etc., as well as the setting up of a given social institution. All institution, he suggests, should be understood in a double sense: it refers us both to a beginning and to an end, a realization and a destruction. If to institute is to open something, then an institution is also that which has begun; it is both the order already given to things and something that disturbs an order of things, a reordering is a new ordering. As Rosalyn Diprose eloquently describes, for Merleau-Ponty, "meaning is both instituted (dependent upon being 'exposed to' an already meaningful world) and instituting (involves 'initiation' of the new, the opening of '*a* future')."[2] Merleau-Ponty's concern with doubleness—with showing how change and creativity become possible only as or in relation to what has already been assembled or begun—both characterizes his work in general and makes his work especially well suited to understanding the logics of what institution means. In this chapter, I will, however, not address all the aspects of institution Merleau-Ponty is interested in, but will focus on how his broad notion of institution helps understanding what we commonly call (social) institutions.

Across a range of social science disciplines, including economics and political science, as well as sociology, we have witnessed the emergence of "the new institutionalism," concerned precisely with how we can understand institutions as processes or even as effects of processes. Indeed, Victor Nee argues that the new institutionalism "seeks to explain institutions rather than simply assume their existence."[3] To explain institutions is to give an account of how they emerge or take form. Such explanations require a thick form of description—a way of describing not simply the activities that take place within institutions (which would allow the institution into the frame of analysis only as a container, as what contains what is described rather than being part of a description), but how those activities shape the sense of an institution or even institutional sense. To do this, I propose to return to Merleau-Ponty's approach to the habitual body as found, for example, in *Phenomenology of Perception*, which I think is an important moment in the project of making sense of institutions. Indeed, I explore how Merleau-Ponty's reflections on habit can be developed to account for "institutional bodies," by which I mean not only how bodies come to inhabit institutional spaces, but the mechanisms whereby certain bodies come to be assumed as the right bodies by an institution. If the development of this argument is to offer a rethinking of habituation as an institutional process, then as a development it is attuned to Merleau-Ponty's own double sense: as both continuing and changing the terms I have inherited from him.

More specifically, in this chapter I want to think through how institutions become habits by drawing upon research I completed on diversity work within educational institutions.[4] I mean diversity work in two senses: firstly, I consider diversity work as the work done by those who are appointed to institutionalize commitments to diversity. In this sense, diversity workers could be described as "habit changers." Secondly, diversity work is the work we might do when we do not quite inhabit the norms of an institution. Some might be diversity workers in both senses: those who do not quite inhabit the norms of an institution who are often given the task of transforming those norms. For example, people of color tend to be diversity workers in both senses: because we tend to embody diversity for institutions of whiteness, we are often given the task of doing diversity.

The Habitual Body

We can call institutional norms "somatic norms."[5] Merleau-Ponty's work on the habitual body can help us to reflect on how bodies incorporate the worlds they inhabit. In *Phenomenology of Perception*, Merleau-Ponty offers powerful descriptions of the intelligence of bodies, of how we learn through our body. In dance, he suggests, "You don't learn the formula intellectually first," but, "[I]t is the body which 'catches' (*kapiert*) and 'comprehends' movement."[6] To carry out an action is to catch its significance: "The acquisition of habit is indeed the grasping of significance but it is the motor grasping of motor significance."[7] I think it is important that we do not rely here on a distinction between mental and motor. Even tasks often deemed mental (such as the labor of thought) involve motor movement. To think might require we write our thoughts, moving our hands and arms as we lean on the desk, and in the activity of writing, in the motor of the movement, we might even "catch" the thought.

If we have a tendency to divide the mental activities from motor ones, as well as to elevate the former over the latter, then Merleau-Ponty teaches us to be attuned to the motor of the mental. He shows how bodies are engaged in the world practically. It is through the tasks that are on the way to being completed that a body reveals a stance or attitude. As he describes:

> [M]y body appears to me as an attitude directed towards a certain existing or possible task. And indeed its spatiality is not, like that of external objects or like that of "spatial sensations," a *spatiality of position*, but a *spatiality of situation*. If I stand in front of my desk and lean on it with both hands, only my hands are stressed and the whole of the body trails behind them like the tail of a comet. It is not that I am unaware of the whereabouts of my shoulder or back, but these are simply swallowed up in the position of my hands, and my whole posture can be read so to speak in the pressure they exert on the table.[8]

Here, the directedness of the body toward an action, which is a leaning of a body toward a thing such as a desk (that has its own leanings), is how the body "appears."[9] The body is "habitual" not only in the sense that it performs actions repeatedly, but in the sense that when it performs such actions, *it does not command attention*, apart from at the "surface" where it "encounters" an external object (such as the hands that lean on the desk or table, which feel the "stress" of the action). In other words, the body is habitual insofar as it "trails behind" in the performing of action, insofar as it does not pose "a problem" or an obstacle to the action, or is not "stressed" by "what" the action encounters. The postural body for Merleau-Ponty is the habitual body: the body that "does not get in the way of an action" is *behind an action*.

We can explore the relation between what is behind social action and the promise of social mobility. Merleau-Ponty uses as his example objects that enable bodies to extend their motility, such as "the blind man's stick." A habit is when something has been incorporated into the body, becoming part of the body: "The blind man's stick has ceased to be an object for him, and is no longer perceived for itself."[10] We must note here that the extension of motility through objects means that the object is no longer perceived as something apart from the body. The object, as with the rest of the body, trails behind the action, even when it is literally "in front" of the body. When I am writing I might not then notice the pen, even if it is before me, as it has to be, for me to write. When something becomes part of the habitual, it ceases to be an object of perception; it is simply put to work. Such objects in being incorporated into the body also extend its horizon, or what is within reach: "The position of things is immediately given through the extent to the reach which carries him to it, which comprises besides the arm's own reach the stick's range of action. If I want to get used to a stick, I try it by touching a few things with it, and eventually I have it 'well in hand,' *I can see what things are within reach or out of reach of my stick*."[11] Habits involve not only the repetition of actions that tend toward things, but also involve the incorporation of that which is "tended toward" into the body. Reachability is hence an effect of the habitual: what is reachable depends on what bodies "take in" as objects that extend their bodily motility, becoming like second skin.

Objects that we "tend toward" become habitual insofar as they are taken into the body, reshaping its surface. Merleau-Ponty describes, "Habit expresses our power of dilating our being-in-the-world, or changing our existence by appropriating fresh instruments."[12] The process of incorporation is certainly about what is familiar, but it is also a relationship to the familiar. The familiar is that which is "at home," but also how the body feels at home in the world: "Once the stick has become *a familiar instrument*, the world of feelable things recedes and now begins, not at the outer skin of the hand, but at the end of the stick."[13] When bodies are oriented toward objects, those objects may cease to be apprehended as objects, becoming extensions of bodily skin. As Merleau-Ponty further suggests:

> We grasp external spaces through our bodily situation. A "corporeal" or postural schema gives us a global, practical and implicit notion of the relation between our body and things, and our hold on them. A system of possible movements, or "motor projects" radiates from us to the environment. Our body is not in space like things; it inhabits or haunts space. It implies itself to space like a hand to an instrument and when we wish to move about we do not move the body as we move an object.[14]

The language implies here that bodies provide us with a tool, as that through which we "hold" or "grasp" onto things, although elsewhere Merleau-Ponty suggests that the body is not itself an instrument, but a form of expression, a making visible of our intentions.[15] What makes bodies different is how they inhabit space: space is not a container for the body; it does not contain the body, as if the body were "in it." Rather, bodies are submerged, such that they become the space they inhabit; in taking up space, bodies move through space, and are affected by the "where" of that movement. It is through this movement that the surface of spaces as well as bodies takes shape. Bodies as well as objects take shape through being oriented toward each other, as an orientation that may be experienced as the cohabitation or sharing of space.

How does this model of the habitual body help us to think through institutions? At one level we could think of institutions as dwelling spaces; they are thus inhabited or even haunted by bodies. Bodies are extended through the work of inhabitance. We can certainly think through how these mechanisms involve incorporation: as bodies become attuned to an organization, they acquire practical skills and know-how. The very idea of "institutionalization" (of becoming institutional) might even denote those tendencies or habitual forms of action that are not named or made explicit. We can thus think of institutions in terms of how some kinds of action become automatic at a collective level; institutional nature might also be "second nature." When an action is incorporated by an institution it becomes natural to it. Second nature is "accumulated and sedimented history," as "frozen history that surfaces as nature."[16] We might describe institutionalization as "becoming background," when being "in" the institution is to "agree" with what becomes background. It is this becoming background that creates a sense of ease and familiarity, an ease that can also take the form of incredulity at the naïveté or ignorance of the newly arrived or of the outsiders. The familiarity of the institution is a way of inhabiting the familiar. Institutions become familiar, and certain instruments come to extend the capacities of bodies, as an extension of the domain of the reachable. Institutions are designed to enable certain kinds of tasks to be completed. To design a space for work is also to create a space for the working body. Merleau-Ponty describes: "What counts for the orientation of my spectacle is not my body as it in fact is, as a thing in objective space, but as a system of possible actions, a virtual body with its phenomenal 'place' defined by its task and situation. My body is wherever there is something to be done."[17]

If the body is where something is to be done, then the body that is performing its tasks also requires things to be handy. Think not only of the tools that becoming part of an institution might require you to use (the communication technologies, for instance, that allow you to communicate or "sign" with others, creating lines or pathways in their trail) but also of the incorporation of the institution *as an idea*: you might come to think of yourself as being from such and such an organization, such that the edges between you and it ceases to be experienced as such; it becomes part of you, part of the bodily horizon. When good things happen to it, you might feel inflated; when bad things happen to it, you might feel deflated.

But who is this "you"? Can anyone in and over time experience this kind of ease of passage? Let us return to the question of habit. Following Gail Weiss, I would suggest that William James's approach to habit as the gradual loss of plasticity could be usefully brought into conversation with Merleau-Ponty's phenomenology.[18] A loss of plasticity is not simply a loss; it is how certain kinds of movements become easier or less trouble through repetition. James cites the work of a M. Léon Dumont on habit:

> Everyone knows how a garment having been worn a certain time clings better to the shape of the body than when it was new. A lock works better after being used some time; at the outset a certain force was required to overcome certain roughness in the mechanism. The overcoming of their resistance is a phenomenon of habituation. It costs less trouble to fold a paper after it has been folded already. This saving of trouble is due to the essential nature of habit, which brings it about that, to reproduce the effect, a less amount of the outward cause is required.[19]

The description of habituation can be understood in terms of attunement. A garment becomes attuned to the body that wears it. It is not just things happen to fall this way or that: through repetition, things acquire certain tendencies. Things cling *better* or become clingy in time. If a shape is acquired through the repetition of an encounter, then repetition becomes direction. Although William James considers habits as socially conservative (he famously describes habit as "the enormous fly-wheel of society, its most precious conservative agent"),[20] he also suggests that habits enable the conservation of energy. When more actions become habitual, subjects are free to attend to other matters, including those matters that might matter in a morally significant way. For James, even if habits are socially conservative, they make a dynamic psychic life possible.

Maybe an institution is like an old garment: if it has acquired the shape of those who tend to wear it, then it becomes easier to wear if you have that shape. The ease of movement, the lack of a stress might describe not only the habits of a body that has incorporated things, but also how an institution takes shape *around a body*. If a body is oriented *toward* things, an institution might be orientated *around* that body. We might be thinking of this bodily inhabitance as "fit." Take the example of the reduction over time of the force required to work a locking mechanism. The more you use the mechanism, the less effort is required; repetition, if you like, smoothes the pass of the key. James describes this reduction of force or effort as essential to the phenomenon of habituation. "Fitting" could also be thought in these terms: *as an energy-saving device*. If less effort is required to unlock the door for the key that fits the lock, so too is less effort required to pass through an institution for bodies that already fit. The lessening of effort might be essential to the phenomena of fitting. After all, institutions come to have their own tendencies: they tend toward the bodies that tend to inhabit them. Once a certain body is assumed, then a body that fulfills this assumption can more easily take up a space even if the space is imagined as open to anybody. Writing these words as I am, in Cambridge University, an institution that seems to sweat privilege from the very architecture of its space, from the pores of its skin, I am reminded how much inhabiting an institution involves garments, how class can be the comfort of wearing the right jumper with the right body, a "fit" acquired over and in time, in the comportment and postures that bodies *remember without having to think*.

We can re-pose the question of whiteness in terms of the institutional body.[21] What does it mean to talk about whiteness as institutional problem or as a problem of institutions? When we describe institutions as being white, we are pointing to how institutional spaces are shaped by the proximity of some bodies and not others; white bodies gather and create the impression of coherence. Think of the "convene" in convention. A convention is a meeting point, a point around which bodies gather. Whiteness is a name we give to how some gatherings become conventions. Institutional norms can refer to the explicit rules or norms of conduct enforced by an institution (through a system of awards and sanctions). If we think of institutional norms as somatic, then we can show how institutions, by assuming a body, can generate an idea of appropriate conduct without making this idea explicit. The institute "institutes" the body that is instituting, without that body coming into view. If institutional whiteness describes an institutional habit, then whiteness recedes into the background, just like Merleau-Ponty's comet that trails behind, not feeling the stress of an encounter.

Whiteness then can become something that we encounter, almost as if it is a tangible thing in the world. When I walk into university meetings, that is just what I encounter. Sometimes I get used to it. At one conference we organize, four black feminists arrive. They all happen to walk into the room at the same time. Yes, we do notice such arrivals. The fact that we notice such arrivals tells us more about what is already in place than it does about "who" arrives. Someone says: "It is like walking into a sea of whiteness." This phrase comes up, and it hangs in the air. The speech act becomes an object, which gathers us around. When an arrival is noticeable, we notice what is around. I look around, and re-encounter the sea of whiteness. I had become so used to this whiteness that I had stopped noticing it. As many have argued, whiteness is invisible and unmarked, as the absent center against which others appear as points of deviation.[22] Whiteness could be described as a habit insofar as it tends to go unnoticed.[23] Or perhaps whiteness is only invisible to those who inhabit it, or those who get so used to its inhabitance that they learn not to see it, even when they are not it.

The word *comfort* suggests well-being and satisfaction, but it can also suggest an ease and easiness. Comfort is about an encounter between bodies and worlds, the promise of a "sinking" feeling. If white bodies are comfortable it is because *they can sink into spaces that extend their shape*. Whiteness becomes, in other words, not only a phenomenon of habituation (how an individual body repeats actions and catches their significance) but also a means of creating an institutional space in which some bodies more than others can "fit." Whiteness is more than a body count, even when bodies being counted are those for whom whiteness has become a habit. Rather, what is repeated is a very style of embodiment, a way of inhabiting space, which claims space *by the accumulation of gestures of "sinking" into that space.*

Diversity Work and Habit Change

In this section, I want to explore diversity work in the first sense: as the work that is done by those appointed to institutionalize a commitment to diversity. I have already described such workers as "habit changers." We can immediately identify the paradox in this work: if you are employed to change the habits of the organization, then you are employed to change the employer. The means by which you are given the task might thus restrict your capacity to complete the task. If to institutionalize diversity is a goal for diversity workers, it does not necessarily mean that it is the institution's goal. I think this "not necessarily" describes a paradoxical situation that is a life situation for many diversity practitioners. Having an institutional goal to make diversity a goal can even be a sign that diversity is *not* an institutional goal.

The institutional nature of diversity work is often described in terms of the language of integrating or embedding diversity into the ordinary work or the daily routines of an organization. As one practitioner explains, "My role is about embedding equity and diversity practice in the daily practice of this university. I mean, ideally I would do myself out of a job but I suspect that's not going to happen in the short term, so I didn't want to do that and I haven't got the staff or money to do it anyway." The diversity worker has a job because diversity and equality are not already given; this obvious fact has some less obvious consequences. When your task is to remove the necessity of your existence, then your existence is necessary for the task.

Practitioners partly work, then, at the level of an engagement with explicit institutional goals, that is, of adding diversity to the terms in which institutions set their agendas, what we might think of as an institutional purpose or end. An institution will give form to its aims in a mission statement. If diversity work is institutional work, then it can mean working on mission statements, getting the term *diversity* included in the statements. This is not to say that a mission statement simply reflects the aims of the university; as Marilyn Strathern has shown, mission statements are "utterances of a specific kind" which mobilize the "international language of governance."[24] Giving form to institutional goals involves following a set of conventions. This is not to say that mission statements are any less significant for being conventional; the aim of a convention is still directive.

When I participated in an equality and diversity committee, some of our discussions were based on how to get "equality" and "diversity" into the university's mission statement and the other policy statements that were supposed to derive from it. We aimed not only to get the terms in, but also to get them up: to get the terms *equality* and *diversity* cited as high up the statement as possible. I recall the feeling of doing this work; in retrospect or in abstract what we achieved might seem trivial (I remember one rather long discussion about a semicolon in a tag line!), but the task was still saturated with significance. The significance might be thought of as a distraction (you work on something you can achieve as a way of not focusing on—and thus being depressed by—what you cannot achieve), but also could point to how institutional politics can involve the matter of detail; perhaps, diversity provides a form of punctuation.

However, institutionalization was not simply defined by practitioners in terms of the formal or explicit goals, values, or priorities of an institution. In contrast, many spoke about institutionalization in terms of what institutions "tend to do" whatever it is they say they are doing or should be doing. They address the institutional body as a "habitual body" in Merleau-Ponty's terms. Institutionalization "comes up" for practitioners partly in their description of their own labor; diversity work is hard work, as it is can involve within institutions what would not be otherwise done by them. As one interviewee describes, "You need persistence and I think that's what you need to do because not everyone has an interest in equity and diversity issues so I think it needs to be up there in people's faces; well, not right in their faces, but certainly up there with equal billing with other considerations, so that it's always present, so that they eventually think of it automatically and that it becomes part of their considerations." The aim is to make thought about equality and diversity issues "automatic." Diversity workers must be persistent precisely because this kind of thought is not automatic; it is not the kind of thought that is normally included in "how institutions think," to borrow an expression from the anthropologist Mary Douglas.[25] Or, as Ole Elgström describes in a different but related context, such thoughts have to "fight their way into institutional thinking."[26] The struggle for diversity to become an institutional thought requires certain people to "fight their way." Not only this: the persistence required exists in necessary relation to the resistance encountered. The more you persist, the more the signs of this resistance. The more resistance, the more persistence required.

The institution can be experienced by practitioners as resistance. One expression that came up in a number of my interviews was "banging your head against a brick wall." Indeed, this experience of the brick wall was often described as an intrinsic part of diversity work. As one practitioner describes, "So much of the time it is a banging your head on the brick wall job." How interesting that a job description can be a wall description! The feeling of doing diversity work is the feeling of coming up against something that does not move, something solid and tangible.[27] The institution becomes that which you come up against. If we recall that most diversity practitioners are employed by institutions to do diversity (though not all, some practitioners end up having equality and diversity added to their job descriptions), then we can understand the significance of this description. The official desire to institutionalize diversity does not mean that the institution is opened up; indeed, the wall might become all the more apparent, all the more a sign of immobility, the more the institution presents itself as being opened up. The wall gives physical form to what a number of practitioners describe as "institutional inertia," the lack of an institutional will to change.

Perhaps the habits of the institutions are not revealed *unless you come up against them.* I want to take as example an encounter with the institution as a brick wall. In the UK, new legislation on equality has brought about what I have called a new equality regime, in which equality has become redefined as a positive duty. The law seems to embody a will to bring about a new kind of body. But does it? The following is a quote is from a diversity officer based in a British university, who is describing how her institution made a decision to commit to a new equality policy:

> When I was first here there was a policy that you had to have three people on every panel who had been diversity trained. But then there was a decision early on when I was here, that it should be everybody, all panel members, at least internal people. They took that decision at the equality and diversity committee which several members of SMT were present at. But then the director of Human Resources found out about it and decided we didn't have the resources to support it, and it went to council with that taken out and council were told that they were happy to have just three members, only a person on council who was an external member of the diversity committee went ballistic—and I am not kidding went ballistic—and said the minutes didn't reflect what had happened in the meeting because the minutes said the decision was different to what actually happened (and I didn't take the minutes by the way). And so they had to take it through and reverse it. And the Council decision was that all people should be trained. And despite that I have then sat

> in meetings where they have just continued saying that it has to be just 3 people on the panel. And I said but no Council changed their view and I can give you the minutes and they just look at me as if I am saying something really stupid, this went on for ages, even though the Council minutes definitely said all panel members should be trained. And to be honest sometimes you just give up.[28]

It seems as if there is an institutional decision. Individuals within the institution must act as if the decision has been made for it to be made. If they do not, it has not. A decision made in present about the future (under the promissory sign "we will") can be overridden by the momentum of the past. The past becomes momentum that directs action without being given as a command or even in a way that resists a command. Note that the head of personnel did not need to take the decision out of the minutes for the decision not to bring something into effect. Perhaps an institution can say "yes" when there is not enough behind that "yes" for something to be brought about. It is simply that a "yes" does not bring something about, but that the "yes" conceals this not bringing under the sign of having brought.

A will can become a wall: what blocks an action. *A wall can be an expression of what the institution is not willing to bring about.* The will is made out of sediment: what has settled and accumulated over time. Let's return to Merleau-Ponty's own description of the habitual body. It is a body that is leaning a certain way. When an action is being completed, the body can be what trails behind. Perhaps we can think of this "behind" not only in terms of what does not come into view, but also as a form of momentum. An action is being completed because it has energy and momentum behind it. A decision does not need to be made for the action to be completed; indeed, a decision cannot easily intervene in its completion. You have to *become pushy* if you are to push against what has acquired momentum. As another practitioner describes, "You can put all policies in place and put all the training in place and assume it will all happen and it has not happened."[29] Even with effort, you do not get through. No wonder diversity work feels like banging your head against a wall. If the wall keeps its place, it is you that gets sore.

One way of thinking of diversity work would be as a *practical phenomenology*. It is not simply that diversity workers are philosophers—in the sense of being reflexive and critical—in their attitude toward institutions (though they are). It is not simply that they become conscious of what ordinarily recedes from view. Rather, diversity workers acquire a critical orientation to institutions in the very process of *coming up against them*. They become conscious of "the brick wall," as that which keeps its place even when an official commitment to diversity has been given. It is only the practical labor of "coming up against" the institution *that allows this wall to become apparent*. To those who do not come against it, the wall does not appear: the institution is lived and experienced as being open, committed, and diverse; as happy as its mission statement, as diverse as its equality statement.

Breaking the Feather

Diversity work is also the work we do when we do not quite inhabit the "norms" of an organization. When you don't quite inhabit norms, or you aim to transform them, you notice them as you come up against them. We can return once more to Merleau-Ponty's description of the habitual body as an "I can." Merleau-Ponty notes: "Consciousness is in the first place not a matter of 'I think' but of 'I can.'"[30] The "I can" expresses not only a practical orientation, but also competence or capacity. Both Iris Marion Young and Frantz Fanon supplement this focus on "I can," with a view of the "I cannot," a viewpoint of the body that does not extend into space: a female body, a black body: a black female body.

Let's think more with Merleau-Ponty's own examples. His primary example is the blind man's stick. The blind man's stick is a prosthesis that becomes handy, enabling the blind man to get about by feeling the world. The extension of mobility is for a body whose mobility is already compromised (the compromise is not necessarily "in" the body but as a relation of a body to a world that assumes the capacity for sight). The stick is a *walking stick*: incorporated into the body horizon; it becomes a means that enables the disabled body to reach an end, to become more mobile in a world that tends to assume an able body in the design of public and social space. Vivian Sobchack describes in *Carnal Thoughts*, "The prosthetic becomes an object only when there is a mechanical or social problem that pushes it obtrusively into the foreground of one's consciousness."[31] The "point" of the prosthesis is to recede, to allow a body to inhabit a world that does not assume that body as a norm.

Merleau-Ponty also offers two other examples: that of a driver and his car, and a woman with a feather in her cap. In the case of the driver of the car, the object is a self-evident extension of the motility and range of the human body. The driver is competent when the steering wheel is not perceived as something being held, but becomes part of the body of the driver, allowing him to think while driving of things other than driving. What of the woman with a feather in her cap? The feather has no function; it does not enable her to move around in the world. The woman, however, as the example suggests, feels the feather; she "knows" where the feather ends; she is able to walk without breaking the feather: "A woman may, without any calculation, keep a safe distance between the feather in her hat and things which might break it off. She feels where the feather is just as we feel where our hand is."[32] The feather has been incorporated into a body horizon. It might be here that we can understand the mechanisms of incorporation as not simply about the extension of bodily capacity. The incorporation of the feather seems bound up in some way not only with the achievement of femininity, but of how some bodies become *what appears*; or how appearance matters to the negotiation of social as well as bodily space. It might be that "appearing right" can become the aim; a body that *can do* is one that appears to others as doing what it can to appear in the right way.

I have suggested that phenomenology can help us explore bodies that are not at home in the world. When a category allows us to pass into the world, we might not notice that we inhabit that category. When we are stopped, or held up, by how we inhabit what we inhabit, then the terms of habitation are revealed to us. We need to rewrite the world from the experience of not being able to pass into the world. I called in *Queer Phenomenology* for a phenomenology of "being stopped," a description of the world from the point of view of those who do not flow into it.[33] I suggested that if we begin with the body that loses its flesh (*chair*), the world we describe will be quite different.[34] Or perhaps we might begin with a body that breaks the feather, that has not "felt" the things that are supposed to be part of its horizon.

In the first section of this chapter I explored an experience of fitting as comfort, drawing on Merleau-Ponty's description of the habitual body as the one that trails behind an encounter. How does it feel when you inhabit a space that does not extend your shape? To inhabit whiteness as a nonwhite body can be uncomfortable; you might even fail the comfort test. You won't trail behind, you feel the stress of an encounter. You come up against a world by not being received into that world. It can be the simple act of walking into the room that causes discomfort. Whiteness can be an expectation of who will turn up. A person of color describes: "When I enter the room there is shock on peoples' faces because they are expecting a white person to come in. I pretend not to recognize it. But in the interview there is unease because they were not expecting someone like me to turn up. So it is hard and uncomfortable and I can tell that they are uneasy and restless because of the way they fiddle and twitch around with their pens and their looks. They are uncomfortable because they were not expecting me—perhaps they would not have invited me if they knew I was black and of course I am very uncomfortable. I am wondering whether they are entertaining any prejudice against me."[35] They are not expecting you. Discomfort involves this failure to fit. A restlessness and uneasiness, a fidgeting and twitching, is a bodily registering of an unexpected arrival.

The body that causes their discomfort (by not fulfilling an expectation of whiteness) is the one who must work hard to make others comfortable. You have to pass by passing your way through whiteness, by being seamless or minimizing the signs of difference. If whiteness is what the institution is oriented around, then even bodies that do not appear white still have to inhabit whiteness. One person of color describes how she minimizes signs of difference (by not wearing anything perceived as "ethnic") because she does not want to be seen as "rocking the boat."[36] The invitation to become more alike as an invitation of whiteness is about becoming more comfortable or about inhabiting a comfort zone.

Bodies stick out when they are out of place. Think of the expression "stick out like a sore thumb." To stick out can mean to become a sore point, or even to experience oneself as being a sore point. To inhabit whiteness as a not-white body can mean trying not to appear at all: "I have to pretend that I am not here because I don't want to stick out too much because everybody knows I am the only black person here."[37] When you stick out, the gaze sticks to you. Sticking out from whiteness can thus reconfirm the whiteness of the space. Whiteness becomes obtrusive, what gets in the way of an occupation of space. When we fail to inhabit a category (when we are questioned or question ourselves whether we are "it," or pass as or into "it") then that category becomes more apparent, rather like the institutional wall: a sign of immobility or what does not move.[38]

Diversity work thus can take the form of description: it can be to describe the effects of inhabiting institutional spaces that do not give you residence. An example: we are at a departmental meeting with students to introduce our courses. We come up, one after the other, to the podium. A colleague is chairing, introducing each of us in turn. She says: this is Professor So-and-so; this is Professor Such-and-such. On this particular occasion, I happen to be the only female professor in the room. And I am the only professor introduced without using the title. She says: "This is Sara." And in taking up the space that has been given to me, I feel like a girl, and I giggle. It is a "girling" moment, to use Judith Butler's evocative term.[39] "Girling" moments do not stop happening, even after we have been pronounced girls. We can feel this assignment as atmosphere. When you look like what they expect a professor to be, you are treated like a professor. A somber and serious mood follows those who have the right kind of body, the body that allows them to pass seamlessly into the category, when the category has a certain affective value, as somber and serious.

I could add here that I was the only professor of color in the room (as the only professor of color in the department, this detail was not so surprising). Other critics have documented what it means to occupy the place and position of a professor of color. Pierre Orelus, for example, offers a moving account of how being a professor of color causes trouble, as if being one thing makes it difficult to be seen as the other: "After I formally introduce myself in class, I have undergraduate students who ask me, in a surprised tone of voice, 'Are you really the professor?' I sometimes overhear them asking their peers, 'Is he really the professor?'"[40] Orelus compares this mode of questioning, this sense of curiosity and astonishment, with the questions typically asked of immigrants about "funny accents." Or we could think of the questions asked of strangers, "Where are you from?" as if to say, or more accurately, which is to say, you are not from here. When we are asked questions, we are being held up, we become questionable. Being asked whether you are the professor is also a way of being made into a stranger, of not being at home in a category that gives residence to others.

Diversity work can involve an experience of hesitation, of not knowing what to do in these situations. There is a labor in having to respond to a situation that others are protected from, a situation that does not come up for those whose residence is assumed. Do you point it out? Do you say anything? Will you cause a problem by describing a problem? Past experience tells you that to make such a point is to become a sore point. Sometimes you let the moment pass, because the consequences of not letting it pass are too difficult.

Some have to "insist" on belonging to the categories that give residence to others. If you point out the failure to be given the proper name, or if you ask to be referred to by the proper name, then you have to insist on what is simply given to others. Not only that; you are heard as insistent, or even for that matter as self-promotional, as insisting on your dues. If you have to become insistent in order to receive what is automatically given to others, then your insistence confirms the improper nature of your residence. We don't tend to notice the assistance given to those whose residence is assumed.

Conclusion: Diversity Work and Disorientation

To catalogue these incidents is not a melancholic task. I realize how much we come to know about institutional life because of these failures of residence, how much the categories in which we are immersed as styles of life *become explicit when you do not quite inhabit them*. Diversity work can be disorientating, a way of making the familiar strange. Bodies that don't fit, bodies that are tripped up, caught out, are bodies to whom the institution is revealed. If we are disoriented by this work, what about the institutions?

If our arrival can cause discomfort, and even if it is uncomfortable to cause discomfort, it can be how things can happen. You learn to fade into the background, but sometimes you can't or you don't. As Nirmal Puwar shows, when bodies arrive who seem "out of place" in institutional worlds there is a process of *disorientation*: "People are 'thrown' because a whole world view is jolted."[41] Or, as Roderick A. Ferguson suggests, the presence of minorities and racialized others has an "eccentric" effect, given they such bodies are placed outside the logic of normative whiteness.[42]

When bodies "arrive" that don't extend the lines already extended by spaces, those spaces might even appear "slantwise" or oblique. It is worth noting here that Merleau-Ponty himself considers moments of disorientation. He notes: "If we so contrive it that a subject sees the room in which he is, only through a mirror which reflects it at an angle at 45 degrees to the vertical, the subject at first sees the room 'slantwise.' A man walking about in it seems to lean to one side as he goes. A piece of cardboard falling down the door-frame looks to be falling obliquely. The general effect is 'queer.'"[43] By discussing a number of spatial experiments that "contrive" a situation so that a subject does not see straight, Merleau-Ponty asks how the subject's relation to space is reoriented: "After a few minutes a sudden change occurs: the walls, the man walking around the room, and the line in which the cardboard falls become vertical."[44] This reorientation, which we can describe as the "becoming vertical" of perspective, means that the "queer effect" is overcome and objects in the world no longer appears as if they were "off-center" or "slantwise." The queer moment, in which objects appear slantwise, and the vertical and horizontal axes appear "out of line," must be overcome not because such moments contradict laws that govern objective space, but because they block bodily action: they inhibit the body, such that it ceases to extend into phenomenal space. So, although Merleau-Ponty is tempted to say that the "vertical is the direction represented by the symmetry of the axis of the body,"[45] his phenomenology instead embraces a model of bodily space in which spatial lines "line up" only as effects of bodily actions on and in the world. In other words, the body "straightens" its view, in order to extend into space.

In one footnote, Merleau-Ponty refers to Stratton's *Vision without Inversion*, to provide both an analysis of the way in which orientation happens, and what happens when it fails to happen. As he puts it: "We remain physically upright not through the mechanism of the skeleton or even through the nervous regulation of muscular tone, but because we are caught up in a world. *If this involvement is seriously weakened, the body collapses and becomes once more an object.*"[46] The "upright" body is involved in the world, and acts on the world or even "can act" insofar as it is already involved. The weakening of this involvement is what causes the body to collapse, and to become an object alongside other objects. We can learn from this: we can learn that disorientation is unevenly distributed; that some bodies more than others have their involvement in the world called into crisis. This shows us how the world itself is more "involved" in some bodies than others, as its takes such bodies as the contours of ordinary experience.

Perhaps to be involved with institutions as diversity workers is an attempt to call them into crisis, to render institutions into the objects that appear slantwise, or as objects that appear insofar as they register as obtrusive. Our aim is to bring what we are not into view to those who are not this "not." It might be that institutions are *not* transformed by our work; that they defend themselves from the process of being revealed. Institutions might even recover from our involvement. We might in this recovery become the objects yet again, those who are obtrusive or willful. But the very effort to transform institutions, the effort not to reproduce what we inherit, cannot leave us untransformed. And perhaps in how we are transformed by diversity work as diversity workers, we start again. We might start with what is old, but in being startled by the old, we start again.

Notes

1. *IP*, 7.

2. Rosalyn Diprose, "Review of Institution and Passivity," *Notre Dame Philosophical Reviews* (2010).

3. Victor Nee, "Sources of the New Institutionalism," in *The New Institutionalism in Sociology*, ed. Mary C. Brinton and Victor Nee (Stanford: Stanford University Press, 1998), 1.

4. For further details about this research project please see: Sara Ahmed, *On Being Included: Racism and Diversity in Institutional Life* (Durham: Duke University Press, 2012). For any quotes that I use in this chapter I will provide page numbers from this text.

5. Nirmal Puwar, *Space Invaders: Race, Gender, and Bodies out of Place* (Oxford: Berg, 2004).

6. *PP*, 165.

7. Ibid.

8. *PP*, 115.

9. It is worth noting here that the word *habit* comes from the Latin for condition, appearance, and dress.

10. *PP*, 165.

11. *PP*, 166.

12. Ibid.

13. *PP*, 176.

14. *PrP*, 5.

15. Ibid.

16. Russell Jacoby, *Social Amnesia: A Critique of Contemporary Psychology* (New Brunswick: Rutgers University Press, 1997), 31.

17. *PP*, 291.

18. Gail Weiss, *Refiguring the Ordinary* (Bloomington: Indiana University Press, 2008).

19. William James, *The Principles of Psychology, Volume 1* (New York, Dover, 1950), 105.

20. Ibid., 121.

21. In drawing on Merleau-Ponty's work to develop a phenomenology of institutional whiteness, my work is indebted to the work of scholars who have offered a phenomenology of race, in particular the work of Linda Martín Alcoff. See Linda Martín Alcoff, *Visible Identities: Race, Gender, and the Self* (Oxford, Oxford University Press, 2006).

22. See Richard Dyer, *White* (London and New York: Routledge, 1997) and Ruth Frankenberg, *White Women, Race Matters: The Social Construction of Whiteness* Minneapolis: University of Minnesota Press, 1993).

23. Shannon Sullivan, *Revealing Whiteness: The Unconscious Habits of White Privilege* (Bloomington: Indiana University Press, 2006), 1. There are a number of recent studies on whiteness as a habit; in addition to Sullivan, see Terrance MacMullan, *Habits of Whiteness: A Pragmatist Reconstruction* (Bloomington: Indiana University Press, 2009).

24. Marilyn Strathern, "Bullet-Proofing: A Tale from the United Kingdom," in *Documents: Artifacts of Modern Knowledge*, ed. Annelise Riles (Ann Arbor: University of Michigan Press, 2006), 194–95.

25. Mary Douglas, *How Institutions Think* (Syracuse: Syracuse University Press, 1986).

26. Ole Elgström, "Norm Negotiations: The Construction of New Norms Regarding Gender and Development in EU Foreign Aid Policy," *Journal of European Public Policy* 7, no. 3 (2000): 458.

27. It is interesting to consider the brick wall in relation to the glass ceiling: both are metaphors for institutional limits that derive their sense with analogy not only to physical objects but also to the means by which internal spaces are delineated and contained. The glass ceiling refers to the institutional processes that stop certain categories of people from moving up (vertical mobility) while the brick wall refers to the institutional processes that stop certain values from moving across (horizontal mobility). Both metaphors also point to the significance of visibility and invisibility: the point of the ceiling being made of glass is that you can't see it. The transparency of glass means, however, that you can see through it; you see above to the places you cannot reach. With the brick wall, you cannot see it, unless you come up against it. The metaphor of the brick wall points to how what is tangible and visible to some subjects, something so thick and solid that *you cannot see through it*, does not even appear to others. What some cannot see through, others cannot see.

28. Ahmed, *On Being Included*, 124–25.

29. Ibid., 126.

30. *PP*, 159.

31. Vivian Sobchack, *Carnal Thoughts: Embodiment and Moving Image Culture* (Berkeley, Los Angeles, London: University of California Press, 2004), 211.

32. *PP*, 165.

33. Sara Ahmed, *Queer Phenomenology: Orientations, Objects, Others* (Durham: Duke University Press, 2006), 140.

34. Ibid., 139.

35. Ahmed, *On Being Included*, 40–41.

36. Ibid., 158.

37. Ibid., 41.

38. I am acknowledging here that it is possible not to inhabit fully a category of privilege even if one is privileged by a category. For example, if men do not inhabit the category of masculinity properly or fully, *then the category appears as an institutional wall*, as a physical barrier that is revealed in coming up against it. I should also note that it is possible not to inhabit fully a category without becoming conscious of the restriction of that category: the psychic work of accommodating to a world that does not take your body as norm can involve precisely not even registering those norms as a way of protecting oneself from them.

39. Judith Butler, *Bodies that Matter: On the Discursive Limits of "Sex"* (London: Routledge, 1993), 7.

40. Pierre Orelus, *Transnationals of Color: Counter Narratives against Discrimination in Schools and Beyond* (New York, Peter Lang, 2011), 31.

41. Puwar, *Space Invaders*, 43.

42. Roderick A. Ferguson, *Aberrations in Black: Toward a Queer of Color Critique* (Minneapolis, London: University of Minnesota Press, 2004), 26. See also: José Esteban Muñoz, "Feeling Brown: Ethnicity and Affect in Ricardo Bracho's The Sweetest Hangover (and Other STDs)," in *Theatre Journal* 5, no. 21 (2000): 68.
43. *PP*, 289.
44. Ibid.
45. *PP*, 291.
46. *PP*, 298; emphasis added.

Art and Creation

Art after the Sublime in Merleau-Ponty and André Breton

Aesthetics and the Politics of *Mad Love*

GALEN A. JOHNSON

The strife and the hope that mark the relation between aesthetics and the political have, in our time, reached an apotheosis. Plato thought the artist so dangerous as to require expurgation from the *polis*. Marcuse thought the artist so redemptive as to provide the only refuge against capitalist materialism. In between, John Dewey and Friedrich Nietzsche promoted aesthetic experience to the status of a replacement for the sacred in a secular age. This essay seeks to explore the theme of art and politics within the framework of Merleau-Ponty's aesthetics. We are construing "politics" very broadly to mean the politics of everyday life and personal life as well as the politics of the public realm, which includes the region of government and law, both national and international, but is not reducible to it. Though across this range there will be multiplicities, we can provisionally follow Merleau-Ponty's image of social "fields" of "forces," within which we aspire to Dewey's ethical ideal of a body politic in which every human being "has a truly infinite chance to become a person."[1] Merleau-Ponty will caution about moralism in politics, but that is about calling oneself good while labeling another or others evil. Borrowing a title from Lyotard: What is the place of art in political life in an era "after the sublime?"

I

In *The Prose of the World* and again in *Signs*, Merleau-Ponty had said that the arts and language are the model for understanding human history: "We would undoubtedly recover the concept of history in the true sense of the term if we were to get used to modeling it after the example of the arts and language. For the fact that each expression is closely connected within one single order to every other expression brings about the junction of the individual and the universal."[2] And in the preface to *Sense and Non-Sense,* he raised the example of Cézanne to an inspirational power for grasping history and politics. Cézanne had "won out against chance, and men, too, can win provided they will measure the dangers and the task."[3] I want still to agree with Merleau-Ponty that the politics of our time requires the arts, though it is not so much the fine arts themselves, which Merleau-Ponty celebrated, that we require in an age "after the sublime"; rather, an aesthetic sensibility of experimentation, intercorporeal community, challenge, confrontation, subversion, and joy that the arts can embody. It is the poets, the songsters, and the painters among us—and in ourselves—who are the makers and builders of worlds. It is not only in the museums that house fine arts and paintings where we will find transformation, as Merleau-Ponty himself contended. "One should go to the museum," he wrote, "as the painters go there, in the sober joy of work; and not as we go there, with a somewhat spurious reverence."[4] To the question, "Can phenomenology as a descriptive philosophy be critical?" here is one of the most poignant instances of critical theory in the phenomenology of Merleau-Ponty. His critique of the museum distinguishes between a "historicity of life" and a cruel, pompous, and official "historicity of death" that removes all the vehemence, struggle, suffering, and sacrifice from actual, living art work and turns it into "works" and "messages," vying with one another in a space out of time and place. It lends the "works" a false prestige and makes of the living artist a creature from another world "as mysterious for us as octopi or lobsters."[5]

Lyotard has written: "As for a politics of the sublime, there is no such thing. It could only be terror. But there is an aesthetic of the sublime in the political."[6] The actors and heroes of political drama are always suspect and should be suspected of pursuing particular and interested motives. "But the sublime affection the public experiences for the drama is not to be suspected."[7] On the one hand is the smell of cynicism, on the other is the invitation of hope. "Politics is the modern tragedy,"[8] Merleau-Ponty wrote in *Signs*, at once speaking of politics in terms of an art form, but a page earlier he had expressed skepticism about philosophy: "The politics of philosophers is what no one practices."[9] For Merleau-Ponty's aesthetics of history and the political, the challenge is skepticism and criticism of the frozen Medusa of authoritarianism and moralism in political life, and yet belief in love and hope in our relations with others. "Underneath the clamor a silence is growing, an expectation. Why could it not be a hope?"[10] How, we might ask, in our day and in these times, is this possible?

II

We have written of a retrieval of the beautiful, of Cézanne and strong beauty, of Paul Klee and mortal beauty.[11] We have spoken of the experience of the "contagion" created by the beautiful as an interpretation of Kant's *Third Critique* and notion of "subjective universality," available in the aesthetic of Merleau-Ponty as judgment "without concepts," the "sensible ideas."[12] Contagion is this desire, this demand that imposes itself without our will for our experience of beauty to be shared with others, for them to see what we have seen, to hear what we have heard, to read what we have read. We now want to prolong this vector of strong beauty and mortal, suffering beauty toward André Breton's surrealism and his notion of "convulsive beauty." So doing will shed light on the significance of the experiences of the beautiful and sublime for the formation and development of intersubjective community and love, what Merleau-Ponty called an "anonymous intercorporeity." Throughout, we must be cognizant of Benjamin's warning regarding the dangers of the "aestheticization of the political,"[13] as we must be aware of Merleau-Ponty's own warnings regarding the dangers of a narrow, puerile, and nostalgic surrealism. In *Signs*, he wrote: "There was a Surrealism which sought for miracles in a crude state in every disorganization of the constituted world. At the limit, this is the art of farces and hoaxes. The Surrealism which endured was not satisfied to tear the customary world apart; it composed a different one."[14]

Though Merleau-Ponty's engagement with surrealism is much less well known than his engagement with Cézanne, Klee, Rodin, Matisse, and others, nevertheless that engagement was long and deep. When we speak this way, we are making a shift from the art of painting to that of literature, namely, novels and poetry, and principally mean to indicate the surrealism of André Breton, author of the first *Manifesto of Surrealism* (1924) and the *Second Manifesto of Surrealism* (1930). We also find references to Rimbaud, particularly his *Letters of a Seer* (*Lettres du voyant*), and to Jean Paulhan, a lesser-known writer on the fringes of the surrealist movement proper, which dates from the end of World War I, flowering in the 1930s and 1940s, with still significant works and influence into the early and mid-1960s.[15] Claude Lefort's "Preface" and "Editorial Note" at the beginning of *The Prose of the World* tell us that Merleau-Ponty had planned for it to be a much longer work with a second section containing five literary studies—Montaigne, Stendhal, Proust, Breton, Artaud—and with a third section considering the significances of the redefined categories of prose and poetry in their generality for "love, religion, and politics."[16]

Merleau-Ponty was a reader of manifestoes and published an article about the *Communist Manifesto* of Marx and Engels on the occasion of its centenary anniversary in 1948.[17] Nevertheless, the work by Breton that Merleau-Ponty references and repeatedly returned to was not the surrealist manifestoes, rather the short and captivating work Breton had titled *Mad Love*.[18] Merleau-Ponty discusses particularly that work's concepts of "convulsive beauty," the "sublime point," and the "found object" (*la trouvaille*). Though Breton strove to marshal passionate sexual love, convulsive beauty, and the sublime point for a revolutionary politics, we will find Merleau-Ponty more fascinated with the significances of the found object for possibilities of humans living well together.

Merleau-Ponty's first mention of surrealism in his published writings comes in *The Structure of Behavior* (1942), found in a passage contrasting adult ordinary reality with ways in which that reality can be interrupted and momentarily replaced by a "surreality."

In adults, ordinary reality is a human reality and when use-objects—a glove, a shoe—with their human mark are placed among natural objects and contemplated as things for the first time, or when events on the street—a crowd gathering, an accident—are seen through the panes of a window, which shuts out their sound,

> and are brought to the condition of a pure spectacle and invested with a sort of eternity, we have the impression of acceding to another world, to a surreality [*une surréalité*] because the involvement which binds us to the human world is broken for the first time, because a nature "in itself" [*en soi*] is allowed to show through. . . . It should be noted that infants are unaware of the use of many objects even when they have seen them handled; we ourselves can remember the *marvelous* [my emphasis] appearance which things had when we did not know what they were for.[19]

When the window pane closes out the sound of the spectacle outside, our normal sensory synesthesia, which renders sight and sound simultaneous, is interrupted. Camus mentions a similar instance of seeing a person talking and gesturing in a phone booth but not being able to hear him. He looks mechanical, robotic. Merleau-Ponty's footnote to the word *surreality* says the use that surrealist poetry has made of these themes is well known.

Reading Merleau-Ponty and finding so frequently words such as "magic," "miracle," and "metaphorsosis," one must be struck by Breton's stress upon surreality as the *marvelous*. In the first *Surrealist Manifesto*, he writes: "Let us not mince words: the marvelous is always beautiful, anything marvelous is beautiful, in fact only the marvelous is beautiful."[20] Breton locates the marvelous in history and notes that it is not the same in every historical period. It includes romantic *ruins,* equally the modern *mannequin* and Baudelaire's couches.

Surreality takes multiple forms in the discourse of Breton and it is foolhardy to attempt to reduce it to a univocal meaning. Breton's *First Manifesto* speaks of a surreality that is the merger of dream states and reality, the free play of the imagination and associations with regard to images and verbal word play, from childhood memories the sentiment of being unintegrated, the absentmindedness of Kant regarding women, and complete nonconformism.[21] Surrealist images "come to one spontaneously, despotically. He cannot chase them away; for the will is powerless now and no longer controls the faculties."[22] The first *Manifesto* gives the often cited definition that Breton declares "once and for all":

> Surrealism, n. Psychic automatism in its pure state, by which one proposes to express—verbally, by means of the written word, or in any other manner—the actual functioning of thought. Dictated by thought, in the absence of any control exercised by reason, exempt from any aesthetic or moral concern.[23]

The "once and for all" must be qualified, for Breton continued to develop and hone the definition of surrealism, and in *Communicating Vessels* (1932) offered an image adapted from electricity, that of a "conductor" (*un fil conducteur*) between dream and reality: "I hope that it [surrealism] stands as having tried nothing better than laying down a *conductor* between the far too separated worlds of waking and sleeping, of exterior and interior reality, of reason and madness, of the calm of knowledge and of love, of life for life and the revolution, etc."[24] By identifying surreality with the irrational bifurcated from the opposed polarity of the rational—"the absence of any control exercised by reason"—surreality includes equally the images induced by opium and mescaline,[25] as well as certain pathological states of mind where sensorial disorders occupy the patient's complete attention.[26]

L'Amour fou [*Mad Love*], Merleau-Ponty writes in *Signs*, "is to be created, beyond self-love, the pleasure of dominating, and the pleasure of sinning."[27] In Breton's words expressing the meaning of mad love, and there can be no better:

> Delirium of absolute presence. How could one not find oneself wishing to love like this, in the bosom of reconciled nature? . . . Love, only love that you are, carnal love, I adore, I have never ceased to adore your lethal shadow, your mortal shadow.

And then Breton speaks, as did Aristophanes in the *Symposium* of Plato, of love as fusion:

> And it is there—right there in the depths of the human crucible, in this paradoxical region where the fusion of two beings who have really chosen each other renders to all things the lost colors of the times of ancient suns.[28]

Breton had imagined a "new beauty envisaged exclusively to produce passion,"[29] found in the beloved of mad love from the time of *Nadja*, that earlier autobiographical work dedicated to the woman whose name is the beginning of the Russian word for hope. In "*L'Homme et l'objet*" ("Man and Object") (1948), Merleau-Ponty had written: "Like Breton, we must be aware that a lamp has a physiognomy, a "convulsive beauty."[30] Breton is clear, as are we today, that this new beauty is categorically opposed to that classical, formal conception of beauty based upon perfection. "On the contrary, I have never stopped advocating creation, spontaneous action, insofar as the crystal, nonperfectible by definition, is the perfect example of it."[31] As perfection is replaced by the imperfectible crystalline work of art with its "hardness, rigidity, regularity, the luster on every interior and exterior facet,"[32] convulsive beauty is conceived in motion, in the reciprocal relations linking the object in motion and in its repose. Breton combines experiencing the beloved, like the work of art, from many angles of repose together with experiences in motion, in action.[33] In sum, again in the poetic words of Breton: "Convulsive beauty will be veiled-erotic, fixed-explosive, magic-circumstantial, or it will not be."[34] This is all about desire, and clearly in this case we are speaking of sexual desire. Breton argues that real objects, things, and persons do not exist just as they are independently from the "phosphorescent letters" of desire," but as the *actual* ways in which they arise for our desire: "Desire, the only motive of the world, desire, the only rigor humans must be acquainted with, where could I be better situated to adore it than on the inside of a cloud?"[35] The surrealist association of desire with being on the inside of a cloud is drawn from a stanza of Baudelaire's poem, "Voyage:"

> None of the famous landscapes that we saw equaled the
>   mysterious allure
> of those that chance arranges in the clouds . . .
> And our desire would let us have no peace![36]

Such thoughts on love and desire are not distant to the author of *Phenomenology of Perception*, though we will mark a difference as well. At the beginning of its chapter on "The Body as a Sexed Being," Merleau-Ponty wrote: "If we wish to reveal the genesis of being for us, then we must ultimately consider the sector of our experience that clearly has sense and reality only for us, namely, our affective milieu. Let us attempt to see how an object or a being begins to exist for us through desire or love, and we will thereby understand more clearly how objects and beings can exist in general."[37] In *Signs*, Merleau-Ponty, writing of Freud, speaks of the body as an enigma of absolute desire: "The body is enigmatic: a part of the world certainly, but offered in a bizarre way, as is dwelling (*son habitat*), to an absolute desire to draw near the other person and meet him in his body too, animated and animating, the natural face of mind [*figure naturelle de l'esprit*]."[38] Love and beauty involve body and desire in a double opening both to the other and to ourselves, that is an awareness and "knowing by sentiment" (*connaissance par sentiment*), as Merleau-Ponty expressed it in the working note of *The Visible and the Invisible* of May 1960 titled "Flesh of the world—Flesh of the body—Being."[39] In all fairness, we must also mark a distance between Breton and Merleau-Ponty on love and desire, for Breton's *Nadja* is, in this light, a very strange work in which Nadja loves him "like the sun" but it is a pitifully one-sided love story in which Breton finds her less and less interesting. In spite of this, *Mad Love* devotes a lengthy analysis to the supposed inevitable cooling or "falling off" of erotic love, noting the harmless complaints that grow into a "stone of silence."[40] But Breton argues this depressing conception is founded on two great errors, the social error of a materialist economic base of society that is violently antagonistic to anything having to do with something permanent and eternal, and the moral error of the infamous Christian idea of sin. "There has never been any forbidden fruit. Only temptation is divine."[41] He rejects, therefore, the excuse of habit, of weariness, and concludes that true reciprocal love is an absolute love in which there is an inexhaustible depth. Even stranger, therefore, Nadja.

The concluding section of *Mad Love* is a surprise, and one that captured Merleau-Ponty with its image of the "sublime point." Breton writes a letter to his daughter, born to himself and his second wife, Jacqueline Lamba, the daughter, age two at the time of publication of *Mad Love* but projected forward in the letter to age sixteen when she might be tempted to open his book: "Dear Hazel of Squirrelnut [*Chère Écusette de Noireuil*]."[42] What author with children has not thought of this anxiety?

Near the beginning, he writes: "let me believe that these words, 'mad love,' will one day correspond uniquely to your own delirium."[43] It is a beautiful letter expressing many memories and intimate thoughts about a love he believes is the only miracle that gives a chance for escaping the meanness of the human condition, telling her how deeply and certainly she had been brought into the world: "You were thought of as possible, as certain, in the very moment when, in a love deeply sure of itself, a man and a woman wanted you."[44] The letter's last sentence is as dramatic and overwhelming as Breton's own love for her: "I want you to be madly loved! [*d'etre follement aimée*]."[45]

This letter is the source of the image of a sublime point that guides eternal love, to which the expression *forever*, Breton claims, is "the master key." This impossible word, "I will love you *forever*," not for a long time but "*forever*," is the word, Breton writes, that wears his colors. "Forever, as on the white sand of time and through the grace of this instrument which is used to measure it, reduced to a stream of milk endlessly pouring from a glass breast."[46] Immediately following, Breton writes of the sublime point:

> I have spoken of a certain "sublime point" on the mountain. It was never a question of establishing my dwelling on this point. It would, moreover, from then on, have ceased to be sublime and I should, myself, have ceased to be a person. Unable reasonably to dwell there, I have nevertheless never gone so far from it as to lose it from view, as to not be able to point it out. . . . I have never ceased to identify the flesh of the being I love and

the snow of the peaks in the rising sun. I have tried only to know the hours of love's triumph.[47]

This beautiful image of the snow of the mountain's peaks warmed by the heat and illuminated by the rays of the rising sun is the capstone guiding point for the meaning of mad love and convulsive beauty.

Merleau-Ponty referred to Breton's "sublime point" in "Man and Adversity" in *Signs* (1951) and again in the "Preface" to *Adventures of the Dialectic* (1955). In the latter, he was writing in the context of the disappointment of the Marxist dialectic and revolutionary politics. "Revolutionary politics was the *sublime moment* [*le point sublime*] in which reality and values, subject and object, judgment and discipline, individual and totality, present and future, instead of colliding, would little by little enter into complicity."[48] One of the striking shared features of *The Communist Manifesto* and *Surrealist Manifesto* is that both sought a revolutionary politics that would achieve the abolition of the same three structures: family, religion, country. Earlier in "Man and Adversity," Merleau-Ponty had expressed the rationale for the surrealist revolutionary politics:

> It [surrealism] sought to recall language and literature to the whole extent of their task by freeing them from the literary world's petty formulas and fabrications of talent. It was necessary to go back to that point of innocence, youth, and unity at which speaking man is not yet man of letters, political man, or moral man—to that "*sublime point*" Breton speaks about elsewhere [my emphasis], at which literature, life, morality, and politics are equivalent and substituted for one another, because in fact each of us is the same man who loves or hates, who reads or writes, who accepts or refuses political destiny.[49]

In *Adventures of the Dialectic*, when Merleau-Ponty spoke of Breton's sublime point, he asked: "What is left of these hopes?" [50] Yet Merleau-Ponty had stated the rationale perfectly that links the individual with the universal, the personal or private with the public: life and politics are equivalent because all of us are the same ones who both love or hate and who accept or reject political structures and destiny.

Breton believed fervently that mad love and convulsive beauty could transform the social world, and his rationale is very much as Merleau-Ponty summarized it. In the letter to his daughter, he referred to love and beauty as life's *raison d'être*, which is

> worth fighting for collectively and not just individually. . . . This blind aspiration towards the best would suffice to justify love as I think of it, absolute love, as the only principle for physical and moral selection which can guarantee that human witness, human passage shall not have taken place in vain.[51]

He extends the argument to "the whole world that will be newly lit from our loving each other, because a chain of illuminations passes through us."[52] Breton recruits Marx's *Communist Manifesto* and Freud's *Civilization and Its Discontents* on behalf of the argument: "These two testimonies, which present a conception, less and less frivolous, of love as a fundamental principle for moral as well as cultural progress, would seem to me by themselves of such a nature as to give poetic activity a major role as a tried and tested means to fix the sensitive and moving world on a single being as well as a permanent force of anticipation."[53] Too bad if that offends the mockers and scoundrels, Breton writes, "the recreation, the perpetual re-coloration of the world in a single being, such as they are accomplished through love, light up with a thousand rays the advance of the earth ahead. Each time a person loves, nothing can prevent everyone's feelings being involved. In order not to let them down, the involvement must be entire."[54] Other passages can be cited and multiply. An individual failure to engage and sustain carnal love lets the whole world down, according to Breton.

Reading these ideas and their rationale today in our times, these times of confusion and crisis, of famine, war, and terror, from one point of view, they sound familiar, for Breton knew that the problem was no longer, as it used to be, "whether a canvas can hold its own in a wheat field, but whether it can stand up against the daily paper."[55] Breton was writing in the aftermath of World War I, at a time when he could see the signs of Europe again coming undone and a second world war imminent. One of these very visible signs was ongoing in 1937 as he was finishing *Mad Love*, the war of Franco's forces and fascism against Republican Spain. Nevertheless, from another point of view, Breton's words and view seem as though they are from an altogether other place and a faraway time, a place and time of myth. Here we mean by "myth" a historical illusion, such as when Merleau-Ponty asked: "Is it then the conclusion of these adventures that the dialectic was a myth [= illusion]?"[56] We do not mean the "mythic," the past that belongs to "a mythical time, to the time before time, to the prior life, farther than India and China,"⁵⁷ as Baudelaire had written in his poem "Moesta et Errabunda" ("Grieving and Wandering") in *Les fleurs du mal,* and Merleau-Ponty attributed to the "origins" of art, to "involuntary memory" in Proust, and the Freudian idea of the unconscious as "indestructible." In politics, the social imaginary is contaminated by myth: the "myth of the proletariat," the "myth of the Aryan race," the "myth of Social Darwinism," the "myth of the people."

Needless to say, Merleau-Ponty never endorsed such a "myth" linking sex love with political revolution and the formation of more just political arrangements. In the "Preface" to *Adventures of the Dialectic,* he had invoked Breton's "sublime point" as a revolutionary moment that had become a lost hope. By the time of the "Epilogue," he famously wrote: "Revolutions are true as movements and false as regimes."⁵⁸ "As established regimes they can never be what they were as movements; precisely because it succeeded and ended up as an institution, the historical movement is no longer itself: it 'betrays' and 'disfigures' itself in accomplishing itself."⁵⁹ Merleau-Ponty was speaking of revolution generally here, of Marxism in particular, and not of surrealism in particular. Others have been openly cynical or sarcastic about surrealist revolutionary poetry and love. Kundera's novel *Life is Elsewhere* (1973) caustically caricatures the naive hopes and dreams of young poet Jaromil and the celebrated slogan of surrealism, "Life [existence] is elsewhere," written as the last sentence of Breton's first *Surrealist Manifesto.*⁶⁰ Benjamin's essay on surrealism refuses the name of "literature" for surrealist writing—"demonstrations, watchwords, documents, bluffs, forgeries if you will, but at any rate not literature."⁶¹ He describes surrealism as an effort to win the energies of "intoxication" for the revolution, but faults it for "an inadequate, undialectical conception of the nature of intoxication." He asks, "poetic politics?" And answers, "We have tried that beverage. Anything rather than that!"⁶² He argues that to place the accent exclusively on intoxication mistakenly subordinates "the methodical and disciplinary preparation for revolution entirely to a praxis oscillating between fitness exercises and celebration in advance . . . pernicious romantic prejudices."⁶³

Sounding a different note, Benjamin accepts the distinction articulated by the surrealist writer Louis Aragon between metaphors and images and believes it must be extended to the realm of politics where artists can make important contributions in the sphere of imagery. He writes: "To organize pessimism [i.e., to organize those who are pessimistic about and opposed to bourgeois politics and culture—my insertion] means nothing other than to expel moral metaphor from politics and to discover in political action a sphere reserved one hundred percent for images."[64] In his article titled "On Fascination: Walter Benjamin's Images," Ackbar Addas comments: "Metaphors explain, while images provide evidence. Metaphors reconcile us to power with stories about newness: images show us that the Emperor has no clothes."[65] Thus, surrealist image production, drawn from dreams and the unconscious, brings images into history as a form of action. In spite of his searing twofold critique of surrealism for its adoration of intoxication and lack of dialectical rigor and discipline, in the end Benjamin grants to the surrealist poet and artist revolutionary power as social criticism to the extent they dwell in images. Benjamin concludes his essay:

> The collective is a body, too. . . . Only when in technology body and image so interpenetrate that all revolutionary tension becomes bodily innervation, and all the bodily innervations of the collective become revolutionary discharge, has reality transcended itself to the extent demanded by the *Communist Manifesto*.[66]

III

Here, however, we must reverse the field against the critics of surrealism who are skeptical, cynical even, about love as a political power, for, in *Mad Love*, Breton opens an investigation of the power of another kind of love for community life. Here we will find an intersubjectivity, an intercorporeity in the body politic, which Merleau-Ponty himself also sought to articulate. The starting point comes from the unexpected and remarkable claim by Breton in the first *Surrealist Manifesto* that "the forms of Surrealist language adapt themselves best to dialogue."[67] The claim regarding dialogue is unexpected because one would suppose the kind of "automatic writing" associated with surrealism would best emerge from monologue. In fact, in the section of the first *Manifesto* discussing the methods of Freud, Breton does link the method of "free association" with surrealist technique as "a monologue spoken as rapidly as possible without any intervention on the part of the critical faculties, a monologue consequently unencumbered by the slightest inhibition and which was, as closely as possible, akin to *spoken thought*."[68] However, as the Surrealist movement unfolded, automatic writing became less and less favored as a surrealist practice for the generation of images and Merleau-Ponty says exactly this in an important passage regarding the "*pathos of language*" found in "Man and Adversity" (1951) published in *Signs*.

In our century this *pathos of language* is common to writers who mutually detest one another but whose kinship is from this moment on confirmed by it. In its first stages, surrealism certainly had the air of an insurrection against language, against all meaning, and against literature itself. The fact is that Breton, after a few hesitant formulations which he quickly corrected, proposed not to destroy language to the profit of non-sense but to restore a certain profound and radical usage of speech, which he realized all the writings called "automatic" were far from giving an adequate example of.[69]

Immediately following this text is found Merleau-Ponty's reference to the surrealist "sublime point" discussed above in relation to Breton's letter to his daughter in the concluding section of *Mad Love*. Much could be made in surrealist word play fashion of the word *insurrection*: "surrection" (rebellion, uprising, but "rising" in general), "resurrection."[70] What Merleau-Ponty means by the *pathos of language* is made precise in the immediately preceding text: "As Baudelaire already said, there are finished works which we cannot say have ever been *completed*, and unfinished works which say what they meant. What is proper to expression is to never be more than approximate."[71]

Unfinished works take many shapes: interrupted with the intention to return, abandoned or discarded, taken up in a different project. In whatever shape, Merleau-Ponty means to bring to our attention that *all* works are unfinished in the sense that they are approximate, never perfect. In the words of Maurice Blanchot, the work is "the absence of the work"; this paradoxical expression only means that in the work there is an incomplete residue that will become future work that remains to be done, to "go further." In *Eye and Mind*, Merleau-Ponty asks, "What is that dimension which lets Van Gogh say he must go 'still further' [*veut aller 'plus loin'*]."[72] When we return to *The Prose of the World* below we will note the remarkable role played in that work by Jean Paulhan, whom Breton lists among the occupants of his surrealist "castle," whether the castle had been real or imagined.[73] It was Paulhan who puzzled Merleau-Ponty in a way that launched *The Prose of the World* by saying the very opposite from Baudelaire and Merleau-Ponty on the always unfinished nature of expression. In Paulhan's *Les Fleures de Tarbes* (*The Flowers of Tarbes*), he had adopted the statement of La Bruyère: "Of all the possible expressions which might render our thought, there is only one which is the best. One does not always come upon it in writing or talking: it is nevertheless true that it exists." Of this claim, tellingly, Merleau-Ponty asks: "How does he know this?"[74]

Returning to surrealism's elevation of dialogue, perhaps now it is no longer so unexpected. Breton suggests two very different models of how dialogue works. In the first, two thoughts confront each other, and one takes up the thought of the other only giving it cursory attention as the occasion for one's own reply. My attention treats the other's thought as an enemy and puts me in a position to turn it to my good advantage, actually thereby distorting the thought of the other. The goal is simply and only to get the better of the exchange. Breton pushes the limits of this form of "dialogue"—Should one call it dialogue at all?—by offering two pathological cases where sensorial disorders occupy the patient's attention completely:

Q: "How old are you?" A: "You." (*Echolalia*)

Q: "What is your name?" A: "Forty-five houses." (*Ganser syndrome, or beside-the- point replies*).[75]

Echolalia is the compulsion to repeat, a normal form of word imitation in young children learning to speak, but a speech disorder when prolonged into adulthood. It invokes the tragic story of Echo whose curse it was to be denied original speech, only and always to repeat, therefore unable to express her love for Narcissus.

The second meaning of dialogue Breton describes he affirms as the "absolute truth" of Poetic Surrealism. Here both speakers are freed completely from any obligations of politeness and each pursues his remarks without trying to impose anything whatsoever upon the other. "The words, the images are only so many springboards for the mind of the listener."[76] In *Mad Love*, Breton mentions the surrealists' love of games of definitions, supposition, or foresight: "'What. . . . If. . . . When . . .'—which has always seemed to me the most fabulous source of images otherwise *unfindable*."[77] Even of this second form of dialogue, which is called the true surrealist form, one still might be led to ask, Is any real listening going on? That kind of listening would mean the real effort to think along with or according to the words and thoughts of the other.

In *Mad Love*, Breton tells a remarkable story about a springtime stroll through a flea market with none other than Alberto Giacometti, the great artist who at the time was working on an enigmatic statue of the female figure. The story records their visit and walk as an experience of *shared preoccupations*.[78] To abbreviate an experience that Breton describes in several lovely pages, Giacometti and Breton made two *finds*, one by each: Giacometti purchased a half-mask made of rigid metal with horizontal, angled strips of metal to create visibility. The mask was of unknown purpose. Breton purchased a large wooden spoon that he found quite beautiful, of peasant fabrication, whose handle rose at the end from a little shoe that was part of it. This *finding* of an object, the found object (*la trouvaille*), is "invested with the sense of the marvelous, as one 'hits on something.' "[79] Breton compares it with the same purpose of the dream, freeing one from affective scruples that were supposed to be an insurmountable obstacle. This is the "*catalyzing* role of the found object"[80] as a "crystallization of desire." Through a narrative of their friendship and discussion of the Eros and Thanatos instincts in Freudian psychoanalysis, the details of which I will leave to the curious reader, Breton realizes the links both between Giacometti and himself, and both of them together, with the story of Cinderella's glass slipper. Thus, Breton is able to realize the "marvelous slipper potential in the modest spoon."[81] What I want to emphasize about this story of the flea market is Breton's experience of the stroll with Giacometti and their purchases as a mutually shared desire: "These two discoveries Giacometti and I made *together* respond not to a desire on the part of one of us, but rather to a desire of one of us with which the other, because of particular circumstances, is associated."[82] I think we can all understand the way in which such a found object in an antique store, perhaps, or a visual event such as a movie or paintings in a museum or gallery, and many more such things, can crystallize (or condense, as in the dream) the wishes and desires of two or more who share a life. I think this can be true as well of the *found gift*, that unexpected event of coming across something perfectly suited to a friend or family member perhaps, even though he or she is not present yet present in mind. Breton adds: "I would be tempted to say that the two people walking near each other constitute a single influencing body, *primed*."[83] This unusual mathematical expression, which I take it to be, seems to me to mean that the two separate individuals, Breton and Giacometti, had been raised to a higher power as a single body functioning together: BretonGiacometti.

Subsequently, Breton names this experience of the body *primed* the experience of "sympathy existing between two or several beings," and it leads to solutions "they would never have found on their own."[84] It puts in play what Breton calls a *second finality* that links our own will with another human will. The word *finality* seems to have an Aristotelian sense of final cause, referring to a final goal or purpose secondary or subsidiary to the primary purpose of purchases at a flea market. To these terms, *found object, catalyst of desire, body primed, sympathy*, and *second finality*, Breton now adds two older and less enigmatic terms, *friendship* and *love*: "For individuals as for societies, friendship and love, the relations created by the community of suffering and the convergence of demands, are alone capable of favoring this sudden dazzling combination of phenomena that [seem to] belong to independent causal series. Our fortune is scattered in the world, and able to spread out over everything."[85] Here immediately follows a surrealist image of the poppy, which also makes us think of the night of the sunflower shared with Nadja. Our fortune is scattered in the world, "but is wrinkled like the bud of a poppy. When we are alone in seeking it, it closes the gate of the universe upon us, deceives us with the pitiful resemblance of all the leaves, and takes on, along the highways, the garb of so many pebbles."[86] These are images drawn from the surrealist imagination of Breton that defeat transparent understanding, for such images are not meant for the rational mind but ultimately, it seems to me, reflect and refract one another as a composite picture of loneliness: wrinkled, the closed poppy bud as the closed gate of the universe, the leaves all the same, the pebbles along the highway. The found object is like the found words of the poem, the "actual *trouvaille* of words,"[87] and the found "aura" of a painting."[88]

"This *trouvaille*, whether it be artistic, scientific, philosophic, or as useless as anything, is enough to undo the beauty of everything beside it. In it alone can we recognize the marvelous precipitate of desire ["*merveilleux précipité du désir*"]."[89] Breton treasured his simple wooden spoon for it brought with it the presence of his friend, Giacometti, of BretonGiacometti. Merleau-Ponty referred many times to Breton's notion of the found object (*la trouvaille*). In "Man and Object," he mentioned specifically the found objects of the flea market from *Mad Love*: "An object found at the flea market, whether mask or spoon, is a 'wonderful precipitate of the human face,' fraught with reminiscences. Without stretching this to the point of occultism, we must admit that every object is also a 'find' that allows us to decipher ourselves."[90] In the Mexico lectures of the same year, 1948, he repeated the reference to the flea market and wrote: "Poetry of the found object, of the human object reclaimed by nature (abandoned locomotive in the forest, covered by plants). . . . All objects reside in us. The thing is not in front of us, but with us, it wounds our body.[91] The image of the abandoned locomotive in the forest is drawn directly from *Mad Love*, where Breton describes it as the most magical "monument to victory and to disaster."[92] In the same time period, Merleau-Ponty's lectures for French radio, published as *Causeries* and translated as *The World of Perception*, comment on Francis Ponge's poem "Water" as an example of what Merleau-Ponty meant by "element."

He referred to Gaston Bachelard's writings on the psychoanalysis of the elements of air, water, fire, and earth as "sacraments of nature," and stated: "These studies have all grown out of the surrealist experiment, which, as early as thirty years ago, sought in objects around us and above all in the found objects to which, on occasions, we become uniquely attached, what André Breton called the 'catalysts of desire': the place where human desire manifests itself, or 'crystallizes.' "[93] References to surrealism multiply and continue into Merleau-Ponty's late writings.[94]

    The Prose of the World takes up the question of dialogue in its chapter titled "Dialogue and the Perception of the Other" and the question of language more generally in the preceding chapter on "The Algorithm and the Mystery of the Other." Both are vitally important to understanding Merleau-Ponty's position regarding intercorporeity, interpersonal understanding, and life with others. In some ways, the chapter structure of *The Prose of the World* is enigmatic, for its movements from painting to literature to scientific and mathematical expression, and for its movement from these written or symbolic forms of signification to speech, as we find it predominantly in the chapter on dialogue. In our reading, we are persistently reminded of the unfinished nature of this work. In spite of these transitions, as we have seen, Merleau-Ponty himself wanted to create, in a projected but never completed Part Three, a philosophy of politics based upon his newly defined ideas on prose and poetry, a "flesh of politics," we would call it, founded upon genuine dialogue. As Breton moved from the found object to shared life and desire, we can look for a flesh of politics in Merleau-Ponty's views on the mystery of language, the nature of true dialogue, and active listening.

    In the chapter on the algorithm in *The Prose of the World*, the mystery of language is the "metamorphosis" speech undergoes "through which words cease to be accessible to our senses and lose their weight, their noise, their lines, their space (to become thoughts)."[95] From the side of thought, it "renounces (to become words) its rapidity or its slowness, its surprise, its invisibility, its time, the internal consciousness we have of it. This is indeed the mystery of language."[96] This two-way, not one-way, exchange between words and thoughts means that when we speak, we do not think of the words we are saying or are being said to us, but comprehend immediately their signification. Merleau-Ponty compares this to shaking another's hand, which is felt not as a bundle of flesh and bone but as "the palpable presence of the other person."[97] This is the "incantation of language."[98] To put it another way, Merleau-Ponty says that "the mystery is that, in the very moment where language is thus obsessed with itself, it is enabled, through a kind of excess, to open us to a signification."[99] Nowhere is this more true than in poetic language, where the poet, obsessed with the words, both their sound and their sense, achieves the lightning of new significations and the poem opens us to an excess of meanings, an incantation of rhythm and light. The same is true, Merleau-Ponty argues, of mathematical integers, geometry, and algorithms even though they possess a purity, Merleau-Ponty argues, that tempts us to assign them a timeless truth and a totality of meaning. Because mathematical expression is equally an exploration of the world as is literary expression, an *event* that *opens* on a truth, "mathematical truth, reduced [brought back] to what we truly establish [*ramenée à ce que nous constatons vraiment*], is not of a different kind"[100] than perceptual truth. It is purer, cleaner, and less cluttered perhaps, yet it is not of a different order. Therefore, "mathematical thought rests upon the sensible but it is creative."[101] The blend of the mathematical imagination with the artistic, poetic imagination means, we might say, that there is a poetry of mathematics.

When Merleau-Ponty spoke of the "mystery of language," he cited Jean Paulhan, which comes as a bit of a surprise since it was he whom Merleau-Ponty had questioned regarding the perfect word, perfect expression discussed above.[102] "Paulhan is the first to have seen that in use speech is not content with designating thoughts the way a street number designates my friend Paul's house. Speech in use really undergoes 'a metamorphosis.'"[103] Merleau-Ponty's notes cite Paulhan's *Les Fleurs de Tarbes* (*The Flowers of Tarbes*) and *Clef de la poésie* (*The Key to Poetry*). The full title of the first is *Les Fleurs de Tarbes ou La Terreur dans les Lettres* (*The Flowers of Tarbes or Terror in Letters*). This work by Paulhan is a consideration of the turning point in French literary history, around the time of the French Revolution and Terror, away from rule-bound imperatives of rhetoric and genre to the gradual abandonment of these rules in Romanticism and its successors, including Surrealism, searching for greater originality of expression. Paulhan names these literary rebels "terror" as a quixotic and somewhat ambiguous provocation. His analysis provides a way of clarifying what Merleau-Ponty meant by the "excess" of signification as part of the miracle of poetic language, namely, that language retains an untamed element, try to tame it as we might, or, equally and paradoxically, try to celebrate it as we might. Merleau-Ponty cites the last page of *The Flowers of Tarbes*: "[T]he signification of language consists in 'rays sensible to him who sees them but hidden from him who watches them,' while language is made of 'gestures which are not accomplished without some negligence.'"[104]

Immediately following in the "Dialogue" chapter, Merleau-Ponty begins by stating a theme he will emphasize throughout the chapter, the "violence" of speech, its transgressions, and its encroachments upon others. To speak, equally to write, is to break in on an other's world, which may be welcome or unwelcome. "We shall completely understand this trespass [*enjambement*] of things upon their meaning, this discontinuity of knowledge which is at its highest point in speech, only when we understand it as the trespass [*empiètement*] of oneself upon the other and of the other upon me."[105] We find this notion of trespass in Merleau-Ponty's writings from the time of the Mexico lectures in 1948 forward, and it is a theme never relinquished. The French word *empiètement* indicates a range of aggressive social interactions, from crowding or invading someone's social space to encroaching upon their rights, such as encroaching upon property rights as damage or theft, or usurping the right to one's own body as in hitting or even biting. In fact, there is a remarkably strong passage in Merleau-Ponty's text that uses this word *biting* to speak of the "bite" of the world and its wound or injury. He describes observing a person sleeping then waking up in the heat of a scorching sun: "If I am forever incapable of effectively living the experience of the scorching the other suffers, the bite of the world [*la morsure du monde*] as I feel it upon my body is an injury [*blessure*] for anyone exposed to it as I am—and especially for this body which begins to defend itself against it."[106] This text expresses a universality of feeling between oneself and another, yet the example and language is very harsh—scorching, bite, wound—and it escalates: "As long as it [the world] adheres to my body like the tunic of Nessus, the world exists not only for me but for everyone in it who makes gestures toward it. There is a universality of feeling."[107] The "tunic of Nessus" is the poisoned shirt that killed Hercules, unwittingly given him by his wife; the shirt burned him so severely he leaped onto his funeral pyre. We can understand Merleau-Ponty's "realism" about human relationships as a remnant of the influence of the philosophy of being-for-others of Sartre in *Being and Nothingness* as conflict, struggle, and wound, and from *Nausea* the image of the drain-hole in which my own being leaks away. Nevertheless, this must be qualified, for Merleau-Ponty rejected the necessary pervasiveness of bad faith in human relations and the inevitability of masochism and sadism as alternating forms of domination.

Yet from these passages we also must note the severe problem of intersubjectivy, sympathy, and empathy that has arisen, a problem that has haunted Western philosophy as the ghost of Descartes's *cogito*. We see that at the beginning of the chapter in these texts, Merleau-Ponty is thinking of intersubjectivity as a movement beginning from the self outward to the other, in which the other person will be made in my own image, we might say. He writes, for example: "The other's body is a kind of replica of myself, a wandering double which haunts my surroundings more than it appears in them. The other's body is the unexpected response I get from elsewhere, as if by a miracle things began to tell my thoughts."[108] There are many passages that confirm such a reading and there is a real philosophical struggle that Merleau-Ponty is undergoing in this text, which I regard as a crucial transitional text, perhaps *the* crucial transitional text, for understanding Merleau-Ponty's philosophy of intersubjectivity and the political. How, Merleau-Ponty asks himself, "How can I decenter myself?"[109]

We get a first inkling of an answer to this "how" and the beginning of an alternative view when Merleau-Ponty combines the egocentric position with a different one. He begins: "Every other is a self like myself. He is like that double which the sick man feels always at his side, who resembles him like a brother."[110] But then comes a glimmer of that decentering for which Merleau-Ponty was searching: "Myself and the other are like two *nearly concentric* circles which can be distinguished only by a mysterious slippage."[111] He adds this decentering and slippage will be inconceivable if our approach to an other is direct, "like a sheer cliff," which mean a one-to-one face-off. In *Corporeal Generosity*, Rosalyn Diprose has commented on the transition and double bind in which Merleau-Ponty finds himself in this chapter: "Upon close scrutiny," she writes, "it is not so clear that for Merleau-Ponty the self as a perceiving body comes before and so dominates the other."[112]

There are two crucial discoveries or experiments, we might call them, that Merleau-Ponty undertakes to get to his "corrected" or mature view of genuine otherness and genuine dialogue. The first is the notion of social fields. Diana Coole has stressed its importance in *Merleau-Ponty and Modern Politics After Anti-Humanism*.[113] Merleau-Ponty writes: "Neither the body of the other nor the objects he regards have ever been pure objects for me. They are internal to my field and to my world, and they are altogether variations of that fundamental relation."[114] And Merleau-Ponty hastens to add: "One field does not exclude another the way an act of absolute consciousness, a decision, for example, excludes another. Rather, a field tends of itself to multiply, because it is the opening through which, as a body, I am 'exposed' to the world."[115] Our body is "non-closed"; it is fundamentally an "openness." Merleau-Ponty made this clear in a rare moment of praise for Cartesianism, in *The Visible and the Invisible* in a Working Note, February 1, 1960, titled

"Human body—Descartes." "The Cartesian idea of the human body as human *non-closed,* open inasmuch as governed by thought—is perhaps the most profound idea of the union of the soul and the body."[116] The open body is the transcendental condition that makes possible the discovery of the social field that is shared and multiplies itself. This social field is comprised of common cultural institutions and, most importantly, a shared language; it is a linguistic field. Here in the "Dialogue" chapter is an early occurrence of the notion of "institution," to which Merleau-Ponty would devote an entire course in 1954–55 titled "Institution in Personal and Public History." There, he would progressively stress "instituting" as a feeling, particularly the feeling of love, then instituting a work of art, then a domain of knowledge, before arriving at "the field of culture." These are the cultural objects and apparatuses we receive from our historicity to which we lend our own accent and style. "Here to receive is to give, in effect, but to give is to receive. [Such is the sense of the] notion of field and institution: they give what they do not have and what we receive from them, we bring to them."[117] The social field, therefore, is a culture of receiving/giving, passivity/activity. *The Prose of the World* names this field an "anonymous corporeality" and stresses our membership in a "common universe of language." Through commonly shared institutions and language, we are able to conceive the self—other relationship "in a much more radical sense,"[118] Merleau-Ponty writes. An arresting passage in *The Visible and the Invisible* truly shows us how radically Merleau-Ponty was rethinking the social field: "I do not perceive any more than I speak— —Perception has me as has language— —And as it is necessary that all the same *I* be there in order to speak, *I* must be there in order to perceive— —But in what sense? As *one* [Fr: *on*]."[119] "One," the French pronoun *on* is the third-person pronoun of passive voice in which there is no specific performer of the action but an anonymous "we": "*ici one parle français*" means "French is spoken here." I would argue this anonymous corporeity is the experience Breton was seeking to express that he named "body *primed*" and we have written as "BretonGiacometti."

The social field of an anonymous corporeity enables Merleau-Ponty's second discovery or experiment in this chapter, and that is the discovery of other persons as genuinely other, as genuinely different and not merely made in my image as sprouts or branches of my life. "If the book really teaches me something, if the other person is really another, at a certain stage I must be surprised, disoriented. If we are to meet not just through what we have in common but in what is different between us—which presupposes a transformation of myself and of the other as well—then our differences can no longer be opaque qualities. They must become meaning."[120] He goes on to make this surprise, disorientation, and transformation more precise: "In the perception of the other, this happens when the other organism, instead of 'behaving' like me, engages with the things in my world in a style that is at first mysterious to me but which at least seems to me a coherent style because it responds to certain possibilities which fringed the things in my world."[121]

Furthermore, such a decentering and slippage of self offers a different account of rationality and irrationality. "Rationality, or the agreement of minds, does not require that we all reach the same idea by the same road, or that significations be enclosed in definitions. It requires only that every experience contain points of catch for all other ideas and the 'ideas' have a configuration. This double requirement is the postulation of a *world*."[122] When Merleau-Ponty says "world" in this context, he means the cultural world, chief among which is our power of speech. The interesting expression, "points of catch" is *points d'amorçage*, which refers to the energizing points or striking points of an electrical arc. The social field is "charged" like an electrical field with positive and negative polarities, which as opposites, yet only together create electrical current. "Field" is a concept that runs throughout Merleau-Ponty's writings from *The Structure of Behavior* throughout *Phenomenology of Perception*, where it is associated with Gestalt theory of perception as a field of vision organized by foreground and background *charged* with value and sense. Things perceived are organized by a tacit set of spatiotemporal horizons against which the things appear and are hidden. In *The Visible and the Invisible*, Merleau-Ponty writes, "[M]y body . . . is a *charged field*."[123] Therefore, a social field is a dynamic arena of interaction between a plurality of agents and structures, always immanent and taken for granted, not available in total either to reflection or an objectified gaze. It is an interplay of agents and forces, and what matters is the lines, dimensions, pivots, hinges, harmonies, frustrations, and oppositions *between* them. In naming these interactions, we are remembering "encroachment" and "trespass," therefore we see their dialectic, both openness and cooperation on the one hand together with frustration and challenge on the other. Diana Coole puts it this way: "In a field of forces, every form is subtended by a plethora of material, temporal and imaginary or virtual relationships that crisscross the social (or the visual). Invisible relationships both situate actors and engender or incite agentic efficacies that are more or less fleeting and ambiguous but always contingent." She adopts the marvelous term *choreography* for this play and interplay in a social field.[124]

The new and revised view of dialogue as a linguistic field within a social field is simply this, in the conclusion of *The Prose of the World*: "Speech concerns us, catches us indirectly [*nous atteint de biais*], seduces us, trails us along, transforms us into the other and him into us, abolishes the limit between mine and not-mine, and ends the alternative between what has sense for me and what is non-sense for me, between me as subject and the other as object."[125] Our relationship with an other is not a relation of two positivities but a relation of "two opennesses" that are charged and together create an attraction, an expectancy. "In reality there is neither me nor the other as positive, positive subjectivities. There are two caverns [*antres* = caverns, lairs, dens, hideouts], two opennesses, two stages where something will take place—and which both belong to the same world, to the stage of Being. . . . They are each the other side of the other. This is why they incorporate one another."[126]

Such a revised and radical view of intersubjectivity and rationality led Merleau-Ponty on to a view of genuine dialogue that would remain with him right into *The Visible and the Invisible* when he wrote of the method of philosophy itself as a kind of listening, auscultation, or palpation in depth.[127] "Palpation" refers to the touch of the parent or physician and "auscultation," based on the Latin verb, *auscultare*, "to listen," means listening to the inside of the body, particularly to the heart and lungs. These terms propose the method of the philosopher as touching and listening to others and the world rather than imposing, dominating, and grasping. In *The Prose of the World*, this is about active listening: "I am not active only when speaking; rather, I *precede* [my emphasis] my thought in the listener. I am not passive while listening; rather I speak according to

> what the other is saying. Speaking is not just my own initiative, listening is not submitting to the initiative of the other, because as speaking subjects we are *continuing*, we are resuming a common effort more ancient than we, upon which we are grafted to one another and which is the manifestation, the growth, of truth.[128]

The word *precede*, which I have emphasized, means the experience of active listening with such focus and fascination—and no doubt long history together, I would add—that we become able to complete one another's sentences, to anticipate the significations.

Genuine dialogue joins us to a cultural world more ancient than we: in my speech and voice, as in yours, are all the voices of all those we have ever known and all those we have never known. In the "Introduction" to

Signs, Merleau-Ponty, again thinking about this anonymous "one" (*on*), wrote: "Things are said and are thought by a Speech and by a Thought which we do not have but which has us. . . . All those we have loved, detested, known, or simply glimpsed speak through our voices."[129] In the last paragraph of the "Dialogue" chapter, Merleau-Ponty asks this remarkable question: "In the end, what should we call this power to which we are vowed, and which, however we feel, pulls significations from us?" "This power to which we are vowed,"[130] what is this power, this charge and magnetism? He answers this way: "Certainly, it is not a god, since its operation depends upon us. It is not an evil genius, since it bears the truth. It is not the 'human condition'—or, if it is 'human,' it is so in the sense that man destroys the generality of the species and brings himself to admit others into his deepest singularity. It is still by calling it speech and spontaneity that we best designate this ambiguous gesture which makes the universal out of singulars and meaning out of our life [*et du sens avec notre vie*]."[131] Merleau-Ponty's expression here ever so close to "the meaning of life," bears an echo of Breton's argument for love and beauty as life's *raison d'être*.[132]

Based on passages such as these in *The Prose of the World*, Fred Dallmayr makes the case for what he calls Merleau-Ponty's "integral pluralism," a way of being and thinking about unity and diversity, of the singular in the universal, that includes Dewey, Gadamer, and Gandhi.[133] As to what all this implies for the practices of a "flesh of politics," as Dallmayr says, "The expressive operation, and speech in particular, establishes a 'common situation' that is not merely a juxtaposition or a relationship of knowing but a 'community of doing.'"[134] And, he adds, the common world fostered by the language of dialogue involves not only sharing ideas and points of view but also a sharing of practices, including unfamiliar practices and customs. This does not lead to any one particular political system or revolutionary politics; rather, the multiple practices of dialogue and openness, revolutionary enough in themselves, indeed, a permanent revolution.

For practical politics, both the politics of everyday life and personal life as well as the politics of the public realm, Merleau-Ponty indicated that what is required is a politics without moralism, but one that also does not collapse into immoralism or nihilism. This position is articulated powerfully both in "The War Has Taken Place" published in *Sense and Nonsense* and "A Note on Machiavilli" published in *Signs*, written in 1945 and 1949, respectively, in the aftermath of war. In these essays, he insisted we grant that the fundamental condition of politics and political virtue is that they unfold in the realm of appearances where there is always an element of contingency, which hides the meaning of history from even the strongest and most intelligent of human beings. Machiavelli, Merleau-Ponty claims—not without controversy, we well know—was the first to form the theory of "collaboration," which is "a relationship of consultation and exchange with others which is not the death but the very act of the self."[135] There is a way of speaking to others that suppresses and essentially enslaves the other person. However, "The prince communicates with others; and others can rally around the decision he makes, because it is in some respects their decision."[136]

Perhaps it was unwitting that Merleau-Ponty incorporated the aesthetic image of the ephemeral play of the "fairyland" to express the nature of communicative collaboration and political truth: "As mirrors set around in a circle transform a slender flame into a fairyland, acts of authority reflected in the constellation of consciousnesses are transfigured, and the reflections of these reflections create an appearance which is the proper place—the truth, in short—of historical action. Power bears a halo about it, and its curse is to fail to see the image of itself it shows to others."[137] Breton had also spoken of mad love as a system of mirrors with a thousand angles of reflection and refraction; a "system of mirrors which reflects for me, under the thousand angles that the unknown can take for me, the faithful image of the one I love."[138] At the end of his Sorbonne lecture on "The Child's Relations with Others," Merleau-Ponty spoke of adult or mature love, and says this: "From the moment when one is joined with someone else, one suffers from her suffering. . . . One is not what he would be without that love, the perspectives remain separate—and yet they overlap. One can no longer say, 'This is mine, this is yours;' the roles cannot be absolutely separated. . . . [Love] tears me away from my lone self and creates instead a mixture of myself and the other."[139]

Dialogue, literature, art, science, and math are the "prose of the world" and dialogue is the "flesh of politics." Together they are the fabric of a "prose of truth," and dialogue is the truth of "mad love." Rather than the ecstasy of carnal love, it is the love created in a kind of friendship that yet dares risk the word *forever*.

Notes

1. John Dewey, "The Ethics of Democracy," in *Pragmatism: A Reader*, ed. Louis Menand (New York: Vintage, 1997), 201. Originally published in *University of Michigan Philosophical Papers* 1: 1888.

2. *S*, 73, orig. 91; *PW*, 85, orig. 120.

3. *SNS*, 5, orig. 10.

4. *S*, 62. orig. 77–78.

5. *S*, 63, orig. 78.

6. Jean-François Lyotard, "Postscript to Terror and the Sublime," in *The Postmodern Explained* (Minneapolis: University of Minnesota Press, 1993), 71. For a discussion of the sublime in Merleau-Ponty in comparison with Lyotard, cf. my article, "The Beautiful and the Sublime in Merleau-Ponty and Lyotard," *Chiasmi International: Trilingual Studies Concerning the Thought of Merleau-Ponty* 10 (2008): 207–26, and with regard to their differences on surrealism and Paul Klee, cf. 211–12. At the time of this article, I was contrasting Merleau-Ponty and Lyotard with regard to surrealist painting and had not yet undertaken the study of surrealist literature and poetry, which this essay undertakes.

7. Lyotard, "Postscript to Terror and the Sublime," 71.

8. *S*, 6, orig. 11.

9. *S*, 5; orig. 10.

10. *S*, 23; orig. 32.

11. Cf. Galen A. Johnson, *The Retrieval of the Beautiful: Thinking Through Merleau- Ponty's Aesthetics* (Evanston: Northwestern University Press, 2010), esp. chapters "Paul Cézanne: On Strong Beauty" and "Paul Klee: Mortal Beauty."

12. Ibid., ch. 8: "Beauty and the Sublime," especially section I: "Kant 1: Contagion and the Beautiful," 210–18.

13. Walter Benjamin, "The Work of Art in the Age of Mechanical Reproduction," in *Illuminations: Essays and Reflections*, ed. Hannah Arendt, trans. Harry Zohn (New York: Schocken, 1968), 141—42. German original published by Suhrkamp Verlag, Frankfurt, 1955.

14. *S*, 309, orig. 386.

15. Cf. Maurice Nadeau, *Histoire de surréalisme* (Paris: Éditions du Seuil, 1945) and André Breton, *Surrealism and Painting*, trans. Simon Watson Taylor (New York: Harper and Row, 1972). French original: *Surréalisme et la peintur* (Paris: Éditions Gallimard, 1965).

16. Cf. Claude Lefort, "Preface," *PW*, xvi, and "Editorial Note," *PW*, xxiv.

17. Maurice Merleau-Ponty, "Le manifeste communiste à cent ans," in *Maurice Merleau-Ponty: Parcours, 1935–1951* (Paris: Éditions Verdier, 1997), 103–108. Originally in *Le Figaro Littéraire*, 3 avril 1948.

18. André Breton, *Mad Love*, trans. Mary Ann Caws (Lincoln: University of Nebraska Press, 1987), 76. French original: *L'Amour fou* (Paris: Éditions Gallimard, 1937).

19. *SB*, 167, orig. 181.

20. Breton, André, "Manifesto of Surrealism (1924)," in *Manifestoes of Surrealism: André Breton*, trans. Richard Seaver and Helen R. Lane (Ann Arbor: The University of Michigan Press, 1969), 14.

21. Ibid., 14, 40, 47.
22. Ibid., 36.
23. Ibid., 26.
24. Cited in Mary Ann Caws, *André Breton*, New York: Twayne, 1971.
25. In *The Structure of Behavior*, as part of his discussion of "surreality," Merleau-Ponty mentions that mescalin intoxication can give animal appearances to objects and "*make* an owl out of a clock without any hallucinatory image whatsoever" (*SB*, 168, orig. 182). The footnote cites "an unpublished observation of J. P. Sartre."
26. Breton served during World War I working with patients suffering from hysteria at the Centre neurologique de la Pitié, in 1917.
27. *S*, 309, orig. 386.
28. Breton, *Mad Love*, sec. I, 8.
29. Ibid.
30. We have only a written summary of Merleau-Ponty's lecture published as "'L'homme et l'objet' ("Man and Object"), an unpublished lecture given by Merleau-Ponty at the Pavillon du Marsan, in introduction to a cycle on "L'objet et poésie" ("The Object and Poetry"), resumé by J. L. Dumas, "Les Conférences," *La Nef*, 5th année, no. 45 (August 1948): 150–51. I express my thanks to Emmanuel de Saint Aubert for a digital copy of this text.
31. Breton, *Mad Love*, sec. I, 11.
32. Ibid.
33. Mary Ann Caws has written regarding convulsive beauty: "As cubism can be thought to be the picturing of an object many times from many angles of repose, and futurism to be the picturing of it in action, surrealism combines the two tendencies." Cf. Mary Ann Caws, *André Breton*, 124.
34. Breton, *Mad Love*, sec. I, 19. Cf. José Pierre, "'Such is Beauty': The 'Convulsive' in Breton's Ethics and Aesthetics," in *André Breton Today*, ed. Anna Balakian and Rudolf E. Kuenzli (New York: Willis Locker and Owens, 1989), 19–27.
35. Breton, *Mad Love*, sec. 5, 87–88.
36. Ibid., 88–89.
37. *PP*, 156, orig. 180.
38. *S*, 229, orig. 290.
39. *VI*, 249, orig. 297.
40. Breton, *Mad Love*, sec. 6, 99.
41. Ibid., sec. 5, 93.
42. Ibid., sec. 7, 129/111.
43. Ibid., 112.
44. Ibid., 119.
45. Ibid., 137/119.
46. Ibid., 114.
47. Ibid., 115–16.
48. *AD*, 7, orig. 14–15.

49. *S*, 233, orig. 296.
50. *AD*, 7, orig. 14–15.
51. Breton, *Mad Love*, sec. 7, 116–17.
52. Ibid., sec. 5, 89.
53. Ibid., 76–77.
54. Ibid., 79.
55. Cf. André Breton, *Surrealism and Painting*, 11, regarding Braque. Cited by Mary Ann Caws in *André Breton*, xii.
56. *AD*, 205, orig. 300.
57. *VI*, 243, orig. 296.
58. *AD*, 207, orig. 303.
59. Ibid.
60. Breton, *Manifesto of Surrealism 1924*, 47.
61. Walter Benjamin, "Surrealism," in *Reflections: Essays, Aphorisms, Autobiographical Writings* (New York: Schocken, 1978), 179.
62. Ibid., 190.
63. Ibid., 189.
64. Ibid.
65. Ackbar Abbas, "On Fascination: Walter Benjamin's Images," *New German Critique* 48 (1989): 53.
66. Benjamin, "Surrealism," 192.
67. Ibid., 34.
68. Ibid., 23.
69. *S*, 233, orig. 295–96.
70. Cf. Emmanuel de Saint Aubert, "A Poetics of Co-naissance via André Breton, Paul Claudel, and Claude Simon," forthcoming in *Merleau-Ponty's Poets and Poetics* (New York: Fordham University Press).
71. *S*, 233, orig. 295.
72. *OE*, 15/*PrP*, 123.
73. Breton, *Manifesto of Surrealism 1924*, 17.
74. *PW*, 6, orig. 11.
75. Breton, *Manifesto of Surrealism 1924*, 34.
76. Ibid., 35.
77. Breton, *Mad Love*, sec. 3, 34.
78. Ibid., sec. 3, 33.
79. Caws, *André Breton*, 126, n. 3.
80. Breton, *Mad Love*, sec. 3, 32.
81. Ibid., 34.
82. Ibid., 32.
83. Ibid., 32–33.
84. Ibid., 34.
85. Ibid., 34–35.

86. Ibid., 35.
87. Ibid., 56–57.
88. Breton interpreted the paintings of Cézanne in terms of their "aura," and comments particularly on the painting titled *The House of the Hanged Man*. "Here, I open a parenthesis to declare that contrary to the current interpretation, I think Cézanne is not above all a painter of apples, but the painter of *The House of the Hanged Man*. I insist that the technical preoccupations, which everyone starts to talk about as soon as it is a question of Cézanne, make us too systematically forget the concern he showed, on several occasions, to treat these subjects having an *aura*. . . . I willingly admit that, because of his particular aptitude to perceive these auras and to concentrate his attention on them, Cézanne was led to study them in their immediacy, considering them in their most elementary structure. Such an aura exists, just as well, around an apple, even if it is only constituted by the desire it might arouse to eat it." Ibid., sec. 6, 105–107. What Breton means here by an aura would become a topic and paper in its own right. For Breton, "aura" comes down to "relations of light". . . . in order to pinpoint it, we might think it better to stand hypnotized before an Iceland spar than to take immediate account of a mirage." Ibid., 107. I take it we are considerable distance away from Benjamin's meaning of the loss of "aura" in cinema.
89. Ibid., sec. 1, 16/15.
90. Merleau-Ponty, "Man and Object," 151.
91. I express my thanks to Kerry Whiteside for sharing his transcription of the Mexico lectures, included in the list of titles in his table of contents of the early unpublished writings found in *Merleau-Ponty and the Foundation of an Existential Politics* (Princeton: Princeton University Press, 19880, 312–14. In the abbreviation system for the Merleau-Ponty *inédits* established by Emmanuel de Saint Aubert, this particular citation is from the second Mexico lecture: Mexico II, [158] (44).
92. Breton, *Mad Love*, sec. 1, 10.
93. *WP*, 65–66, *C*, 31.
94. Cf, references to Max Ernst and Rimbaud in *Eye and Mind* (*OE*, 128–29, *PrP*, 30–31), the lectures on *Nature* with regard to Schelling's concept of an *Erste Nature* or *Übersein* ("Over-Being") (*N*, 38/62), and *La Philosophie aujourd'hui* ("Philosophy Today"), Course of 1958–59, regarding Rimbaud and Breton (*NC*, 47–48).
95. *PW*, 116, orig. 162–63.
96. *PW*, 163/116.
97. *PW*, 116, orig. 162.
98. Ibid.
99. *PW*, 115, orig. 162.
100. *PW*, 123, orig. 173.
101. *PW*, 126, orig. 177.
102. *PW*, 6, orig. 11.
103. *PW*, 116, orig. 162.

104. Ibid. Cf. Jean Paulhan, *Les Fleurs de Tarbes ou la terreur dans les lettres* (Paris: Éditions Gallimard NRF, 1941), 168. English translation, 94.

105. *PW*, 133, orig. 185.

106. *PW*, 137, orig. 190–91.

107. Ibid.

108. *PW*, 134, orig. 186.

109. *PW*, 135, orig. 188.

110. *PW*, 134, orig. 186.

111. Ibid.

112. Rosalyn Diprose, *Corporeal Generosity: On Giving with Nietzsche, Merleau-Ponty, and Levinas* (Albany: State University of New York Press, 2002), 182.

113. Diana Coole, *Merleau-Ponty and Modern Politics after Anti-Humanism* (New York: Rowman and Littlefield, 2007), ch. 8, 233–55. By stressing the concept of the social field in Merleau-Ponty's political thought, she seeks to bring it together with Foucault's genealogies of power.

114. *PW*, 137–38, orig. 191.

115. Ibid.

116. *VI*, 234, orig. 288.

117. *IP*, 60, orig. 101.

118. *PW*, 140, orig. 194–95.

119. *VI*, 190, orig. 244.

120. *PW*, 142, orig. 197–98.

121. Ibid.

122. *PW*, 143, orig. 198–99.

123. *VI*, 264, orig. 318.

124. Coole, *Merleau-Ponty and Modern Politics after Anti-Humanism*, 238, 239. For a discussion of the meaning of "force" articulated by Judith Butler in relation to Hegel and Nietzsche, cf. 233.

125. *PW*, 145, orig. 202.

126. *VI*, 263, orig. 317.

127. *VI*, 128, orig. 170.

128. *PW*, 143–44, orig. 200.

129. *S*, 19, orig. 27.

130. Cf. Scott Marrato, " 'This Power to Which We are Vowed:' Subjectivity and Expression in Merleau-Ponty," in *Time, Memory, Institution: Merleau-Ponty's New Ontology of Self*, ed. David Morris and Kym Maclaren (Athens, OH: Ohio University Press, 2015), 160–79.

131. *PW*, 146, orig. 203.

132. Breton, *Mad Love*, sec. 7, 116–17.

133. Fred Dallmayr, *Integral Pluralism: Beyond the Culture Wars* (Lexington: University of Kentucky Press, 2010), Chapter 6: "Hermeneutics and Cross-Cultural Encounters, Integral Pluralism in Action," esp. 118–22.

134. Ibid., 121–22.
135. *S*, 215, orig. 271.
136. Ibid.
137. *S*, 216, orig. 273.
138. Breton, *Mad Love*, sec. 5, 93.
139. Maurice Merleau-Ponty, "The Child's Relations with Others," in *The Merleau-Ponty Reader*, ed. Ted Toadvine and Leonard Lawlor (Evanston: Northwestern University Press, 2007), 182. Also cf. *CPP*, 260, orig. 228.

Institution and Critique of the Museum in "Indirect Language and the Voices of Silence"

Rajiv Kaushik

One could argue that the theme of expression indicated by style is key to Merleau-Ponty's oeuvre. All the various philosophical problems that occupy his work, from the late 1930s to 1961 in *The Visible and the Invisible*, can coalesce around what he eventually calls "the paradox of expression"[1] in which every act of expression is ultimately chiasmatic with some capaciousness that it does not fully express and that exceeds its activity. In his engagement with Malraux in "Indirect Language and the Voices of Silence," this paradox particularly concerns the chiasm between expression and its muteness or the mute arts, and also between the execution of a specific style and its place in history. Another fundamental motive for Merleau-Ponty to adopt and recalibrate Malraux's notion of style here is thus also to avoid "the historical" in Hegel's sense.[2] To understand the standpoint Merleau-Ponty stakes out, it is important to note that, in a crucial passage of "Indirect Language and the Voices of Silence," he says that the movement of history is just a movement between articulated styles, each referring more basically to what he calls institution (*Stiftung*). He refers to institution in "Indirect Language and the Voices of Silence" in the following oft-quoted passage:

> It is always only a question of advancing the line of the already opened furrow and of recapturing and generalizing an accent which has already appeared in the corner of a previous painting

or in some instant of his experience, without the painter himself ever being able to say (since the distinction has no meaning) what comes from him and what comes from things, what the new work adds to the old ones, or what it has taken from the others and what is its own. This triple resumption which makes a sort of provisory eternity of the operation of expression is not simply a metamorphosis in the fairytale sense of miracle, magic, and absolute creation in an aggressive solitude. It is a response to what the world, the past, and the completed works demanded. It is accomplishment and brotherhood. Husserl has used the fine word *Stiftung*—foundation or establishment—to designate first of all the unlimited fecundity of each present which, precisely because it is singular and passes, can never stop having been and thus being universally; but above all to designate that fecundity of the products of a culture which continue to have value after their appearance and which open a field of investigations in which they perpetually come to life again. It is thus that the world as soon as he has seen it, his first attempts at painting, and the whole past of painting all deliver up a *tradition* to the painter—*that is*, Husserl remarks, *the power to forget origins* and to give to the past not a survival, which the hypocritical form of forgetfulness, but a new life, which is the noble form of memory.[3]

Merleau-Ponty's usage of institution means to get underneath this retroactive point of view and see the articulation of a style from within the arising of what institutes it. To the extent that both Hegel's and Malraux's positions on history and subjectivity are parasitic on and ignorant of precisely this primal-institution, Merleau-Ponty's critique of style in terms of institution refers to a "crisis" in the Husserlian sense of being blind to the very grounds that gives one's position meaningful sustenance. Referring to institution, Merleau-Ponty describes Husserl's *Crisis* in his 1958 *Philosophy Today* lectures in the following way:

> [T]he transcendental is no longer immanent consciousness of constituting *Auffassungen* [opinions]. This would be what he calls in the *Vienna Conference* "*einseitige Rationalität*" [unilateral rationality]—there is, furthermore, for example, history which

functions in us, not processes, chains of visible events, but intentional or "vertical" history with *Stiftungen* [institutions], forgetting which is tradition, reprisals [*reprises*], interiority in exteriority—*Ineinander* of the present in the past. As long as we have not recovered this transcendental, rationality is in crisis.[4]

Here, institution has a double sense of the instituted/instituting—it is both that which *has been instituted* and that which *does the instituting or institutes*. It refers to institution in the ordinary sense of an assemblage of traditional values and practices that coalesces a meaning we take to be exterior from us. It also, and more profoundly, refers to an event whereby we take this exterior assemblage of meaning to be our own, interior to us, and thus in fact reciprocally allow it to be the assemblage of tradition and value we take it for. Only in this way do traditions and values and their institutions appear as inevitabilities—as a supervenient foundation, truth, ideality, or fixed norm. They do so on the basis of some more profound event—which is not essentially different from our interiority—that inaugurates and give them their look of fixity. Here, we can speak about institution as *instituting*, a ground that for its part lacks fixity and definiteness. Merleau-Ponty might say that, at this level, any idea of ground could only express the idea of "trudging in a circle," a condition that never really reaches an end nor is itself an end because it itself is contained by the movement of an instituted expression without being reduced merely to what is already instituted or to having been instituted.

This lack of foundationalism may be phenomenologically borne out: when words surge up within me and I speak, this event of expression is never—can never be—transparent; like all expressions, my speech stands in need of clarification or can be further elaborated, but clarification and elaboration are always possible only as the basis of a meaning that was hitherto unseen, unnoticed, or invisible in the first act. It is only retroactively that this unexplicated meaning may be posited as having the transcendental character of being deducible or axiomatic—something that all along I was trying to say. To undercut this transcendental view, however, Merleau-Ponty's institution dispels its presumptive myth, that of a reason to which any previously unexplicated meaning could suddenly lose its opacity and instead become transparent and immediately available. His phenomenology was always one of ambiguity, and, as long as the ambiguity of the unexpressed is forgotten and ignored as such, reason will be in crisis, ignorant of what makes it possible and deeply inhumane. But let us also be clear that Merleau-Ponty's notion of institution not only indicates the paradox of expression at work in every single articulated style of the artist; because it does this, it also undercuts the very notion of a museum as an institute. Ignoring the ambiguity of every act of expression, the museum is as much in a state of crisis as reason itself: it remains insensitive to the contexts of sense that initially motivated the works it contains; it remains disentangled from the very community and history it purports to congeal; and it stops from exposing the existential significance of its works, becoming just like an esoteric, abstract system of generating propositions. All of this implies that the museum will always, without a deeper sense of institution, remain ignorant of the basic ambiguity and plurality of alternative meanings available to it, so that, if ever they are presented, they are only so revealed as a threat to its already established norms.

Yet the space of *dissensus* is the space of the political. Neither the hegemonic character of the museum nor its alienation from the concrete acts of creation can be ignored in Merleau-Ponty's account. This leads us to think that Merleau-Ponty's project in "Indirect Language and the Voices of Silence" is eminently dialectical, and suggests that the effects of national ideals expressed by the museum-institute can and ought to be undone. Though the museum-institute at least implicitly bears the themes of hegemony and alienation for Merleau-Ponty, its deeper circular structure forces us to call into question dialectic itself. One of the points of his essay is that it is ultimately only from within the structure of dialectic that the problem of the museum has so far been thought. We have either history in Hegel's sense or the ahistorical in Malraux's sense of subjectivity and radical creativity. With a view toward getting at institution in the deep sense, Merleau-Ponty would rather place under critical regard the very structure of this tension. This requires him to plunge more profoundly into the trajectory of Western philosophy toward dialectic. Since he first sees it necessary to collapse and dismantle this philosophy from within, Merleau-Ponty's project may be linked to Hegel while also complicating Hegelian critique. In fact, it could be argued, this is precisely what for Merleau-Ponty the phenomenological discovery of institution does, and is the only way of averting the crisis of the philosophy of history to which the museum adheres. To place under critical regard the very structure of the problem of the museum is also to place under critical regard the very structure of philosophizing itself.

Institution and the Critique of Philosophical Spectation

Hegel famously describes Greek philosophy as a phase in "immediacy"—that between which nothing intervenes—that, consequently, has not yet thematized any notion of the subject to whom objects appear. Such a philosophy thus remains "unreflective," and not until Descartes does it first reach solid ground with the initial thematic moment of the cogito. Merleau-Ponty's project begins as a deeply anti-Cartesian project aiming to show that the reflexive subject is never truly transparent to itself and so never really can fully *comprehend* itself as the ground of appearings. Indeed, for Merleau-Ponty, there is nothing like a happy consciousness, since the supposed first moment of intervention in immediacy, when subjectivity becomes thematized or comprehensible to itself, always includes something of which it is unreflective, and so something always possibly further intervening even on it.

Nestled in the heart of reflection is something unclear, and a suspension of certainty to any philosophical position is required, including any position that demands speculative reconciliation. Merleau-Ponty's phenomenology is instead linked to immanental philosophy only to show how reflection is always due to some excess of it already having transpired—to show how reflection betrays an incapacity to master that upon which it reflects. True to this, an ontology for Merleau-Ponty must be a concrete rather than happy one. It must concern being without the assumption of its fullness or transparency to thought, a being that is always farther, in constant displacement, and where what is displaced always slips out from underneath reflection. In *The Visible and the Invisible*, Merleau-Ponty famously describes his ontology as one of divergencies (*écart*), and instead of providing a principle that functions as a unifying or foundational principle, ontology is finally to be understood variously in terms of separation, spread, deviation, gap, etc.—a distance from and even within reflection without which reflection would in fact be impossible. This distance is not itself something positive, in other words, but something that only comes to be in terms of any explicit expression precisely as its latency. This is in fact a distance that has proximity. It is thus neither a deducible a priori nor an external limit of things; being is at work in every expression as the interruption of its lucidity. Rather than a full presence that absorbs differences into it, finally, Merleau-Ponty's account of being instead has a history and a future—it is always differential, having a time and place and is not until then predictable or deducible. Its predictability or deducibility is never its affirmation.

It is here that Merleau-Ponty's phenomenology merges with artworks, engaged in the same project of making us witness to this very interruption, the point at which the sensible field opens up and is formalized—made predictable—even though it itself resists formalization. Merleau-Ponty makes this point another way in "Indirect Language and the Voices of Silence," when he says, succinctly, "There is no painting before painting."[5] In other words, painting, which has its own set of formal rules and techniques, is self-constitutive, spontaneous, and so apparently structurally unencumbered. Yet precisely because it is self-constitutive, Merleau-Ponty would point out that it is also the development of a set of formal rules—a revelation that its form is constantly in development, historical, in the hazards of something instead of just pure and autonomous experimentation. To see *what* this form is developing, though, requires that we pay attention once again to what Merleau-Ponty means by "style." The term *style* may very well refer to a formal act, but it is one that is so only by virtue of its differentiation from other similar and formal acts. In this sense, style emerges by way of some hypercritical stance it must take with respect to itself and its separation from other styles; it is new in the sense that it places itself on the horizon of previous similar acts and futural ones. Its newness is thus genealogical in the sense that, if it is so, it is not at all conscious of being so. In fact, I suggest that "no painting before painting" is a phrase about a contingency of the art form highlighted precisely when a new style articulates itself while being unconscious of its newness. I would go so far as to say, in fact, that, rather than an inevitability or deducibility, the form of the artist's style is impossible without the materiality we would normally call its "content." I believe Nancy echoes this point when he writes that the intelligibility of a drawn line, "is nothing other than a more demanding, more intense grasp of sensible propriety itself . . . the point or moment of interruption of the movement and opening up of sense," and that "[m]atter—to recall word that remains inseparable from 'form'—is the name of the form's resistance to its deformation. It is not a formless 'content' that form comes to mold or model but rather the thickness, texture, and force of form itself."[6] There is the need to explicate the arising of formal structures and say how they do not dispense with but arise from their media—in Merleau-Ponty's terms, how their formal intelligibility is a kind of foreground to the sensible field, a way of grasping that field alongside and in the middle of other ways—so that intelligibility is no longer the privileged and direct way of accessing form.

According to Merleau-Ponty, for this reason the project of art is deeply philosophical, more than philosophy itself, since it exposes philosophy to its own formal limitations. It does this without revealing itself just as its "external limit" to philosophy precisely so that, in the face of works of art, the very "object" of philosophy has to change. Thus, Merleau-Ponty writes in "Eye and Mind":

> What is depth, what is light, *ti to on*? What are they—not for the mind that cuts itself off from the body but for the mind Descartes says is suffused throughout the body? What are they, finally, not for the mind but for themselves, since they pass through us and surround us? Yet this philosophy still to be done is that which animates the painter—not when he expresses his opinions about the world but in that instant when his vision becomes gesture, when, in Cézanne's words, he "thinks in painting."[7]

To think *in* painting, rather than *about* it, is precisely to be at the intersection with the opening up of sense. It is furthermore to concede that this opening poses a difficulty for any particular expression to ever be in full possession of itself. Rather, expression is ongoing or always farther on, always needing to find ways to make explicit what does not get expressed by the expression. To think *in* painting is in this way the development of a practice that likewise develops a way of expressing and also exhibits *this way*. I think we can bear witness to the same dynamic when we consider light, which Merleau-Ponty also mentions here. The activities of applying paint matter are inevitably bound and subservient to the drying characteristics of different colors of pigment and hence to a chromatic exposure to light; and this exposure is also itself put on display. This really is a most profound sense of reversibility: ordinarily, we think that light is shed on things, allowing them to turn up and to be visible, but the act of applying paint matter has also found a way to allow this light itself to turn up. *It lets show how everything appears.*

Here we must be careful to stress again that, for Merleau-Ponty, there is no way to directly see that which lets everything appear. It is simply that we are constantly asked by works of art to inspect how we are being made to see, and it does not follow—in fact, this is precisely what is prevented—that our vision is the certain and straightforward one, the only vision. There is no way for vision to end where it begins and close its loop, and no way for it to foreclose its alternatives and render it unambiguous or transparent and without darkness. Instead, we are being made to accommodate our vision "according to, or with,"[8] as Merleau-Ponty writes in "Eye and Mind" about the cave paintings of Lascaux. In his excellent book, *The Flesh of Images:*

Merleau-Ponty between Painting and Cinema, Carbone explains describes this seeing "according to, or with":

> Merleau-Ponty goes so far as to call this seeing farther "*voyance,*" explaining that this "*voyance*" "renders present to us what is absent." Beware, though: the *voyance* consists in seeing "farther than one sees," in showing us the invisible as "the outline and the depth of the visible." Precisely for this reason, the *voyance* "renders present to us what is absent" not simply by *presentifying it,* but rather in *creating it* as a particular presence which, as such, had never been present before. In my opinion, what Merleau-Ponty also calls "quasi-presence" should be understood in this way. That is to say, not as a weakened presence, but rather as "the pregnancy of the invisible in the visible," as an effective and insisting "latency"; in short, as the "flesh of the imaginary." In fact, this happens because seeing "farther than one sees" is seeing "according to, or with" what one sees.[9]

It is more appropriate for my vision to depend on a newly opened or configured space that could not have been present before my vision and yet is not reducible to what I see. To take this point seriously, we would have to admit that in the depths of what I see there is nothing denoted. Furthermore, this lack of denotation pertains to both my looking and the things that I look at. Rather than some privileged access to a being that has always been, we may say with Merleau-Ponty that vision is "farther than one sees,"[10] where both my looking and the things that I see are not exactly identical with themselves and each proceeds downward into some aphotic depth. I will come back more directly to this point at the end of this chapter when speaking about the newly erupted *voyance* and understanding it as a nondialectical vision. Now, following Carbone's insights and placing them in terms of Merleau-Ponty's critique of the museum, one could say that in the latter we have an articulation of vision that interrogates the museum as well as its static version of seeing, and maybe even a way to resist any sort of idealism of museological spaces and the spaces from which we look. This space is itself configured by the work, and *this very way of configuration* may always be sudden and new. The question should arise as to whether there are curatorial methods adequate to the task of elaborating exactly this alternative feature of vision, allowing us to bear witness to this seeing "according to, or with," the fact that we are being made to see in a specific way.

Merleau-Ponty and New Curation

In her 1990 article "The Cultural Logic of the Late Capitalist Museum," Rosalind Krauss argued that encounters with artworks had been subordinated to their containers, the museums that hold them.[11] Taking her cues from Fredric Jameson's logic of late capitalism, for Krauss this subordination meant that spaces of exhibition were no longer organized around or even made with the exhibited works in mind. It meant, in other words, the suppression of the specificities and materiality of these works. The effect, for her, was that museums now traded in *dis*-embodiment, *de*-contextualization, *dis*-placement, etc., and this was all for the sake of the unencumbered flow of global capital. Against this same backdrop, there emerged a curatorial criticism in the 1990s that aimed at giving critical precedence to the curator and the curated space of exhibitions over art objects.[12] Such analysis was of the so-called curatorial gesture in which curation itself provided a nexus for discussion, critique, and debate. The understanding was that the activity of exhibiting artworks was a unique and autonomous form of investment.[13] One can wonder how much this way of conceiving the space of exhibition has had to do with the last decades' explosion of museological scale, designed by so-called starchitects, making them tourist destinations themselves. People seem to want to publicize that they've been in these spaces too. There is plenty of debate as to whether or not a "selfie" should be allowed in museum spaces. Never mind that, at least at the time of writing this, a museum in Manila called *Art in Island* is entirely made up of three-dimensional reproductions of famous paintings that one can touch or step inside, with the sole purpose of unhindered self-portrait opportunities.

What has happened to the idea that the work of art configures and interrogates how we see, that we see according to it, that it puts on display and calls into question its space or the spaces from which we look? Consider how appropriate Merleau-Ponty's critique of the museum is still today:

> The Museum gives us a thieves' conscience. We occasionally sense that these works were not after all intended to *end up* between these morose walls, for the pleasure of Sunday strollers or Monday "intellectuals." We are well aware that something has been lost and that this self-communion with the dead is not the true milieu of art—that so many joys and sorrows, so much anger, and so many labors were not *destined* to reflect one day the Museum's mournful light.[14]

He even says that the museum

> is the historicity of death. And there is a historicity of life of which the Museum provides no more than a fallen image. This is the historicity which lives in the painter at work when with a single gesture he links the tradition that he recaptures and the tradition that he founds. It is the historicity which in one stroke welds him to all which has ever been painted in the world, without his having to leave his place, his time, or his blessed or accursed labor. The historicity of life reconciles paintings insofar as each one expresses the whole of existence—insofar as they are all successful—instead of reconciling them insofar as they are all finished and like so many futile gestures.[15]

One notices here again the demands of Merleau-Ponty's project, to take back from the museum and its official sense of art history the concrete activities of an artist's work—to return to the event of the development of her own style. Re-emancipating these acts, putting them on display from the perspective of their execution—this would be a properly antihegemonic museology because we would get to bear witness to the concrete situations of art works and the opportunities these situations have to proliferate in meaning for a population or over time.

Merleau-Ponty does not himself speak about specific curatorial techniques that would do justice to the "history of life" he describes. Yet I think, given the way I have explicated his stance this far, one can notice in the current literature on "the contemporary" a real connection at least to Merleau-Ponty's concerns, if not to his methodology. For instance, in her recent book *Radical Museology*, Claire Bishop describes three contemporary art museums—the Van Abbemuseum in Eindhoven, the Museo Nacional Centre do Arte Reina Sofia in Madrid, and Muzej sodobne umetnosti Metelkova in Ljublana—which, according to her, are doing the individual work of reversing the misfortune that's befallen artworks at the hands of their museums, calling into question the latter's role either as nationalistic monuments and forces of hegemony or "to disrupt the relativist pluralism of the current moment, in which all styles and beliefs are considered equally valid."[16] "Rather than simply claim that many or all times are present in each historical object," they "ask *why* certain temporalities appear in particular works of art at *specific* historical moments."[17] Their aim, then, is to develop a contemporaneity that has to do with the way in which a value is staked out and made evident. They ask how artworks express and are established by certain historical values, and furthermore, how and in what conditions these same works might express other values in other times. Hence, the contemporary under consideration in *Radical Museology* "does not designate a style or period of the works themselves so much as an *approach* to them."[18] Notice that the term *approach* here does not exclude Merleau-Ponty's specific use of the word *style*: because this approach would rather see artworks as bearing a tendency to articulate itself in different epochs, it "requires us to think in several tenses simultaneously: the past perfect and the future anterior."[19] Bishop calls this a "dialectical contemporaneity," and describes it as a "non-presentist, multi-temporal contemporaneity."[20]

Much of Bishop's aim is to show a new notion of the contemporary that undermines the Eurocentricity of a museology in which Western Europe is the marker for all other historical periods of art and art forms. Take, for example, one of her primary examples, the Reina Sofia: "The starting point for this museum," she argues, is "*multiple modernities.*"[21] Indeed, the initial difficulty of curating the contemporary is to note that our time is split up. It is Agamben who seems to best describe for Bishop this aspect contemporaneity when he writes that "contemporariness *is that relationship with time that adheres to its past through a disjunction and an anachronism,*" and thus one can view one's own time only as a "dyschrony." As such, contemporaneity is marked by a certain "darkness" or impossibility of unity.[22]

Curating the contemporary, Bishop notes in reference to the Reina Sofia, means giving a special place to an art form such as performance that is "no longer conceived in terms of avant-garde originals and peripheral derivatives, since this always prioritizes the European center."[23] Instead, as she says in *Artificial Hells: Participatory Art and the Politics of Spectatorship*, performance art

> formally aims . . . to challenge traditional artistic criteria by reconfiguring everyday actions as performance; to give visibility to certain social constituencies and render them more complex, immediate and physically present; to introduce aesthetic effects of chance and risk; to problematize the binaries of live and mediated, spontaneous and staged, authentic and contrived; to examine the construction of collective identity and the extent to which people always exceed these categories.[24]

This last formal feature, to display an excess of categorial distinctions, would seem to subsume the other features. It would be the most general formal feature under which the everyday is reconfigured, the marginal made visible, chance and risk are turned into aesthetic features. If curating performance were noteworthy, furthermore, it would be because it critiques these categories and troubles them as essential or decisive. This might be precarious, since, for example, giving visibility to otherwise invisible social constituents might also mean making use of invisibility itself. A performance, as Bishop says in another context might, "reify *precisely in order to discuss reification*, or . . . exploit *precisely to thematise exploitation itself*," and so each category is constantly critiqued even as it is being used.[25]

But, then, the very act of exhibiting these formally distinct artworks means at another level calling into question the very exhibiting institution itself, and so in *Radical Museology*, for instance, Bishop is interested in the Reina Sofía's handling of the archive of the Chilean performance art group CADA (Colectivo Acciones de Arte, 1979–1985); the museum ensures that CADA has a place in an institution in Chile in exchange for a copy of an archive of their work for itself.[26] The aim for the Reina Sofía, she points out, is to reconceive itself as "an *archive of the commons,* a collection available to everyone because culture is not a question of national property, but a universal resource," and "rather than being perceived as hoarded treasure, the work of art would be mobilized as a 'relational object' (to use Lygia Clark's phrase) with the aim of liberating its user psychologically, physically, socially, and politically."[27] In her summative comments, she asks, "Can a museum be anti-hegemonic?" and suggests that, with the employment of different curatorial methodologies, "by juxtaposing texts, cartoons, prints, photographs, works of art, artifacts, and architecture in poetic constellations," the three contemporary museums in *Radical Museology* ultimately propose "a spectator no longer focused on the auratic contemplation of individual works, but one who is aware of being presented with augments and positions to read or contest." In doing so, they "defetishize objects by continually juxtaposing works of art with documentary materials, copies and reconstructions. The contemporary becomes less a question of periodization or discourse than a *method* or practice, potentially applicable to all historical periods."[28] Its aim is to point to new techniques that undermine a form of curation that is uncritical with respect to its own normative and political entrenchments, and is so because it does not understand itself to be shaped in any way by artworks themselves.

How should we understand this "shaping"? The problem with Bishop's radical museology, it seems to me, is that she provides no framework to account for its dialectical nature. She has referred to the Brazilian artist Lygia Clark and the notion of a "relational object," which was radically concerned with the interpositionality between art, body, and societal norms. In *Artificial Hells: Participatory Art and the Politics of Spectatorship*, she also contrasted her position with the "relational aesthetic" one outlined by Nicolas Bourriaud. The latter would account for a dialectic in terms of what he calls the "materialistic tradition," and the idea of a "materialism of encounter, or random materialism."[29] Escaping Hegel's historical system and his enigmatic statement that it marks "the end of art," Bourriaud writes that this materialism of encounter or random materialism instead

> [t]akes as its point of departure the world of contingency, which has no pre-existing origin or sense, nor Reason, which might allot it a purpose. So, the essence of humankind is purely trans-individual, made up of bonds that link individuals together in social forms which are invariably historical (Marx: the human essence is the set of social relations). There is no such thing as any possible "end of history" or "end of art," because the game is being forever re-enacted, in relation to its function, in other words, in relation to the players and the system which they construct and criticize.[30]

For a relational aesthetics, then, there really is no necessary need for a fixed art object, and the revelation of aesthetic value instead arises only dialectically, from a host of other kinds of relations and values.[31] One can point out a deeper problem of explanation that pertains to both the radical museology and relational aesthetics. To refuse the notion of an "end of art" or "end of history" is supposedly to refuse to appeal to a supervenient explanation apart from the contingency of human bonds—a condition of their possibility that is not inherent to them. But what if, following Merleau-Ponty, a complete and transparent end or intention of art is impossible to begin with? Why should we have to negate such a position unless we accept it as a possibility from the start? It is impossible to deny that there is an "end of art"—or impossible to say that there is "no end of art"—unless we also assume the transparent end or intention *as that which is to be denied*. This logic leads to problematic consequences; we might very well find that *using* categories in performance art such as reification and exploitation is unsettling exactly because they aestheticize and further justify them and never get us away from Krauss's criticism of the museological space to begin with.

It is precisely this logic, though, that Merleau-Ponty's formulation of institution undermines. What he initially said with respect to the history of the philosophy of reflection as described by Hegel he can also say with respect to art: if art for Hegel only ever functions to overcome itself, it is also never on the way to anything greater than itself. There is no happy consciousness of art, and the very *acceptance* of an "end of art"—an intention, or a moment where it becomes clear to us what it is and what it is for—is premised on a basic and hidden fact of art, which forces us to be oriented to it a certain way or makes us think about it in a certain way. In other words, instead of subjecting contingency to abstract and unaccounted-for notions, institution is instead about interrogating contingency from within it once and for all. In doing so, institution in fact counters the positions of Bishop, Bourriaud, Malraux, and, above all, Hegel. I would submit that it alone gives us the ontology adequate to the demands of a properly radical museology that exposes an event—nonintentional, incoherent, and especially concrete or multiplicitous—which nevertheless forces us to try and make it otherwise.

To return to Carbone's point about *voyance*: the brute and eventful fact of artwork is really the "farther than one sees," or "the outline and the depth of the visible." It is in fact the means or configuration by which things appear. This configuration does not happen at the level of sense-vision but rather in advance of vision by an event that is not there, in fact never was there, to be seen. This implies that sight can stand on the thither side of itself, that it can be distant from itself, and that it contains an obscurity, insensibility, or what Merleau-Ponty calls its "blind-spot."[32] This obscure, insensible, and blind spot is both the weakness and strength of vision: it is its weakness because it can never be undone, and so speaks to a dyschrony that prevents vision from exceeding itself and transitioning into an objective view that is certain and straightforward; and it is its strength because it is also precisely the spot at which vision is being made to see the things that it sees and the manner in which those things are apprehended. Because of exactly this tension, because what makes the visible possible is not itself visible, it is also possible that we could at any time be forced to turn our attention to the alienness within our sight, to the ways in which are being made to see. Now, although exactly as its marginalia, such witnessing would also always opened up to its alternatives, to other ways of seeing and being, without taking this to be the collapse of our present sight.

Merleau-Ponty's critique of the museum is ultimately in the service of exposing exactly this moment of vision, and it is thus a proposition for other museological techniques that aim to undermine the philosophical sense of spectation. Another way to say this, it seems to me, is that Merleau-Ponty's critique of the museum serves to expose the possibility of alternative discourses and histories without flattening them out and grasping them merely in terms of the present discourse and history. If we say with Merleau-Ponty that we see "according to, or with" the artwork, this is because the artwork calls into question the very place in which it is seen, and this place is not apart or somehow opposed to the other possible interpretations of its artwork. Thus, following Merleau-Ponty, the vision that is "according to, or with" the artwork leads us at the very least to reject as foundationally prior any one particular story we tell about it.

Notes

1. *VI*, 144.
2. *S*, 60–62, 80.
3. *S*, 59.
4. "Mais, en tout cas, le transcendantal n'est plus conscience immanente des *Auffassungen*. Ceci serait ce qu'il appelle dans *Conférence de Vienne* '*einseitige Rationalität*'—Il y a en outre, par exemple, l'histoire qui fonctionne en nous, non pas processus, chaîne d'événement visibles, mais histoire intentionnelle ou 'vertical' avec *Stiftungen*, oubli qui est tradition, reprises, intériorité dans l'extériorité—*Ineinander* du présent et du passé. Tant qu'on n'aura pas retrouvé ce transcendantal, la rationalité sera en crise" (*NC*, 84).
5. *S*, 63.
6. Jean-Luc Nancy, *The Pleasures of Drawing*, trans. Philip Armstrong (New York: Fordham University Press, 2013), 6–7.
7. *PrP*, 178.
8. *PrP*, 164.
9. Mauro Carbone, *The Flesh of Images: Merleau-Ponty between Painting and Cinema*, trans. Marta Nijhuis (Albany: State University of New York Press, 2016), 6.
10. Ibid.
11. Rosalind Krauss, "The Cultural Logic of the Late Capitalist Museum," *October* 54 (1990): 3–17.
12. Paul O'Neill, "The Curatorial Turn: From Practice to Discourse," in *Issues in Curating in Contemporary Art and Performance*, ed. Judith Rugg and Michele Sedgwick (Chicago, University of Chicago Press, 2008), 15.
13. Ibid.
14. *S*, 62.

15. *S*, 63.

16. Claire Bishop, *Radical Museology, or What's "Contemporary" in Museums of Contemporary Art?* (London: Koenig Books, 2014), 23.

17. Ibid.

18. Ibid., 9.

19. Ibid., 24.

20. Ibid., 23.

21. Ibid., 43.

22. Ibid., 19.

23. Ibid., 43.

24. Claire Bishop, *Artificial Hells: Participatory Art and the Politics of Spectatorship* (London: Verso, 2012), 238–39.

25. Ibid., 239.

26. "CADA's works primarily consists of performances, actions and interventions, and such work has increasingly defined the most politically engaged art of the late 20th Century. The Reina Sofia is thus attempting to legally recategorize works of art as 'documentation' with the aim of increasing accessibility to artworks—for example, the public can go to the library and handle them, alongside publications, ephemera, photographs of works of art, correspondence, prints, and other textual materials." Bishop, *Radical Museology*, 44.

27. Ibid., 43.

28. Ibid., 58–59.

29. Nicolas Bourriaud, *Relational Aesthetics*, trans. Simon Pleasance and Fronza Woods, with the participation of Mathieu Copeland (Dijon: Presses du réel, 2002), 18.

30. Ibid.

31. Ibid., 19.

32. *VI*, 78.

Deleuze's "Philosophy-Cinema"

A Variation on Merleau-Ponty's "A-Philosophy"?

MAURO CARBONE

There is a little-known text by Merleau-Ponty, published for the first time in 1945, that helps to clarify, indirectly but decisively, the point at which his reflections on the arts and literature were traversed, from then on up to his death, by certain constant themes, which have not yet been sufficiently noted by commentators. The text in question is a brief article titled "Cinéma et psychologie,"[1] that was published in the weekly cinema journal *L'ecran français* on October 24, 1945. In this text, Merleau-Ponty "summarizes"—this is the word used in the editorial header—the talk titled "The Film and the New Psychology" that he gave on March 13, 1945, at the *Institut des Hautes Études Cinématographiques* in Paris. It is only in 1947 that Merleau-Ponty published the text of the talk in *Les Temps Modernes*.[2] In anticipation of this, in his brief article for *L'écran francais,* Merleau-Ponty makes explicit, specifies, and synthesizes certain considerations that are found scattered throughout his writings of the same period. Indeed, he declares in it: "There are great, classic works which reach man from the outside, like cinema, modern psychology and the American novel do."[3]

Merleau-Ponty thinks these cultural domains search, each in its own way, to "express man through his visible behavior," as he writes later in the text. The same idea comes back in the conclusion of the text, with a nuance concerning the spirit of the times: "If the cinema, psychology and literature agree in expressing man from the outside, it is not a whim of fashion, it is a demand of the human condition that even classical art did not ignore."[4]

269

A similar but more pronounced nuance appears in a much more famous passage by Merleau-Ponty dating from the same period and concluding the "Preface" of the *Phenomenology of Perception*, which explains that

> [i]f phenomenology was a movement prior to having been a doctrine or a system, this is neither accidental nor a deception. Phenomenology is as painstaking as the works of Balzac, Proust, Valéry, or Cézanne—through the same kind of attention and wonder, the same demand for awareness, the same will to grasp the sense of the world or of history in its nascent state. As such, phenomenology merges with the effort of modern thought.[5]

This passage is formally similar to the sentence cited above, but its content does not refer to cinema or psychology. Rather, it makes reference to phenomenology, to the painting of Cézanne, and to literature—in this case, rigorous French literature. Despite this difference of content, it is necessary, above all, to note that by associating these passages with one another, we rediscover the group of cultural domains addressed in the section titled "Arts" in *Sense and Nonsense*, the book that gathers the essays published by Merleau-Ponty in the preceding years. Indeed, we encounter in this section of *Sense and Nonsense* the painting of Cézanne, of course, but also "the film and the new psychology," to which the last part of the essay of the same title adds phenomenology and more generally "contemporary philosophy."[6] It makes this addition by finding as their common denominator the demand to "make us *see* the bond between subject and world, between subject and others, rather than to *explain* it."[7] But we also find, in this section of the book, two essays dedicated to the novels of Sartre and Simone de Beauvoir, "A Scandalous Author" and "The Novel and Metaphysics" respectively. From its first paragraph, this last essay discovers in literature too the demand to "make us see" [*faire voir*] when it maintains that "since the end of the 19th Century,"[8] "philosophical expression assumes the same ambiguities as literary expression, if the world is such that it cannot be expressed except in 'stories' and, as it were, *pointed at*."[9]

Thus, the article in *L'écran français* where we left off confirms to us the idea that, in the aftermath of World War II, Merleau-Ponty's reflections on the arts and literature do not constitute a varied assortment of contributions and remarks, but rather rest on some very precise guiding ideas that confer on them a very recognizable organicity. Among these guiding ideas we can group at least three: first of all, in our epoch it is possible to recognize a convergence between the novel, painting, and cinema; secondly, such a convergence also extends to the psychology of Form and contemporary philosophy, in particular phenomenology; thirdly, this convergence is essentially a matter of attending to the visible.

The first and third of these points will give rise to significant constant themes in Merleau-Ponty's thought, which I made allusion to earlier, while the second will produce a discontinuity that is no less significant.

We can evaluate the first and third of these themes as much as the second by referring to the notes prepared by Merleau-Ponty for a lecture dated February 23, 1961. This lecture was given during his last course at the *Collège de France*, titled "Cartesian Ontology and Ontology Today" ("*L'ontologie cartésienne et l'ontologie d'aujourd'hui*"), which was interrupted at the start of May by his sudden death. In this lecture, which represents the hinge between the first and second parts of the course, we find again the thesis according to which contemporary culture distinguishes itself by a convergence—interpreted, this time, in an ontological sense—between the novel, painting, and cinema. Let us note here that the cinema was considered by commentators, some years ago, as a domain that did not give rise to any important developments in Merleau-Ponty's later thought.[10] Moreover, in this lecture we find again the claim that this convergence between art forms manifests itself precisely in the investigation into the visible; or rather, as we read in the just-cited footnote, in the investigation into the "relations of the visible and the invisible." It is through this convergence that the novel, painting, and cinema express a "spontaneous philosophy" that Merleau-Ponty sought to make explicit for himself in order to better escape what he calls "official philosophy in crisis."[11] On this point, both the constant themes and the discontinuity announced above become evident. Unlike what had taken place in the aftermath of World War II, among the domains of research that converge to express, in their products, the "mutation within the relations of man and Being"[12] at the dawn of the 1960s, the "official" philosophy no longer has its place because, according to Merleau-Ponty, it remains closed inside the categories of thought that condemn it to a radical "backwardness."[13] This is why, in the other course, which was interrupted the same year by his sudden death and titled "Philosophy and Non-philosophy since Hegel," he refers instead to a "true philosophy" that, echoing Pascal, "mocks philosophy" and is "a philosophy which wants to be philosophy by being non-philosophy" and which he christens "a-philosophy."[14]

At the end of the same decade, Gilles Deleuze seems to glimpse, in his own way, an epochal backwardness of philosophy as standardized knowing in relation to "certain arts," of which he evokes theatre and cinema in the final part of the "Preface" of *Difference and Repetition*, published in 1968:

> The time is coming when it will hardly be possible to write a book of philosophy as it has been done for so long: "Ah! the old style. . . ." The search for new means of philosophical expression was begun by Nietzsche and must be pursued today in relation to the renewal of certain other arts, such as the theatre or the cinema.[15]

Some years later, in 1975, he added on another occasion, alluding to himself and Félix Guattari: "Together we would like to be the Humpty Dumpty of philosophy, or its Laurel and Hardy. A 'philosophy-cinema.'"[16] In the cinema, in short, Deleuze saw the projection of questions that philosophy asks itself, not only concerning our relations to ourselves, to others, to things, and to the world, but also, inevitably, in relation to itself: in relation to its own style of expression and, thus, to the very style of its own thought.

Nevertheless, it must be said that when the research of Deleuze ends up directly encountering the cinema—in the two volumes titled *The Movement-Image*[17] and *The Time-Image*[18]—he adopts an attitude that finishes by leaving open the question concerning what "a philosophy-cinema" ultimately is. As is well known, in the "Preface" of *The Movement-Image*, Deleuze states that "the great directors of cinema may be compared, not merely with painters, architects and musicians, but also with thinkers."[19] It is a strange formulation, because it seems to imply that it is not evident to compare "painters, architects, musicians" with thinkers, as he suggests we should do with filmmakers. Deleuze certainly emphasizes that the thought of filmmakers has a specificity, which consists in being inseparable from cinematographic expression. Nevertheless, a similar claim could be made for all other forms of artistic practice, each expressing itself in a particular manner which alone makes the practice one with its own manner of *thinking*.

In the text titled "The Film and The New Psychology," Merleau-Ponty attempts to characterize the cinematographic expression by making reference to the definition of "aesthetic ideas" given in section 49 of Kant's *Critique of the Power of Judgment*. Produced by the imagination of the artist and incarnated in the beauty of the work that he or she creates, aesthetic ideas occasion "much thinking-through"[20]—Kant explains—without being completely conceptualizable and conceptually expressible. In the case of cinema, on Merleau-Ponty's interpretation, this means that "the meaning of a film is incorporated into its rhythm just as the meaning of a gesture may immediately be read in that gesture: the film does not mean anything but itself. The idea is presented in a nascent state,"[21] that is to say, in its form without concept. Therefore, the idea shows itself to be indiscernable from its sensible manifestation:

> [It] emerges from the temporal structure of the film as it does from the coexistence of the parts of a painting. . . . As we saw above, a movie has meaning in the same way that a thing does: neither of them speaks to an isolated understanding; rather, both appeal to our power tacitly to decipher the world or men and to coexist with them.[22]

From these premises, Merleau-Ponty arrives at the conclusion that even "*contemporary philosophy consists not in stringing concepts together* but in describing the mingling of consciousness with the world, its involvement in a body, and its coexistence with others; and . . . this is movie material *par excellence.*"[23]

Deleuze is more concerned with affirming the specificity of cinematographic expression in relation to the philosophic, explaining that "the great directors of cinema . . . think with movement-images and time-images instead of concepts."[24] In any case, as we just noted, Merleau-Ponty, as much as Deleuze, excludes the possibility of characterizing cinematographic expression by reference to conceptual thought.[25]

Moreover, it must be observed that during the period of "The Film and The New Psychology" and the other essays gathered in *Sense and Nonsense*, Merleau-Ponty seemed to find in the cinema, just as in the painting of Cézanne, artistic research converging with the philosophical research of phenomenology. This is no different from what we see in Deleuze's books on cinema, which he approached through Bergson's philosophy. This tendency is particularly clear in the following passage from *Cinema 1*, which I must cite in its entirety:

> Another path, however, seemed open to Bergson. For, if the ancient conception [of movement] corresponds closely to ancient philosophy, which aims to think the eternal, then the modern conception, modern science, calls upon *another* philosophy. . . . This

is a complete conversion of philosophy. It is what Bergson ultimately aims to do: to give to modern science the metaphysics which corresponds to it, which it lacks as one half lacks the other. But can we stop once we have set out on this path? Can we deny that the arts must also go through this conversion or that the cinema is an essential factor in this, and that it has a role to play in the birth and formation of this new thought, this new way of thinking? This is why Bergson is no longer content merely to corroborate his first thesis on movement. Bergson's second thesis—although it stops half way—makes possible another way of looking at the cinema, a way in which it would no longer be just the perfect apparatus of the oldest illusion, but, on the contrary, the organ for perfecting the new reality.[26]

During the period of *Sense and Nonsense*, Merleau-Ponty is, like Deleuze, interested in emphasizing the historical convergence between the novelty of the cinema and his philosophy of preference, which in his case is of course phenomenology. The former is more interested in emphasizing this historical convergence than in focusing on the "fundamental thought" at work in cinema. It is necessary, however, to note that Merleau-Ponty's attitude seems to change in the final phase of his reflection. In this period, he utilizes precisely the expression "fundamental thought" in order to indicate a type of "thought of the *Ungedachte*,"[27] where he sees at work a relation between man and Being that thought codified as philosophical has not yet truly taken into account. In this period, Merleau-Ponty ends up leaning on such a "fundamental thought," namely, the thought that operates in the domains which are supposed to be "non-philosophical" (such as literature, painting, and cinema), because according to him they express what we earlier heard Merleau-Ponty call "spontaneous philosophy." In other words, the reasons for the change, which I pointed out above, in Merleau-Ponty's attitude become clearer when one links them to the negative evaluation that he comes to about the capacity of philosophy proper to propose a thought in line with the challenges of that era. This is why we know that he himself comes to forge the word *a-philosophy* as a way of avoiding the traditional metaphysical dualism that separates and opposes philosophy and non-philosophy, and in order to develop a style of thought and expression having the concrete efficacy of experiences and knowledges "without concepts." These experiences and knowledges are sedimented in certain images no less than certain modes of speech. Therefore, what Merleau-Ponty wrote concerning the latter can only be valid as the former:

[T]he words most charged with philosophy are not necessarily those that enclose what they say, but rather those that most energetically open upon Being, because they more closely convey the life of the whole and make our habitual evidences vibrate until they disjoin.[28]

It is in this "a-philosophical" direction that Merleau-Ponty's interest in the a-conceptual nature of Kantian "aesthetic ideas," which we have seen evoked in order to characterize the cinematographic expression itself, becomes its theorization of Proustian "sensible ideas,"[29] on the subject of which he utilizes precisely the Kantian expression *without concept*. Rather than a cohesion due to the fact that they "enclose what they say," he attributes to them "a *cohesion without concept*, which is of the same type as the cohesion of the parts of my body, or the cohesion of my body with the world."[30]

In the pages of the *Recherche* that Merleau-Ponty makes allusion to, in his opinion Proust characterizes an order of ideas that—just like aesthetic ideas for Kant—cannot be reduced to concepts, ideas that the intelligence, as such, cannot grasp, because—as Merleau-Ponty emphasizes—they "are without intelligible sun."[31] Indeed, he insists, "it is essential to this sort of ideas that they be 'veiled in darkness' "[32] and not let themselves "be erected into a second positivity"[33]—precisely the positivity that permits the concept to enclose what they talk about—because we cannot "see [them] without the veils,"[34] to the extent that it is these veils which make the ideas radiate.

Unlike what Proust calls "ideas of intelligence"—namely, concepts— Merleau-Ponty believes that "these ideas, do not let themselves be detached from sensible appearances,"[35] which is where the designation "sensible ideas" comes from. On this subject he emphasizes in fact that "there is no vision without the screen: the ideas we are speaking of would not be better known to us if we had no body and no sensibility; it is then that they would be inaccessible to us."[36] In short, it is a question of ideas that can only be *experienced*—because knowing them means having their bodily experience—by encountering them in one of their sensible manifestations: encountering them on some kind of "screen" or of "veil," we could say, even if it will be a question of a metaphorical screen such as the listening in case of a piece of music or the reading in that of a literary work. The experience of the screen reveals itself thus as exemplary for this thought without concept.

Regarding the cinema in particular, the direction of Merleau-Ponty's "a-philosophical" research just evoked seems to imply, notably, the reflection of André Bazin, given that the name of the latter is the only one that he cites in the context of this research.[37] We can consequently claim that, for the reasons I indicated up to this point, in the final period of his production he intended to elaborate a thought supplied by the "implicit philosophy" at work in reflections such as those of André Bazin.[38]

We could be tempted to say that Deleuze develops a similar operation to Merleau-Ponty's, for example, at the beginning of *The Time-Image*, where he takes up and elaborates in an autonomous way the indications and the remarks that Bazin had dedicated to Italian neorealism.[39] Moreover, in an interview titled "On the time-image," Deleuze also claims that we can find in certain critical reflections on cinema a sort of spontaneous philosophy:

> Yet cinema critics, the greatest critics anyway, became philosophers the moment they set out to formulate an aesthetics of cinema. They weren't trained as philosophers, but that's what they became. You see it already in Bazin.[40]

Despite this element of convergence, we must note that the evolution of the thought of Deleuze concerning the relations between philosophy and cinema seems to go in a direction opposed to that of the evolution of Merleau-Ponty. Indeed, the latter comes to give a similar task to the one Deleuze gives to the philosophy of "today" in the conclusion of the "Preface" of *Difference and Repetition*: "The search for new means of philosophical expression."

On the other hand, fifteen years after the publication of this work, the assertion of the "Preface" of *The Movement-Image* mentioned above—according to which "the great directors of cinema . . . think with movement-images and time-images instead of concepts"[41]—shows the tendency to revive the identity of philosophy as conceptual knowing. This tendency is confirmed in the very final pages of *The Time-Image*.[42] Of course, Deleuze emphasizes there that it is necessary to understand "philosophical theory" as "a practice of concepts"; and, of course, he clarifies that "the theory of cinema is not about the cinema, but about the concepts of cinema." Nevertheless, he asserts there that it is "the great directors of cinema . . . who speak the best about what they do"—a highly disputable claim, because it seems to ignore the hermeneutic principle concerning "what the author does not know."[43] Yet more contestable, he suggests that *they speak of their work through concepts*—he who, however, tells us that they "think with movement-images and time-images"—these "concepts of cinema" that, for him, philosophy, as the practice of concepts, can grasp, as he wrote in accordance with the most traditional approaches, as "its object."[44]

We can thus wonder: What do we make of the "philosophy-cinema"? And of this hyphen? If we leave behind the theoretical stake expressed by this hyphen—making "a philosophy-cinema"—do we not risk writing, once again, books of philosophy "as it has been done for so long," to speak with Deleuze himself, taking, not cinema, but quite simply "the concepts of cinema" for their object?

In order to avoid this risk, it would be necessary to radically develop the problematization of the ideas of "philosophy" and of "concept" that Deleuze had undertaken in the course of the 1960s,[45] which might mean, in turn, exploring the history of the very notion of concept. We might observe that the modern conception of the latter is modeled on the German term that designates it, namely, the term *Begriff,* the roots of which refer to the gesture of "grasping" (*greifen*). Additionally, in such a conception we might be able to see the product of a process of *abstraction* from the notion of Idea begun by Plato himself: this process consists in the separation and opposition of the essence and the existence, of the intelligible and the sensible, of the universal and the particular, and it marks the manner of thinking that we call *Platonism,* which continually dominates Western culture. Furthermore, this process of *abstraction* of the notion of Idea was at the same time the process of its *reification,* that is to say, its transformation into a positive entity, a sort of object. Of course, this is an "ideal object," but, as such, ideally graspable—as the German etymology of the term *concept* suggests—in all the domains of our experience that philosophy claims to define, such as (the concepts of) cinema, for example.

In conclusion, in order to avoid such a risk it would be necessary to fully develop the program of the *reversal of Platonism,* which is the title of a famous 1967 text by Deleuze republished in the appendix to *The Logic of Sense,*[46] precisely the book of 1969 of which the author's "Note for the Italian edition" posits, as we saw, the notion of "philosophy-cinema." On the contrary, in the first half of the 1980s, when Deleuze devoted himself to his two books on cinema, his research seems to have left behind the intention of radically problematizing philosophy as conceptual knowing, and it finishes by also leaving open the question concerning what is ultimately "a philosophy-cinema." Perhaps it is this modified theoretical horizon that also explains the implicit criticism that Slavoj Žižek puts to the Deleuzian reflection on cinema: that it does not fully understand the philosophical importance of Alfred Hitchcock.[47] Or, as Merleau-Ponty would have said, the "spontaneous philosophy" of the latter. Žižek's criticism of Deleuze is summarized when he reproaches Deleuze for not having seen that "*Vertigo* is, in a sense, the ultimate anti-Platonic film, a systematic materialist undermining of the Platonic project, akin to what Deleuze does in the appendix to *The Logic of Sense.*"[48] In short, Žižek reproaches Deleuze for not having seen that the cinema of Hitchcock, and *Vertigo* in particular, can contribute effectively to the effort of *reversing Platonism,* which he had encouraged fifteen years earlier. In the conclusion of *The Time-Image,* Deleuze shows, instead, the tendency to come back to a model of philosophy as *subject which must think its objects*: "Cinema itself is a new practice of images and of signs, of which philosophy must make the theory."[49] Ah! the old style . . .

(*English translation by Joseph Barker revised by the author*)

Notes

1. Published for the first time as Maurice Merleau-Ponty, "Cinéma et psychologie," *L'écran français* 17 (1945): 3–4.
2. Maurice Merleau-Ponty, "Le cinéma et la nouvelle psychologie," *Les Temps Modernes* 26 (1947): 930–47; reprinted in *SNS*, 48–59, orig. 61–75.
3. Merleau-Ponty, "Cinéma et psychologie," 4.
4. Ibid.
5. *PP*, xvi, orig. lxxxv.
6. *SNS*, 58, orig. 75.
7. *SNS*, 58, orig. 74.
8. *SNS*, 27, orig. 35.
9. *SNS*, 36–37/28; my emphasis.
10. *NC*, 391. The couple "painting-cinema" is once again evoked by Merleau-Ponty in the preparatory notes of the third course, which he dedicated to the "Concept of Nature," titled "Nature and *logos*: the human body" (1959–60). It is evoked as a double domain that he expects to explore further in *The Visible and The Invisible:* "These relations of the visible and the invisible, of the logos of the visible world and of the logos of ideality, will be studied (*The Visible and the Invisible*) only in the next years with language, with other systems of expression (painting, cinema), with history and its architectonic." *VI,* 291, orig. 391.
11. *NC*, 391.
12. *OE*, 63.
13. *NC*, 163.
14. *PNP*, 275. For more on this theme, one can turn to the second chapter of my book *The Thinking of the Sensible: Merleau-Ponty's A-Philosophy* (Evanston: Northwestern University Press, 2004), 14–27. Concerning Pascal, see Blaise Pascal, *Pascal's Pensées,* [1669], bilingual edition, trans. H. F. Stewart (London: Routledge and Kegan Paul, 1950), 498–99.
15. Gilles Deleuze, *Différence et répétition* (Paris: P.U.F., 1968), 4. Translated as *Difference and Repetition,* trans. Paul Patton (New York: Columbia University Press, 1994), xxi.

16. Gilles Deleuze, "Note pour l'édition italienne de *Logique du sens*" [1974], French translation by D. Lapoujade, in *Deux régimes de fous. Textes et entretiens 1975–1995* (Paris: Minuit, 2003), 60; translated into English as "Note for the Italian Edition of *The Logic of Sense*," trans. James Cascaito, in *Two Regimes of Madness* (New York: Semiotext(e), 2007), 66.

17. Gilles Deleuze, *Cinéma 1. L'image-mouvement* (Paris: Minuit, 1983); translated as *Cinema 1: The Movement-Image*, trans. Hugh Tomlinson and Barbara Habberjam (Minneapolis: University of Minnesota Press, 1986).

18. G. Deleuze, *Cinéma 2. L'image-temps* (Paris: Minuit, 1985); translated as *Cinema 2: the Time-Image*, trans. Hugh Tomlinson and Robert Galeta (London: Athlone, 1989).

19. Deleuze, "Movement-Image," xiv, orig. 7.

20. Immanuel Kant, *Critique of the Power of Judgment*, trans. Paul Guyer and Eric Matthews (Cambridge: Cambridge University Press, 2000), § 49, 143–44. On this subject, it is necessary to recall that, for Kant, aesthetic ideas operate in a symbolic manner, which means indirectly and analogically (see ibid., § 59, 174).

21. *SNS*, 57, orig. 73.

22. *SNS*, 57–58, orig. 75.

23. *SNS*, 59, orig. 75; my emphasis.

24. Deleuze, *The Movement-Image*, xiv, orig. 7–8.

25. For more on what Deleuze is concerned with here, see also Gilles Deleuze, "What Is the Creative Act?" in *Two Regimes of Madness: Texts and Interviews 1975–1995*, ed. David Lapoujade, trans. Ames Hodges and Mike Taormina (New York and Cambridge, MA: Semiotext, 2007), 312–24.

26. Deleuze, *The Image-Movement*, 7–8, orig. 17.

27. *NC*, 391.

28. *VI*, 102, orig. 137; translation modified.

29. The sixth chapter of my book *La visibilité de l'invisible. Merleau-Ponty entre Cézanne et Proust* (Hildesheim: Georg Olms Verlag, 2001), is devoted to this subject.

30. *VI*, 152, orig. 199; my emphasis.

31. *NC*, 194.

32. *VI*, 150, orig. 197.

33. *VI*, 149, orig. 196.

34. *VI*, 150, orig. 197.

35. Ibid.

36. *VI*, 150, orig. 194.

37. *NC*, 391.

38. In what sense could we say that the writings of certain film critics are animated by a thought without concept such as I have tried to characterize up to now? In the sense that Deleuze imputes to Godard: "Godard likes to recall that, when the future directors of the new wave were writing, they were not writing about cinema, they were not making a theory out of it, it was already their way of making

films." Gilles Deleuze, "Sur *L'image-temps* [1985]," in *Pourparlers: 1972–1990* (Paris: Minuit, 1990); translated as "On the Time-Image," in *Negotiations: 1972–1990* (New York: Columbia University Press, 1995), 365/280.

39. Ibid., 1, orig. 7.
40. Ibid., 57, orig. 82.
41. Deleuze, *The Image Movement*, 7–8, orig. xiv.
42. Deleuze, "On the Time-Image," 280, orig. 365–66.
43. Afterward, Deleuze will rather claim: "The only people capable of thinking effectively about cinema are the filmmakers and film critics or those who love cinema" ("What Is The Creative Act?" in *Two Regimes of Madness*, 313).
44. "Philosophical theory . . . is no more abstract than its object." Deleuze, "On the Time-Image," 280, orig. 365.
45. On this subject, I direct the reader to my contribution titled "Mais quelle 'création de concepts'?" in *La Géophilosophie de Gilles Deleuze entre esthétiques et politiques*, ed. M. Carbone, P. Broggi, and L. Turarbek (Paris: Mimesis France, 2012), 17–25.
46. See Gilles Deleuze, "Renverser le platonisme," *Revue de Métaphysique et de Morale* 4 (1967), republished under the title "Platon et le simulacre," in *Logique du sens* (Paris: Minuit, 1969), 292–307; translated as "Plato and the Simulcrum," in *The Logic of Sense*, ed. Constantin V. Boundas, trans. Mark Lester and Charles Stivale (New York: Columbia University Press, 1990), 253–65.
47. Deleuze, *L'image-mouvement*, ch. 12, esp. 202, orig. 269.
48. Slavoj Žižek, *Organs without Bodies: Deleuze and Consequences* (New York: Routledge, 2004), 157.
49. Deleuze, "On the Time-Image," 280, orig. 366.

Strong Beauty

In Face of Structures of Exclusion

VÉRONIQUE M. FÓTI

> The work of art effects an upheaval of the transcendental illusion and its acceptance of the given purely as such . . . and thinks from before the thought that tends toward absolutization and totalization.
>
> —Rajiv Kaushik, *Art, Language, and Figure in Merleau-Ponty*

The critique and eclipse of beauty as an artistic aim and ideal, prominent since the early twentieth century, is interlinked with what Jean-Luc Nancy speaks of as "the magnitude and intensity of the transformations to which the history of art has exposed us within a single century."[1] This single century spans, for him, roughly from 1850 to 1950, so that "it cuts across Auschwitz" and other genocidal events of the twentieth century. On a global scale, such events did not, of course, reach a point of exhaustion by mid-century (one need only recall Cambodia, Tibet, and Rwanda), nor of course has there been any more recent dearth of radical innovation in the arts. It may rather be that the eclipse of beauty in art and art-theoretical discourse—whether in favor of innovative ways of art making such as conceptual art, or of a quest for sublimity in beauty's stead—reflects not only beauty's seeming irrelevance to a world gripped by atrocities, but also an awareness of its possible, and actualized, complicity with evil. One thinks here of what Nancy characterizes as Nazism's, and specifically Hitler's, quest for a worldview that would galvanize the masses, being "placed before [their] eyes and given presence in its totality, its [supposed] truth, and its destiny."[2] The artist who paradigmatically accomplished this sort of (re)presentation is, of course, Leni Riefenstahl who, to the end of her long life, named beauty as the sole aim and absolute value of her work in film and photography—an aim that supposedly left her blameless for the spectacular success of her Nazi propaganda. To cite Nancy once more, the vision that Nazism advocated is one that repudiates any sort of "withdrawn invisibility."[3] As such, it is antithetical to Merleau-Ponty's thought of the intricate inter-involvement of visibility with invisibles; and the contrast highlights the political relevance of Merleau-Ponty's ontology.

At the very outset of his insightful book *The Retrieval of the Beautiful*, Galen A. Johnson points out the long-standing confusion of beauty with hierarchies of perfection that lend themselves to the idolization of ideological, racist, sexist, and other prejudices.[4] Even Heidegger, in *Besinnung* of 1938, satirizes the National Socialist ideal of male beauty and comments memorably that beauty functions here as "what pleases and must please the power-essence [*dem Machtwesen*] of the beast of prey, man."[5] Beauty understood in terms of ideals of perfection can readily function as an instrument of propaganda, manipulation, and dominance. François Cheng, in his *Five Meditations on Beauty*—meditations initially carried out in a dialogical manner within a circle of artists, writers, psychoanalysts, and other professionals—states that a specific form of evil stems from such perversion and abuse of beauty.[6]

Mindful, perhaps, not only of the marginalization or eclipse of beauty in twentieth-century art and art-theoretical discourse, but also of beauty's ambiguity and sinister potential, Merleau-Ponty maintains an almost unbroken silence concerning beauty. Johnson traces the few instances in which the philosopher mentions it, showing that they function either as quotations from other writers or else in the context of his informal 1948 radio program *Causeries*.[7]

If Merleau-Ponty's silence concerning beauty feels strained at times, his thought nonetheless offers a challenging conceptuality and vocabulary for rethinking and, perhaps, ultimately renaming it, to shed the burden of its trivialization. In "Eye and Mind," and in his posthumous manuscript, *The Visible and the Invisible*, he speaks oxymoronically of carnal essences and recognizes an opening without concept to the anteriority or the sheer donation of "there is," as well as of a deflagration of being and of the painter's self "pierced through" by the universe, in a piercing (*percée*) that opens unto the very heart of being.[8] The challenge to the reader is not only that of sensitive and adequate interpretation, but of thinking both forward to address contemporary art and also, as it were, downward to explore the ontological depth of Merleau-Ponty's thought, in quest of an understanding of beauty capable of revealing its richness, power, and ethical import.

Johnson, drawing on the vision, work, and thought of artists whom Merleau-Ponty favored, notably Cézanne, Rodin, and Klee, suggests an understanding of strong beauty that would not juxtapose it to sublimity but would rather cast it as not only sublimity's equal, but as indissociable from it. Rodin, Johnson points out, rejected any understanding of beauty based on the dichotomy between bodily perfection and the rejected ugliness of its innumerable shortfalls, recognizing that art transfigures, but does not belie the entire scope and truth of reality.

Taking the notion of strong beauty as the mark of a central insight that calls for further exploration, I propose to address the following questions: What makes for the power and strength of beauty? Is strong beauty found in nature (which is, of course, the locus of the Kantian sublime) or does it require art? If the latter, must any art capable of strong beauty respond explicitly to the conflicts, violence, and agonies that pervade contemporary life, or can it irradiate an art that is meditative, or even somewhat hermetic? Finally, and importantly, by what strength can beauty resist becoming an instrument of exploitation and domination? Can it become genuinely and incorruptibly ethical?

In the limited format of this study, I will explore these questions chiefly with regard to painting (which is, of course, Merleau-Ponty's artistic focus), rather than to the plethora of media in contemporary visual art, but hopefully they will, in future, be addressed not only to visual art as a whole but also to the entire spectrum of art, whether visual, literary, or performative.

On Strong Beauty

So long as beauty functions chiefly or exclusively as a source of pleasure, exciting or gratifying desire, it is not strong beauty. Rather than being a quality, and thus something objectively given, strong beauty has the character of an *event*. What it manifests is not representational but revelatory. Its apparitional moment is characterized by an absence of transparency and by imprevisibility, which jointly frustrate any attempt at manipulation or control.[9] For this reason, rather than just offering delight, it brings with it, in its presencing, an intensity akin to pain that may border on the scarcely bearable. It does so even in artworks that do not show anything intrinsically distressing. Furthermore, visual works of art radiating strong beauty may be experienced, by those incapable of responding to their challenge, as just, boringly, "more bottles" in a still life by Morandi, or as seemingly sketchy or even awkward, such as Li Fangying's ink paintings of flowering plum.[10]

Nonetheless, and even though strong beauty in a work of art is independent of what it may (re)present, or of whether or not it is figurative at all (recalling Merleau-Ponty's point that the dichotomy between figuration and abstraction is ill conceived)[11] certain works that thematize horrific and distressing situations or events remain outside the pale of beauty. One may think here of Goya's *Disasters of War* or of Picasso's iconic *Guernica*, to say nothing of photographic or cinematographic works that addresses the Shoah or recent terrorist events. To seek to appreciate such works in terms of beauty is to aestheticize horror and pain, which is not only ethically objectionable but is complicit with enlisting beauty for purposes of manipulation and domination. The complicity stems from beauty's being stripped, in these contexts, of any aspect of enigma or nontransparency, together with its elemental character. Although, once again, Merleau-Ponty does not address beauty directly, he reflects that perception fundamentally is "of elements (water, air . . .)," or of "dimensions," rather than of anything prosaically identifiable.[12]

Strong beauty's enigmatic elementality is linked to the fact that its apparitional moment is one of sheer encounter—an encounter that is refractory to possession and that is, as Henri Maldiney stresses, oriented not solely toward the human Other but also toward the entire spectrum of living beings, and ultimately (beyond Maldiney) toward what Whitehead speaks of as the "ether of events" that pervades the cosmos.[13] Meditating on this play of energies in relation to the key function of voids in the sculpture of Henry Moore, Merleau-Ponty speaks of "a certain constitutive void . . . [that] supports the pretended positivity of things."[14] It is the empty yet dynamic insubstantiality of the open dimension of manifestation that fundamentally gives strong beauty its strength.

In this context, it may be important to distinguish between *aisthēsis*, in the double sense of sensory receptivity and feeling (approximated by the French term *sentir*), and perception, which, in the history of thought, tends to occlude the complexity of *aisthanesthai*. Merleau-Ponty's subtle interrogations of the "participations" that inform even basic sensory givens, and of the painter's "secret science" aim to uncover a level of pure donation, or of the upsurge of "wild being" beneath, and disruptive of, the perceptual quest (a quest characteristic of what he calls "profane vision") for objectification. His terminological assimilation of *aisthēsis* to perception tends thus to obscure its anteriority to perceptual faith and to the quest for identification. *Aisthēsis*, unlike perception, involves a moment of sheer exposure and *pathos*; and this moment allows strong beauty to seize and grip her who experiences it, leaving her shaken or, in Merleau-Ponty's phrasing, "pierced through" by beauty's apparitional moment.[15] In this sense, and in the words of Rilke's first Duino Elegy (cited by Johnson), "The beautiful is nothing / but the beginning of the terrible."[16]

Nature and Art

As Cheng felicitously expresses it, the universe appears in its beauty in the manner of a gift, and not as a mere fact.[17] In his second lecture course on Nature of 1957–58, Merleau-Ponty takes up Portmann's researches on animal appearance as being, not a byproduct of biological processes geared toward species survival, but rather as the creative expression of the organism's distinctive life energy.[18] Portmann reflects that this quest for visual innovation and refinement may even sometimes be at odds with the aim of survival and that, moreover, nature abounds in "unaddressed appearances" or visual creativity not addressed to any possible eye.[19] In contrast to the Cartesian notion of a *creatio continua* that reduces nature to utter dependence on the divine creative act (thereby encouraging the theistic argument from design), nature emerges, from these researches, as dynamically self-creating and as striving for beauty.

One hesitates, nonetheless, to ascribe strong beauty to nature purely in itself, even when contemplating, say, majestic mountains traditionally held to be sacred, or the starscapes of the Southern sky. The reason is that, while nature offers beauty in the manner of a granting or favor, strong beauty requires the encounter between nature and human exposure, or *pathos* and creative response. As Henri Maldiney puts it, "The irruption of being has meaning [*du sens*] only within the space of a human act."[20] Within the art work itself, nonetheless, any dualism between action and passion is overcome, so that, as Merleau-Ponty writes, in painting "it is mute Being that comes of itself to manifest its own sense."[21] Similarly, Rajiv Kaushik reflects that the art work discloses "a site of being prior to subjectivity and objectivity," and thus to the problematic of constitution in transcendental phenomenology.[22]

In this context, it is instructive to cast a quick glance at the arts of the garden. Gardens are, on the whole, suffused with a beauty that enchants, supports contemplation, and optimally offers restoration or healing. Nonetheless, a search for strong beauty purely within the parameters of the garden remains nearly fruitless, unless perhaps one turns to almost counternatural dry Zen gardens such as Kyoto's iconic *Ryōan-ji*, created austerely out of rocks and raked sand, in a denial of nature's vegetal exuberance, yet with an acknowledgment of the elemental and tensional interplay of sea and land.

Strong beauty can characterize only an expressive work, that is to say, a work of art, at a greater remove from nature than most gardens. In the words of Jean-Louis Chrétien, its strength and power derive from the viewer's "being seized by the there-is," or being gripped by a donation that is fundamentally ontological.[23] In the moment of encounter, this donation exceeds both intentionality and cognitive grasp, together with one's own preformed possibilities. It is therefore experienced as transgressive and enigmatically transformative. In these respects, it is close in kind to the sublimity that Barnett Newman envisages as the aim of art—an aim that was, for him, incompatible with a quest for beauty, given how, in mid-twentieth century, beauty was understood.[24]

Strong Beauty in Art

Merleau-Ponty holds that whether or not art is figurative is of no relevance to its fundamental elision of positivity.[25] It is noteworthy that, within the global art-historical spectrum, nonfigurative work possessed of strong beauty predates the modern era. Prominent examples include Chinese and Japanese calligraphy, such as, within the Chinese tradition, Huang t'in- chien's (1451–1505) handscroll of biographies of Lien P'o and Ling Hsing-ju (undated), or within the Japanese tradition, the Zen-inspired *Bokuseki* (ink-trace) works of the Shingon Buddhist monk Jiun Onkō (1718–1804). On the other hand, strong beauty also characterizes contemporary figurative work, such as Lucian Freud's career-long engagement with the human figure that problematizes beauty, or Kiki Smith's haunting focus, in sculpture and installation, on female and animal bodies. There is perhaps a certain sense today that, as Arthur Danto puts it, art has for too long "given ashes in place of beauty—the reverse of Isaiah's 'good tidings,'" and that "to withhold beauty is no less of a moral infraction [than] what deliberately de-beautified art-criticism."[26] This realization has motivated some contemporary artists to cultivate beauty anew within their work, investing it with searing significance. Given the need, however, to stay clear of the multiple exclusionary and sexist politics often associated with beauty in figuration, as well as figuration's proneness to illusionism, which tends to mask the sheer event of beauty, strong beauty today tends to privilege nonfigurative art.

One might perhaps wonder, recalling Cézanne's well-known pronouncement that he owes his viewers "the truth in painting," and that he will deliver it,[27] whether an abandonment of figuration may be detrimental to pictorial truth. Cézanne himself evidently did not consider pictorial truth to be univocal, given his highly differential explorations of key motifs, such as Mt. Ste. Victoire, the figure of his wife, Hortense Fiquet, or his oneiric scene of nude bathers in a landscape. His painterly truth is not one of adequation but rather is akin to Merleau-Ponty's own ontological interrogation, in that it seeks to recover an obliterated stratum of "wild being" on which humanity and culture have established themselves.[28] In a tribute to Cézanne, Maldiney writes that the painter has made of space "a fabric of events which are encounters, at once pictorial and cosmic."[29] His pictorial truth, being devoid of univocity and positivity, is indifferent to the supposed dichotomy between figuration and abstraction.

To counteract the further temptation to think of strong beauty as forceful, assertive, or confrontational, it will be instructive to cast a brief glance at the nonfigurative art of Agnes Martin. In her extensive writings, she expresses a central, unquestioning devotion to beauty as "the mystery of life," and as indissociable from artistic validity, which in turn is linked for her to joy and to an intuitive (rather than intellectually mediated) contact with transcendent perfection.[30] Perfection remains for her insubstantial and beyond grasp, thus resisting hierarchization. The empty form, she writes (with reference to a pair of Chinese ceramics), "goes all the way to heaven"; and if one understands her praise of "Humility, the beautiful daughter" as a validation of her own work, one has to agree with her that "all her ways are empty."[31]

When Martin took up painting again around 1974 in New Mexico after a hiatus, having left New York's art world, she had also exchanged oil paint for acrylics and had shifted to mathematically articulated broad plane divisions in place of her earlier closely spaced linear grids. The geometries of her horizontal or vertical bands were no longer marked necessarily by penciled lines nor enclosed within a demarcated frame. Barbara Haskell notes that, in these works, "lines and grids disappear into "subtly active fields of color," citing Rosalind Krauss's comment that they form "luminous containers for the shimmer of line."[32]

One owes to Krauss a perceptive analysis of Martin's work. Building on Kasha Linville's phenomenological study of how viewing distances alter the work's appearance, in a progression from a close-up foregrounding of materiality and facture to a middle-distance veiling as though by mist, and finally, from far distance, to impenetrable opacity.[33] Krauss understands these changes as effects within a painterly system that *must exclude* what is opposed to it, while nevertheless requiring and continually invoking it. Drawing on Hubert Damisch's work on Brunelleschi's depiction of the Baptistery in Florence,[34] she reflects on perspective construction (which abidingly fascinated Merleau-Ponty) as a system of exclusions that marks the excluded (for Brunelleschi, the changeable sky, which, in his rendering of the Baptistery, is mirrored rather than depicted) as unknowable and unrepresentable within the canons of the system. The all-over grid, Krauss reflects, highlights these tensions by conjoining a quest for classical clarity and lucid definition, irrespective of vantage point, with a dissolution of the figure/ground articulation—a dissolution incompatible with classical clarity. It thus inscribes within its systematicity the excluded unformed as a lack (echoing the Derridean supplement) that nonetheless enables the system's self-articulation.[35]

An acknowledgment of the way that systems of form remain dependent on the excluded unformed is integral, and perhaps essential, to strong beauty. Such a marking or acknowledgment contrasts with the sort of complacent self-absolutizing "positivity" that Merleau-Ponty consistently rejects. Even though his insistence on the irrecusable primacy of the upsurge of the world or life-world is in tension with an art that seeks, like Martin's, to turn its back on the world in a quest for transcendent perfection, the very acknowledgment of the lack symbolized by a differential marker that frustrates the "positivity" of a given system in fact unites these divergent perspectives in enabling strong beauty.

In conclusion, Krauss considers that the grid has tended, in recent art history, to merge more and more with its material support, giving rise to an "objectivist opticality." Thus, whereas Martin's effort to safeguard a classical ideal of perfection led her to define the grid structure in terms of a subtle acknowledgment of what it excluded, Ellsworth Kelly proceeded to materialize the grid itself.[36] This approach is exemplified for Krauss by Kelly's 1951 painting *Colors for a Large Wall*, which consists of sixty-four discrete monochrome panels, with the color sequence left to chance.[37] Unlike Martin (with whom, incidentally, he cultivated a warm friendship while they both lived at Coenties Slip in Manhattan during the late 1950s and early 1960s), Kelly rarely expresses an explicit concern for beauty. Quite apart from the issue of materializing the grid, the way that chance functions for him (despite his practice of meticulous advance planning of his work) as an important interlocutor is essential to his achievement of strong beauty.

Kelly began to integrate chance into his work during his formative years in France (1948–1954). His encounter with Dadaism and surrealism—movements that, in the wake of World War I, rejected rationality and systematicity—was influential, as was his contact with Jean Arp's practice of creating collages based on chance (a practice later taken up by Cy Twombly). Chance informed Kelly's work in two ways: firstly in his turn, around 1949, from figuration to an abstract visual language that relied on forms found serendipitously within the natural and built environment, and secondly by becoming integral to his creative process, in particular with respect to color. *Colors for a Large Wall* was preceded by *Spectrum Colors Arranged by Chance I*,[38] which not only tensionally juxtaposes the geometric rigidity of the square grid, together with the mathematical perspicacity of the spectrum, with chance in the position of the unpredictable excluded. Kelly's engagement with chance is complemented by his sustained engagement with nature (which is once again refractory to systematicity) through his almost career-long practice of drawing plant forms from nature—a practice that constituted, in his own words, "the bridge to the way of seeing that brought about the paintings of 1949 that are the basis of all my future work."[39] His dual and tensional integration of nature and chance with systematicity served also to distance his art from the formalist practices of Mondrian and Vantongerloo, and even of Malevich, to which critics had assimilated it, in oblivion of its strong beauty. As he himself states the point: "My color use, and the object quality of the 'painting,' and the use of fragmentation is closer to birds and beetles and fish than to De Stijl and the Constructivists." More fundamentally, his dual involvement with nature and chance allows Kelly's work to display its formal refinement over against "the unknowable and unrepresentable," to recall Krauss's words, which guards it against self-absolutization. Incidentally, this implicit acknowledgment of the precariousness of its own constraints is also integral to what sets it, as a key achievements of painterly abstraction, apart from what Merleau-Ponty criticizes and rejects as abstraction's negation and refusal of the world.[40]

Kelly's first large-scale sculpture, *Sculpture for a Large Wall*,[41] was originally commissioned for the lobby of the Transportation Building at Penn Center, Philadelphia. It echoes both the titles and concept of the paintings that preceded it. Within its four horizontal bands, it combines rectilinear and curvilinear forms in polished or anodized aluminum. Although Kelly had devoted much time and energy to planning the work, its final execution was not dictated by plan. In his own description, his working process was "like a trance: my curves came at the right time. It was like writing."[42] His recognition of chance as an epistemological marker of the excluded within the structure of a visual system allows his work to achieve the impact of strong beauty.

In "Eye and Mind," Merleau-Ponty reflects that, had Descartes examined "this other and more profound opening upon things given to us by the secondary qualities, notably color," he would have faced a universality without concept and might have been motivated to treat Albertian perspective as "a special case of a vaster ontological power."[43] In view of perspective construction, and of the classical Florentine ideal of *disegno* as a whole, Merleau-Ponty tends to treat color as a constructivist system's essential excluded. Color, however, functions uneasily in this position since, within the legacy of seventeenth-century optics, it has itself been quantitatively analyzed and systematized. Newton's quantification of the color components of pure white light was greeted as aesthetically significant, in that it opened up the possibility of assimilating the harmonics of color to those of music, and ultimately perhaps to the music of the spheres.[44]

Powerful tensions traverse what Merleau-Ponty calls "the dimension of color,"[45] including not only that between the energy fields of color and color's quantitative systematization, but also between the chromas of the spectrum and those of pigmentary materiality (which offers its own register of expression). How then does color enter into painting's alchemy of strong beauty?

One artist whose work addresses these issues is Gujarati-born Natvar Bhavsar who, moreover, is also centrally concerned with beauty. Upon arriving in the United States in 1962, Bhavsar was drawn to the color-field tendencies within abstract expressionism, as well as to soak-and-stain color field painting, as practiced by Helen Frankenthaler and Morris Louis. Unlike the critic Clement Greenberg, who championed color field painting, however, Bhavsar did not consider "opticality" to be incompatible with "tactility," or with painting's self-assertion of its own materiality. He sought instead a method of working with color that acknowledged both color's manifestation of the sheer luminous energy of the spectrum and its pigmentary physicality.

He developed a technique of sifting pure powdered pigments onto large-scale canvases soaked in a clear acrylic solution functioning as a binder. Color is thus treated as a material substance in its own right, one whose rhythms and densities of application to the prone canvas (by means of screens, sieves, or funnels) configure the image as a record of bodily movement rather than as circumscribed form. Bhavsar's chromatic environments are nonetheless sensitive to viewing distance, in a manner similar to Martin's work as discussed by Linville and Krauss. Up close, the viewer experiences the material granulation, densities, or dispersal of pigments. Taking her distance, however, she finds herself immersed in luminous chromatic fields.[46] Bhavsar's art keeps in play the contrary tensions of color without any attempt at subjugation or exclusion. As he has himself acknowledged, he works *from within* color itself; rather than within systematic constraints and their concomitants of exclusion. Doing so, he is entranced by the beauty "of what just happens" (although such happening is always in dialogue with the artist's critical evaluation).[47] In his own view, the beauty attained does not negate or fall short of sublimity.[48] It has the event-character of strong beauty and addresses the viewer within the space of what has been called "an oasis of contemplation."[49] Bhavsar's is not an acknowledgment of the excluded but instead an undercutting of the very need for exclusion, which is perhaps what consummates the alchemy.

The Resilience of Strong Beauty

Strong beauty's foregrounding of its own event-character is integral to its resilient resistance against being made an instrument of manipulation and domination. Its strength involves, somewhat paradoxically, a refusal to shrink from and cover over its own vulnerability, marked as it is by its invocation of the unfigurable excluded, or else by suspending the exclusionary structure of a visual system together with its systematicity. Commenting on Maldiney (rather than on strong beauty), Jean-Louis Chrétien offers a felicitous formulation:

> It is also a question of disengaging within ourselves this deep-seated fragility of exposure to the world, which is our only resource, covered over and obfuscated as it is by fears and prejudices of every sort—derisory fortifications that set up against the ravaging [*la déchirure*] of existence.[50]

For Merleau-Ponty, however, the sheer event character of strong beauty realized in art is more radically ontological. Kaushik, taking up Merleau-Ponty's reflection in "Eye and Mind" that a painting is first of all *autofigurative* and, as such, "a spectacle of nothing," argues that what he calls the autofigure marks being's intrinsic lack of self-sufficiency: it cannot "enact itself" without issuing into appearances.[51] The basic reason is that "its fundamental moment is no more than genesis."[52] The art work can directly and sensibly reveal this ontological movement of autofiguration, and in doing so, Kaushik writes, it discloses depth itself as the multidimensional field structure of things.[53] It also discloses strong beauty in the tensional interrelation between delimitation and depth.

When Merleau-Ponty writes, in "Eye and Mind," that "the painter's vision is a continual birth,"[54] he is not casting it as a matrix of creative initiatory acts. Rather, in the context of his reflections on the reciprocity and reversibility of seeing and being seen, and of action and passion becoming indiscernible, so that "one no longer knows who . . . paints and who is painted,"[55] birth is paradigmatically the (always immemorial) event, not of giving birth, but of coming to birth, or being born. As Merleau-Ponty notes in his 1954–55 lecture course on Institution and Passivity:

> Birth [is not an act] of constitution, but institution of a future. Reciprocally, institution resides in the same *genre* of Being as birth, it is no more an act than it.[56]

Birth is also not the solitary ex nihilo eruption of a subjectivity, but rather, it reveals that, as Merleau-Ponty points out, there is no absolute privilege of subjectivity or the self. We are situated not only in a field with multiple entry points but also at the multiple thresholds of other and self.[57]

Since strong beauty eventuates in and through a work of art, and thus neither as a given at one's disposal, nor in the manner of exemplary actions and accomplishments, but within a field marked by divergent and incompatible orientations, as well as by ellipses and lacunae, it cannot be taken hold of for purposes of manipulation. More crucially still, since in its very articulation of meaningful form it constantly acknowledges what such form, in its very self-assertion, excludes and must exclude, it places that form, however compelling, under the aegis of transience and erosion. The conjunction of compelling fascination and power with an inalienable fragility is not only essential to strong beauty but renders it refractory to any attempt at absolutization.

In visual art, strong beauty comes into its own at the precarious juncture between visual presencing and the invisibles that it brings into play. To be sure, nothing is masked or concealed, whether within the register of enigmatic beauty in classical painting, such as the works of Leonardo or Giorgione, or within the contemporary works discussed. One can look at the classical figures or landscapes, at Brunelleschi's mirrored panorama of sky, or at the entracements of chance, viewing distances, or rhythms of light and color in contemporary works without having to respond to the presencing within absence of invisibles of the visible. The challenge to respond to their solicitation is, nonetheless, offered unceasingly; and strong beauty is realized only in the ensuing response.

Merleau-Ponty searchingly explores also the interrelation of artistic creation with contingency and adversity, showing that the relations between an artist's life, with its inevitable components of adversity, and the transcendent import of his or her work, is neither causally nor rationally explicable. It is centered, rather, on the enigma of expression that is at the core of Merleau-Ponty's thought. In an insightful study of the relations between artistic creation and adversity, Anna Caterina Dalmasso finds that the inextricable complicity of meaning or significance (*sens*) with contingency reveals "the inauthenticity of any absolute point of view."[58] This revelation shows itself to be complementary to the impact of strong beauty.

One might think, perhaps, that an artistic engagement with contingency, adversity, and with the position of the excluded would solely valorize an art of social and political consciousness and commentary, rather than the sort of detached "formalism" that artists such as Kelly have sometimes been indefensibly accused of. Martin's paintings have in fact not infrequently been defaced by viewers annoyed at their refusal of any graspable image or content. My focus here on Martin, Kelly, and Bhavsar is not intended to privilege their artistic idiom, but rather to make the point that, whatever an artist's vision or style, his or her work has the power to bring one face to face with strong beauty, which is challenging and not for the fainthearted.

Notes

1. Jean-Luc Nancy, "Forbidden Representation," in *The Ground of the Image*, trans. Jeff Fort (New York: Fordham University Press, 2005), 35.
2. Ibid.
3. Ibid., 38.
4. Galen A. Johnson, *The Retrieval of the Beautiful: Thinking Through Merleau-Ponty's Aesthetics* (Evanston: Northwestern University Press, 20100, 5, 10.
5. Martin Heidegger, *Besinnung*, ed. W. F. von Herrmann, *Heidegger Gesamtausgabe* (*GA*), vol. 66, 30, 34. Translations from both German and French are mine unless otherwise indicated.
6. François Cheng, *Fünf Meditationen über die Schönheit*, trans. Judith Klein (Munich: C. H. Beck, 2009), 18. The volume was originally published as *Cinq Méditations sur la beauté* (Paris: Editions Albin Michel, 2006). I translate from the German version.

7. *WP*, section 6.

8. *PrP*, 171, 172, 180; *OE* 41, 43, 65.

9. See here Emmanuel Alloa, *Resistance of the Sensible World. An Introduction to Merleau-Ponty* (New York: Fordham, 2017).

10. See Siri Hustvedt, "Giorgio Morandi: Not Just Bottles," in *Mysteries of the Rectangle* (New York: Princeton Architectural Press, 2005), 121–34. Li Fangying (1696–1755), whose paintings did not favor veriimilitude, is counted among "The Eight Eccentrics of Yangzhou."

11. *PrP*, 188; *OE*, 69.

12. *VI*, 271; orig. 221, my translation.

13. See Merleau-Ponty's comments on Whitehead in *N*, 186–89. See also Henri Maldiney, "Tal Coat: Solitude de l'Universel," in *Regard, Parole, Espace*, ed. Christian Chaput, Philippe Grosos, and Maria Villela-Petit (Paris: Les Editions du Cerf, 2013), 53–60, and 167–74. Tal Coat is the pseudonym of the painter Pierre Louis Jacob (1905–1985).

14. *PrP*, 184; *OE*, 76.

15. *SNS*, 16.

16. Rilke, "Denn das Schöne ist nichts / als des Schrecklichen Anfang"; verses 5 and 6 of the First Elegy of Duine.

17. Cheng, *Fünf Meditationen*, 30.

18. *N*, 186–89.

19. Adolf Portmann, *Die Tiergestalt: Studien über die Bedeutung der tierischen Erscheinung*, 2nd rev. ed. (Basel: Verlag Friedrich Reinhardt, 1960). This revised edition appeared too late for Merleau-Ponty to be able to respond to its discussion of unaddressed appearances.

20. Maldiney, "Tal Coat," 56.

21. *PrP*, 188; *OE*, 87.

22. Rajiv Kaushik, *Art, Language, and Figure in Merleau-Ponty: Excursions in Hyper-Dialectic* (London: Bloomsbury, 2013), 58.

23. Jean-Louis Chrétien, "Introduction," in Henri Maldiney, *Œuvres philosophiques*, 4 vols. (Paris: Éd. Cerf, 2012), 29.

24. Barnett Newman's 1948 statements that "The Sublime Is Now" and that "the impulse of modern art is to destroy beaurty" are extensively discussed in Nick Benezra and Olga M. Viso, *Regarding Beauty: The View of the Late Twentieth Century* (Washington, DC: Hirshorn Museum and Hatje Cantz Publishers, 1999), 17, 21. It is also discussed extensively in Johnson, *The Retrieval*.

25. *PrP*, 188; *OE*, 87.

26. Arthur C. Danto, "Beauty for Ashes," in *Regarding Beauty: A View Of the Late Twentieth Century*, ed. Nick Benezra and Olga M. Viso (Washington, DC: Hirshhorn Museum and Hatje Cantz Publishers, 1999), 184.

27. See Cézanne to Emile Bernard, 23 October 1905, in *Conversations with Cézanne*, ed. Michael Doran, trans. Julie L. Cochran (Berkeley: University of California Press, 2001), 148.

28. *PrP*, 163; *OE*, 19.
29. Maldiney, "Tal Coat," 171.
30. Agnes Martin, *Agnes Martin, Selected Writings*, ed. Barbara Haskell (New York: Harry N. Abrams, 1992), 10.
31. Ibid., 13, 26.
32. Barbara Haskell, "Agnes Martin: The Awareness of Perfection," in *Agnes Martin, Selected Writings*, 106. Haskell's reference is to Rosalind Krauss and Marcia Tucker, "Perceptual Fields," in *Critical Perspectives in American Art*, exh. Catalogue, Amherst Fine Arts Center Gallery, University of Massachusetts, 1976, 15.
33. Rosalind Krauss, "The /Cloud/," in, *Agnes Martin, Selected Writings*, 155–65. Krauss's reference is to Kasha Linville, "Agnes Martin: An Appreciation," *Artforum* 9 (June 1971): 72.
34. Hubert Damisch, *Théorie du nuage* (Paris: Seuil, 1972).
35. Maldiney, "Tal Coat," 164.
36. Ibid.
37. *Colors for a Large Wall*, 1951. Oil on canvas, 64 joined panels, 94 ½ x 94 ½ in, New York: The Museum of Modern Art.
38. *Spectrum Colors Arranged by Chance, I*, 1951. Graphite and collage on paper, 19 ½ x 39 in. Philadelphia Museum of Art.
39. Ellsworth Kelly, "Notes of 1969," in *Theories and Documents of Contemporary Art: A Sourcebook of Artists' Writings*, 2nd rev. and exp. edition, ed. Kristine Stiles and Pete Selz (Berkeley: University of California Press, 2012), 129.
40. *S*, 56.
41. *Sculpture for a Large Wall*, 1957. Polished and anodized aluminum, 104 panels, 188 x 785 x 13 in. New York: Museum of Modern Art.
42. Tricia Y. Paik, "In New York City, 1954–70," in *Ellsworth Kelly*, ed. Tricia Y. Paik (London: Phaidon Press, 2015), 121.
43. *PrP*, 172; *OE*, 43; my translation.
44. See here John Gage, *Color and Meaning: Art, Science, and Symbolism* (Berkeley: University of California Press, 1999), 139.
45. *PrP*, 180; *OE*, 67.
46. Irving Sandler, "Natvar Bhavsar: Painting and the Reality of Color," in *Natvar Bhavsar: Poetics of Color*, ed. Paola Gribaudo (Milan: Skira, 2008), 43.
47. Ibid. 38.
48. Ibid. 44.
49. Ibid., 47.
50. Jean-Louis Chrétien, "Introduction," in Henri Maldiney, *Œuvres philosophiques*, 4 vol. (Paris: Éd. Cerf, 2012), vol. I, 29. This tearing or rift is, of course, reminiscent of Heidegger's Riss in "The Origin of the Work of Art," without, however, involving Heidegger's reference to a given historical people.
51. *PrP*, 181; *OE*, 69. Drawing on a metaphor by Henri Michaux in *Aventures de lignes*, Merleau-Ponty says that painting "breaks through the skin of things" and reveals how things become a spectacle of themselves only by first being a spectacle

of nothingness. This comment in *Eye and Mind* is echoed by a working note to *The Visible and the Invisible* dated from November 1959, which speaks of nonfigurative painting as being "without the skin of things, but giving their flesh" (*VI*, 218). See also Kaushik, *Art, Language, and Figure in Merleau-Ponty*, 13–14, 37.

52. Kaushik, *Art, Language, and Figure in Merleau-Ponty*, 37.
53. Ibid., 56.
54. *PrP*, 168; *OE*, 32.
55. Ibid.
56. *IP*, 8, orig. 38.
57. *IP*, 179, orig. 134. See here Sanja Delanovic, "Through the Fold: A Jointure of Gilles Deleuze and Jean-Luc Nancy," *Philosophy Today* 60, no. 2 (Spring 2016): 325–45. Delanovic writes: "[The] manner in which Nancy articulates the event as a kind of restlessness [is] best encapsulated by the verb to be born, to never cease being born" (330).
58. Anna Caterina Dalmasso, "L'artiste et l'adversité: hasard et création chez Merleau-Ponty," *Chiasmi International* 17 (2015): 201–22.

Epilogue

Merleau-Ponty

An Attempt at a Response

Jean-Luc Nancy

How many times have I been questioned about my relation to Merleau-Ponty—I mean, to his thought, for there is no question of my knowing the man (I arrived in Paris as a student, shortly before his death)! How many times have I been asked why I talk about the "body" and not the "flesh"! Every time I am asked these questions, I admit that they are somewhat justified. Every time I try to sketch out an answer, but do so barely, and without ease. I do not feel at all capable of analyzing the proximity between Merleau-Ponty and myself that the questioners have noticed. I do not deny them, but I am too unfamiliar with his œuvre to justify a response.

I must also admit that such questions contain something that makes me uneasy, or rather two things. The first is that it seems to me a little meaningless to compare a great, recognized thought, one that is even, if I may say so, canonized (not in the ecclesiastical sense, but in the sense of being fixed in a registry of notable authors, such as we see in the *Alexandrine Canon*), with my own thought, which is too close to even be identified properly (I say this regardless of other differences between his thought and mine and in order to avoid false modesty, not to mention anything else, and to steer clear of a modesty that is ever-sly). The second reason for my discomfort is broader: I experience this discomfort with all attempts at comparison, parallels, and confrontation between authors. It seems to me that one never gains very much from them because every author—whatever he is worth—is only worth anything with reference to what he is. In short, his value is absolute, like the value of anyone. This is why comparative studies have never yielded much profit, unless it is a matter of delineating the contours of an epoch.

In this latter sense, it is very obvious that I come from a time when Merleau-Ponty—alongside Camus, Sartre, Kojève, Aron, Alquié, Guéroult, Jankélévitch, to name but a few—composed a landscape that one would only improperly call "the Sixties." But this was the landscape of my philosophical prehistory. Of course, I was instructed and nourished by it, but it was not my intellectual horizon. The *Phenomenology of Perception* and *The Structure of Behavior* were on the reading list, just as were books by Gurvitch. The latter bored me, but I was interested in the former, although they remained ensconced within the confines of the academic prism. My Socratic torpedoes were, rather, things that reached me from outside the institution, such as a bit of Heidegger or Bataille, or *Arguments*.

Just a few years later, I discovered Deleuze, Althusser, and Derrida. I experienced—even more so with regard to the latter—the feeling of listening to the music of the present. An unprecedented sensation: it turned out that philosophy did not simply succeed itself.

Such empirical considerations obviously have a transcendental role. In the case of my relation to Merleau-Ponty, this role is extremely complex and I cannot aspire to reconstruct it. I would say that the German tradition was too overbearing for me—which means that my points of reference at the time were metaphysical. Merleau-Ponty belonged to another space, the space from which Deleuze emerged. This was the space of a turn of thought rather than the space of answers to questions regarding principles and ends. I was impressed by Deleuze's reading of Nietzsche, but I did not find in it what was, as I discovered at the very same time, the "question of being." Soon it would become the question of "writing" in the sense of Derrida.

How did this shift take place even as Derrida did not expressly refer to the question of being? Even more, how did it take place even as one might characterize his thinking as a deliberately and expertly displaced reappraisal of this question under the guise of the "originary and existential synthesis" of the subject (in the language of his 1954 thesis), which then becomes the question of "originary difference" in 1961, before becoming that of "différance" in 1967? Without attempting an answer, one must simply remark that, in the interim, the reading of *Sein und Zeit* was decisive, as Derrida clearly states in *Speech and Phenomenon*.

On his side, and approximately in the same time period, Merleau-Ponty followed a very different path. My knowledge of this path is very rough, but it is clear to me that if he himself did talk of ontology it was without any primordial reference to Heidegger (although of course, not without any reference at all). He wanted to emphasize "existence" not in the sense of *Da-sein* but in the direction of "life" and of this "flesh" that seems only a partial reprisal of Husserl's *Leib*. For even Husserl was not the primordial ground of his own growth. It seems that Gabriel Marcel, who also spoke of existence and ontology in the Thirties, although in a very different register, could be regarded as fundamental. Very roughly again, I would suggest that the theme of a "participation in being" stood clearly apart from the "putting into play of the meaning of being in the being of *Dasein*." This very narrow and fragile suggestion—which I venture to propose without further investigation—may perhaps be said to contain the reason for the dehiscence between a thought of being as foremost in the world and a thought of being as foremost in play. On the one side, an inherence to the world (according to a phrase Merleau-Ponty used in connection to the dream); and on the other, a "transcendence of being," which is or performs an "appropriating event."

Certainly, this difference is as wide as it is narrow. One must be able to pass from side to side in an almost imperceptible way, or to brush against both. Yet, there is a difference, which also projects us toward a gap between a German and a French climate, between—if one wishes to play on words—a physical style in the sense of the presence of the "me" in the world, and a metaphysical style in the sense of a distance opened within presence. The "me" asks itself, under a Biranian mode, why and how it is itself and not another. The distance, then, continues to dig and be, in a Heiedggerean way, its own proper/improper spacing.

I have certainly received the imprint and the incitations of the two sides, simultaneously, confusedly, and without trying to situate myself with reference to them. In any case, I did indeed find myself traveling alongside Merleau-Ponty without ever crossing his path. He himself had always taken his own path, one that would take him ever more toward the visibility of the invisible. It was in this way that he would later touch me the most, as he continues to do, for me as well as for many others. How can one not experience the strength of these words: "Vision is the means given to me to be absent from myself, to witness from within the fission of being"? The sentence, however, concludes thus: "at the end of which I alone close myself onto myself"—and this remains alien to me for I do not know what such a "closure" might represent, any more than this "me."

And yet, I have just traced back "my" trajectory. But this mineness, insofar as it is empirically closed, does not provide anything to be thought. It is, on the contrary, given from its outside, given from the same outside that all stimulations, pulsions, and excitations come from and from where they conspire to outline a few exploratory signs, to attempt a few explanations from across the unknown regions that are indefinitely open, not so much by a "fission of Being" as by fissurations, wanderings, and expropriations that *are*—a verb whose infinite transitivity entrances us.

This is why Merleau-Ponty's lecture notes on passivity interested me: because their publication came—against my expectations, I confess—after Levinas's and Derrida's insistence on passivity, whereas they had in fact in many ways preceded their works. I became more clearly aware of the fact that passivity (partly on the basis of a posthumous Husserlian text published in the Eighties) had been a long continuous baseline of the time that it needed to be reconnected with Heidegger (although in his work it bears another name), and, in another way, to Bergson, Wittgenstein, and even Freud. In other words, if it is given that passivity implies non-self-presence, it is one of the axes or ways of naming a displacement of the "metaphysics of presence."

The notes on dreams, published at the same time, also struck me in another way: away from the Freudian theme of interpretation, the dream becomes, in the notes, the mode of a present which, here again, isn't "one's own" and which is, as Merleau-Ponty says, "neither ignorance nor knowledge." For me, this certainly is the most novel in Merleau-Ponty: this decided and deep distance taken from the Freudian orientation (directed toward a knowledge/non-knowledge opposition), in favor of a perceiving always already caught into the world before any subject/object partition—a perception that is a "coexistence with the world and with the others." His novelty, once again, radiates through Derrida, Deleuze, and even Levinas. It does so because it affords the possibility to distance ourselves from the deep solidarity that links all the thoughts of the "subject" and of "knowledge" (including Freud and Lacan) just as well as it distances itself from the appeals, recent as they are, to a "real" or to a thought "directed at the object," which are also naïvetés overcome in advance. It is true that this constitutes a "step acquired" that I fully recognize—albeit with some lexical discomfort. For me, "perception" is a word that has been foreclosed for too long a time, and this is due, probably in part wrongly, to the academic effect of the author Merleau-Ponty whom one once was required to study. By contrast, his relationship to art is undoubtedly a decisive incitation for me, for he seems to me to have been the first to have penetrated the gesture of the artist in and vis-à-vis the world rather than vis-à-vis the determinations of the work.

As you can see, I cannot separate an account of an author from my sensitivity to the tectonic movements that mobilize a whole philosophical planet. This doesn't mean that I ignore the irreducible and singular mark made by each author. Therefore, one encounters a paradox: singularity constitutes at once an invitation to compare or contrast as well as an insurmountable obstacle to these very endeavors. Indeed, there always remains a degree of incommensurability in everyone just as there always remains something common to all of those who share an epoch (perhaps even the whole "epoch" of philosophy itself). This paradox cannot be bypassed . . . it is inherent to thinking.

P.S.

> If the sexual history of a man gives the key to his life, this is because his manner of being toward the world—that is, toward time and toward others—is projected in his sexuality . . . Neither the body nor existence could pass for the original model of the human being, since each one presupposes the other . . . In particular, when it is said that sexuality has an existential signification or that it expresses existence, this should not be understood as if the sexual drama [*drame sexuel*] were, in the final analysis, merely a manifestation or symptom of an existential drama. The same reason that prevents us from "reducing" existence to the body or to sexuality also prevents us from "reducing" sexuality to existence: it is because existence is not an order of facts (like "psychical facts") that one could reduce to other facts or to which these others could be reduced; rather, it is the equivocal milieu of their communication, the point where their boundaries merge, or again, their common fabric [*trame commune*].[1]

These lines by Merleau-Ponty, to which I returned when the time came to finish my book on sex, finally put my conscience at ease. They struck me as the best possible epigraph for their affirmation of the reciprocity between sex and existence, this "common *fabric*" [*trame commune*] engaged by the "sexual drama" [*drame sexuel*]—these are so many expressions whose force astonished me over the distance of sixty years and including one "sexual liberation." In a sense, my work is concerned with nothing else than this fabric [*trame*] and this drama [*drame*].

Translation by Frank Chouraqui

Notes

1. *PP*, 161 and 169, orig. 185 and 194.

Contributors

Sara Ahmed is an independent feminist scholar. She has held previous appointments at Goldsmiths, University of London, and Lancaster University. She works at the intersections between feminist theory, queer theory, critical race theory, postcolonialism, and phenomenology. She is the author of nine books including *Queer Phenomenology. Orientations, Objects, Others* (Duke University Press, 2006), *Living a Feminist Life* (Duke University Press, 2017), and *What's the Use: On the Uses of Use* (Duke University Press, 2019).

Emmanuel Alloa professor in aesthetics and philosophy of art at the University of Fribourg. His research focuses on phenomenology, contemporary philosophy, aesthetics, and politics, with a special emphasis on questions related to images. He has been awarded the Latsis Prize 2016 and the Aby-Warburg-Wissenschaftspreis 2019. He has edited a dozen volumes and authored four monographs, among them *Resistance of the Sensible World. An Introduction to Merleau-Ponty* (Fordham University Press, 2017).

Renaud Barbaras holds a chair in contemporary philosophy at the University Paris 1 Panthéon-Sorbonne. He is a prominent voice in contemporary French phenomenology, and is largely credited for the Merleau-Ponty "renaissance" in the early 1990s. His latest books and seminars have moved from what he calls a "phenomenology of desire" toward a "phenomenology of life," which has metaphysical implications. A senior member at the Institut Universitaire de France from 2010 to 2015, Renaud Barbaras was awarded the Grand Prix in philosophy of the French Academy for his research in 2014. Among his books translated into English: *The Being of the Phenomenon: Merleau-Ponty's Ontology* (Indiana University Press, 2004) and *Desire and Distance: Introduction to a Phenomenology of Perception* (Stanford University Press, 2005). His *Introduction to a Phenomenology of Life* is forthcoming in English.

Jocelyn Benoist holds a chair in contemporary philosophy and epistemology at the University Paris I Panthéon-Sorbonne and has held numerous visiting professorships. His work covers a wide range of topics, from Kant to phenomenology, early analytic philosophy and philosophy of mind, theories of meaning, and philosophy of language. He is the author of more than a dozen monographs in those areas. Lately he has developed, in the context of the debate around new realisms, his own version of contextual realism. His book, *Le bruit du sensible* (Ed. Cerf, 2013), deals more specifically with Merleau-Ponty and the limits of intentionality.

Mauro Carbone is professor at the Faculté de Philosophie of the University Lyon 3-Jean Moulin in Lyon, France. Since 2012, he has been a senior member of the Institut Universitaire de France. Carbone is the founder of the journal *Chiasmi International. Trilingual Studies concerning Merleau-Ponty's Thought*, which he has co-directed since its foundation in 1999. Among his books in English: *An Unprecedented Deformation* (State University of New York Press, 2010). Carbone is also author of *The Thinking of the Sensible: Merleau-Ponty's A-Philosophy* (Northwestern University Press, 2004), of *The Flesh of Images* (State University of New York Press, 2015), and of *Screen Philosophy. From Cinema to the Digital Revolution* (State University of New York Press, 2019). His present research focuses on the connections between philosophy and contemporary visual experience.

Frank Chouraqui is assistant professor in Contemporary Continental Philosophy at Leiden University, the Netherlands. His research focuses on Nietzsche and phenomenological concerns including phenomenological ontology and the theory of belief. He is the author of *Ambiguity and the Absolute, Nietzsche and Merleau-Ponty on the Question of Truth* (Fordham University Press, 2014) and *A Philosophical Guide to the Body and Embodiment* (Rowman and Littlefield International, 2020).

Annabelle Dufourcq is assistant professor of fundamental philosophy at Radboud University Nijmegen. She has published works on the relation between the real and the imaginary in contemporary continental philosophy, with special interest in a phenomenological approach. She is the author of *Merleau-Ponty: une ontologie de l'imaginaire* (Springer, 2012) and *La dimension imaginaire du réel dans la philosophie de Husserl* (Springer, 2010), as well as the editor of *Est-ce réel? Phénomenologies de l'imaginaire* (Brill, 2016). Her most recent and current work investigates the ontological status and the ethical and political implications of the imaginary of animals.

Bernard Flynn has been teaching political philosophy at the New School (New York), particularly the political thought that emerged in Europe from the seventeenth century to the present. He focuses on the concept of modernity and its relation to premodern forms of political organization. Flynn is interested in the form of philosophical reflection elaborated by the major thinkers of the tradition of phenomenology, including Husserl, Heidegger, Merleau-Ponty, and Derrida, and in particular in the philosophy of Claude Lefort. He has published two books: *Political Philosophy at the Closure of Metaphysics* (Humanities Press, 1992) and *The Philosophy of Claude Lefort: Interpreting the Political* (Northwestern University Press, 2007) and he is the co-editor of *Merleau-Ponty and the Possibilities of Philosophy* (State University of New York Press, 2009).

Veronique M. Fóti is a professor of philosophy emerita at Penn State. Her areas of specialization are contemporary European philosophy, continental rationalism, philosophy of art, and philosophy and literary theory. She is the author of, among other books, *Vision's Invisibles: Philosophical Explorations* (State University of New York Press, 2003), *Epochal Discordance: Hölderlin's Philosophy of Tragedy* (State University of New York Press, 2006), and *Tracing Expression in Merleau-Ponty: Aesthetics, Philosophy of Biology, and Ontology* (Northwestern University Press, 2013).

Regula Giuliani is the director of the Waldenfels Archive at the Albert-Ludwigs-Universität Freiburg. She is the author of *Sprache und Erfahrung in den Schriften von Maurice Merleau-Ponty* (Peter Lang, 1983) and she has co-edited Edmund Husserl's *Wahrnehmung and Aufmerksamkeit* (Husserliana XXXVIII, 2004).

Galen A. Johnson is professor of philosophy at the University of Rhode Island. His research interests include phenomenology, aesthetics, American philosophy, and recent French philosophy. He is the author of numerous articles in contemporary continental philosophy and has held fellowships from the National Endowment for the Humanities, the American Council for Learned Societies, and the American Philosophical Society. He has published four books that deal with phenomenology and aesthetics, the last of which is *The Retrieval of the Beautiful: Thinking Through Merleau-Ponty's Aesthetics* (Northwestern University Press, 2010). He is co-editor of *Chiasmi International: Trilingual Studies in the Thought of Merleau-Ponty.*

Rajiv Kaushik is professor of philosophy at Brock University in Canada. He has published widely in the areas of language, hermeneutics, and aesthetics and on the phenomenologies of Edmund Husserl and Maurice Merleau-Ponty. He has three books on Merleau-Ponty's aesthetics and ontology: *Art and Institution: Aesthetics in Merleau-Ponty's Late Works* (Continuum, 2011), *Art, Language, and Figure: Excursions in Hyper-Dialectic* (Bloomsbury, 2013) and *Merleau-Ponty between Philosophy and Symbolism: The Matrixed Ontology* (State University of New York Press, 2019).

Jennifer McWeeny is associate professor of philosophy at Worcester Polytechnic Institute. Her research interests are in the areas of phenomenology, philosophy of mind, ontology, feminist philosophy, and decolonial theory. She is co-editor of two books and has published more than twenty-five articles or book chapters in venues such as *Hypatia, Continental Philosophy Review, Chiasmi International,* and *Journal for Critical Animal Studies*. She has served as executive secretary for the Eastern Division of the Society for Women in Philosophy and is currently editor-in-chief of *Simone de Beauvoir Studies*.

Jean-Luc Nancy is professor emeritus at the University of Strasbourg and is one of France's foremost philosophers. In more than forty books, he has explored both the continental tradition (with a special emphasis on Kant, Hegel, and Heidegger) and the margins of philosophy, namely, the relationship of philosophy and art and the question of the political. While taking Heidegger's notion of being-with (*Mitsein*) a step farther toward an ontology of co-existence, and undertaking the ambitious endeavor of a deconstruction of Christianity, he has also developed an original theory of the body and of fleshly exposure. Among his latest books are *Que faire?* (Galilée, 2016) and *Sexistence* (Galilée, 2017).

Bernhard Waldenfels is professor emeritus at the Institute for Philosophy at Ruhr University Bochum, and he is widely recognized as one of the most original voices in German phenomenology. Having studied with Merleau-Ponty himself, Waldenfels has developed a phenomenology of responsivity which has been documented in thirty authored books. He has received numerous awards and prizes for his work. Among his most important works translated to English are *Phenomenology of the Alien* (Northewestern University Press, 2011), *The Question of the Other* (State University of New York Press, 2007) and *Order in the Twilight* (Indiana University Press, 1996). He has also contributed to the book *Refugees* (University of Chicago Press, 2016), a collaboration with the photographer Roland Fischer and the sociologist Stephan Lessenich.

Stephen Watson is professor of philosophy at the University of Notre Dame. His areas of specialization include: contemporary continental thought, nineteenth-century philosophy, and aesthetics. He is the author of several books, including: *Traditions I* (Indiana University Press, 1997), *Traditions II* (Indiana University Press, 2001), *Reinterpreting the Political* (State University of New York Press, 1998), *Crescent Moon over the Rational: Philosophical Interpretations of Paul Klee* (Stanford University Press, 2009), and *Writings after Merleau-Ponty vol. I & II* (Continuum, 2011).

Index

Abram, D., 121, 122, 123, 135, 136, 140, 143
Addas, A., 232
Agamben, G., 263
Ahmed, S., 12, 197ff
Alberti, L. B., 290
Alexandre, 57, 298
Alloa, E., 1ff, 8, 61ff
Alquié, F., 298
Althusser, L., 298
Aristotle, 38, 80, 82, 180, 181
Aron, J.-P., 107, 298
Augustine, 38, 39, 50, 54, 56, 181

Bachelard, G., 59, 237
Bannon, B., 123, 135, 138, 140, 143, 144
Barbaras, R., 7, 10, 17ff, 56, 126, 141, 142, 143
Bataille, G., 86, 167, 298
Bateson, G., 149
Baudelaire, C., 225, 227, 231, 233
Bazin, A., 275, 276
Beauvoir, S., 79, 270, 306
Benjamin, W., 96, 97, 105, 107, 223, 231, 232, 246, 248, 249
Benoist, J., 9, 10, 111ff
Bergson, H., 37, 38, 39, 46, 48, 49, 50, 51, 54, 57, 59, 60, 80, 81, 82, 103, 140, 273, 274, 300

Berkeley, G., 65, 80
Bhavsar, N., 14, 290, 291, 293, 295
Binswanger, L., 44, 45
Bishop, C., 262, 263, 264, 266, 268
Bitbol, M., 122, 123, 140
Blanchot, M., 86, 103, 233
Bourriaud, N., 265, 266, 268
Breton, A., 6, 12, 13, 221, 223, 224, 225, 226, 227, 228, 229, 230, 231, 232, 233, 234, 235, 236, 237, 239, 241, 243, 244, 245, 246, 247, 248, 249, 250, 251
Brown, W., 181
Brunelleschi, F., 288, 292
Butler, J., 213, 217, 250

Cage, J., 96
Camus, A., 225, 298
Carbone, M., 13, 260, 266ff
Carnap, R., 93
Cassirer, E., 85, 90, 103, 104
Castoriadis, C., 172, 175, 182
Celan, P., 100
Cézanne, P., 14, 67, 138, 222, 223, 246, 249, 259, 270, 273, 279, 283, 287, 294
Cheng, F., 282, 285, 293, 294
Chouraqui, F., 1ff, 11, 178, 182, 183ff
Chrétien, J.-L., 286, 291, 294, 295
Clark, L., 264, 265

Index

Clarke, M., 123, 135, 136, 140, 143
Claudel, P., 49, 248
Coole, D., 240, 242, 250

Dallmayr, F., 244, 251
Dalmasso, A. C., 293, 296
Damisch, H., 288, 295
Danto, A., 286, 294
Dastur, F., 123, 140, 185, 186, 195
Deleuze, G., 2, 3, 4, 10, 13, 54, 269, 271, 272, 273, 274, 275, 276, 277, 278, 279, 280, 296, 298, 300
Derrida, J., 4, 10, 55, 57, 171, 174, 182, 288, 298, 300, 305
Descartes, R., 10, 44, 55, 56, 57, 64, 89, 91, 118, 137, 138, 139, 172, 173, 239, 240, 241, 257, 259, 271, 285, 290
Dewey, J., 221, 244, 245
Dillon, M. C., 123, 127, 135, 136, 140, 141, 143
Diprose, R., 197, 215, 240, 250
Douglas, M., 207, 216
Dufourcq, A., 10, 145ff
Dumont, L., 203

Ehrenfels, C. von, 69
Elgström, O., 207, 217
Emmeche, C., 148, 163
Engels, F., 224

Fangying, L., 284, 294
Fanon, F., 210
Faulkner, W., 61, 80, 172, 182
Ferguson, R. A., 214, 218
Fichte, J. G., 95
Fink, E., 47, 52, 54, 57
Flasch, K., 54
Flynn, B., 11, 171ff
Fóti, V., 14, 106, 141, 281ff
Foucault, M., 2, 4, 10, 175, 176, 182, 185, 186, 250

Frankenthaler, H., 290
Frege, G., 97, 112
Freud, Lucian, 286
Freud, Sigmund, 45, 46, 47, 52, 53, 76, 101, 106, 107, 174, 179, 182, 194, 227, 230, 231, 232, 235, 300
Fukuyama, F., 179, 182

Gadamer, H.-G., 244
Gandhi, M., 244
Giacometti, A., 234, 235, 236
Giorgione, 292
Giuliani, R., 7, 8, 35ff
Goethe, J. W., 79, 173
Goldstein, K., 44
Goya, F., 284
Greenberg, C., 290
Guattari, F., 272
Guéroult, M., 298
Gurvitch, G., 298

Habermas, J., 178, 182
Haskell, B., 287, 295
Hegel, G. W. F., 49, 60, 70, 91, 94, 103, 106, 115, 116, 118, 124, 194, 195, 196, 250, 253, 254, 256, 257, 265, 266, 271, 306
Heidegger, M., 37, 38, 39, 47, 48, 49, 51, 58, 107, 156, 159, 166, 282, 293, 295, 298, 299, 300, 305, 306
Henry, M., 19, 34, 35, 59, 105, 284
Hitchcock, A., 277, 278
Hobbes, T., 172, 176
Hofmeyer, J., 145, 146, 147, 148, 161, 162, 163, 164
Hölderlin, F., 100, 305
Huang t'in-chien, 286
Hume, D., 69
Husserl, E., 9, 3, 4, 7, 14, 17, 19, 20, 29, 30, 34, 35, 37, 38, 41, 42, 43, 47, 48, 49, 50, 52, 55, 56, 57, 63, 74, 76, 77, 78, 81, 84, 85, 87, 89,

Index

90, 91, 93, 94, 95, 96, 99, 100, 101, 102, 103, 105, 106, 107, 108, 112, 120, 125, 126, 142, 144, 172, 175, 186, 254, 299, 300

James, W., 9, 10, 38, 73, 81, 142, 143, 203, 204, 279
Jameson, F., 261
Jankélévitch, V., 298
Jiun Onkō, 286
Johnson, C., 183
Johnson, G., 12, 13, 221ff, 282, 283, 285, 293, 294

Kafka, F., 174, 175, 179, 181, 182
Kant, 41, 55, 88, 90, 92, 94, 95, 100, 103, 125, 156, 163, 275, 283
Kant, Immanuel, 38, 41, 47, 48, 55, 58, 69, 84, 85, 87ff, 100, 103, 105, 106, 125, 156, 163, 195, 196, 223, 225, 246, 272, 275, 279, 283
Kantorowicz, E., 176
Kaushik, R., 1ff, 13, 253ff, 281, 285, 291, 292, 294, 296
Kelly, E., 14, 142, 288, 289, 293, 295
Kentridge, W., 175, 176
Klee, P., 223, 246, 283, 307
Kleisner, K., 152, 153, 164, 165
Kofka, K., 54, 69, 73, 81
Köhler, W., 54, 69
Krauss, R., 261, 266, 267, 287, 288, 289, 290, 295
Kull, K., 148, 163, 164
Kundera, M., 231

La Bruyère, J., 233
Lacan, J., 49, 91, 101, 107, 300
Lefort, C., 5, 11, 81, 100, 171, 172, 173, 174, 175, 176, 177, 179, 180, 181, 182, 224, 246
Leibniz, G. W., 10, 73, 124, 129, 130, 131, 132, 133, 138, 141, 142

Leonardo da Vinci, 292
Levinas, E., 48, 54, 55, 57, 58, 60, 76, 250, 300
Lévi-Strauss, C., 49
Lien P'o, 286
Ling Hsing-ju, 286
Linville, K., 287, 290, 295
Locke, J., 64, 80
Louis, M., 290
Lyotard, J.-F., 4, 221, 222, 246

Machiavelli, N., 173, 181, 184, 190, 192, 193, 245
Maldiney, H., 78, 82, 284, 285, 287, 291, 294, 295
Malebrache, N., 75
Mallarmé, S., 86
Malraux, A., 13, 92, 253, 254, 256, 266
Maran, T., 149, 153, 161, 164, 165
Marcel, G., 57, 299
Marcuse, H., 221
Martin, A., 14, 166, 176, 287, 288, 290, 293, 295
Marx, K., 60, 173, 175, 181, 192, 224, 230ff, 265
Matisse, H., 223
McDowell, J., 116, 117, 118, 119, 120
McWeeny, J., 7, 9, 10, 121ff
Minkowski, E., 44, 54
Morris, D., 122, 123, 140, 250

Nancy, J.-L., 14, 78, 258, 267, 281ff
Nietzsche, F., 47, 60, 178, 179, 182, 221, 250, 272, 298, 304
Novalis, 99, 107

Orelus, P., 213, 217

Patočka, J., 30, 31, 34
Paulhan, J., 223, 233, 238, 250

Peirce, C. S., 145, 148, 163
Piaget, J., 40
Picasso, P., 284
Plato, 48, 157, 167, 221, 226, 277, 280
Plessner, H., 44
Ponge, F., 236
Portmann, A., 10, 148, 149, 150, 151, 152, 153, 154, 155, 156, 157, 159, 160, 161, 164, 165, 167, 285, 294
Proust, M., 37, 46, 47, 52, 57, 224, 231, 270, 275, 279
Puwar, N., 214, 216, 217

Reid, T., 68, 79
Richir, M., 96, 105
Ricoeur, P., 54
Riefenstahl, L., 282
Rilke, R. M., 285, 294
Rimbaud, 223, 249
Rodin, A., 223, 283
Rousseau, J.-J., 192, 193, 195

Saint Paul, 181
Sartre, J.-P., 12, 47, 48, 50, 58, 86, 89, 91, 98, 103, 104, 107, 192, 193, 195, 239, 247, 270, 298
Scheler, M., 39, 124, 125, 126, 130, 131, 132, 133, 136, 137, 138, 142, 143
Schelling, F. W. J., 88, 98, 99, 103, 127, 249
Schilder, P., 44
Schlegel, F., 99, 107

Sellars, W., 111
Simondon, C., 71
Smith, K., 55, 57, 58, 103, 120, 286
Strathern, M., 206, 216
Stratton, G. M., 215
Straus, E., 44, 182
Strauss, L., 173

Toadvine, T., 107, 123, 135, 140, 141, 143, 251
Tompson, E., 123, 140
Twombly, C., 289

Uexküll, J.v., 10, 39, 54, 145, 148, 156, 159, 160, 162, 166, 167

Valéry, P., 46, 57, 58, 270

Waldenfels, B., 7, 8, 35ff, 76, 77, 82
Watson, S., 8, 9, 83ff, 246
Weber, M., 173, 177
Weiss, G., 203, 216
Weizsäcker, V.v., 39, 54
Wertheimer, M., 69, 81
Whitehead, A. N., 38, 56, 59, 284, 294
Wittgenstein, L., 90, 93, 97, 104, 105, 106, 140, 300

Young, I. M., 210

Zahavi, D., 123, 126, 140, 141
Zeno, 47
Žižek, S., 277, 280